# Mentoring with a Coaching Attitude

# Mentoring with a Coaching Attitude

**International corporate mentorship that works**

*Sylviane Cannio, Cicero Carvalho and Fisher Yu*

Mc Graw Hill

Open University Press

Open University Press
McGraw Hill
Unit 4,
Foundation Park
Roxborough Way
Maidenhead
SL6 3UD

email: emea_uk_ireland@mheducation.com
world wide web: www.openup.co.uk

First edition published 2023

A catalogue record of this book is available from the British Library

ISBN-13: 9780335252077
ISBN-10: 0335252079
eISBN: 9780335252084

Library of Congress Cataloging-in-Publication Data
CIP data applied for

Typeset by Transforma Pvt. Ltd., Chennai, India

# Praise page

*"A compelling read to help make corporate mentoring not just good practice, but also common practice."*

*Dr Mark Hiatt, Vice President, Guardant Health, USA*

*"There are few books that provide a practical guide to linking coaching and mentoring as a basis for organisational learning and improvement. Mentoring with a Coaching Attitude bridges the gap between the two forms of personal development, thereby proposing a more impactful approach to meeting the needs of today's organisations that are managing in a volatile, uncertain, changing and ambiguous world. The inclusion of a truly international selection of case studies increases the both the interest and value of the book, providing insight into a range of country-specific paradigms while also identifying the commonalities that exist in the diverse implementations. This is an important book that provides clear, unambiguous guidance in a 'how to' structure which can assist any company that is committed to unlocking the hidden potential of its people."*

*Frank Nigriello, Director of Corporate Affairs, Unipart Group, UK*

*"Such a timely and forward-looking book, especially in the era of twin transition. Only by creating an inclusive society can we find sustainable solutions to the challenges caused by climate change and digital transformation. And mentoring is the best tool to reach that goal: As a two-way, non-judgmental learning experience covering a wide variety of contexts, mentoring is an inclusive mutual partnership for co-value creation that values differences. I genuinely hope this book will serve as a resource for inspiration for all practitioners in every aspect of modern life."*

*Dr Riza Kadilar, EMCC Global President, Netherlands*

*"I am particularly pleased to support this multicultural book on Mentoring, which shows that this relationship is a wonderful human adventure and gives useful tips on how corporations should implement their mentoring programmes."*

*Nadia Bouyer, CEO of Action Logement, France*

# Contents

# List of figures

# Foreword: The era of mentoring

*Professor David Clutterbuck*

Mentoring happens when one person uses their wisdom to help another become wiser. For most of its 3000-plus[1] year history, mentoring has been an informal relationship, associated especially with the achievement of personal and ethical maturity. Formal mentoring programmes appeared less than 50 years ago, driven by corporations wanting to build generation-spanning cultures and retain young talent.

The first formal programmes quickly spawned a wide variety of applications, often with social aims, such as enabling people from disadvantaged groups to have equal access to work and the corridors of corporate power. The recent decades have seen the emergence of many more applications, including:

- Maternity mentoring – women on maternity leave are more likely to return to their jobs and integrate better and faster on return.
- Ethical mentors – to help mentees work through complex ethical dilemmas and choose wise paths going forward.
- Entrepreneurial mentoring – to support people starting businesses. A key element here is ensuring that the entrepreneur undergoes personal growth commensurate with the growth of their business – so they can handle success! Another is helping them develop resilience when things don't go as planned.
- Reverse mentoring – this pairs a junior person from a disadvantaged group with a senior person from a privileged group, with the aim that the latter learns to see the world through different eyes. The junior person in exchange gets to understand how to work within the corporate or professional culture. Reciprocal meeting goes further. It places much more emphasis on co-learning and encourages both parties to work together to change the system that creates inequalities.
- Professional mentoring – with this, retiring executives gain a similar or greater level of skill than professional coaches. Leadership can be very lonely and professional mentors provide empathetic and wise sounding boards for enterprise leaders.

We have also seen major trends in mentoring. The first, in the 1980s, was a push-back from Europe and elsewhere to the interpretation of mentoring from North America. Probably through confusion between Athena in her personae as goddess of wisdom and goddess of martial arts, North American writers conflated

---

1   The term Mentor comes from the Ancient Greek oral history, but many other cultures of the time have similar tales of a hero's older and wiser companion helping them to make sense of their experiences and become a more complete human being.

mentoring with sponsorship – a different set of behaviours and relationships, largely incompatible with 'pure' mentoring. Where sponsorship emphasises the power imbalance in a relationship, mentoring works best in an environment where any hierarchical power is 'parked' and where co-learning occurs. It's very close to modern coaching (historical coaching is a form of directive instruction) and increasingly referred to as 'coaching plus' – the plus being the mentor's store of accumulated experience and wisdom.

Other significant trends include the development of mentoring standards by the EMCC Global (European Mentoring and Coaching Council) – first for mentoring programmes, then for mentors and more recently for managers of mentoring programmes. Mentoring programmes increasingly give mentors access to professional supervision, to support them in their continued growth in the role and maintain ethicality.

Technology has also changed mentoring, firstly through telephone mentoring, then email and now platforms, such as Zoom or Microsoft Teams. I have begun to experiment with the next technological advance for mentoring – Virtual Reality. While 'clunky' right now, technology is advancing to the level where it will soon become easier and more commonplace. The level of connectedness between mentor and mentee is much greater than with meeting software and the potential to use concepts such as constellations to explore issues is unprecedented.

One of the challenges mentoring faces is the rise of Fast Knowledge Transfer (FKT), which is often inaccurately described as mentoring. Mentoring is in essence a long-term developmental relationship, whereas FKT is a short-term transaction. For me, however, the biggest challenge is in bringing the benefits of mentoring to a much wider audience. My 1985 book, the first to explore mentoring programmes from a developmental mentoring perspective, had the title *Everyone needs a mentor*. That statement is even more accurate now. Effective career self-management involves multiple mentoring relationships, aligned to the phase of a person's development. I estimate that, in developed economies, fewer than one person in five has access to a mentor in the formative stages of their careers; and fewer than one in eight people at more senior levels in organisations. In terms of *trained* mentors, the proportion is far less. In less developed economies, access to mentors is even more limited, with few, if any, trained mentors available.

With the dilution of traditional support relationships in rural communities, mentoring represents the most powerful and effective way of helping people cope with the complexity of modern life. It's part of my life's ambition to widen the scope and availability of mentoring. My *Cool Coaching and Mentoring* project has been testing out approaches to educating school children to be mentors to peers. We aim to achieve 5 million school age mentors over the next decade. It's not just the children who are the beneficiaries in terms of self-awareness and self-confidence. A school benefits from less pupil disruption and future employers from knowing that young recruits already have many of the people skills that are not typically trained in until employees reach their late twenties.

It's an exciting time to be engaged in the world of mentoring. I recommend it to anyone who wants to make a difference in the world and to any corporation that wants to bring out the best in its people and retain its talent!

# Introduction

The World Economic Forum describes the current period as the Fourth Industrial Revolution[2] where previous advances are merging physical, digital and biological worlds. The 'VUCA[3]-ness' of this age suggests that no individual holds the key to the solution, and the global experience of the pandemic, in addition to international conflicts and climate emergency changes are a reminder of our interdependencies and interconnectedness. This context presents an urgent call for everyone, including leaders in corporations to transform, build new capabilities and upskill their people. In addition, many corporations will lose the 'baby boomers', born in the late 1950s and 1960s, as they retire and this means that not only experience, memory and technology will step away but also, mainly the 'tacit knowledge', namely all that cannot be transmitted via trainings or tutorials, only by real individual transmission and by accompanied, thus mentored, on-the-job implementation.

## Our intention is to support talent development and retention

The intent behind this book is to promote mentoring as a profession for a better world and inspire people to adopt mentoring for the transferring of knowledge, experience and know-how to the learning generation to reduce the trail of mistakes, the learning costs of the society and to help to create a better world.
  According to the EMCC Global:

> Mentoring is a learning relationship, involving the sharing of skills, knowledge, and expertise between a mentor and mentee through developmental conversations, experience sharing, and role modelling. The relationship may cover a wide variety of contexts and is an inclusive two-way partnership for mutual learning that values differences.[4]

On reflection, mentoring is not just a solution bridge, it has potential to bring a fractured world together to co-create a world that is inclusive, honouring and

---

2   www.weforum.org/focus/fourth-industrial-revolution
3   VUCA is the acronym describing today's environment: Volatile, Uncertain, Complex and Ambiguous.
4   https://www.emccglobal.org/leadership-development/leadership-development-mentoring/ - Established in 1992, EMCC Global is the professional federation for coaching, mentoring and supervision, present is 85 countries. It has its own Code of Ethics, proposes accreditations for practitioners and for programmes, and was a key player for the regulation of coaching in Europe.

leveraging different voices and ideas. It is a demonstration or move towards a more evolved and sustainable world.

Mentoring is also an answer to the call to support talent development and retention in a sustainable way, including the wellbeing of individuals. If asked, most organisations will claim to be doing some form of mentoring, albeit in an informal manner. An increasing number of companies are now seeking ways of institutionalising mentoring through alignment with their corporate strategy and reaping the benefits at an organisational and individual level. Readers will be introduced to overcome some of the common pitfalls of corporate mentoring programmes through a longer term, structured and culturally aligned approach.

## Mentoring for a more balanced power relationship

Mentoring is re-emerging in the world, this time in a new form as we have moved from the mentor–protégé relationship to a more adult-to-adult relationship, namely with a 'coaching attitude'.

This book aims to show how it is possible to set up mentoring programmes that endure over time. Mentoring is today what coaching was 15 years ago. Increasingly, companies have understood its usefulness, especially in the transfer of knowledge and tacit knowledge between generations of managers, the transmission of human leadership through strong values, and mentoring is part of it.

The mentor is like a running buddy or pacer, where their experience provides insights to focus the learning dialogue; for example, approaches to consider a situation, potential pitfalls to watch out for and resources that might be useful, and others. With humility and self-awareness, the mentor remains curious about the needs of the mentee and appreciates that the mentee is working in a different context, which although similar, is never the same.

**The mentoring relationship is a power-balanced relationship where both parties may appropriately contribute questions and insights to advance the learning goal of the mentee.** Apart from the commitment of the mentee to the mentoring exercise, the other key influence that impacts a mentoring session is a mentor's ability to hold a safe space for learning by knowing when to provide appropriate guidance and when to ask insightful questions to support the mentee's learning. This empathetic way of working, in full partnership, promotes psychological safety for learners, especially those who are traditionally trained in a 'teach' or 'must have a right answer' learning environment.

**Mentors need coaching skills to activate the learning muscles in their mentees to encourage expanded and sustainable learning abilities.** At the same time, mentors' expertise, experience and wisdom are acknowledged, recognised and passed on to the next generations. We believe this inclusive and synergistic approach to mentoring in corporations and beyond will support people and organisations to flourish in this new era.

*Mentoring with a Coaching Attitude* encapsulates a university course and online programme developed by MentoringCo, enriched by inputs from mentoring professionals who share their own processes, experiences and learnings from implementations of in-house mentoring programmes around the world.

# An international network of mentors with a coaching attitude

This book is a collaboration between 24 world-class mentors and coaches who are well known in the coaching and mentoring community, keynote speakers, book authors and/or active in the EMCC-Global and/or the International Coaching Federation (ICF).

## Contributors

On board are, in alphabetical order:

**Arshad Ali**, CEO MentoringCo, Senior Practitioner EMCC, former Global Director at Pfizer Inc., mentor, consultant.

**Raja'a Yousef Allaho**, mentor and professional coach in the Middle East and owner of a mentoring school in Kuwait.

**Dominique Cancellieri-Decroze** and **Danielle Deffontaines**, authors and architects of several large mentoring programmes in France, co-owner of a mentoring school.

**Prof. Sylviane Cannio**, Master Certified Coach ICF and Master Practitioner EMCC, Accredited supervisor ESIA from EMCC, co-founder and Chief Learning Officer of MentoringCo, President of GO-TKM (Global Think-tank on Organizational Tacit Knowledge Management), former Vice President of ICF Global, keynote, author of several books translated into different languages.

**Cicero Carvalho**, Senior Partner MentoringCo, Certified Master Coach IAC, former Latin America Business Excellence at Pfizer, and former National Learning and Development Lead (Brazil) at Bristol Myers Squibb, mentor, consultant, Vice-President of GO-TKM.

**Piotr Ciacek**, Senior Practitioner EMCC, Professional Certified Coach ICF, owner of the first school in Poland with European Quality Award (EQA) EMCC with a pure mentoring profile.

**Dr Julie Haddock-Millar**, Associate Professor of HRD at Middlesex University Business School, Work Group Lead for International Standard for Mentoring and Coaching Programme, EMCC Global.

**Dr Neil Kaye**, Research Fellow, University College London Institute of Education.

**Dionysia Lagiou**, mentor, coach, and former Principal Administrator – R&I Policy Officer in European Public Administration, European Commission.

**Felicia Lauw**, Master Practitioner EMCC and Accredited Supervisor ESIA from EMCC, Senior Partner MentoringCo, EMCC Award winner 2020 for supervision, and representative of a supervision school in Singapore.

**Dr Lise Lewis**, Master Practitioner and Accredited Supervisor EMCC, Global Past President of EMCC and special ambassador, owner of a supervision school.

**Dr Robin Owen,** Associate Professor of Entrepreneurial Finance, Middlesex University Business School.

**Samira Siham Raïssouni**, a leading figure in mentoring and coaching in Morocco, former president of Maroc-Coaching (ICF), partner of MentoringCo for Maghreb and French-speaking Africa.

**Dr Chandana Sanyal,** Senior Lecturer in Human Resource Management and Development at Middlesex University Business School, Work Group Lead for European Individual Accreditation, EMCC Global.

**Dr Leandro Sepulveda**, Associate Professor in Socioeconomic Development, Middlesex University Business School.

**Dr Stephen Syrett,** Deputy Dean, Research & Knowledge Exchange, Middlesex University Business School.

**Fisher Yu**, President of EMCC China, CEO of MentoringCo China, a mentoring pioneer and market leader in China (providing EQA programmes), Treasurer of GO-TKM, and recipient of the EMCC Global Mentoring Award in 2021.

There are also contributors from three major organisations who present their successful respective mentoring programmes:

- **Euroclear** with **Sophie Bocquet**, Lead Coach and Head of Mentoring
- **Médecins sans Frontières** with **Wiet Vandormael,** Mentoring and Coaching Programme manager, mentor and coach and **Aurélien Maréchal**, Logistics Workforce Coordinator, mentor and coach
- **Bharatiya Yuva Shakti Trust** with **Lakshmi Venkataraman Venkatesan,** Founding and Managing Trustee.

Each contributor brings their own experiences and expertise to provide unique and deep insights based on a diversity of industries, geography and culture.

## Who should read this book?

Our target readers are numerous: team leaders, executives, CEOs, CFOs, COOs, CIOs, HR specialists, consultants, internal and external mentors, future mentors, mentees, internal and external coaches, consultants, lecturers, students … But also, any professional who seeks to help their peers or colleagues in the role of the mentor with a coaching attitude. And, finally, educators and parents who are daily mentors with their students, pupils and children.

The book is intended to be both practical and theoretical so that it can be used in both academic and corporate settings.

## Overview of the sections of the book

*Mentoring with a Coaching Attitude* is divided into three main parts.

**Part One** includes:

- Introduction to *Mentoring with a Coaching Attitude*: the why, the why now? The difference from other professions, such as counselling, training, supervision, psychotherapy, coaching.
- The mentoring process: the stakeholders, the agreement and its conditions for success, the overall mentoring process and the three main types of indicators.
- Building the relationship and the tools of Transactional Analysis that sustain this approach.
- The competencies needed by an effective mentor, such as genuine presence and refined listening skills, strategies for asking powerful questions, providing constructive feedback, encouraging mentees to move towards action, monitoring progress and evaluation.
- Installing successful, effective and long-lasting mentoring programmes inside organisations, the roles of the mentor, the mentee, the programme manager and the conditions for success.

**Part Two** considers the history and the philosophy behind *Mentoring with a Coaching Attitude* – the higher purpose:

- Two chapters trace the history of mentoring in the West, starting from Greece, and in the Far East, starting from China.
- One chapter provides answers to the question: 'How can mentoring help us in our quest for deeper self-knowledge and understanding?'
- And one chapter illustrates the motto 'Mentoring is a way of life.'

**Part Three** comprises numerous applications on mentoring and cases from around the world and in different sectors:

- corporate mentoring (a global approach): changing the paradigm
- the supervision of mentors and coaches: main challenges and learnings
- the key role of the programme manager in the light of cases in the French market

- mentoring at Bristol Myers Squibb in Brazil
- mentoring at Kuwait Oil Company
- mentoring with a coach attitude at Médecins sans Frontières
- mentoring at Euroclear
- mentoring at Bosch and at Unilever in Poland
- turning job seekers into job creators in India
- mentoring at the University Hassan II of Casablanca and mentoring political parties
- mentoring in two universities in China.

We hope that all these applications will provide you with the inspiration to create sustainable mentoring programmes inside your organisations and that you will therefore contribute to a better transmission of knowledge, tacit knowledge and way of life.

December 2022

# Part 1

## Introduction to mentoring with a coaching attitude

# 1 Mentoring with a coaching attitude: what is it exactly?

This first chapter encompasses an introduction to the mentoring profession, its origins, its benefits, and its foundation values and models, a comparison with other professions, as well as the structure of a mentoring session.

## What is mentoring?

The roots of the practice of mentoring are lost in antiquity. The word itself was inspired by the character of Mentor in Homer's *Odyssey* (see Chapter 13). Though the Mentor in the story is a somewhat ineffective old man, the goddess Athena takes on his appearance in order to guide young Telemachus in his time of difficulty. As explained in Chapter 14, mentoring technologies are also derived from the Chinese *Analects of Confucius* in the ancient period, which means to teach students in accordance with their aptitude.

### Some definitions

'**Mentoring** is a learning relationship, involving the sharing of skills, knowledge, and expertise between a mentor and mentee through developmental conversations, experience sharing, and role modelling' – European Mentoring and Coaching Council (EMCC) 2022.

'**Mentorship** is a process for the informal transmission of knowledge, social capital, and the psychosocial support perceived by the recipient as relevant to work, career, or professional development; mentoring entails informal communication, usually face-to-face and during a sustained period of time, between a person who is perceived to have greater relevant knowledge, wisdom, or experience (the mentor) and a person who is perceived to have less (the protégé)' – Wikipedia.

'**Mentoring** is a helping relationship based on exchange of knowledge, experience and goodwill. Mentors help someone less experienced gain confidence, clearer purpose, insight and wisdom' – David Clutterbuck (2014).

'**Mentoring** is an Alliance and a Learning partnership between two people with different levels or kinds of experience, where both can achieve new learning, new insights and personal growth' – Kirsten M. Poulsen.[5]

---

5    Kirsten M. Poulsen, (2008) *A New Way of Seeing Mentoring – benefits for mentors: Mentor+Guide*, KMP+ Forlag.

# The benefits of mentoring

Especially in the workplace, there are many benefits for an employer in developing a mentoring programme for new and current employees. Those benefits apply in different domains, which we will look at now.

### Career development mentoring

In this domain, mentoring has the following benefits:

- Enables an organisation to help junior employees to learn the skills and behaviours from senior employees that the junior employees need to advance to higher-responsibility positions.
- Can help to align organisational goals with employees' personal career goals (of progressing within the organisation).
- Gives employees the ability to advance professionally and learn more about their work.
- Provides employees with a feeling of engagement with the organisation, which can lead to better retention rates and increased employee satisfaction.

### High potential mentoring

In this domain, mentoring offers two major benefits:

- The most talented employees in organisations tend to be difficult to retain, as they are usually seeking greater challenges and responsibilities.
- Granting them one-on-one guidance from senior leaders can help to build the engagement of these talented employees, give them the opportunity to develop and increase their retention in the organisation.

### Diversity mentoring

In this domain, there are several interesting outcomes:

- Mentoring is a good way to innovate by bringing in new ideas from senior employees and leaders from underrepresented groups (e.g., women, ethnic minorities, etc.) – who is included in an underrepresented group depends on the industry sector and the country.
- Mentors from underrepresented groups can empower employees from other underrepresented groups to increase their confidence to take on higher-responsibility tasks and prepare for leadership roles.
- By developing employees from diverse groups, it can give the organisation access to new ideas, new ways of looking at problems and new perspectives.
- It also brings cultural awareness and intercultural dialogue into the workplace.

- Mentor/mentee relationships between homogenous groups (majority/majority or minority/minority) can provide a sense of security and belonging within an organisation. These relationships tend to lead to success within the organisation and increased job satisfaction.

## Reverse mentoring

In this domain, mentoring generates surprising results:

- While mentoring generally involves a more experienced, typically older employee or leader providing guidance to a younger employee, the opposite approach can also be used. It is particularly true in the 2000s, with the rise of digital innovations, internet applications and social media.
- In some cases, new, young employees are more familiar with these technologies than senior employees in the organisations.
- Younger generations can help the older generations to expand and grow towards current trends.
- Everyone has something to bring to the table; this creates a 'two-way street' within companies where younger employees can see the larger picture, and senior employees can learn from younger employees.

## Knowledge transfer mentoring

In this domain, mentoring generates under conditions:

- Employees must have a certain set of skills in order to accomplish the tasks at hand.
- Mentoring is a great approach to help employees get organised and give them access to an expert who can give feedback and help answer questions that they may not know where to find answers to.

# The competencies of the mentor

According to the European Mentoring and Coaching Council (EMCC), there are eight competencies that are common to coaching. See Figure 1.1. Two specific competencies for mentoring could be added upon the results of the poll held in 2022 with the members[6] – 'Being a Role Model' and 'Using One's Professional Experience'.

---

6   As announced during the EMCC Mentoring Day on 28 October 2022, those two new competencies were confirmed by an internal enquiry with the EMCC members. However, the decision to add them in the accreditation competencies or to create a separate accreditation journey for mentors still had to be made by the EMCC Global Board when the final draft of this book was completed in December 2022.

**Figure 1.1** EMCC Mentoring Competencies (as of August 2022)

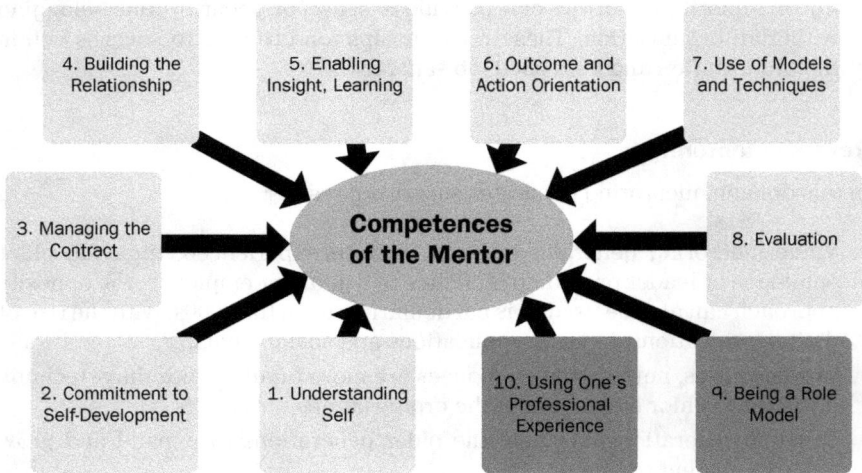

| | | | |
|---|---|---|---|
| 4. Building the Relationship | 5. Enabling Insight, Learning | 6. Outcome and Action Orientation | 7. Use of Models and Techniques |
| 3. Managing the Contract | **Competences of the Mentor** | | 8. Evaluation |
| 2. Commitment to Self-Development | 1. Understanding Self | 10. Using One's Professional Experience | 9. Being a Role Model |

# Compared to other professions: what mentoring is or is not

Mentoring is a stand-alone profession with its own rules, ethics and special training. Serious training courses provide the basic competencies, particularly the eight competencies that are common for two professions (mentoring and coaching) plus the two additional competencies for mentoring as defined by the EMCC (see Figure 1.1). Mentoring is completely different from other techniques, but also embeds some of them.

## Individual training

Training means the transfer of knowledge from the trainer to the trainee. The trainer adopts a dominant position and remains in control of the interaction.

This is also found in mentoring; however, it is the mentee who decides what subjects are to be dealt with, and there is no prior preparation – outside of the definition of objectives and the signing of the contract.

## Consulting – advice

In the case of consultancy, the expert is familiar with the activity sector in which they have developed acknowledged experience. They analyse, benchmark and compare. They make recommendations.

Advice is offered in mentoring. However, it is far more empowering that the mentor also allows the mentee to select their own path. The mentee should be involved in their own solution. They are not *given* a fish – they learn to fish and thus become autonomous.

## Supervision of mentors and coaches

Supervision of mentors and coaches is an activity undertaken by a more experienced practitioner with the aim of spotlighting the practices leading to the assimilation of new methods. It mainly focuses on the relationship between the practitioner and their client's or mentee's system. It is a didactic method intended to acquire greater personal capacity to provide beneficial services.

In fact, the mentor and the coach are in a process of continuous training and constant supervision. Supervision is a specific professional contract that deals with the practice of the person being supervised. If, for example, a mentor is in supervision, the contract will focus on how they mentor someone and their system, or how they established their mentoring contract, or what type of emotions resonate with them, for instance.

## Psychotherapy

Although it may be the case that mentoring is also a supportive relationship, it differs from therapy in that it is not directed at people who are suffering, have problems that they cannot solve or suffer from pathological disorders. Therapy explores the past with a view to isolating a pattern and explaining it. Mentoring concentrates on the present and the future. Therapy is not concerned with the objectives to be achieved, even if a patient's desired condition is clearly defined at the beginning of the therapy process.

A therapy session generally lasts 30, 45 or 60 minutes and sessions are frequent (often once a week); while mentoring sessions are typically longer but less frequent.

## Mentoring versus coaching

Because of their experience, the mentor gives an example and communicates knowledge and skills. In this sense, the word *mentor* usually refers to older and more experienced individuals who are in positions to be able to communicate their professional skills and business know-how to younger candidates, the mentees or apprentices. Some call mentoring 'Coaching Plus'.

Coaching, however, adopts the position that the client is perfectly responsible and in full possession of their means. They are mature and know how to take their destiny into their own hands. The coach helps them to organise themselves and set everything in motion, confident in the knowledge that the client is in possession of all the resources necessary to reach the goal.

**Figure 1.2** Comparisons between mentoring and coaching

|  | MENTORING | COACHING |
|---|---|---|
| Goal | Career and personal development via counselling and guidance. | High performance development via problem solving and attaining specific goals. |
| Source | Mentor past experience / Mentor walked the same path the mentee wants to. | Client's resources / Coach does not need to have the same background as the client. |
| Process | Mentor shares expertise and offers possible solutions via storytelling. | Coach helps client to find their own solutions via questioning. |
| Duration | Since it deals with career and personal development, may become lifelong. | Usually as long as it takes to attain a given goal or develop a given skill. |
| Focus | The mentee and his aspirations. | Goal / target attainment. |
| Origin | Greece – mentor tutored Telemachus, son to Ulysses, King of Ithaca. | Greece – Socrates deployed Questioning (Irony) to generate Insights (Maieutic). |

# What the 'coaching attitude' means in practice

Since ancient Greece and the recognition of the role of Mentor, the friend of Ulysses, the philosophy of mentoring has always been based on a relationship between an experienced elder and an inexperienced younger person. One would transfer their knowledge and the other would listen and apply what they received.

This approach has lasted through the centuries but is no longer applied in the same way today. Indeed, the leadership style has changed. We are no longer in the era of 'telling' (listen and obey) but rather in the era of 'asking' (what are you doing to meet this challenge?)

This is especially true for millennials, the generation born around the year 2000, who want more meaning and purpose in their work, but also for their elders, whose desire for more ecology is becoming increasingly prevalent. Traditional mentoring is becoming 'mentoring with a coaching attitude'.

## What is meant by 'coaching attitude'?

A coaching attitude is based on a series of principles that form the basis of this profession, which has its roots in sports and in Socrates' theory of maieutic.

**Coaches have the firm conviction that their clients know more than they believe.** Their role is therefore to help clients to 'give birth' to solutions that they probably have already mentally or intuitively elaborated. Through powerful questioning, coaches lead their clients to formulate their thoughts and objectives, to overcome possible barriers and to transform their intention and objectives into action plans. In this way, coaches reverse the stages of learning explained by the anthropologist Gregory Bateson: clients do not know that they already know, and coaches are there to bring out this knowledge (see the steps of the Learning Process).

**Coaches never judge; they ask questions, provide constructive feedback**. Their goal is to make their clients feel comfortable in all circumstances so that their full creative potential can be unleashed.

**Coaches have developed strong listening skills and are able to hear the words and what is said between the words** – body language, emotions, beliefs, moods, etc.

**Coaches put themselves at par with their clients**. They feel neither superior nor inferior, in skills or in achievements. If they feel their clients are losing parity, they do everything to restore it. They are in perfect OK-ness with their clients (see the theory on Life Positions below).

Importantly, **they encourage their clients to experiment** (see David Kolb) and to **take action**.


### Coaching is about inverting the steps of the Learning Process[7]

In coaching, steps 3 and 4 of Bateson's Learning Process are reverted as the coach helps the coachee become aware that they know a lot already. This approach can be embedded in the mentoring process.

1 **Unconscious incompetence**
   I don't know that I don't know.
   I don't know that I cannot do it.
2 **Conscious incompetence**
   Now I know that I don't know.
   Now I know that I cannot do it.
3 **Conscious competence**
   Now I know that I know.
   Now I know that I can do it.
4 **Unconscious competence**
   It's obvious, it is completely intuitive.
5 **Incompetence made conscious again**
   Well, I need to learn again as the technology has changed.

---

7    Gregory Bateson (1972) *Steps to an Ecology of Mind: Collected Essays in Anthropology, Psychiatry, Evolution, and Epistemology*, University of Chicago Press.

## Life Positions:[8] finding the OK-ness with the mentee for better mutual respect

Many mentors have a sincere admiration and respect for their mentees and transfer their knowledge with simplicity and care. They consider that they just have more experience and that their mentee is a specialist-to-be. They are in a relationship where both deploy their 'OK-ness', a concept created by Franklin Ernst Jr, and which is a wonderful model of Transactional Analysis.[9]

Life Positions are basic beliefs about self and others, which are used to justify decisions about ourselves and others, and to justify our own behaviour.

This life position is defined in childhood. By the way they are treated in their families, schools and environment, children make choices about their existential position. This choice guides their way of seeing themselves and others. This position is in some ways the basic postulate of themselves and others and goes as far as their way of seeing the world beyond their own behaviour. 'The world is like that.' The good news is that a wrong perception can always be corrected by a good mentor, a good coach or, if more deeply rooted, by a good psychotherapist.

Everyone can be in any position of life at any time. Therefore, simply because someone has been seen two or three times in a given position of life, it cannot be generalised that any of those life positions is their normal position. What is fundamental when communicating with someone is to understand what position they find themselves living at moment T.

At one moment T, to say **'I'm OK, they are OK'** or **'be in ++'** means that there is a potential source of wellbeing for oneself and for others. Here, we are on an existential level: the person feels good about themselves, regardless of their behaviour. They fully accept the consequences of their actions. The decision 'I'm OK, they are OK' was made by the child raised in a family where there is perceived love, fairness and kindness. When punished, they know this is fair and done because their parents love them and want them to be well-educated. At another moment T, to say 'You're OK' means that the other person is the source of wellbeing for themselves and for us (they wish us well). However, this does not mean that we accept everything they do.

*For the mentors in OK-OK position or* **++**: the relation is fluid, ego-free, they share with humility yet accepting their competence and experience. They are open, vulnerable and top transmitters.

---

8   Concept by Franklin Ernst Jr. (1971) The OK Corral: The Grid for the Get-on-With, *Transactional Analysis Journal*, 1, 4.

9   Transactional Analysis (TA) is a discipline created in the late 1950s by the Canadian psychiatrist Eric Lennard Bernstein, better known as Dr Eric Berne. It is a psychoanalytic theory and method of therapy wherein social interactions (or 'transactions') are analysed to determine the ego state of the communicator (whether parent-like, child-like, or adult-like) as a basis for understanding behaviour. In transactional analysis, the communicator is taught to alter the ego state as a way to solve emotional problems. The method deviates from Freudian psychoanalysis which focuses on increasing awareness of the contents of subconsciously held ideas – Wikipedia.

***For the mentees in OK-OK position*** **++**: they feel the joy of being supported by a highly qualified mentor and they accept being an apprentice, a learner. They are at peace with themselves and with the process. They speak openly and do not hesitate to display their doubts, fears, flaws and areas for development.

At another moment T, to say **'I'm not OK, they are OK'** or **'be in -/+'** means that I am fundamentally wrong, that nothing of value can come from myself, whatever I do. The person is inferior to the other. If they do not feel OK when others are OK, they say to themselves that they are worthless, that others are better than they are and that the feeling could develop into an inferiority complex. Here the child has been educated in a family where there is blame and humiliation. It could emanate from a parent who always compares the little one to elder siblings for instance. As a result, the child develops an inferiority complex and becoming adult, tends to find themselves in difficult situations where they might be ridiculed or humiliated.

***For the mentors in a 'non-OK-OK' or '-/+ position'***: they may feel uncomfortable in the relationship, not daring to provide feedback or ask the adequate question at the adequate time. They hold themselves back. Or they might be demanding too much, wanting to be too perfect, holding too fast to their mentee, not for the performance itself but to prove to themselves that they are good effective mentors.

***For the mentees in a non-OK-OK or -/+ position***: they feel worthless, like a dummy, and place their mentor on a pedestal (even if the mentor does nothing to gain this honour), they do not dare to show vulnerability or mistakes, they wear a mask of performance as they seek recognition, or they hide mistakes and areas for development. They lose the opportunity to be a learner and do not take full benefit from the mentoring process – like a curse: 'This is not for me; I do not deserve this.'

At another moment T, to say **'I am OK, you're not OK'** or **'be in +/-'** means that the other person could be the source of bad things, of mistakes. If the person feels that they are OK, and that others are not OK, they begin to despise the others, become arrogant and develop a superiority complex at that time. Here the child has been educated by parents who repeatedly say that their family is above the others; for instance 'We are noble, or much brighter than others or we come from the capital city'. Grown up, the child will continue despising others and feel superior. Importantly, some people seem to be in a +/- 'plus-minus' relationship but in fact, are hiding a -/+ 'minus-plus' position – they take a lot of space, they move a lot when speaking as they do not feel at ease and need to recomfort themselves.

***For the mentors in 'OK-non-OK' or +/- position***: they will speak a lot about themselves, displaying their successes, their achievements and leave little space to their mentee. They tend to impose their opinion and are poor listeners or might be using the mentee's words to project their own way of doing – which is the only valid way for them, of course.

*For the mentees in 'OK-non-OK' or +/- position*: first there is little chance that they accept being mentored and will soon disqualify their mentor ('I thought he was competent, but I am very disappointed') or the mentoring process ('This is not what I need for the time being'). Or they will pretend that the mentor's suggestions do not match the reality of today, or find arguments to counter the mentor's opinion and place themselves in competition with their mentor, etc.

At another moment T, to say **'I'm not OK, you're not OK' or 'be in -/ -'** means that the person believes in neither themselves nor the other person at that moment. Here the child was born in a terrible and unhappy environment (starvation, war, perpetual conflict, rape, etc.) and concludes that they are not worth living in that horrible environment and that others are bad as well. They might become addicted to drugs, violence, or commit an act against themselves, and there is very little chance that they could be a candidate for mentoring (however, when they engage in mentoring, results are incredibly positive in very little time).

**Figure 1.3** The OK-Corral

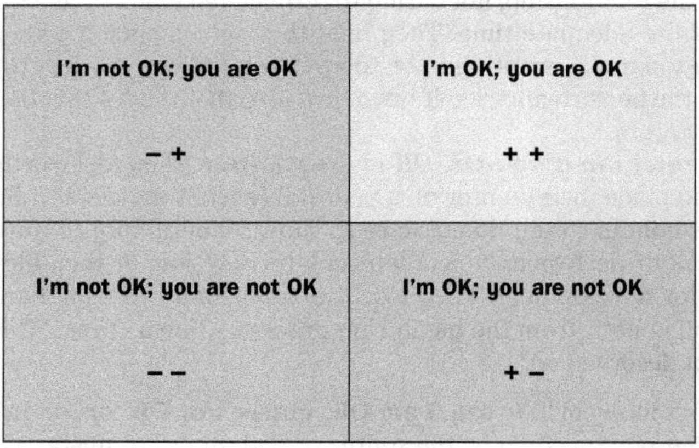

| | |
|---|---|
| **I'm not OK; you are OK**<br><br>**– +** | **I'm OK; you are OK**<br><br>**+ +** |
| **I'm not OK; you are not OK**<br><br>**– –** | **I'm OK; you are not OK**<br><br>**+ –** |

The position 'I'm OK; you're OK' or 'to be in ++' is the best for long-term viability. It allows the resolution of problems and conflicts. We can all experience a non-OKness position but it never lasts for a long time. To be aware of our vulnerability and to accept is a further proof of OK-ness.

> **Mentor's take-away**: It is always possible to change a non-OK position into an OK-OK position through good mentoring and supervision, and above all with lots of agape (humanistic) love and respect. It is our job as mentors to be the safeguards of the OK-ness in all circumstances and it starts with ourselves (see Chapter 16). If it is too difficult for us to restore our mentee's ++ position, it might mean that the mentee needs psychotherapy – and perhaps the mentor needs some supervision or therapy as well …

## Kolb's Stages of Learning to push the mentee into experimentation and action[10]

Just as one moves from one level of learning (subconscious incompetence to conscious incompetence – Bateson), the mentee is invited to pass through the learning stages described by David Kolb (2015). The coaching attitude is precisely that invitation towards immediate action.

Kolb presents learning from experience (or experiential learning) as a four-stroke cycle, each 'stroke' corresponding to a specific learning style.

**Figure 1.4** The process of experiential learning proposed by S. Cannio based on D. Kolb and K. Lewin (Kolb published his experiential learning theory (ELT) in 2014, inspired by the work of the gestalt psychologist Kurt Lewin.)

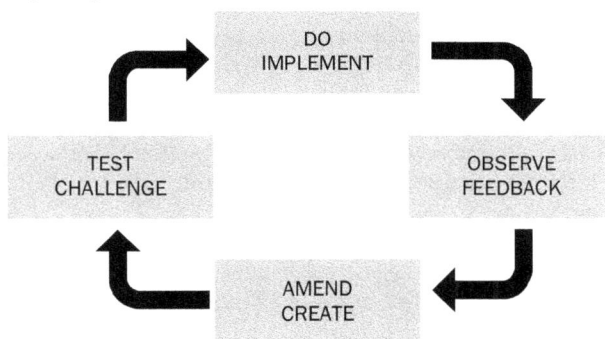

**Concrete experience – Do/Implement**: in this phase, the person 'lives' the experience; they record information about what they discover; it is a receiving phase, the taking in of information.

**Reflective observation – Observe**: the person analyses the situation they have just experienced, compares it with previous situations, and tries to make sense of it.

**Abstract conceptualisation – Think/Amend/Create**: this is a theoretical stage; the person develops concepts to analyse the experience they have just lived.

**Active experimentation – Test/Dare**: the person has developed several hypotheses; they will prove or disprove them through a new experience. The cycle can then start again.

This circular process does not necessarily occur in the order shown here. The experience of one person varies from another, and from one phase to another.

Kolb states that everyone has their preferred learning style.

---

10   David Kolb: *Experiential Learning: Experience as the Source of Learning and Development*, Pearson Education, 2015. The verbs Do-See-Think-Dare were added by the authors of this book.

What is important in mentoring is to verify that the mentee passes through the four learning stages effectively. There must be experimentation in order to achieve the integration of new behaviour; in the same way, the mentee needs to pass through the observation and then the conception phases to consolidate a change in their habits.

# The balance of power between coaching and mentoring

Despite the long history behind mentoring, coaching has retained the attention of many corporates and HR professionals for the past thirty years. In recent years, the pendulum has shifted, and more companies are now turning to mentoring as an important and effective people development and retention tool. Coaching maintains its role and indeed, the two terms are often used interchangeably. There are, however, some clear differences but each remains a powerful and valuable approach to people development. The key is to use the right approach for the situation and many companies are now considering both in a blended manner.

The other context of power relating to coaching and mentoring is the dimension of the relationship between coach–coachee and mentor–mentee. The notion that 'knowledge is power' informs us that in the classic mentor–mentee relationship, where the mentor is normally more senior and experienced than the mentee, then the 'power' sits more with the mentor. On the other hand, the coach does not require in-depth technical expertise on what the coachee does. Whichever approach is taken, having insights on the power shift at the start, during and towards the end of the relationship is important. This is even more relevant in the mentor–mentee relationship since these continue over a longer period of time and are more holistic than the coach–coachee relationship, which are shorter in time, and skills- or performance-focused.

A coach asks instead of tells and a mentor shares personal experiences and guides. Both approaches have their place depending on the development needs of the individual.

In a coaching relationship, there 'should' be no power relations; both 'should' be in full parity. The coach does not share their story nor experience, and their true power relies on the quality of their questioning in order to stretch the coachee's views and raise their level of awareness.

A 'traditional' mentor will merely adopt a parental posture: 'I have been there before you, I have experience and pretty well know the technology that you need for your professional development.'

In a more contemporary approach, namely mentoring with a coaching attitude, we find a blending of mentoring and coaching – core competences are key to good mentoring (listening skills, impactful questioning) and sharing feedback based on personal experience – warning the mentee about the benefits and the pitfalls, sometimes looking to receive information and an answer to their question.

In reference to power, let us remember that there are various types of power:

- Positional power: I am your boss and I tell you what you do.
- Technical power: you come to me so that I share my competences.
- Expert power: I have a specific technology, e.g., accountancy (a mentor can have expert power).
- Referent power: I have power because you trust me – this is important in mentoring.
- Personal power: I love what you say and I want to support you.

In mentoring with a coaching attitude, the mentor can rely on their power but will do it in a more subtle way, preferably by sharing experience with detachment, by inspiring, encouraging, supporting, and less by advising or suggesting.

From their side, it is important for the leader to determine whether they need more coaching or more mentoring, or a blend of both.

# 2 The mentoring process

In this chapter, we will see how the traditional mentoring process can be augmented by some elements of the coaching process. We will analyse the types of contracts, the process itself and how to measure its effectiveness through well-determined indicators.

## The types of relationships and contracts

### From self-initiated relationships[11] to better-structured mentoring programmes

Many mentoring journeys are generated by mentors and mentees themselves. 'I need a mentor; would you be mine?' or 'I am ready to help younger executives and would like to dedicate time to help them grow. It is my passion' are the types of statements that are often heard inside the corporation. This type of informal 'good old fellowship' could sustain for a period; however, either the relationship lasts for many years due to a wonderful chemistry within the pair, or the process fails rapidly due to a lack of structure, clear objectives and indicators, and follow-up.

The upside is that the pair can set up their own framework for mentoring, including those well-determined objectives and indicators, and the relationship remains free from any expectation generated by a third party.

The downside is that without some more formal structure and process, the journey might quickly fail due to a lack of motivation from one or both parties, and a lack of visibility of the possible outcomes of the mentoring journey. As analysed by Arshad Ali in his chapter on the New Paradigm (see Chapter 17), informal mentoring is more focused on the benefit to the individual rather than on the organisation's benefit. While this is good for the individual, less well-networked employees and minorities can be side-lined. This can result in non-egalitarian treatment of employees that can have a very negative and detrimental impact on morale.

With the rise of in-house mentoring programmes, we often see that both the mentors and mentees appreciate so much this form of development that they

---

11   This paragraph is inspired by Kirsten Poulsen's webinar provided during the Mentoring Day organised in October 2019 by EMCC.

actively seek out the role again, or that mentees apply to become mentors, and mentors try to find mentees or find mentors for themselves. When they have taken part in a formal, organised mentoring programme, they have a much better understanding of the framework and ground rules required by a mentoring alliance. Therefore, they are better prepared for self-initiated mentoring relationships after participating in the programme. They are also much more likely to get good results from their self-initiated relationship.

### Inviting a friendly witness

The principle of a mentoring journey is that it will always remain voluntary, confidential and without control, except in terms of process by the Programme Manager (making sure pairs are well matched, monitoring the number of sessions, etc.). However, there is one element of the coaching process that could be introduced to make it more involving: inviting one or two 'friendly witnesses' of the mentee's development. Usually, the invitation is made to the mentee's line manager and/or a member of the HR department. The line manager is the best-positioned person to witness the mentee's development over time based on clear behaviour indicators (see below). There is one condition though: the line manager is not included in the process for any kind of control but rather to encourage and support the adoption of new habits and behaviours. This is a further reason to include the line manager in the training sessions organised to sustain the mentoring programme (see Step 3 below, as well as Chapter 12).

If a friendly witness is invited aboard, the mentor would first meet separately with the mentee to establish initial contact and main mentoring objectives. They would then meet the witness(es) in an 'alignment meeting' or 'intake meeting' to determine the contract altogether. This would include the standard contractual terms, including duration of the mentoring; number and frequency of sessions; location; context and objectives; evaluation methodology; financial terms (for external mentors); confidentiality, rules of ethics, etc. It is also recommended to include a cancellation clause and a way to solve any conflict should it occur.

In recent times, management in organisations has invested significant time in the following activities related to mentoring programmes:

* Matching the mentee with a neutral and experienced mentor and creating the objectives.
* Creating a supportive and confidential learning environment where both parties can explore their skills, opportunities and ambitions.
* Challenging the participants – both mentors and mentees – to get to know themselves better by seeing themselves through another person's eyes.
* Giving mentors the opportunity to develop their leadership skills and competences by practising the mentor role.

# The mentoring process

The literature contains several examples of mentoring processes – generally in four or five steps – and specific ones are sometimes developed by mentoring consultants, as you can read in several cases in Part Three of this book. In this chapter, we shall rely on the MentoringCo Mentoring Process (MMP), as it was generated by the authors of this book and is based on the company's best practices for establishing impactful mentoring programmes.

## The MentoringCo Mentoring Process (MMP)

**Figure 2.1** MentoringCo Mentoring Process (MMP)

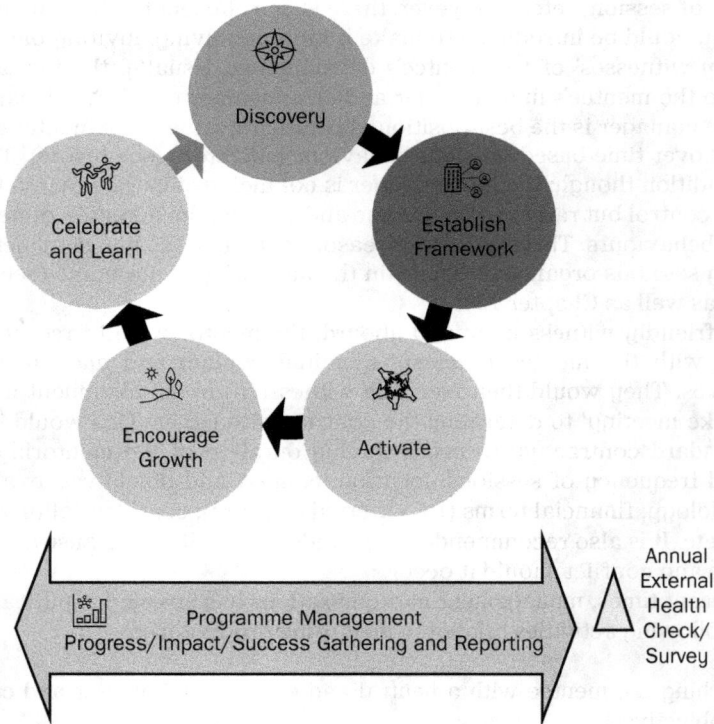

## Step 1: Discovery

This first step is organised with the input of senior stakeholders and direct sponsors – business or functional heads. It encompasses three major elements:

1 A needs analysis.
2 Governance.
3 The scope.

A **needs analysis** is performed to define the overall purpose of the mentoring programme as well as its strategic intent (see Chapter 17, explaining how to align a mentoring programme to the corporate strategy). The analysis will also determine the expected business impact, as a mentoring programme should serve the business and not only individuals. And it should also establish its ROI/Cost-benefits.

The **governance** includes three elements: who is sponsoring the programme, the composition of the Steering Committee – roles, expectations, etc. – and the nomination of a Programme Manager who will lead the project, from inception to concluding report. During this important phase, the company either relies on internal forces or appoints an external consultant.

The third element is the **scope**: what are the boundaries of the project, deliverables, outcomes and timelines? Who are the first target groups – do we start with a pilot programme, or do we immediately roll out? What is the timeline, and which will be the major milestones?

### Step 2: Establish framework

We are still in the preparation phase, and this needs clarity on several elements:

1  Stakeholder enrolment.
2  Communication.
3  Governance.
4  Operating scope.
5  Impact / result tracking.

**Stakeholder enrolment**: Who and how are we going to recruit? Which profiles? The team needs to establish the roles of mentors, mentees, the support team as well as the ground rules. The Programme Manager should be appointed (See Chapter 19 on the key role of the Programme Manager). And the potential barriers should be addressed so that we reach a win-win situation for all stakeholders.
**Communication**: A strong communication plan should be elaborated, explaining the rationale behind the mentoring programme, with the aim of motivating both mentors and mentees to enrol.
**Governance**: All stakeholders must be aware of the scope of their roles and responsibilities. There should be consensus and compliance to clear ground rules. Also, precise ways of working must be established for all parties, including elements of contracting, following-up and reporting.
**Operating scope**: Under this umbrella, we find measurement elements, learning events, supervision and supporting application/software.

- Measurement and evaluation: it must be clearly indicated how mentees' progression will be assessed. Quite often, organisations organise pre-mentoring measurement including pre-assessments, 360 degree or 180 degree enquiries and personality tests, for example MBTI, PCM, Insight, etc.
- Learning events: determine the length, the rhythm, the duration and the audience of the learning events. These should be punctuating the whole duration

of the process in order to offer support to all parties. Usually, corporations organise one event per quarter for a programme lasting one year.

- Support and supervision must be organised for the mentors; they need to have a space where they can obtain support in case of difficulty with their mentee and reinforce methods that are working well.
- Specific software or applications (APPs) should be used to follow up the process. Today, several APP designers have created supporting tools for effective mentoring programmes including a 'matching list' of mentors and mentees, a calendar for sessions' follow-up, and key statistics and reporting tools so that the Programme Manager and HR can monitor the process.

**Impact/result tracking**: This element of measurement should be facilitated by customised software or an application as mentioned above. It is a discipline to install this as early as possible in the whole process.

## Step 3: Activate mentoring

We are now in the implementation phase of the process. It implies four stages:

1 Recruit mentors and mentees.
2 Match.
3 Train.
4 Launch the programme.

**Recruit**: There must be sufficient mentors to satisfy the mentees' needs and have them committing to the programme in terms of responsibility as a mentor, the time allocation and the priority they confer to their role as a mentor. The programme management should create the lists of mentors and mentees and start matching.

**Match**: The closer the background and the personality, the better will be the matching. However, the opposite – different backgrounds and personalities – leads to far more interesting learning (see Chapters 10 to 12 about installing programmes inside corporations).

**Train**: Training must be organised for three populations: the future mentors, the future mentees and the line managers. Each individual must have full clarity on their respective role, the way they get involved to ensure the success of the programme, what it means in terms of commitment and respect of the confidentiality rule, etc. Especially mentors must know what is meant by a 'good mentor,' what are the competences they already have or must acquire to fulfil the requirement of the mentoring programme – especially if it is on special techniques – what to expect from the mentoring programme and how they could also learn from it; how they can prioritise so that the mentee knows that the mentor remains available, how to manage progress and, perhaps, frustration if the mentee doesn't comply with the standards and speed of learning. Usually, they are invited to meet former mentors who will share their experience.

This preparation phase is of paramount importance to make sure that mentors are fully aware of what represents a fruitful mentoring relationship. The time consumption must be clear in terms of number of meetings foreseen; the necessity to prioritise so that the mentee doesn't feel abandoned when mentors are confronted with a heavy workload and might not leave time for their mentoring meetings. Clarifying the use of time guarantees that there are no surprises for both parties – mentor/mentee – about their respective expectations.

**Launch the programme**: The programme should be launched officially by management – the higher the better. The sponsorship of senior leaders, especially with their own stories of how they have benefited from mentoring, tends to have a big impact on the mentoring culture of the company. Is the company launching a full-fledged programme or a first pilot? Clarity of communication is key to manage expectations.

### Step 4: Encourage growth

Time will fly and the programme management must follow up with:

1 Learning events.
2 Supervision.
3 Feed-forward.
4 Checking the course and finetuning if needed.

**Learning events**: After basic training has been provided to stakeholders, more specific training sessions could be organised to address the prioritised themes: leadership, increasing visibility through new digital techniques, communication techniques, etc.

**Supervision**: Mentors should vent their doubts and fears about their practice in case they are faced with negative energy or game playing by the mentee (playing 'victim' for instance – see Chapter 8 on autonomy). Supervisions offer a safe space, the temenos (see Chapter 3) for the mentee to share their emotions, their sensibility and the challenges faced during the mentoring process and sessions. Either the corporation can rely on an internal supervisor or appoints external supervisors depending on organisational contexts and needs. Common challenges met in mentoring are further explored and addressed in supervision (see Chapter 18 on mentor supervision).

**Feed-forward**: At several moments during the mentoring process, the Programme Manager (PM) should enquire on several points:

- Enquire on the perception of both parties on the process, the sessions, listen to their feelings.
- Reflect on the impact of the learning events: should their content be revised? Should they be adapted to environmental changes?
- Check the satisfaction level of all stakeholders.
- Monitor the efficiency of the follow-up.

**Checking the course and finetuning if needed**: Conclusions after each learning event should be analysed with great care and processed. This allows further events to be well adapted to expectations, new requirements by the business or the environment (e.g., sanitary rules), new techniques and technologies, etc.

### Step 5: Celebrate and learn

This last step includes three elements:

1  Review the business impact.
2  Consolidate wins and learning.
3  Conduct closing event.

**Review the business impact**: When Key Performance Indicators (KPIs) are clearly established – both quantitative and qualitative – it will be easier to assess the impact of the programme. This reporting phase is important as it might motivate the corporation to launch additional programmes in other departments or business lines for instance.

**Consolidate wins and learning**: Success should be modelised and anchored in 'best practice' documentation to be transferred to next generations of PMs and mentors. Learning is key at all levels of the process, from inception to the reporting phase and conclusion. 'I never fail,' says Nelson Mandela, 'Either I succeed, or I learn.' This motto should be applied to the corporation as well to pave the way to succeeding programmes.

**Conduct closing event**: It is important to celebrate and to communicate about the success and learnings of the programme. This is a good way to have mentors and mentees join to share their personal experiences, their progress, and express their gratitude for their mentors and for the corporation. It will also be the time to determine what will happen next. Many mentor–mentee pairs pursue their relationship on a friendly basis; they meet inside or outside the organisation, they still enjoy being together. However, and especially if the mentor has a heavy workload, the mentoring programme should have an end and promote the mentee's full autonomy – this is the scope of Chapter 8 on autonomy.

# The three main types of indicators

Three types of indicators are seen during the mentoring process:

1  The Key Performance Indicators (KPIs) of the programme itself.
2  The Key Behaviour Indicators (KBIs) of each individual mentoring journey.
3  The indicators of each mentoring session.

### The KPIs of the programme itself

When the mentoring programme meets the strategic focus of the corporation, it is easy to establish Key Performance Indicators as the programme should have a clear impact on the business. It is important to note that mentoring is an intervention taken to support the achievement of these KPIs. It would be the joined-up impact of the efforts of the mentoring programmes, the respective functional and department heads to achieve the set KPIs. Review of KPIs are just one of the three levers of success in mentoring. Here are three examples:

One company wants to decrease its turnover rate among the generations X and Z. They offer a mentor to 20 employees. The KPIs, in this case, are rather easy to determine:

- Increase the retention rate among the selected population from x per cent to y per cent.
- Increase the satisfaction rate at work by xx per cent.
- Promote xx of them within the mentoring programme period.

A second company wants to enhance diversity into its middle management. Several KPIs are established:

- Increase promotion rate by xx per cent within the target groups: women leaders, specific ethnic groups, people with lower management skills, executives with specific backgrounds.
- Ensure that xx per cent of the target population are keen to increase their visibility, enhance their leadership and communication skills.
- Organise x learning events in addition to mentoring sessions.

A third company would like to create bridges between two newly acquired units, and decides upon these KPIs:

- Through the mentoring programme, organise 50 pairs originated from the two new acquisitions.
- Make sure mentoring allows the dissemination of key corporate values and helps newcomers mix with old timers daily.
- Transfer ways to do (behaviours) to build a new corporate culture.

These KPIs are quantitative and qualitative and are rather easy to measure by the end of the mentoring programme.

## The KBIs of the individual mentoring journeys

Individual objectives and KBIs are part of the agreement signed by the mentor and their mentee. They are established together with all the actors of the mentoring process during the Alignment or Intake meeting. And they are written in the agreement signed by all parties. Here we speak about Key *Behaviour* Indicators; this means some **newly installed behaviours** that the mentee performs at work.

In coaching, those KBIs are accurately detailed as directly relating to a better performance. It could be a leader who needs to improve their leadership skills; in this case, a KBI could be their 'new' ability to provide feedback, to develop their team members and to ensure a good life balance among their team members, especially young parents.

In mentoring, since it is a more holistic relationship, and not only based on improving short-term performance, KBIs will automatically be more general. Still, it is important that the mentor takes extreme care with the quality of the objectives – and this could be an input from the coaching process that we advocate in this book. The objectives must be SMARTEC (smart + ecological + under the mentee's control – see Chapter 8) and therefore easy to measure. And the KBIs, those new behaviours taken as indicators, should be installed by the end of the mentoring process, a few months later.

Take the example of a young executive who is poised to become a member of the Executive Committee. This could be the main objective of the mentoring process and some KBIs could be:

- Develop assertiveness and become a fine negotiator.
- Be more visible inside and outside the company.

A good way to secure this process is either to include those objectives and related KBIs in the mentoring agreement or to make sure that the mentee includes them in their Personal Development Plan (Goal Achievement). For this, we can also refer to the four levels of the Kirkpatrick Model[12] – Reaction, Learning, Behaviour, Results.

In the framework of a mentoring programme, it would be fantastic to obtain that information on an individual basis and then build them up to an organisational level. This process is difficult and cumbersome as it relies on the organisation to be able to observe the behaviours consistently over time and then capture on a centralised dashboard.

## The indicators of each mentoring session

The last type of indicators are the ones that the mentors will develop during each mentoring session. It is a usual practice in coaching and should be introduced in mentoring as well, as it brings clarity for both parties.

---

12   See www.kirkpatrickpartners.com/the-kirkpatrick-model/ for an explanation of the model.

After taking some time for greeting and chit-chat (see Chapter 3), for explaining what happened since the last session (see Chapter 9), the mentor asks their mentee about the objective of the session.

*Mentor*: What could be a good outcome of our session today?
*Mentee*: Well, I would like to prepare for the next meeting with my line manager as I don't really feel at ease.
*Mentor*: Okay, and how will you know, *by the end of our session today*, that you will be well prepared? What would you like to have in your hands, concretely? (Seeking indicators.)
*Mentee*: I would like to know the key messages to convey, the approach to be adopted: may I speak straightforwardly, or would it be better for me to be prudent and wait?
*Mentor* (reformulating to make sure those are well understood): Okay, so you want an approach and to determine some key messages? All right. By the way, how do you feel now when you think about this meeting with your boss? (Mentor seeks an emotion or body indicator.)
*Mentee*: I feel under pressure, my stomach is tied and I have sweaty hands.
*Mentor*: Okay, and what will have changed in your body when you have the approach, the key messages and perhaps also some tools to be more self-confident?
*Mentee* (with a smile): Oh, I'll feel much lighter, I'll be serene, my breath will be easier and my stomach at ease.

Here, the mentor leads the mentee to determine two types of indicators:

• A mental indicator: a concrete way, a strategy, an approach, some key messages, which are all concrete ways to know that the objective is reached.
• An emotional/physical indicator, as the body knows when the mentee is heading in the right direction.

Those indicators have two functions. The first is to benchmark the session itself: the mentor knows exactly what the mentee would like to reach as a satisfactory outcome of the session. The second is that it also helps the mentor monitor if the mentee is moving in the right direction.

**Mentor's take-away**: Always make sure that you have a clear SMARTEC objective and a minimum of two indicators for **each** mentoring session (one mental, one emotional/body). And feel free to recontract at any time during the session if your mentee shifts into a new direction, e.g., 'We have ten minutes left; what would you like to reach in this time?' or 'I see that your objective has changed. Shall we stick to the first objective or move towards this new one?'

# Inside a mentoring session with a coaching attitude

In this book, we shall rely on the MentoringCo Process created by merging two models: the ILLIADA Mentoring Model created by LeaderArt (Cicero Carvalho and Arshad Ali) and the MOVIDA model created by Sylviane Cannio and Viviane Launer[13] for effective coaching sessions.

**LeaderArt's ILLIADA Mentoring Process** is based on five well-defined steps, as shown in Figure 2.2.

**Figure 2.2** LeaderArt's Illiada Mentoring Process

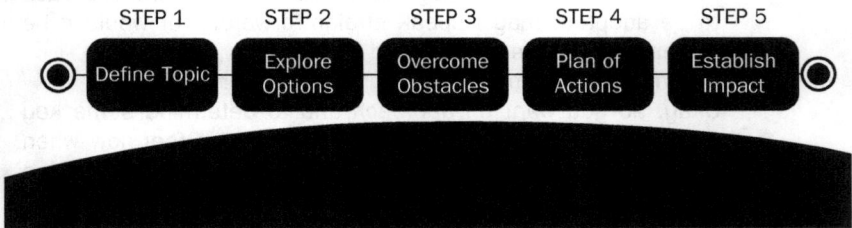

| STEP 1 | STEP 2 | STEP 3 | STEP 4 | STEP 5 |
|--------|--------|--------|--------|--------|
| Define Topic | Explore Options | Overcome Obstacles | Plan of Actions | Establish Impact |

## The Cannio-Launer MOVIDA Model

The Cannio-Launer MOVIDA model briefly summarises what happens during a coaching session on both the coach's side and that of the client. This model perfectly applies to mentoring with a coaching attitude. See Figure 2.3.

**Figure 2.3** The Cannio-Launer Movida Coaching Process

| | For the coach | For the client |
|---|---|---|
| **M** | Monitor | Mobilise yourself |
| **O** | Objectives | |
| **V** | Value the client | Value the experience |
| **I** | Identify options | |
| **D** | Donate space | Decide action |
| **A** | Accompanying | Acting |

## The MentoringCo Mentoring Model

By blending the two models ILLIADA and MOVIDA we can create the MentoringCo model. Figure 2.4 shows the two models combined for a mentoring session with a coaching attitude.

---

13   Sylviane Cannio & Viviane Launer, Coaching Excellence, Lid Publishing London, 2011.

**Figure 2.4** The MentoringCo Mentoring Model

| For the mentor | For the mentee |
|---|---|
| Monitor | Mobilise yourself |
| Define topic and objectives | |
| Value the mentee | Value the experience |
| Identify and explore options | |
| Overcome obstacles | |
| Donate space | Decide action |
| Accompanying | Acting |
| Establish impact | |

### Step 1 – Monitor/mobilise yourself

The session always begins with the establishment of contact and the analysis of the context and of progress made (or not) since the last meeting – if not, what can be developed as a working basis ('what have I put in place to prevent any progress?'). This happens without any judgement, just by analysing facts and pinpointing any possible pattern (repetitive behaviour anchored from the past). On their side, the mentee should have acted and since they have taken the step to see their mentor, they clearly wish to evolve.

Questions that help monitoring the situation and the progress achieved:

- What have you done in this area up to the present?
- What can we celebrate so far? Are you happy with the results?
- (If action was not implemented) What stops you in your current situation?
- Are there some beliefs that prevent you from moving on and do you want to talk about them today?
- Is there any repetitive behaviour that you have adopted for a long time, any fear?
- Is not performing the action to be the objective of our session today?

### Step 2 – Define topic and objectives

Generally, setting the objective of the conversation or mentoring session provides meaning and steering, as well as helping with the structure that the mentee will adopt to reach it.

In addition:

- It helps ensure the mentee's commitment during the conversation.
- It helps establish the focus of what will be discussed.
- It sets forth the criteria to evaluate how productive the discussion was.

Questions that help define the topic:

- At the end of the conversation, what result do you want to achieve?
- What subject would you like to discuss in this meeting today?
- What will you focus on during this conversation?
- What do you expect to specifically achieve when we are done?
- What is the most useful thing for you to take from this session?

*Throughout the session: Step 3 – Value the mentee – value the experience*

Since the first meeting and throughout any mentoring session, the mentor keeps on valuing the mentee and builds on existing foundations, notes the first steps; pushing them to register their available resources, which leads towards greater self-confidence. The mentor constantly looks for supportive underlying behaviour, decodes the strategy put in place to succeed (or not), and assumes that the mentee has all the resources needed to develop and to make the desired changes.

Valuing the mentee helps to:

- Empower them and increase their self-esteem.
- Make them unleash their wings and fly higher.
- Increase the level of energy throughout the mentoring session.
- Make both parties feel good together.

Questions that help valuing the mentee:

- When you analyse your progression so far, which are the lessons learnt?
- Whatever you do, may I invite you to look at you as a great leader? And how can you consolidate this feeling?
- What can you put in place to value your experience?
- Can you see how you have already been capable of overcoming many obstacles and praise yourself?
- Do you see how your foundations are solid? How resilient you are?

*Step 4 – Identify and explore options*

Upon defining the conversation's direction, it is time to investigate possible options to move forward. This is not about finding the 'right' option, because the best option is the one which the mentee feels they have command over and feels responsible for. Based on the mentor's experience, and different from coaching, the mentor may be able to offer some ideas that serve as options for the mentee. In this stage it is important that the mentor functions as a facilitator so that the mentee may find and expand the existing options, and for that it is necessary to observe what comes next:

- Developing awareness of the need for searching for options.
- Obtaining as many options as possible.
- Avoiding opinions and judgement.
- Valuing the options regardless of the level of complexity.

Questions that help to explore options:

- What are your options?
- What could you do differently than you've done so far?
- What went right in the past and could be repeated?
- Is there any additional resource that you need?
- What else could you do?

### Step 5 – Overcome obstacles

According to Sir John Whitmore,[14] the greatest obstacle is the leader's failure in giving up what they have done before, and this impacts the manner of encouraging the follower to implement their new options. On the other hand, the possibility exists of both having an overoptimistic vision, failing to notice possible obstacles that might prevent progress.

The mentor must give the mentee a sense of reality so that they may anticipate possible internal and external obstacles when implementing the options chosen. For that, they should:

- Ask whether possible implementation obstacles exist.
- Keep the optimism based on evidence.
- Investigate other sources of support.
- Identify internal and external barriers.
- Investigate to see if there are any limiting beliefs.
- Encourage learning the new and giving up the old.
- Provide feedback, if necessary, in order to enhance awareness.

Questions that help to overcome obstacles:

- Is there anything that could stop you?
- What evidence do you have that this could work out?
- Who else could help you?
- How can you step away from the risks of failing or the fear of success?
- What should you stop doing to achieve your objective?

---

14   John Whitmore (2017) *Coaching For Performance* (5th edn). London: Nicholas Brealey Publishing.

*Step 6 – Donate space – decide action*

By defining the initial objective and exploring possible options, and overcoming the obstacles that may emerge, the mentee now has a good sense of what must be done to achieve the objective. At this stage, the discussion revolves around the practical actions that will be taken towards this objective. It is important that the mentor lets the mentee state what the actions will be, and that these are not limited to a wish list but include the steps for their effective implementation. To decide on steps to put in place to move forward, the mentee needs space. This is a time for: reflection, awareness, clarification after reframing, a period of silence. It is the mentee's time, which they seek and which they give themselves.

For that, the mentor could:

- Incite the definition of steps with a beginning, a middle and an end.
- Keep the focus on the solution and not on the problem.
- Split great objectives into stepwise goals.
- Push the mentee to achieve the 20 per cent of actions that will show tangible progress. This is based on the famous 80/20 rule of Pareto that consultants are familiar with: generate quick gains ('quick wins') to encourage the mentee and put them in an optimistic mood.
- Offer ongoing support to plan preparation.
- Clarify who is responsible for the execution.
- Stay as silent as possible to let the mentee elaborate their own action plan.

Questions that help to plan actions:

- When are you intending to start and end each step?
- How specifically will you do this?
- Do you already have all the resources necessary?
- What type of action would lead you to extraordinary progress?
- What will be your first action right after this conversation?

*Step 7 – Accompanying – acting*

Now that actions are decided, it is important that the mentor continues being a fervent supporter of their mentee – inspiring, encouraging. It is also necessary to verify that the mentee's body language and energy levels match the willingness to move forward.

For that the mentor could:

- Watch the mentee's body language very carefully to check possible lack of motivation or lack of congruency (e.g., shoulders or chin remain low when explaining the action plan and mentee tends to gaze to the ground).
- Check the level of energy in the room. Normally with a decision to act, energy for both mentee and mentor should be higher.

Questions that help accompanying actions:

- How do you feel about moving towards your solution?
- What is the current emotion?
- How is your level of self-confidence? Your level of energy?
- With whom will you celebrate your first successes?
- Once at the top of the mountain, what will you have achieved?

### Step 8 – Establish impact

Now is the time to wrap up. The mentor encourages the mentee to summarise their next steps so that the whole discussion does not come down to a letter of intent. To contribute to that, the mentor may:

- Ratify the support to the action plan agreed.
- Help the mentee to revise what has been discussed.
- Test the engagement level.
- Go back and simplify the plan, if necessary.
- And continue to check the congruency (walk the talk, talk the thoughts), thus the alignment of body language with speech.

Questions that help to establish impact:

- How will you know that your objective has been achieved?
- In what ways can you ensure the implementation of your plan?
- From 0 to 10, what is your level of commitment to this plan?
- How will you feel when you achieve your goal?
- What new lesson are you taking from our conversation?

# 3 Building the relationship

## Embedding the coaching attitude into the mentoring process

We saw in Chapter 1 that, as defined by the EMCC, eight of the key competencies of mentoring are common with the ones of coaching. This is a further encouragement to embed the coaching attitude into mentoring activities. In a nutshell, those skills encompass the ability to create the trust inside the mentoring pair, to listen actively, to generate awareness, to lead the mentee towards action and to overcome obstacles when they occur. Let's start with building the relationship.

## Ability to create the temenos, the 'sacred space'

A *temenos* (Greek: τέμενος; plural: τεμένη, temenē) is a piece of land marked off from common uses and dedicated to a god, such as a sanctuary, a holy grove or a holy precinct (Wikipedia). Some famous temenos are the sacred valley of the Nile (Egypt), and in Greece, the Acropolis of Athens or the area of Delphi, for instance. A temenos is usually marked by a peribolos fence or wall as a structural boundary.

Carl Jung[15] relates the temenos to the spellbinding or magic circle, which acts as a 'square space' or 'safe spot' where mental 'work' can take place. This temenos resembles among others a 'symmetrical rose garden with a fountain in the middle' in which an encounter with the unconscious can be had and where these unconscious contents can safely be brought into the light of consciousness. Isn't this precisely what the mentor is aiming to do with their mentee? One key competency is therefore this ability to create the safe space, especially when mentoring takes place in the corporate environment.

### Providing the safe space

The safe space is not only a matter of venue; it also depends on the mentor's ability to position themselves in the best parity possible with their mentee and create a friendly relationship based on trust, authenticity and vulnerability.

---

15    Carl Jung (1980) *Psychology and Alchemy* London: Routledge.

Yet, the venue is also of paramount importance. How could a mentee feel at ease if they have to meet their mentor at the top of the office building, at the C-suite level, and enter through a personal assistant's office? And how could the mentee feel at ease and be vulnerable when the mentor spends time on their mobile phone or shows little interest for the mentee's challenging situation? The atmosphere leading to the learning alliance needs to respect a minimum number of conditions: a quiet space, some privacy (not a fishbowl in the middle of an open-space office for instance), and some time slots with the mentor's full attention and presence as well as 'ego-free' meetings where the encountering is made heart-to-heart.

It happened that we witnessed some mentees completely demotivated by the lack of humility of their mentor; it was creating a lack of security for the mentee and some sort of obligation to activate a strong ego and keep on justifying behaviours to save face. The relationship was not built on an OK-OK (++) life position (see Chapter 1). There was a lack of parity between both, and even though experience and seniority were leading to respect, it was up to the mentor to create the safe space so that the mentee could feel at ease and open, with honesty and authenticity. The safe space is both physical and mental.

With the pandemic, it has become even more vital to create the temenos through a screen. Some people are allergic to those virtual meetings and are reluctant to have their mentoring sessions that way. However, more and more mentors and mentees now accept this mode of communication if they want to pair with an executive in another country or region. And they even discover that the temenos can be easily created remotely.

- In many clients' corporations, mentoring is organised on a global basis and mentor–mentee pairs have learned to overcome the technological and/ or psychological barriers of virtual communications. It has been possible to obtain authentic conversations via Zoom, Teams or Skype; and even though both would prefer to meet face to face, they admit how effective and timesaving it is to meet virtually. It is the case of MentoringCo's mentors who managed to convince their mentees. How? Through modelisation of authentic and heart-to-heart mentoring demos performed by their faculty members during their training sessions, either via the EMCC-EQA[16] accredited courses or during the training organised inside corporations. Trainers ask delegates to pop up with a real challenging case and mentor them on their real-life case. This is the best way to show them how to create that safe space in very little time. Several tools are used, relying on Transactional Analysis: Time Structuration, OK-Corral, Signs of Recognition, Ego States – see below.
- One mentor testimonial: 'I uphold the client's safety and privacy in the highest regard, and in doing so, ensure the mentee has a safe and secure

---

16   EQA = European Quality Award, granted by EMCC to programmes matching specific requirements for different levels: Foundation, Practitioner, Senior Practitioner and Master Practitioner.

environment to allow them to be vulnerable, and it is through taking this courageous step that they grow. I easily and quickly create a highly 'safe' environment that enables them to deeply and personally explore, enabling big shifts in their consciousness, beliefs and awareness. Several experiences reminded me of the power of holding the space and being hyper aware of my presence in the mentoring space. My value was not attached to the outcome, but in the quality of my presence.'

- Another testimonial: 'I am working actively on engaging my courage, along with my compassion and curiosity that have served me well in the past. Trusting that the 'safe space' I create with my mentees will permit me to challenge more directly.'
- Self-care is king: 'I have often mentored executives to practise greater self-care as leaders, to ensure that they are in the optimal space for what is required of them as a leader. As a result of this, I'm more conscious of both my own self-care and how my equilibrium serves (or takes away from) my effectiveness in the mentoring environment. I have become more aware of my head space and energy prior to, during and after mentoring engagements.'

## Create a genuine friendly relationship based on trust and complicity

The best mentoring experiences occur when trust has been built quite quickly. It is the responsibility of both parties to reach the stage that will allow effectiveness and high performance in the mentoring process. Yet, it is part of the mentor's role to hold the process and to confer the right tone to the relationship since its inception, namely during the first encounter called the 'chemistry meeting' – unless both parties know each other already, of course. Trust takes place at three levels: mentor, mentee and process.

**Mentor**: The mentor has the adequate experience, has well-accepted credibility and legitimacy, a right-sized ego, strong values, a well-defined role as a mentor, and finds a true rationale behind the intervention (meaning), etc. As a result, the mentee is quickly convinced that they are in the right hands.

**Mentee**: The mentor strongly believes that the mentee knows more than they are aware of (cf. Bateson's learning stages, see Chapter 1). They know that when activating the mentee's functionalities, talents and knowledge, the mentoring will yield high results.

**Process**: The framework of the intervention and the agreement between the mentor and the mentee are crystal clear. Consensus has been reached on the timing/pacing of the sessions, their duration, the venue, the follow-up system, the cancellation policy if one member of the pair cannot commit to the settled date, the delineation of the scope and the territory (when dealing with professional elements, it may have an influence on the private sphere and vice-versa), and all the necessary clauses that must be included in the agreement, including ways to settle possible disputes. And of course, both parties are aware of the rules of ethics established by the EMCC and/or the International Coaching Federation (ICF) and duly respect them.

Both are convinced that mentoring with a coaching attitude is stronger than other disciplines as the mentee commits themselves towards change and action – studies on coaching have proven that coaching yields a Return on Investment (ROI) of more than 700 per cent in the longer run.[17]

Finally, the mayonnaise/the chemistry is present between mentor and mentee since the very first time they met – both are in an OK-OK position.

## The relationship comes first

Mastery in mentoring with a coaching attitude is achieved when the mentor has the skill and the art to immediately connect with the mentee, dive deep in their beliefs and emotions, authentically caring for the mentee, encouraging introspection as well as providing challenging feedback, and therefore obtaining impactful and long-term changes. Both are in an OK position that creates a mutual respect and the willingness to look together in the same direction. As the Little Prince of Antoine de St Exupéry's novel stated: 'Love is not looking to one another, but together in the same direction.' In mentoring, we speak about a friendly learning alliance where both look together at the mentee's professional and personal development.

When OK-ness is not present, it creates several situations that yield negative results for both parties.

When the mentor is in an OK-non OK or +/- position: there is an overprotection of the mentee or lack of trust in their abilities to implement learnings, too many inducing or close questions, mentor speaking of themselves and displaying an oversized ego, etc.

When the mentor experiences a non OK-OK or -/+ position: there is a lack of challenging feedback (fear of wounding) and of powerful questions, too much energy spent during mentoring sessions, very little satisfaction and even sometimes lack of self-confidence.

Importantly, if the chemistry cannot be reached between the mentor and the mentee, it is better to state it out loud, with lots of respect and courtesy of course. Psychological games always yield a negative outcome and automatically lead to a loss of energy for both parties. Both could refuse starting a mentoring journey if there is for instance a clash of values or a potential risk of breaching the code of ethics. The mentoring relationship should be voluntary, in the flow, not forced, and fully accepted by both parties.

---

17   The 700 per cent ROI number appeared in one of the client surveys made between 2004 and 2020 by PwC on behalf of the ICF.

Finally, it is always better to invest in the relationship than in the outcome. Experienced mentors report that their best mentoring experiences occur when there is common appreciation and respect, sometimes forgiveness, when boundaries are clear, when the mentor is empathetic without falling into sympathy,[18] when the mentor knows how to accompany the emotion in the adequate way and when they can make a clear distinction between mentoring with a coaching attitude and psychotherapy.[19]

## Tools of Transactional Analysis used to build the relationship

In mentoring, we mainly use four tools of Transactional Analysis[20] (TA), the discipline created by Dr Eric Berne in the late 1950s, as they contribute to generating a positive energy in the transaction between the mentor and the mentee: the OK-Corral (see Chapter 1), the Time Structuration, the Signs of Recognition and the Ego States.

The philosophy of TA is to enhance the autonomy of a person and to generate respectful transactions: respect for yourself, for others and from others. Negative energy will be created if, in a transaction, the autonomy of one of the two parties is not respected. Negative energy is considered neither good nor bad, moral nor immoral, but simply not supportive of the autonomy of the various players or supportive of respect for others. For example, when one plays a psychological game and then criticises an outsider who cannot defend themselves, it is not respectful of the person and it does not display positive energy.

TA's principle is that everyone is responsible for their thoughts, their feelings and their actions. As a result, we all can instil the right energy in our transactions; this means that a well-trained mentor can instil the right atmosphere in the relationship and this will greatly enhance the quality of the bond.

### Time structuring[21]

According to Dr Eric Berne and Raymond Hostie, when we are awake, there are six types of moments that we can experience during the day, as shown in Figure 3.1.

---

18  An analogy to explain the difference between empathy and sympathy. Empathy: the mentee has fallen in a well. The mentor takes a ladder, goes down and brings the mentee back up. Sympathy: the mentor gets stuck in the well together with the mentee.
19  When the emotion is too heavy, the mentor should invite the mentee to get support from a professional.
20  The TA tools originate from two books written by Dr Eric Berne: *Games People Play* (1964) New York: Grove Press and *What Do You Say After You Say Hello?* (1975) London: Transworld Publishers.
21  Dr Eric Berne, *What Do You Say After You Say Hello?*, op. cit., and Raymond Hostie (1987) *L'âge adulte, Analyse Transactionnelle*, Paris: Interéditions.

**Figure 3.1** Time structuring

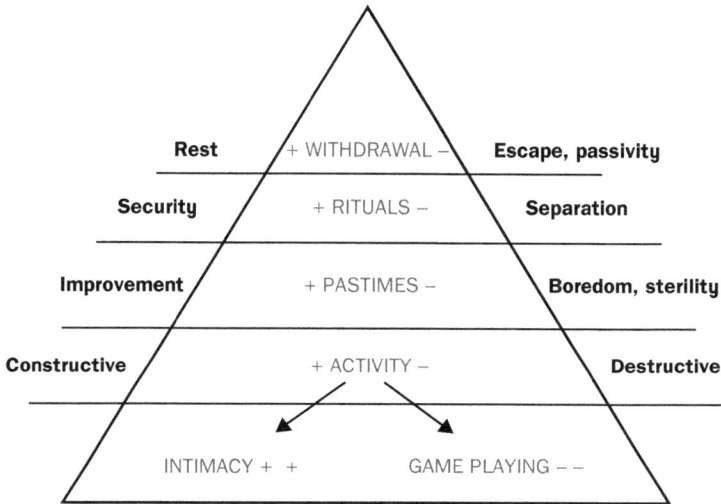

**Withdrawal**: This is the time that we spend out of any contact, when we are alone, in retreat. This time is limited in the day unless we are used to meditating or spend a longer time walking in nature, for instance.

*Advantage*: it allows introspection and quietude.

*Disadvantage*: it can separate us from others if too long.

In a mentoring session, these are times of silence, of introspection, or right after a difficult or highly emotional sequence. The mentee (or the mentor or both) needs a short break or needs some space to recompose themselves. Therefore, we strongly advise mentors to organise their sessions in a remote space, with a buffer time between the mentoring session and the reintegration of the mentee in their working space.

Some mentees withdraw on the inside and are physically present, but emotionally absent. However, we all need time to be with ourselves and regroup, so some withdrawal time is necessary for all of us – it's better not to organise mentoring sessions back to back and allow some time to re-centre.

**Rituals**: These are all the interactions with others with high cultural content. The way two Japanese greet is not the same as two Americans or two Africans. A salutation like 'Hello, how are you?' and a response of 'Thanks, very well, and how are you?' is a pre-programmed ritual.

*Advantage*: they provide structure and security and allow a more intense contact.

*Disadvantage*: they contain little emotional value; the person could exchange hellos with a stranger without much, if any, emotional contact or be lacking authenticity, pretending they feel all right, while it is not the case.

In a mentoring session, the mentor should start by providing a seat; if possible, a drink, or at least make sure the mentee is at ease.

**Pastimes**: This is typically the type of interaction that you nurture with the greengrocer or hairdresser, or the person in the street, or during a cocktail party. It is a polite and easy conversation on culturally agreed topics. Themes are common: weather, traffic, food, travels, sports, games, cinema, VIPs and film stars or singers, etc.

*Advantage*: it allows both parties to feel at ease and on the same wavelength. There is a bit more of an exchange involved, and both parties feel 'in the same tribe', without any controversial or painful topics. This level of interaction fits with casual acquaintances and people recently met.

*Disadvantage*: too much small talk generates boredom.

In a mentoring session: it is the time spent before getting into an activity, to show that we are attuned, we care for one another. This time is key to reach a high quality of authenticity.

**Activity**: This is probably where people spend most of their time with others, mainly in the professional environment. Activity stands for 'goal-directed activity' performed with others: attending a meeting, creating a project together, or practising a sport. It is time we spend *doing* things with others, rather than just *being* with them. Activity may include work or, at home, it could involve running a household or looking after the children.

*Advantage*: when the activity is positive, it is a productive shared time providing satisfaction of the job well done and may include having a lot of fun.

*Disadvantage*: when the activity is negative, it can generate guilt and threaten other people. In addition, any activity might also mean that a person is avoiding authentic presence with the other and meeting them fully.

In a mentoring session, mentors should allow some time for *being* as well as *doing*. This means adopting a slower pacing and rhythm, having some time for breathing together, stop moving forward into action to simply enquire about the emotion present at the moment, and dig into it if it might influence the outcome of the session.

**Psychological games**: As Dr Berne stated, psychological games or stratagems are a sequence of interactions with others which involve a hidden agenda, and which end up with both parties experiencing familiar bad feelings. They usually occur when the stages of time structuration are not respected, e.g., the parties move immediately into action without investing time in rituals and start with mainly pastime conversations. Most common games are victimisation (see the drama triangle, in Chapter 8 on autonomy), or passive aggressivity, or disqualification of the mentor or of the process, and many others that were mentioned in Berne's book[22] *What Do You Say After You Say Hello?* Games can be seen as a failed attempt to be intimate with another person. However, both parties do not take the full risk of being open and authentic with each other and the result is a repetitive pattern of interacting from set roles.

There are no advantages in game playing as the outcome, the bonus, will always be negative and generates negative energy.

---

22   Dr Eric Berne, *What Do You Say After You Say Hello?*, op. cit.

In a mentoring session, games will automatically emerge when a minimum level of trust is not achieved. Both mentor and mentee will remain on the surface, in the appearance, justifying their actions to look good and caring about their reputation. They are far from authenticity and the 'real' thing.

**Intimacy**: This is an authentic encounter with another, a moment of shared openness, trust and honesty. It means expressing genuine emotions in a respectful way for the other, generating understanding, kindness and compassion. It provides the highest level of emotional intensity but also involves risk-taking as we display our vulnerability to the other that could be diverted into humiliation or ridiculing if both parties are not in the same state of openness and showing their true selves. Intimacy and complicity are nurturing a heart-to-heart relationship allowing attachment to take place, and mainly allowing the other person to impact and change us.

*Advantage*: the person feels completely at ease and the energy is highly positive, no games, just authenticity and genuinely shared moments.

*Disadvantage*: it is high risk-taking and both parties must be 100 per cent sure that the other is true, authentic and without any hidden agenda, otherwise it might lead to breach of trust, destroying self-confidence, humiliation and a lot of emotional distress.

In a mentoring session, when both mentor and mentee reach that stage, it leads to deep and sustainable change, with a lifelong impact on both mentor (satisfaction of the result achieved) and mentee (happiness and higher self-confidence).

> **Mentor's take-away**: We strongly recommend mentors to *invest* in pastime during their mentoring sessions, to spend some time to enquire about the mentee's tastes, occupations outside work, to bond with the mentee on a common point of interest in sport, cinema, food, or any other light activity or hobby that can create a bridge between them. When doing this, at the first encounter and at the beginning of each session, intimacy can be easily reached in a very short time.

## Signs of recognition – or strokes

According to Eric Berne (1964), the founder of TA, '*a stroke is a unit of recognition*,' meaning a unit of attention, which provides stimulation to an individual. It is based on the human need for physical and psychological stimulation (Wikipedia). Berne states that 'a stroke may be used as the fundamental unit of social action'. As for the choice of the word 'stroke' in itself, Berne chose it based on the infant's need for touching. As they grow up, humans learn to seek other forms of recognition to compensate for the lack of physical touch that was available to us during infancy.

There are two big categories of strokes: **positive strokes** and **negative strokes**. These can be **unconditional** (whole person) or **conditional** (action, behaviour). According to Berne, unconditional strokes are related to what you *are*, while conditional ones are about what you *do*.

*Some examples:*

- *Unconditional positive strokes*: 'I love you!' 'You are wonderful!' 'I like you!'
- *Unconditional negative strokes*: 'I hate you!' 'You are an idiot!' 'I don't like you!'
- *Conditional positive strokes*: 'You've done a great job!' 'This dress looks fantastic on you!' 'Well done on taking the promotion!'
- *Conditional negative strokes*: 'The level of quality of your work cannot be accepted.' 'You did not meet our expectations.' 'This dress does not fit you.'

Strokes are also verbal and non-verbal, can be physical or psychological, internal (self-praise and other ways of self-stimulation) and external (the ones we receive from others).

In mentoring, strokes are the best way to value the mentee. When receiving positive strokes, the mentee feels empowered and can unleash their wings much faster. It is part of the MentoringCo process, including Cannio and Launer's MOVIDA[23] model to include the mentee's valuation and this should be remembered by all mentors (see previous chapter).

## The 'Ego States'[24]

'Ego States' are the types of behaviour which are manifested by the energy of our mental capacity. These are three different ways in which we react to situations depending on what we have learned, the information available to us, and our feelings and desires: Parent, Adult, Child. These Ego States do not exist; they are practical intellectual tools to understand what is going on inside us and others, and they allow us to be able to live with oneself and with others. They are analytical and developmental tools.

### The 'Ego States' and the distribution of energy

In the TA literature, Ego States are represented in a graph with three circles. The first one describes the parent's behaviours and emotions (normative, nurturing) and their downsides (overprotective and criticising). The middle circle is for the adult. The lower circle is for the child: free child, adapted child, submissive and rebellious child.

In Figure 3.2, we have adapted Berne's model into a slightly modified one, simply reverting the subdivisions inside the circles to make the positive energy parts enter the 'positive energy square'. As a result, the Parent Ego State circle is divided into two positive parts: Normative and Nurturing and two negative parts, Criticising and Overprotective/Rescuing. The same happens with the Child Ego States: there are two positive sides: the Adapted Child and the Free/Spontaneous Child Ego States and two negative parts: the Submissive/Rebellious Child Ego State and the Egotistical Child Ego State.

---

23   Sylviane Cannio & Viviane Launer, *Coaching Excellence*, op. cit.
24   Dr Eric Berne: What *Do You Say After You Say Hello?* op. cit. and *Games People Play*, op. cit.

**Figure 3.2** The Ego States and the positive energy square

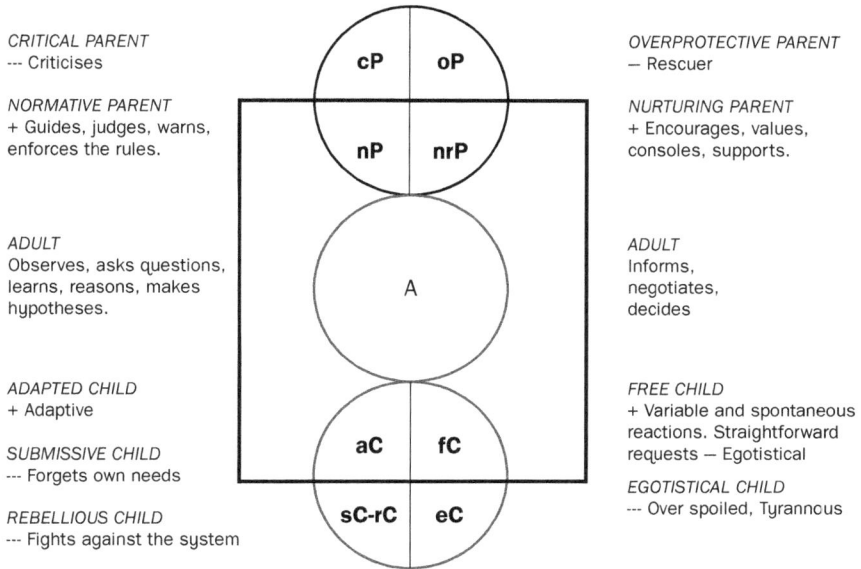

CRITICAL PARENT
--- Criticises

NORMATIVE PARENT
+ Guides, judges, warns,
enforces the rules.

ADULT
Observes, asks questions,
learns, reasons, makes
hypotheses.

ADAPTED CHILD
+ Adaptive

SUBMISSIVE CHILD
--- Forgets own needs

REBELLIOUS CHILD
--- Fights against the system

cP    oP

nP    nrP

A

aC    fC

sC-rC    eC

OVERPROTECTIVE PARENT
— Rescuer

NURTURING PARENT
+ Encourages, values,
consoles, supports.

ADULT
Informs,
negotiates,
decides

FREE CHILD
+ Variable and spontaneous
reactions. Straightforward
requests — Egotistical

EGOTISTICAL CHILD
--- Over spoiled, Tyrannous

To live a life according to the philosophy of Transactional Analysis (TA) and, of course, inside the mentoring journey, is to do our best to operate within a state of maximum positive energy, while avoiding negative energy. This means for the mentor to make sure that only the Ego States that are inside the positive energy square are activated.

### The Transactions and the three Laws of Communication

**First rule**: Communication continues as long as the transactions are parallel or complementary: two Parents/Adults/Children together or a Parent with a Child. See Figure 3.3.

In a mentoring session, most of the time is dedicated to Adult–Adult transactions: looking at an activity together, in a friendly manner but without deep emotions. Or both will be in a transaction Normative Parent–Normative Parent, if they are jointly building the provisions of a contract, for instance. Or both can activate their Free Child Ego State when they start joking for a while or play a game together. It can also happen that a transaction Child–Parent occurs when the mentee (Free Child) narrates a story and expresses a deep emotion, and the mentor (Nurturing Parent) comforts them and provides space for this authentic moment.

**Second rule**: There is an **interruption** when the transactions are crossed. See Figure 3.4.

In the mentoring session, it can happen that the mentee expresses an inappropriate emotion e.g., sadness (tears) that substitutes a fear for instance. In this case, the mentor will obtain better results if they cross the transaction and invite the mentee to be in an Adult Ego State.

**Figure 3.3** Law of Transactions Nr 1

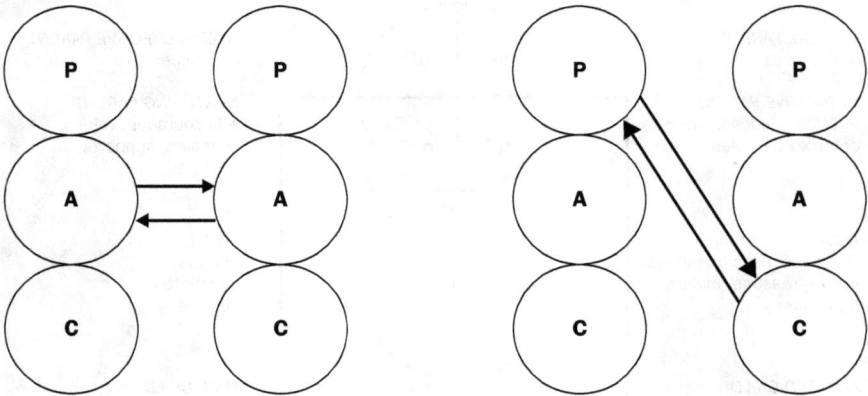

**Figure 3.4** Law of Transactions Nr 2

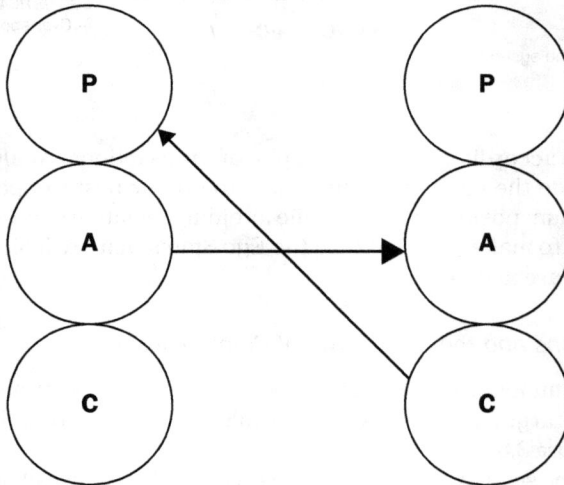

*Mentee:* (starting to cry) I am afraid of my boss when he yells at me.
*Mentor:* I see that you start crying while you tell me that you are fearing his reactions. Are those tears appropriate right now? Do you need me to comfort you? Or do you prefer that we explore your fear and find a solution?
*Mentee:* Ah (drying tears), you are quite right. I tend to cry when I am afraid or angry.

Importantly, it is not to reject an emotion. Here, it is to express the emotion in an adequate way. If the mentee is authentically sad (because their line manager left for another business unit or region, for instance), then the mentor will of course adopt a more appropriate Ego State: Nurturing Parent, for a moment, and grant space for sadness, before getting progressively back to an Adult–Adult transaction.

**Third rule**: A hidden transaction is one in which the communication is played at a psychological level – the interlocutor always perceives the psychological tone and this one is more important than the message itself. See Figure 3.5.

**Figure 3.5** Law of Transactions Nr 3

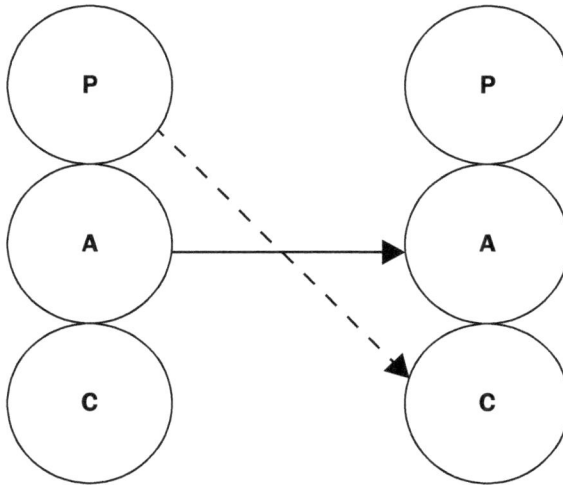

In the mentoring session, the mentor will pay attention to the mentee's body language and the tone of voice. The mentee could perceive a judgement if the mentor looks at them above their glasses, for instance. Same applies to the mentee of course.

# 4 Strong presence and listening skills

A key competence for the mentor is to be able to listen beyond the mentee's words, as they represent only 7 per cent of the message (see below). This means listening to other elements such as: tone of voice, emotions, body language, energy. This competence was developed by Carl Rogers[25] in the 1960s, under his person-centred approach. Rogers showed how to develop empathy, look for congruency and mainly focus on the person; this is valid for numerous situations, including mentoring and coaching.

## Starting by being present to self: the posture and the mindset

How could a mentor be in full presence with their mentee if their mind is polluted by dozens of thoughts and other disturbances: overloaded agenda, phone calls, incoming emails with sound notice, etc.? No one will pretend that it is easy to empty the mind. However, there are techniques that contribute to reaching more serenity and peace of mind and create the void that will help mentors to refine their listening skills: meditation and breathing, focusing on self, having their own rituals and routines for installing the necessary readiness before welcoming the mentee. In the corporate world, this is extremely difficult to organise, especially when the mentor is jumping from one assignment to the other and from one meeting to the other – usually organised back to back and remotely. The same applies to the mentee who might also be running after time and perhaps impressed by the mentor's stature or environment.

As seen in Chapter 3, the mentor's first job is to install the temenos and the space that will allow both to concentrate on the scope of the session. The focus comes from the mind, indeed, but starts with the body: sitting straight forward, feet in contact with the ground, breathing with amplitude, staring at the interlocutor with attention and care.

For the mentor, emptying the mind also allows them to connect with the body. Our body is our first and best mentoring tool: it allows us to 'feel' the

---

25    Carl Rogers (1951) *Client-Centered Therapy: Its Current Practice, Implications and Theory*. London: Constable.

**Figure 4.1** The Computation Index (NLP)

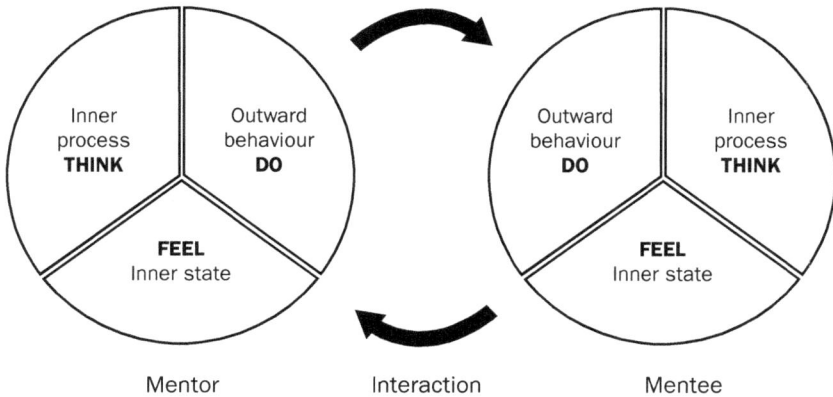

energy of the mentee, the emotions on top of watching the body language (see the section on Calibrating to understand more deeply) and listening to all this provides great information.

To self-centre, you can create your own rituals – and this is easier when referring to the NLP's tool 'Computation Index' (see Figure 4.1).

The mentor can install their self-centring rituals in three domains:

- Their Inner State (FEEL) – to connect with their body: breathing, feeling inside their clothes, feeling their weight on the chair, their feet on the ground, etc.
- Their Inner Process (THINK) – what are their thoughts now, what do they tell themselves to help them to focus? For example, 'Focus!' or 'Let's Go!' or 'I am cool' or 'Watch!' – or any little sentence that they can repeat themselves to focus their attention on the mentee.
- Their Outward Behaviour (DO) – what do they DO to feel centred? Sip their coffee or tea, sit straight forward, put their feet on the ground, write down their thoughts, touch their watch or tie/scarf, etc.

When the mentor is aware of those three elements, they may invite their mentee to do the same to have them completely focused on the session.

This tool is also valid if the mentee (and perhaps the mentor) experiences stage fright before a presentation, an exam or an important meeting. It can also be used at any moment of the session to check if both are still focusing and at the end of the session to check the quality of the action plan, as each action should have a 'do something', a 'think it is feasible' and, therefore, have your own mantra or encouraging thought, and a 'feel' the energy that will be generated by the outcome. As you can see, this wonderful tool can be used in numerous situations and is worth using.

# Listening effectively – empathic listening

'Are you listening to me well?' This question, which we ask to those who have some hearing impairment, would be valid for many other situations of every-day life, especially in contacts with our mentees.

The mentor knows well the importance of empathic listening in the conduct of their work, without which it will not be possible to establish a good connection with their mentee, creating a two-way street where information will come and go smoothly, without edges and turbulences, as it happens when they are only listening instead of hearing.

Empathic listening requires effort to stay in tune with the mentee. This goes far beyond merely being present in body, only simulating interest in what is being said; when, in fact, the mentor is miles away, with their mind focused on other issues and matters. How many times have we seen someone – or ourselves – acting like this?

The mentoring session brings up a lot of information that should be listened to and processed with care and attention. How is this done in practice? The first step for the mentor is to keep their mindset on their mentee, to be aligned with the mentee. This requires a certain personal detachment, an effort not always easy for everyone.

It happens, as the mentor will have to put aside some individual issues in order to direct 'the light of the lighthouse' to the mentee, putting their agenda in the foreground. The intended empathic listening will fail if the mentor only prioritises their own concerns at that moment.

A few tips mentioned below will help to focus the mentor's attention on the mentee.

## Disturbances

The environment can be a powerful distraction generator. Mobile phones, computers and other sources end up attracting and dispersing attention and producing a disconnection in empathic listening.

Therefore, it is worth doing a kind of scan of the environment to identify possible noise-generating places or those that have the capacity to take us away from the desired focus.

In this way, the mentor will build a space free of elements harmful to the mentoring session. This is a constant exercise because there is always the risk of something arising to interfere with the smooth progress of the work. Therefore, the mentor should look carefully at their surroundings to create a place free of factors that could harm the bond to be established with the mentee.

## Listening and not just hearing

Hearing is a mechanical act, performed via autopilot. We hear everything that comes to our ears, without filter or prior distinction. Listening, on the other hand, is an active, controlled process in which we give meaning and sense to the words that are being said to us. It is curious to note that in order to listen, we make use of other senses, such as vision, adding non-verbal data to the conversation and thus make it more robust, complete and enriched.

If the mentor pays attention to the mentee's body language, they will be able to better understand what is being transmitted, adding new icons to the set of information received. This will provide a deepening in empathy, an essential step to make the mentoring session more productive and attractive.

It is always good to highlight some points because we often end up hearing instead of actively listening, and we do not realise that there are factors hindering the smooth progress of our work. A message on the mobile phone or the notification of the arrival of an email radically interferes with the concentration and focus essential for a well-conducted conversation.

## Empathic listening

What the mentee shows is not always what is in fact in their mind and heart. Many times, a certain positive attitude, such as a smile, is minimising or covering up something different from this initial perception.

This is another benefit of empathic listening, as it allows the mentor to identify what is behind gestures or words said by the mentee. Thus, it will be possible to perceive if there is congruence between the information passed and what was not said, no longer emphasising only the technical aspect inserted in the methodologies to put attitude in the foreground. And attitude makes a huge difference!

## Deeper understanding

The biggest gain of active listening will be to exponentially increase the mentor's ability to understand the mentee in a more comprehensive, deep and effective way, providing guidance with greater assertiveness. After all, the mentor could capture with more clarity and depth what was transmitted to them, creating an environment freer from noise and other elements. In a mentoring process, the experience accumulated by the mentor often leads to a lot of time being spent reporting personal cases and experiences.

Illustrating the service with lived references contributes to establishing an inspiring image, but if it happens too much, what follows? It will certainly interfere in the establishment of an empathic relationship, in which the story and demands of the mentee should always be in the foreground. In other words, the mentor should pay attention to not overdoing it by telling their own stories and forgetting to give a voice to the mentee.

It will also be worth reducing the preponderance of internal dialogue and pre-judgements to open fully to the mentee, to their reality and needs. That way the mentor will certainly be more likely to succeed in their efforts to effect an empathic conversation.

## Reformulating to be on the same wavelength

Active listening is also showing the mentee that their narrative is fully under-stood, and the best way to do this is to reformulate what was just said. This way, the mentor can show that they are on the same wavelength, and it also allows the mentee to correct a fact or be more accurate on a key factor. Reformulation starts with listening in silence or just by nodding or saying 'mmm,' 'yes,' then, if needed, by some clarification questions or investigation if more facts are needed to understand the story. Then comes the time of reformulation.

After having listened, clarified and investigated, the mentor is now able to rephrase what the mentee wished to express. This reformulation will ensure that the mentor properly understands, both in terms of arguments and feelings. It could start with these sentences:

- If I understand correctly, you think ... and you feel ...
- Do you think I have understood you correctly?

If the answer is 'yes,' this piece of active listening is finished. Otherwise, the mentor must return to the listening position and repeat the process until the mentee agrees with the reformulation.

### Some examples of rephrasing/reformulation

**'Parrot' what the other person says**: the most effective. It means repeating what the mentee just said, almost word for word. It's fast, but not particularly active and avoids possible new developments. It can also create distrust and annoyance. 'Your boss told you that your presentations are too long and sometimes boring.'
**Silence**: the shortest and the best. A matter of experience: often the mentee takes back the conversation, providing you leave them the space to do so.
**'Flash'**: often sufficient. Here, the mentor just takes a word that symbolises the whole conversation. 'Boring?'
**Empathic**: the most genuine. The mentor only focuses on the perceived emo-tion. 'This must be hard for you.'
**Provocative**: useful to shake up the mentee and put some humour into the relationship. 'Boring as you are right now?' (This should normally be followed by chuckles.)

## Calibrating to understand more deeply

Professor Albert Mehrabian,[26] from the University of California, believes that there are three core elements in the effective face-to-face communication of emo-tions or attitudes: first, non-verbal behaviour (facial expressions, for example);

---

26  Albert Mehrabian (1971) *Silent Messages* (1st edn.). Belmont, CA: Wadsworth.

second, tone of voice; third, the literal meaning of the spoken word. These three essential elements, Mehrabian argues, account for how we convey our liking, or disliking, of another person. His particular focus is on the importance of such non-verbal 'clues' when they appear to conflict with the words used and/or the tone in which they are spoken. Mehrabian developed his early theories on this subject during the 1960s. Drawing on the findings of two experiments he conducted in 1967, he formulated the 7–38–55 per cent communication rule: where 7 per cent are words; 38 per cent voice (pace, rhythm, volume, tone) and 55 per cent non-verbal messages (posture, gestures, face, breathing).

Words are the only element that we consciously select; the tone of voice and non-verbal messages are effective windows into our subconscious. At the end of the day, 93 per cent of our communication is purely subconscious!

Because of this rule, looking at the mentee is therefore of prime importance. The technique, developed by the founders of Neuro-Linguistic Programming (NLP), Richard Bandler[27] and John Grinder, is known as 'calibration' and can help the mentor capture much more information and improve their active listening capabilities.

To calibrate is to recognise the behavioural indicators associated with an internal state in order to use this information. In effect, each sign is an indicator of the mentee's internal state. The mentee will show this sign when reconnecting with the same sensation, such as agreement, fear or shyness. For example, the mentee will not have the same facial expression when they think of a pleasant memory as opposed to an embarrassing situation. Their posture, the position of their head, the look on their face, their skin colour and their breathing are all different.

Although there are many types of calibration in the NLP universe, for this book we will focus on two that are the most useful in the corporate mentoring process: visual and auditory calibration.

## Visual calibration

Visual calibration is used to identify external observable physiological signs. Each sign is an indicator of the mentee's internal state. These micro-signs return every time the mentee experiences the same internal state (e.g., fear, anger, etc.). They are found as much in the body as in the face. They include:

- posture: body position, head position, general attitude
- breathing: strong or weak, rhythm
- muscle tone
- movements
- face: colour of the skin, movements, tilt, facial lines
- eye movements.

---

27  Richard Bandler and John Grinder (1975) *The Structure of Magic I: A Book About Language and Therapy.* Palo Alto, CA: Science & Behavior Books.

The study of gestures is used to reveal our feelings and intentions, notably in the 'law of expansion and retraction'.

Expansion occurs when someone 'buys-in' to a situation, adheres to an idea or a person, has confidence in them and their environment, and is brimming with positive energy. Their actions widen, becoming more expansive and further away from the body.

Retraction happens when the person doubts their ideas or themselves, fears their environment or lacks positive energy. Gestures are then retracted, shapeless and closed. They adopt a closed posture and use blocking gestures to filter information (which may be, for example, considered too novel or destabilising).

## Auditory calibration

In the same way that a mentee expresses their internal state in a visual way, they can also do the same with their voice or their choice of words: tone, rhythm, volume, pitch and interruptions.

Certain words can be highlighted in a particular way, by repetition, phrasing; pausing before or after a word, changes in tone; key words; and predicates (auditory micro-calibration).

These predicates are nouns, verbs, adjectives or adverbs that belong to the sensory register used by the mentee when they express themselves. They allow us to understand the world view of the mentee. So, when they say: 'My project was really clear,' they tell us that they perceive their project in a visual way.

Identifying predicates serves to understand how the mentee perceives what they say. Predicates also allow the mentor to rephrase the words and ask questions in the same sensory register as the mentee. This facilitates dialogue and creates harmony with the mentee, which provides greater impact because communication is established by the subconscious.

Here are some examples to reflect on and for possible use in the calibration with the mentee.

- **Visual references**: 'If I see clearly', 'It seems that', 'In a flash', 'You see the picture', 'To lose sight of', 'Visualise', 'See life as very rosy', 'Make a scene', 'Bring to light'.
- **Auditory references**: 'If I hear correctly', 'It sounds good', 'Makes their opinion heard', 'Gives them a flea in the ear', 'Hear, speak, listen, tell', 'Noise, sound', 'Orchestra', 'Resonate', 'Declare', 'Positive echo'.
- **Kinesthetic references**: 'If I feel good', 'I feel that', 'They are sensitive to', 'Gesture, movement', 'Jumps from one subject to another', 'Goosebumps', 'Takes things in hand', 'This is great', 'Touch of a finger', 'Stay in touch', 'Step by step'.

# Synchronising to talk to the unconscious

Adapting one's behaviour to the other person is talking to the subconscious. Synchronisation is to reflect to the mentee their own image – to send signals that can easily be identified subconsciously and are therefore signs of recognition.

Synchronisation helps to create a climate of confidence; it makes the mentee want to open up because they feel they are being listened to and acknowledged. It allows rapport to be established and improves active listening skills. It occurs in two ways: mirroring and matching.

### Mirroring

This is to discreetly imitate the mentee. The mentor stays standing when their mentee stands, or sits down when the mentee is sitting, taking the same posture, or walking at the same speed, or joins them if the mentee is drinking. This works because such non-verbal signals match a certain mood and internal feeling of the mentee.

When the mentor subtlety imitates the mentee's non-verbal expressions, they can better understand the mentee's state of mind and internal feelings (their model of the world). The goal is not to obtain information in a covert way but to make closer contact with the mentee to establish trust and empathy.

### Matching

This means accepting specific elements: the words, voice and non-verbal mannerisms of the mentee. When the mentor tunes into their mentee, they give them the impression that they are better understood. People who adopt the same tone of voice feel that they understand each other better.

However, the mentor can also decide to 'mismatch'. An example of mismatching is not to look at the mentee. 'Yes' is an expression of matching, and 'no' is likewise an expression of mismatching. Matching is to enter the world of the other. A good mentor enters the interests of the mentee (e.g., their hobbies, their discipline or favourite sport). The mentor uses the jargon of the mentee and their experience to put the messages in order and to position themselves on the same wave length.

Mirroring and matching occur spontaneously and subconsciously between people who understand each other. The mentor who practises mirroring and matching is seen as a sort of magician. Communication becomes intense and real as the mentor and the mentee begin to read each other's thoughts. Intuition is at a high level. It is this form of intimacy and close relationship that happens with a parent or a friend; we already have the skill within us to do this.

It is worth remembering that this attitude will be more efficient if it occurs in a subtle, discreet way, generating rapport and producing a general synergy in each contact. Such movements are strong stimuli when the mentor intends to establish powerful connections, denoting full and true attention to their mentee.

# Mentoring with the linguistic meta-model[28]

When we listen to something, we instinctively apply our internal references (values, beliefs, competences, etc.) in the information filtering process that NLP calls mental filters, which can be activated by both the mentor and the mentee. This attitude often distorts its essence, a harmful factor in empathic listening.

There are three basic types of mental filters which we may highlight – we only take a few examples issued from the linguistic meta-model that best apply to our mentoring experience. These are: generalisation, omission and distortion.

### Generalisation

Generalisation is when the mentee starts replicating some past experience by generalising for all their lives, whether positive or negative. If they use words such as 'always', 'never' or 'nobody' in the composition of some sentences, possibly they will be making use of this generalisation, because there is no specificity. If mentors come across this behaviour, the recommended procedure is to go deeper into the subject, especially by asking questions and making observations, in order to identify the use of the filter.

### Omission

If the mentor notices that a fact was omitted in the presentation made by the mentee, which may occur from a loose phrase such as 'I am very sad …,' it is quite possible that the fact is being covered up. In this case, the recommendation is that the 'de-filter' be carried out in order to clarify what is implied or hidden behind that comment or feeling.

### Distortion

Another benefit of empathic listening is to accentuate the perception of something exposed in a distorted manner, especially in the sense of softening its effects. Instead of passively accepting what is being conveyed by the mentee, the mentor using an empathic purpose should have an investigative posture, breaking down what is being exposed until the essence of the facts is revealed in order to work on it in the best way using the tools available.

---

28  Richard Bandler and John Grinder (1975). *The Structure of Magic I: A Book About Language and Therapy*. Palo Alto, CA: Science & Behavior Books. Ch.3.

# Seeking congruence

An important practice when measuring the perception of the world by the mentee, namely their own perceived reality, is to monitor their congruence; this can be done through a thorough calibration to check if the words are genuinely matching the body language, the tone of the voice and the displayed emotion, if any.

In psychotherapy, congruence is the term used by Carl Rogers to indicate an exact match between experience and awareness. According to NLP, congruence is the agreement between internal beliefs, strategies and behaviour in order to obtain an accurate result. The alignment of speech and attitudes is an essential component of charisma and success. According to the popular motto, congruence can be summarised in a sentence: 'Walk your talk, Talk your thoughts.'

The principle of congruence in communication can be illustrated through the following examples:

- 'I am very happy to be here.' This sentence is congruent; the person gives a clear view on how they feel. Normally, the person expresses joy and usually looks up with a smile, and the body seems expanding with open shoulders.
- 'This place does not displease me.' This sentence is incongruent. At first glance, it seems to testify to the satisfaction of the individual. But there is the presence of the word 'displeased'; the negative meaning is countered by a denial. Here there are two messages expressed. It is likely that this person is unhappy in this place, but for reasons of conscience, they cannot admit it.

The incongruence distorts the communication, while the congruence of a message should enable it to achieve its goal. For example: if the mentee is angry but does not want to express so directly; if their eyes are blazing and their index finger is pointed, the mentor will easily understand that the mentee is angry, even if they don't pronounce a single word.

The mentor can therefore easily presume that even when the mentee does not say anything about their feelings, those can be perceived. The mentor's role is extremely important at this level, including the way they will provide appropriate feedback about aspects of incongruence displayed by the mentee. The mentee is, in fact, very often unaware of their own incongruity. To make the mentee aware of it is the first step towards change in the mentoring exercise. And for this, the mentor has a radical and most effective tool: reframing.

# Reframing, reframing and reframing again

Reframing is one of the mentor's main tools. It starts from the fact that the mentee sees a situation with their own eyes, own context, background and beliefs … In NLP, they call this the 'map of the world', which is not the territory. However, this is only 'one' reality. The mentor might have another vision of the same situation or, at least, complementary information that might modify the meaning of, or the mentee's opinion on, the described situation.

According to Paul Watzlawick, the founder of the Mental Research Institute and of the Brief Therapy Center in Palo Alto (California), reframing can be defined as follows: 'Changing the perceptual point of view, conceptual and/or emotional, through which a given situation is perceived, to move to another part that fits as well, or even better, with the "facts" of the situation and which will change the whole meaning.' (Watzlawick, 1993). As summarised by Laozi: 'Do not rewrite the story, just look at it differently.' (Xiaofen Chen, 2016).

The mentor who wants to reframe the experience of their mentee should immerse themselves in the world view of the mentee, to ensure the best atmosphere for the construction of a new framework. Reframing does not target the truth, but the effectiveness of another point of view. It allows the unblocking of a difficult situation by discovering other possibilities that were inconceivable through the previous way of showing reality. It serves to put a situation in a new light, giving it a new meaning. The method is exciting, both for the mentor who uses it, as well as for the mentee, who discovers other ways of looking at reality. It may be mobilising, offer safety, be educational, provocative, disturbing and humorous. All these attributes are powerful drivers for change.

To be considered, reframing must be ecological at two levels. First, it must respect the psychological balance of the mentee to be accepted and assimilated into their world view. Then it must consider the result of the potentially harmful consequences in the relationships and social life of the person.

To reframe in a meaningful way, the mentor must identify how the mentee has constructed their problem. Reframing may be undertaken at different levels of the construction of reality. According to how the problem is made up, reframing can target the perceptual context (reframing the point of view), the conceptual context (reframing meaning) or the relationship context (reframing behaviour).

## Reframing the point of view

This type of reframing aims at affecting the perceptual level by changing the angle of perception (i.e., the point of view). As we usually think that our view of a situation is central (i.e., typical human egocentricity), our perception of reality is automatically biased. Reframing demonstrates to the mentee that the world is wider and that they have seen only a part of it.

The mentee complains that their boss never provides any positive feedback.

*Mentee:* I never receive any congratulations for a job well done but he is always there to criticise. I am tired of this situation; this is quite demotivating.

*Mentor:* If I understand, when he says nothing, it means that it is a good job! Are you sure he never congratulates?

*Mentee:* No, indeed, he prefers to express gratitude by email.

*Mentor:* You see, some people might have difficulties expressing their satisfaction orally.

Reframing in this way suggests to the mentee that they should select the interpretation of the boss's behaviour that confirms this hypothesis. The fact of anticipating the boss's other ways of communicating satisfaction increases the chances for the mentee that they will behave differently with their boss and subconsciously increase the likelihood of change. By reframing, the mentee sees their boss's behaviour with a different perspective, from a different angle, with perspective and distance, which allows them to envisage new options.

## Reframing meaning

Starting from a fact or a similar experience, the mentor proposes a new meaning to the mentee. This gives new sense to a situation or a word.

Take the example of this mentee who finds that their colleague is very stubborn. They claim that it is really exhausting!

'You mean,' says the mentor, 'that she can defend her point of view, which means she is respected by her peers. You're lucky to have a colleague as assertive as she is because she will always defend your department!'

By showing the mentee the benefits of persistence, it becomes an asset. This reframing is necessary because it is less the behaviour of others which influences our own, but the meaning, assumptions and hypotheses that we attribute to the behaviour.

The psychotherapist Leslie Bandler used this technique with a compulsive housewife who spent her time cleaning the carpet to the entrance of her house. She could not accept that the carpet pile was not in perfect condition. Leslie proposed that she closed her eyes and imagined the carpet to be clean with the pile in perfect order. When she sensed that her patient was satisfied, she added, 'Now you realise that you're all alone in the house and all your loved ones are gone.' The signs of contentment soon disappeared to make room for anxiety. Leslie continued: 'Now put some marks on the carpet. This means that your family is with you.' In this example, Leslie performs a double reframing, changing two complex equivalences:

1 Clean carpet = Everything is right (the patient is happy) becomes clean carpet = I am alone.
2 Carpet with marks = Something is not right (the patient feels bad) becomes carpet with marks = Those whom I love are near me.

## Reframing behaviour

This reframing is based on three basic principles of NLP:

1 Each person behaves according to their capabilities and their world view.
2 A person behaves this way because they adapt to the context.
3 Each kind of behaviour has a positive intention and is useful in the light of a desired change.

When a mentee suffers from a certain kind of behaviour, when they criticise themselves or are being criticised, it usually means 'I would like to change this behaviour (or someone else's), but I cannot.' Then they usually offer a ton of psychological explanations to justify the merits of their position. It is time to ask the question: 'So that I can understand the situation, I wish to know the purpose of this behaviour. I would like to show you that it can be useful in certain situations. Are there any situations where it is useful and where you would like to use it?'

For example: a mentee thinks that he intrudes too much into the lives of his interlocutors when he asks about the progress of a dossier. When his mentor asked him how he felt when others (such as a colleague, client or supplier) asked him about a dossier, he responded that he thought it showed interest on their part, so he answers. By reframing the same behaviour into a different context, the mentor showed how such requests could be viewed in a positive manner.

# Listening to own intuition

Mentors have experience that they can rely on, but also a strong intuition – and this is the same for men and women. What makes them ask a certain question at a given time, or use this analogy or metaphor that will have a genuine impact on their mentee, or make some assumptions not only based on their experience but rather on their 'feeling'?

Frances Vaughan:[29] 'At any time, we are only aware of a small piece of what we know. Intuition allows everyone to tap into the vast reservoir of subconscious knowledge which contains not only all that we have experienced and learned, consciously or subliminally, but also the myriad of materials of universal or collective subconscious which transcend the boundaries of self and the individual.'

Everyone has first-hand experience of intuition and of having either followed it or not – quite often, our state of mind intervenes and makes us despise our own intuition. Hopefully, everyone has intuition at their disposal; some people choose to cultivate it. This is what we suggest that we learn together. By paying attention to it, mentors will improve their ability for intuitive perception. As children need attention, so do adults. Every person needs attention, and so does every part of ourselves – our needs, our desires, our values … and our intuition. If our intuition is not valued, it will not speak to us and pass on messages. In addition, if we ask it to, our intuition is very generous and will send us many messages.

What is strange about intuition is that it has a particular language, not always direct, often unexpected and inappropriate to the present situation.

To access one's intuition, it is important to get away from a logical world view, Cartesian and dualistic. Intuition allows us to pay attention to other

---

29   Frances E. Vaughan (1988) *Awakening Intuition* New York: Anchor Books.

forms of reality. Learning to create a void inside allows us to fill the void with other things.

A quote from Daniel Goleman:[30] 'When the states arising from meditation merge with mental monitoring, intuition will mature. When it has reached full maturity, this state makes durable changes to the consciousness of the meditator, transforming the experience he has of himself and the universe.'

I (Sylviane) usually challenge future mentors to start 'mentoring with their belly'. It means to create the inner silence, the void that will allow them to truly listen to their mentee, especially to their energy level. For me, this level is the very best indicator of change during a mentoring session. With the void, the mentor can easily perceive the change of energy levels, not only through the emotion expressed by the mentee but through their own energy level. They will perceive the lack of congruence – personally, I feel weird, as if the taste of my saliva is changing, I suddenly feel uncomfortable and I immediately analyse the situation in meta-position; this means that I pause, and I observe not only the mentee but also the process. What made us come to this point, which was the trigger that invited the mentee to step away from authenticity and perhaps lie to themselves, create an illusion, get into a fallacy? Also, energy levels automatically decrease with sadness and fear, and will directly increase with anger and joy. Animation shows a drive, a genuine motivation, and this only can lead the mentee to moving into action.

30   Daniel Goleman (2005) *The Varieties of Meditative Experiences*, New York: Most Tarcher/ Putnam Books.

# 5 Asking impactful questions

## The Socratic method

Born in Athens, Socrates (470–399 BCE) is traditionally considered a divisive landmark in the history of Greek philosophy. He is said to have been the son of a sculptor and a midwife, a double heritage that symbolically generated another authentic representation of a human, making him 'give birth' to his own ideas (see Chapter 13).

As in its time, Socrates' method has great value for modern mentoring, since the mentor helps their mentee to question their current mental models, generate new ideas and assume responsibilities; objectives that are well aligned with the two pillars of the Socratic Method: Irony and Maieutic.

### Irony

The first pillar of the Socratic Method, known as Irony, comes from the Greek expression, which means 'to ask, pretending not to know'. The Irony was composed of questions asked to the mentee to make it clear that the knowledge they believed they possessed was nothing more than an opinion or a partial interpretation of reality.

For Socrates, non-knowledge or ignorance is preferable to bad knowledge (knowledge based on prejudices). With that, the questions of Socrates turned around so that the interlocutor realised that they were not sure of their beliefs and recognised their own ignorance.

The same process happens during mentoring sessions, where the mentor often has the role of challenging preconceived or prejudiced ideas, so the mentee realises that often a limiting belief or obstacle in their career was just a preconceived opinion.

### Maieutic

The second pillar of the Socratic Method is known as Maieutic, which means 'childbirth'. In this second moment, the philosopher continues to ask questions, now with the objective that the interlocutor reaches a secure conclusion on the subject and is able to define a concept.

The name 'maiêutica' was inspired by Socrates' own family. His mother, Phaenarete, was a midwife and the philosopher took her as an example and claimed that they both had similar activities. While the mother helped women to give birth to children, Socrates helped people to give birth to new ideas or insights.

Socrates understood that ideas are already within people and that they are known for their eternal soul. However, the right question can remind the soul of its prior knowledge. For the philosopher, no one is able to teach someone else anything. Only they themselves can become aware, give birth to ideas. Reflection is the way to achieve knowledge.

You may be wondering: what is the purpose of talking about Socrates' method in mentoring? The standard answer would be that the method, when used during the session, encourages mentees to develop their critical thinking and have new insights. This is also a pillar of the coaching attitude and considered as a core competency. The questions can be adapted according to the logical level of awareness of each mentee, that we'll see next.

# Beyond closed or open questions

When training future mentors, we seek to go beyond the already known open or closed questions. Of course, both still have their importance during a mentoring dialogue, but to take a step further, we can resort to a few different types. Paul and Elder[31] divided the questions of the Socratic Method into six basic types:

1 Questions for clarification: Why do you say that? How does this relate to our discussion?

2 Questions that probe assumptions: What could we assume instead? How can you verify or disprove that assumption?

3 Questions that probe reasons and evidence: What would be an example? What is … analogous to? What do you think causes … to happen? Why?

4 Questions about viewpoints and perspectives: What would be an alternative? What is another way to look at it? Would you explain why it is necessary or beneficial, and who benefits? Why is it the best? What are the strengths and weaknesses of …? How are … and … similar? What is a counterargument for …?

5 Questions that probe implications and consequences: What generalisations can you make? What are the consequences of that assumption? What are you implying? How does … affect …? How does … tie in with what we learned before?

6 Questions about the question: What was the point of this question? Why do you think I asked this question? What does … mean? How does … apply to everyday life?

---

31    Paul, R., & Elder, L. (2002). *Critical thinking: Tools for taking charge of your professional and personal life*. New Jersey: Financial Times/Prentice-Hall Press.

By expanding the question options with this broader approach, the mentor will expand their arsenal of powerful questions that can be used during the mentoring process. Let's see now another way to improve the ability to ask impactful questions, using an adaptation of the questions according to a hierarchical arrangement developed in the field of NLP (Neuro-Linguistic Programming).

## The logical levels of awareness for deeper change

This hierarchical arrangement, moving through values and beliefs, is the fruit of the work of the American anthropological philosopher Gregory Bateson and Robert Dilts, one of the leading figures in the world of NLP. It is referred to as the logical levels of awareness or change.[32]

Bateson pointed out that the processes of learning, change and communication were natural and hierarchical. The idea is that changing something at the top of the hierarchy would affect everything below it to support the higher level.

From very early in life, the child's attention focuses on their **environment**: where are they, and who is with them? Later, we retain this reflex when we find ourselves in a new place: we notice first the building, the entrance, and the people to be found there, and so on.

As the child grows and enters adolescence, they become more focused on **behaviour**: 'My father is a teacher. My mother writes articles.' 'When we go on holiday, we go hiking.' The same applies to us in the world of business, where we are concerned with behaviour: what should we do?

The young adult is then required to acquire **skills-capacities** (education, first job), show their capabilities, prove themselves. This is the period of the first job and the establishment of the couple. In the workplace, they must continue to acquire new skills and build their future.

When the adult reaches 35 to 45 years of age, they begin to confront their everyday reality in the context of their deeply held **values and beliefs**. 'In my heart of hearts, did I always want to be an engineer, or did I do it to please Dad?' 'I can't bear doing things which conflict with my values.' This is the time of breakups, be they professional or personal. Some people never go through this period because they remain on automatic pilot all their lives. Other people pass through it very early, have been questioning themselves since adolescence, and have aligned their lives with their values from an early stage.

Calm reappears towards the age of 50, when the individual has at last found their way, their **identity**. They also come to realise that this identity is made up of a whole collection of multiple roles: mother or father, partner, son or daughter, colleague, friend, member of a family, of a community, of a club and the like.

---

32   Examples are from the book *Coaching Excellence*, Sylviane Cannio & Viviane Launer, op. cit.

**Figure 5.1** The Logical Levels (Bateson-Dilts)

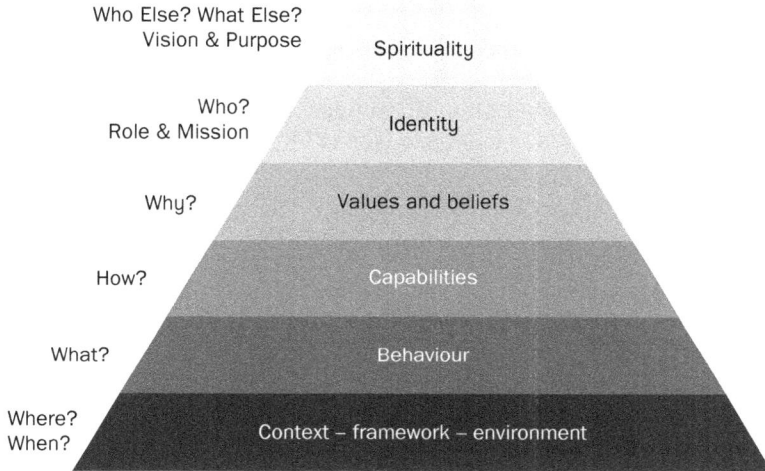

And when life brings wisdom, the period is known as the **spiritual** or **transpersonal** stage, when the person has found their connections: with themselves, with nature, with others, with things that go beyond and that they may refer to as God or something similar. Here we have the old sage who strokes his beard while philosophising about life; the wise woman who is in touch with the forces of nature.

Of course, levels of awareness are not systematically subject to age; these are just possible trends. Some people reach a higher level quite early, finding their vocation and meaning of life during their childhood or adolescence, for instance.

It was Bateson who identified the logical levels of awareness, while Dilts organised them into a pyramid (see Figure 5.1), since the number of people who reach the higher levels becomes smaller and smaller.

## Types of questions to be asked according to the level

### Environment

This level encompasses the physical and emotional environment around us. Our work, community, colleagues, family and living arrangements, as well as the tools and resources we have available. The mentor can access this level by asking the mentee: How does your environment affect your goals? What are your resources and tools? What obstacles do you face? What kind of people do you like to have around you? Where are you? How does it look? Who is with you? When do you arrive/depart? Could you describe the place and its surroundings? How are you dressed? What do you have in your hands?

## Behaviour

This level refers to our actions and behaviours. Here the mentor would ask the following questions: How do you react in each situation? How is your body language towards others? What kind of attitudes do you exhibit to others? What are you doing right now? What are you saying? What are you reading? How are you moving?

## Capabilities

This level reflects the mentee's skills, abilities, talents, knowledge and competencies. All of these will lead to specific actions and behaviours in their life. The mentor can ask: What skills and current knowledge do you possess? What knowledge or training do you need and still must learn? What makes you legitimate to be here right now? What have you learnt that creates your right to be here? What are your resources? What are you putting in place to be skilled at answering questions? Is there anything you are missing to do the job and that you could acquire?

## Values – beliefs

Our beliefs and values drive our behaviours. They play an enormous role in our motivation to act and will impact our outcomes. They define and direct our life. Some thought-provoking questions the mentor could ask at this level could be: What makes you believe these things? What makes you value this and that? What do you believe is right or wrong? What beliefs will help you get better results? What is important for you in this situation? Which are your main values, the ones that overarch your action right now? Do you feel at home with what is requested now by these people? Do you feel comfortable with the actions you have to undertake?

## Identity

Our identity is made up of our core beliefs and values; this gives us a sense of self. Introspective questions such as: By the way, who are you? How do you see yourself? What do you stand for? What is the vision for your life? How would others describe you? What is your role in this situation? Which are the other roles you play in your life? Are there common points between them that builds who you are?

*Spirituality*

This is the highest logical level and reflects the '**big picture**' of life. This is where we begin to question our purpose, ethics, mission and meaning of life. By asking the following questions, the mentor will shed some light on the mentee's purpose of life. What is the meaning of your life? What is your reason for being here? How would you like to be remembered when you are gone? What greater good do you believe in? What is the meaning of this action right now? What is the rationale behind it? What are you seeking? How can it make you evolve and learn? Who, bigger than you, is there to help and support you? And how can you activate their support?

> **Mentor's take-away**: Do your best to define the logical level of the mentee's challenge or issue and ask the questions which correspond to the level **above** it. Or, even better, explore the upper levels of the pyramid: finding the meaning, the rationale behind an action or a move that brings a lot of energy and drive, and motivates the mentee to get into the implementation phase.

# 6 Providing constructive feedback

## What is feedback?

We could say that feedback is a reaction or information that occurs as a result of actions or behaviour undertaken by an individual or even a group. In the mentoring context, both positive and negative feedback is crucial. Feedback provides a sense of engagement and interactivity and allows mentees to take ownership of their development. Effective feedback shows mentees their current level of performance and lets them know what they need to do to reach a higher level.

## The Johari Window

The Johari Window[33] model was created in 1955 by psychologists Joseph Luft and Harrington Ingham as a non-intrusive and empirical method of self-discovery, during a group dynamics programme in the University of California. Luft and Ingham named their model 'Johari' using a combination of their first names, but it is sometimes referred to as an information processing tool or disclosure/feedback model of self-awareness.

The model is based on two fundamental concepts:

1 Trust can be acquired by revealing information about yourself to others.
2 You gain unknown, and perhaps, enlightening insights about yourselves from the feedback you receive from others.

The Johari Window is represented by a chart consisting of four quadrants (areas, zones) that symbolise the behaviours, emotions, sensations and feelings of an individual in relationship to others. See Figure 6.1.

**Public area**: Known to Self and Others. Example: 'I am somebody calm and recognised by others as being calm.'

The information shared here is about the person, their attitudes, behaviour, emotions, feelings, skills and views. It will be known by the person as well as

---

33   Luft, J. (1969) *Of Human Interaction – The Johari Model*. San Francisco: Mayfield Publishing Co.

**Figure 6.1** The Johari Window

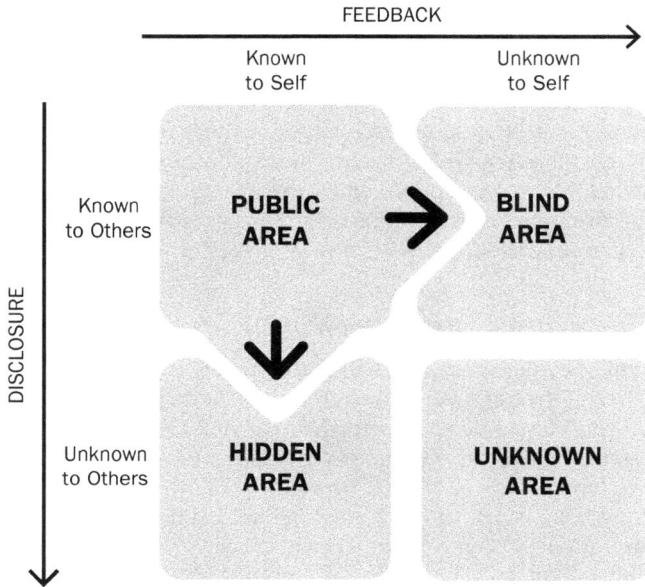

by others. The 'public area' is representative of the richness of communications with others. Actively seeking feedback from others and listening for understanding is a key to decreasing the blind spots while increasing the open area for trustworthy communication; through openly revealing more about oneself to the other person. The goal is simply for us to increase this area by reducing the other three sectors.

**Blind area**: What is known to others and not known to oneself. Example: 'My friend told me I was not attentive to others. I had not realised it.'

This area represents information about us, that other people in that group may know, but of which we're totally unaware. Others may see, interpret, read, feel or think differently about us than we expect. These blind spots in our self-awareness are reduced when we seek honest and constructive feedback from others.

**Hidden area**: What is known to oneself, unknown to others: Example: 'I am a loner, but my friends do not know.'

This area covers the behaviours and attitudes that the individual does not want to share with others. It usually covers holding personal information, including feelings, fears, secrets, past experiences, etc., which we can feel reluctant to reveal. Sometimes feelings and personal information are considered too sensitive or strictly private since their disclosure may have an impact on those relationships. However, in a trustworthy environment that seeks open communication, it is important to reduce this hidden area with open disclosure that moves hidden facts into the public area.

**Unknown area**: What is unknown to oneself, unknown to others. Example: 'Neither others nor I know how I react to death.'

This area could include the information, feelings, capabilities, talents, etc., which may be due to traumatic past experiences or events which can be unknown for a lifetime, or we may be totally unaware of these facts, or information, until at some stage you discover – or others recognise and/or observe – hidden talents, innate qualities or untried capabilities.

Self-knowledge and open communication are an effective way to decrease the unknown area and thus open us and the group to improve effective and rewarding communication.

### Some lessons from the Johari Window

Any change in one quadrant affects the other three.

It takes energy to stop a behaviour from interacting with other behaviours.

A lack of confidence or a perceived threat will tend to inhibit an attitude of awareness and openness. On the other hand, a climate of mutual trust will facilitate the change.

It is not desirable to try to force someone into self-awareness. Moreover, it does not generally lead to the desired result.

The establishment of a dialogue, of communication between two people, results in a change in an area. It then expands at the expense of others.

The larger the public area, the more the parties involved are productive.

Conversely, the smaller the public area is, the weaker are the communications.

We all want to explore our area of personal development; this requires overcoming our fears and inhibitions.

To know oneself, to know others and to empathise is to be aware of our hidden aspects in all quadrants. It is also to respect the wish of others to keep theirs hidden.

If one is able to understand the evolution of a group or an individual – in other words, if quadrant 1 becomes larger – we can measurably improve our relationship with the group or the person.

The value system of a group and its members is reflected in how it addresses the 'unknown' aspects.

I (Cicero) frequently use the Johari Window, in both workshops and one-on-one mentoring sessions to create an atmosphere of safety and trust. I start by sharing a fairly well-known piece of information about myself and I check that everyone was already aware of those facts. I then tell the person or group something about myself that is unlikely to be known by them. Depending on the situation, this may be quite a revealing piece of information, and I then ask them to share, or reveal, something about myself that I either do not already know or do not believe is common knowledge, e.g., I may not be aware that I have a personal idiosyncrasy of playing with coins in my pocket when making a presentation.

Through their willingness to share this quirk with me, I have learnt something about myself that was previously unknown, and I can take appropriate action, if necessary. After duly thanking the person, or persons, you can go through the same process with them and improve your perceptions about them. It is an enlightening and simple technique to encourage open and congruent discussion.

In simple terms, the Johari Window model offers an opportunity for improved self-awareness and for the practice of feedback among individuals when they are in a group – through better understanding of their relationship with themselves and others – while enhancing their perceptions of those others.

# The conditions for constructive feedback

There are so many reasons why a seemingly innocent feedback session can go wrong: strong emotions on both sides, a focus on character rather than on behaviour, a lack of clarity about what needs to change and why. However, we can lessen this risk by creating the necessary conditions for a positive impact on our mentee, such as: precision, construction, sensitivity and responsibility.

### Precision

Giving feedback is to explain to the mentee what is being done correctly, what is not working and what the areas for improvement are. Being vague or avoiding the truth obscures the real message. Better to expose the real situation, dissect it, and talk about the emotion it brings and what can be changed. Precision is as important as appreciation in criticism. Providing nothing but compliments does not make sense; the effect is limited and does not allow the mentee to draw the right lessons.

### Construction

As with any useful feedback, fair criticism serves to indicate how to solve a problem. Otherwise, the mentee feels frustrated, demotivated and demoralised. Fair criticism opens the door to opportunities and options of which the mentee is not aware (see the Johari Window), or simply allows them to take into account points to look out for and should include suggestions about how to solve the problem.

### Sensitivity

The mentor must show empathy, feel the impact of what they say and how it is said. Managers who have no empathy are more inclined to criticise, insulting and denigrating their staff. Such criticism may have a devastating effect on them. Instead of preparing an improvement action, it produces negative effects: the person feels resentful and bitter, becoming defensive and keeping their distance.

## Responsibility

The mentor speaks in the first person 'I': it is in their name that they speak; they do not hide behind the anonymous 'we'. The mentor is responsible for their own feedback.

# Feedforward versus feedback

Feedback can and does have its place. In fact, mentees typically rely on this mechanism to know if their performance aligns with the organisation's vision or the mentoring process and if they are meeting expectations. Without feedback from their mentor, mentees may feel lost or unmotivated.

Feedforward, a concept developed by business educator and coach, Marshall Goldsmith (2012), is now an increasingly popular practice in today's workplaces, including in our MentoringCo ecosystem. This practice can provide the mentor with useful insight and help create a more positive work environment for the future while assisting their mentees in moving past barriers that may be slowing down and negatively impacting their productivity and performance.

When a mentee receives feedback, they get information about how they are presently performing. Feedforward is the reverse exercise of feedback. It is the process of replacing positive or negative feedback with future-oriented solutions. In simple terms, it means focusing on the future instead of the past.

A good way to start a discussion on feeding forward during a mentoring session is to ask the mentee: 'What would you do differently next time?' This leverages your time effectively as it helps shift their focus away from the past and more towards what they need to do, while not being too time intensive for the mentor. A bonus with feeding forward is that the emphasis is on getting better at the task, which avoids the mentee getting defensive and arguing, which often happens if they are feeling personally judged.

Naturally, during the mentoring process, feedback has its time and place. But the whole point of it is that the mentee sometimes leaves the session with a clearer understanding of what it is they need to get better at. If they only get feedback on what they have done, this may be unlikely to occur. Combining feedback with feedforward – with an emphasis on the latter and not the former – is possible to save time for the person giving it and help the person receiving it to improve.

# The power of metaphors

Definition: a metaphor is a story, a recitation that allows transmission of an indirect message. The objective is to get through the mind to bypass any conscious resistance and intellectualisation. It appeals to the subconscious. The mentee recognises themselves through the heroes or the context. It can then project their problems, their questions, their internal or external conflicts, or their dead ends.

A metaphor is a linguistic way to conceive and express something in graphic terms with the objective of opening the spirit towards new paths. Like any fairy tale – and any mentoring situation – a metaphor leaves a difficulty.

## Characteristics

The 'powerful' metaphor has three characteristics:

1 Isomorphism with the real situation.
2 Existence of a solution (outcome).
3 Possibility to link the metaphor to the real situation (connection).

**Isomorphism** is a property that two or more bodies of similar chemical constitution have. Each has a similar crystalline form. For the metaphor to work, its structure needs to be identical to the real situation.

The **outcome** is best when the metaphor indirectly addresses the problem and provides a solution. Often it is the mentee themselves who offer solutions. The mentor offers an outcome, but it is the mentee who applies it to the real situation.

The **connection** is to find a strategy linking the desired outcome to the problematic situation. By connecting the two stories, the mentee can resolve their problem by identifying options. They can reframe the problem, understand its true size and lighten their burden.

A substitute for the metaphor is an analogy. It uses a parallel story to assist the understanding of a situation.

Metaphors are more powerful than advice. They are generally more elegant and are not perceived as threatening. As the communication is indirect, the identity of the other person is respected and is given sufficient freedom for them to find both the link and the solution that suits them.

I (Sylviane) have often used two metaphors/analogies that work rather well. The first is about proactivity versus passivity. 'Do you prefer to be like Sleeping Beauty, waiting for 100 years until the solution comes, or do you prefer to be like Cinderella and be an effective project manager, building her own carriage, dress and relying on a trustworthy person like her godmother?' And for the manager who has difficulty with prioritising, I refer to this wonderful shop found in Jaisalmer, Rajasthan (India): the shop was a genuine cavern of treasures on four floors, displaying a mishmash of clothes, furniture, jewels, and all you can imagine. In this incredible amass of diverse objects, the shop owner knows exactly what to find where: a blue sari? 'Give me one minute' and he would find it. Amazing! The mentee could relate their list of projects to the shopkeeper and find out if they need to order or not – just like some MBTI profiles prefer creativity of the last moment (Perception) and others discipline, planning and order (Judgement).

# 7 Enabling insight and awareness

A major skill to be developed by mentors is the ability to create moments of awareness. These are the shifts of beliefs that were limiting their actions or some 'aha moments'.

## Overpassing limiting beliefs

'We are what we think' says the motto. And our thoughts have been consolidating since we were born through our perception of what we considered as being 'the' reality. Each experience, good or bad, gave birth to a conclusion transformed into a belief. Many of them are excellent drivers: Faith moves mountains – I can do it and ... I am doing it! – It is never too late to learn. However, many can be limiting or sabotaging of our actions: No pain, no gain – Money is happiness – I have reached the peak of my career – Others are better than I am – Showing emotion is a sign of weakness – I need to control everything – Life is a perpetual struggle; and many more.

A good mentor has learned how to track those limiting beliefs. They often come with assertions like 'always', 'never', 'I must' and other elements to be found in the NLP linguistic meta-model (see the section on Mentoring with the linguistic meta-model in Chapter 4). Once a limiting belief is tracked, the best mentor's tool is to reframe; this is to show the mentee that 'their' reality can be seen from another angle and be perceived in another more positive way.

Another useful tool is to extract the belief from a generalisation. 'Are you sure it is **always** like this?', 'Isn't there another moment when the outcome was different?' etc. Or to seek the positive intention behind an action: 'Are you sure that people were laughing at you at that moment? What was their real motive? And when you say that they were laughing at the way you were dressed, are you sure it was directed at you, or was it simply to find a way to feel themselves part of a social group with some sort of a uniform?' etc.

Mentoring can help the mentee to change long-installed beliefs. It happens regularly that a mentor helps their mentee shift a belief that is 10, 20 or more years old. It generates a reaction often guided by guilt or anger – 'I am so angry against myself to have been thinking that silly way for so many years ...' (In this case, the mentor should immediately reframe, telling the mentee that this shift could never happen without their willingness to be mentored.)

The mentee's body also reacts: 'fisheyes' (wide open, with a moment of paralysis), sweat, gallow's laughter (bitter laughter instead of expressing a pain, as defined in Transactional Analysis). A major shift of a limiting belief also generates a 'KO (knockout) moment' with sideration (sudden paralysis), or at the opposite, a wonderful moment of genuine joy. A shift of ancient belief takes a few minutes and is easy (it is a limiting belief to think that shifting a belief is long and fastidious). However, it doesn't mean yet that the person will implement the actions that will translate this new (positive) belief. Here, the mentee needs support and encouragement for implementation to feel convinced of the change and to see the effect it has on their environment.

## Generating wonderful 'aha' moments

Those shifts of beliefs through reframing are best designed to raise awareness. When the mentor revisits a situation from another angle, this can create beautiful aha moments.

Many technicians face difficulties with speaking in public. A good mentor can dare asking the question: 'Do you remember where it comes from? What was the very first triggering situation?' Quite often, the mentee will recall ridiculing or even humiliating experiences when presenting a topic in front of their class during childhood or early adolescence. A mentor has a fantastic opportunity to reframe the situation. 'When you present in front of the Executive Committee, do you find yourself in front of the same pupils who needed to create fun moments since the class was so boring?' To make the mentee aware that the context is not the same usually alleviates the bad anchoring and allows a new freedom to take place.

Importantly, shifts of old beliefs are among the best aha moments that a mentor can generate in a session. Quite often, mentees are stuck in old guilt or humiliation, for instance, for a behaviour or an action or a lack of action they experienced in their childhood or adolescence, and which still has an impact on their adult life.

I (Sylviane) witnessed so many spectacular changes of beliefs, some being anchored for several dozens of years. For example, one mentee, who was convinced that she was at the source of her parents' divorce, or another responsible for their parent's cancer. How could a small child be responsible for such an outcome? How does the adult mentee remain blind to the fact that a child doesn't have the same resources as an adult? I am always surprised that people do not rely on a psychotherapist to move away from such a belief. Is it really in the scope of my job as a mentor? Am I penetrating fields that exclusively belong to psychotherapy? How should I remain silent when the solution is right under my eyes? I consider this is just common sense to share my intuition or, simply, my assumption.

Some other beautiful aha moments are generated when the mentee discovers the graph of the Change Process (Grief – see Chapter 9 on Monitoring Progress and Evaluation). They soon realise that their reactions, their emotions are 'normal' as they are going through grief and need time to process all the related emotions.

After a moment of consideration or real shock/surprise, the mentee feels relieved, and their energy is much higher. In any case, it always leads to a new freedom, a new positive view of life, and this is beautiful to watch as a mentor.

# 8 Leading to action and autonomy

Now that we know what the mentoring process and coaching attitude are, let us look at the relationship itself, namely how the mentor–mentee relationship is managed.

## Reaching interdependence: the stages of autonomy

In most cases, the mentor–mentee relationship is healthy. Both parties know how to function without each other, in full autonomy, and are happy to meet according to a well-defined schedule and a clear framework. But sometimes the relationship is vitiated by more emotional or egotistical elements, and these create a lack of autonomy in one or both parties.

This notion of autonomy is well known to psychologists. It has been widely used over the years and we will retain two theories of autonomy, those proposed by Eric Berne, the father of Transactional Analysis, and by Vincent Lenhardt,[34] a French psychoanalyst who is one of the pioneers of coaching in France.

To further define the four stages culminating in interdependence, we will take three examples: the mother and child, the couple and the mentor–mentee pair.

### Stage One: Dependency

Mother and child: the baby has just been born and is totally dependent on its mother for its survival. For her part, the mother has just 'lost' a part of her body that has been transformed into a small, defenceless being. Her maternal instinct pushes her to nurse the baby 24 hours a day, especially if she is breastfeeding. She finds it difficult to leave her baby in other hands, however benevolent they may be. And if she is prone to postpartum depression, she doesn't want to do anything anyway, and allows herself to become dependent on her baby.

The couple: the two young people who have just met may find themselves in the same addictive relationship that results in dozens of text or WhatsApp messages a day, in the very abandonment of a part of oneself that becomes merged with the other. 'I can't live without you,' 'I feel lost without you' become their key sentences. All activities are done in pairs; they lose the mental and

---

34  Vincent Lenhardt (2002) *Les Responsables porteurs de sens*, Paris: Insep Consulting.

emotional autonomy that would allow them to build boundaries and create their own space. They literally lose themselves in the relationship.

The mentor–mentee pair: it is rare to find such a situation in a mentor–mentee relationship. But it could happen if, for example, the mentee dreamed of working with their idol, high up in the hierarchy, and the mentor loved to play the role of rescuer (see the Drama Triangle, Figure 8.1) or considers themselves as their mentee's spiritual parent. The meetings are organised quite frequently. The mentee systematically calls on the mentor when a decision must be made. As for the mentor, their ego is flattered as soon as they can be of service. The relationship is addictive and far from healthy.

### Stage Two: Counter-dependency

One or both parties slowly start to distance themselves. The young mother needs space and time to recover, to refocus on herself. She decides to go back to her fitness classes, accepts a babysitter and starts to have a social life again. The child, now that they can walk and make themselves understood, sets out to explore the world around them; this is also the time when they are going to be confronted with their first prohibitions: no, you don't put your hand in the socket; yes, you behave properly at the table; yes, you go to bed at the required time, etc.

On their side, the young couple starts activities without each other, still for short periods. Each one finds a space of their own, through work and colleagues, sport and teammates, leisure activities, etc. They appreciate having a little time to themselves. They appreciate having some oxygen to enjoy the reunion.

The mentor–mentee pair has now adopted a rhythm of meetings that better suits the mentee's needs and respective agendas. There is, however, a counter-dependency because both parties still need each other very much and do not necessarily feel free. The relationship has not yet reached a healthy level: for example, procrastination is present when setting the pace of the sessions, each party finds excuses not to organise the session. They see each other less and less, or slowly begin to disqualify the mentoring process or find reasons for dissatisfaction with the achievement of goals, or even with the relationship.

### Stage Three: Independence

The child, now adolescent, moves to a flat or independent home near their school or university. They claim their liberty. The mother has her own activities and space.

The young couple needs a break. They often argue, blaming each other for a lot of things. They feel that the space they have gained so far is no longer enough. So, they decide to separate, either temporarily or permanently. They will then go through the stages of mourning (see Chapter 9).

The same is true for the mentor–mentee pair who decide to take a break or stop the mentoring process altogether.

### Stage Four: Interdependence

Now the child has become an adult and, after distancing themselves, realises that life with their parents was 'not that bad', that the parents' opinions often made sense and that they miss them. As a result, they visit them with pleasure, enjoying their company, while having taken the reins of their life independently.

The same pattern applies to the young couple who, after taking a break from their life together, realise that life is not as meaningful when they live apart. And, while listing each other's needs, they agree to find a fair understanding, an 'Adult-to-Adult arrangement' to live a common destiny but in a much more mature way and respecting each other's space. They feel free in the relationship; each has their own activities. They can travel together or decide to travel separately; each has their own space and well-defined boundaries, and there is trust and harmony in the couple.

This is the same path that the mentor–mentee pair has taken. There is no dependency, but rather the pleasure of sharing a learning project, of support, and of being together. Each party feels free in relation to the other. The relationship is healthy and free. If the mentor proposes solutions, they do so with detachment and the mentee is free to follow them or not, depending on the circumstances. The pace of the sessions reflects the real needs. Communication is fluid and the pleasure of being together is shared.

> **Mentor's take-away**: It is important that the mentor establishes an interdependent relationship from the outset through clear and fluid communication (in Adult-to-Adult Ego States), a common vision and shared responsibilities. It further illustrates the importance of a clear and transparent agreement with clear objectives and indicators.

# The paradigm of the victim

Even though the relationship is sound, some mentees tend to slow down their learning process by claiming that the entire world is against them. They love playing the role of the victim. 'I am powerless and vulnerable in a hostile world, unjust and dangerous. There are lucky individuals and others who are not. Life is unpredictable and dangerous. I have no power over what can happen in my life. It is very difficult to get what one wants in life. The best we can do is to fight, to try to control to the maximum, to protect and defend oneself from others and from life, and eventually pray that the sky will not fall on my head.'

Most such mentees will protest loudly if their mentor tells them that life can be different. They have the proof. Most people who suffer from 'victimhood' do not realise that it is a disease because they believe it to be a normal state. It is contagious and requires continuous care and attention for a long time to be healed. One heals oneself.

**Figure 8.1** Karpman's Drama Triangle

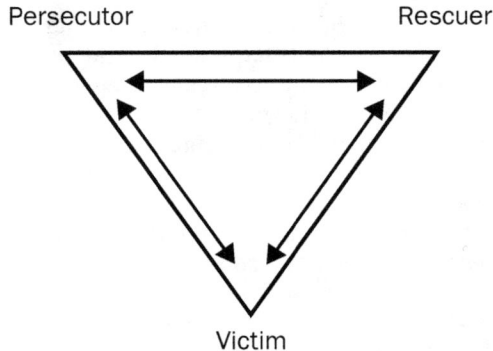

### The cycle of the victim

This can include the following stages:

- They find themselves to be real or imaginary torturers to project their inner reality on the outside.
- Feeling dissatisfied, frustrated and very angry.
- They complain passively or aggressively.
- They blame others or circumstances, silently or out loud.
- They judge and condemn their own torturers and all those in the world who are wrong.
- They avenge themselves (directly or indirectly; subtle sabotage).
- They feel guilty.
- To justify and consolidate the picture, they invent others whom they deem to be rude or other torturers who make them suffer.
- Then they can restart the cycle.

Some mentors like to 'rescue' their mentee and therefore enter in the mentee's stratagem, getting trapped in the famous 'drama triangle' (see Figure 8.1) observed in many life/organisational situations by Stephen Karpman.[35] He realised that it is possible for a person to occupy all three positions in turn when they play psychological games, particularly stratagems.

The roles are:

- the Persecutor who attacks, humiliates and belittles others, whom they see as inferiors

---

35  Stephen B. Karpman M.D.: 'Fairy Tales and Script Drama Analysis', T.A.B., 7; 1968, EBMSA Prize 1972, and 'A Game Free Life', Drama Triangle Publications, San Francisco, https://karpmandramatriangle.com/.

- the Rescuer who also sees others as inferiors and not-OK people and who offers them help from a position of superiority (thus enjoying a feeling of being OK)
- the Victim who feels and positions themselves as inferior, as not-OK, and will make the most of their problems either to seek a Persecutor (by displaying fear), or a Rescuer (by displaying sadness), which will serve to confirm their feelings of inadequacy.

## Questions to ask

To maintain their distance and to stay outside of it, they should have asked themselves some questions.

Here are five questions to ask yourself to reduce the risk of finding yourself in the role of the **Rescuer**:

1 Have I received a clear mandate, a request submitted in the correct and appropriate format?
2 Do I possess the skill to provide the response required?
3 Am I provided with the tools and conditions to provide what is asked of me?
4 Will I be suitably rewarded for the service I am asked to provide? (Even if it comes to a simple 'thank you'.)
5 Do I want to perform this kind of service? (Or am I driven by some form of guilt?)

Five questions to ask yourself to reduce the risk of finding yourself in the role of **Persecutor**:

1 Do I have the authority to act?
2 Do I possess the powers and the right to act?
3 Is it highly likely that my action will be appropriately used?
4 Am I open to reprisals, revenge or other forms of vengeance or punishment?
5 Will my action be appropriately acknowledged?

Five questions to ask yourself to reduce the risk of finding yourself in the role of the **Victim**:

1 Do I really need outside help?
2 Have I exhausted my knowledge and my aptitudes?
3 How will I go about asking for help?
4 To whom shall I address my plea?
5 Am I prepared to pay for the help I seek, at least by proffering appropriate thanks?

# Converting the Drama Triangle into the Virtuous Triangle

**Persecutor to Assertive**: If an individual still clings to the role of the **Persecutor**, it means that they are experiencing a lack of assertiveness, and that they have failed to express their need as a clear request. To achieve this, the best way to extract them from their +/- position (I am the one who knows and the other must obey me) and move them towards a +/+ position (I'm OK and you're OK) is to get them to express their request:

1  What do you need to ask for?
2  From whom?
3  How do you know that this person is able to satisfy your request?

**Victim to Responsible**: If the person already has the role of **Victim**, they need to escape from their -/+ position (the others are better than me because they have the solution which I lack, I can't escape without their help). They must be made to feel responsible, accountable yet vulnerable:

1  What could you set up to escape from this situation?
2  What are your options?
3  What have you decided and when are you going to implement your decision?
4  With whom, where and how?

**Rescuer to Caring**: If the person is already in the **Rescuer** role, they must escape from their +/- position (I know that the others need me) and feel empathy, to care for the other (they are OK, and so am I):

1  What is their problem? What do they feel? What are they suffering?
2  What attitude can I adopt to help them to resolve the problem?
3  What do I need to keep my distance from this problem and the feelings it gives rise to?
4  If I need recognition, what other means are available to me to earn it?

---

Many mentors take the initiative to intervene in a conflict between their mentee and another colleague for instance or want to introduce their mentee into their own circle of peers. In doing so, they automatically enter as rescuers into a drama triangle and will soon become persecutors or victims. A mentor can intervene if there is a clear mandate and request, clear boundaries and expectations, and making sure that the mentee also feels responsible for the outcome.

Kind-hearted mentors lobby for their mentees. If it is clear from the beginning that there is no guarantee of the outcome, the initiative is sound. But if expectations are not defined and the mentor commits without setting clear boundaries, they might soon become persecuted by the mentee, insisting on obtaining quick results, sometimes mobbing the mentor, and the relationship might be damaged.

# Setting SMARTEC objectives and action plans

There is no effective mentoring session without a clear session objective but also an action plan, unless it is clearly stated that no action is foreseen – in case the mentee needs some time for themselves or goes on holiday, for instance. For effectively formulating objectives and action plans, many of us already use the SMART model, disseminated in numerous leadership and management classes. To this acronym, we need to add other questions to verify that an objective or an action is sustainable, as defined by Robert Dilts[36] when analysing the strategies of success of Mozart, Walt Disney or Einstein:

1  **The objective/action must be formulated positively.**

    Being positive is already an action. Example: 'I want to lose weight or stop smoking or stop sending emails after 8 p.m.' is a negative formulation, while 'develop a waistline and longevity, run 5 km or end my daily work at 8 p.m.' is positive. What do I want? What do I have to do? What is it that would give me satisfaction?

2  **The objective/action is specific.**

    Who? What? Where? When? With whom? How much? How long? …

    'I want to learn French' or 'study management' is not specific, while 'I want to gain one level of proficiency in French' or 'I want to follow the class of management provided this year in my university' is far better.

3  **It is entirely under my control.**

    Asking this question of the mentee from the beginning immediately enables verification as to whether the objective is achievable (under their control) or if it is necessary to redefine it.

    Can I achieve my objective with actions that are under my own control?

    On whom does its achievement depend?

    For whom do I wish to achieve this objective?

    A mentee who wants to 'win new clients and increase the sales in their product line by 10 per cent' is misguided because it is not under their control:

---

36    Robert Dilts: Strategies of Genius – free pdf at: www.academia.edu/39219222/Robert_
      Dilts_Strategies_of_Genius_Volume_One_M_E_T_a_Publications_1995_.

to win, the customers must be winnable. There are at least two parties in the relationship. However, what is under their control is: to contact a defined set of customers according to a defined plan so that the turnover could increase by x per cent.

4 **In what context is it applicable? What is the background?**

Date, time, place. There must be a date, otherwise no implementation is compelling and there is no real commitment.

5 **How will I know I have succeeded? (Verifiable – Measurable)**

When the mentee will achieve this objective, what will they feel, see, hear, sense? (Using their five senses and emotions.) How will they know if they have reached their goal?

6 **Is the objective ecological?**

Some mentees tend to be bold in action setting and forget that there might be side-effects, for instance having to sacrifice life balance to fulfil a project, losing sight of their health, rushing into new ambitions without checking the feasibility. The mentor should encourage them to self-reflect on the following questions:

Is there any advantage in not achieving this objective?

What disadvantages could there be in achieving this objective?

What is the impact of the objective on your position within the company? On your colleagues? On your work? On your health?

What are the advantages and disadvantages of achieving this result?

What are the possible adverse side-effects?

7 **What is the price to pay?**

Likewise, the mentee must be aware of the price in time and/or energy and/ or money their objective or action represents: Is it worth it? What does this mean to them? What are they giving up? Is it affordable? And are they really willing to do this?

8 **What resources are at the mentee's disposal?**

In making sure that the mentee can perform the desired action, the mentor should be asking: Which material resources can you rely on? Who can support you? What information sources can you use? What beliefs and support can you count on to feel stronger?

9 **What is the objective of the objective?**

The finality of an action is paramount to make the person move on. We are therefore at the top of the logical level (see Chapter 5). And the following questions should be asked:

What makes it important for you to achieve this? To which broader objective does it relate? Example: reaching a higher proficiency of a foreign language can relate to the broader objective of being promoted to a more international position. What long term changes are targeted as a result of achieving the objective? What changes do you expect should you succeed?

10 **Is it consistent with the mentee's mission?**

Monitoring that there is a meaning to the mentee's actions and objectives is to insert them into their professional/life mission and the following questions could be asked: How is this objective consistent with you becoming the human being that you want to be or to become?

What does the achievement of this objective represent in your personal development?

To what extent does this objective contribute to accomplishing your mission?

11 **Does the objective replace the problem?**

And finally, it is important to check that the objective generates a real change. A wrong example would be to have the illusion that the action will wipe out the problem. Delegating without accepting the right to do wrong does not alleviate the pressure to be perfect, for instance. The mentee needs to accept to let go and trust others.

Is the desired situation worth achieving or will it lead to status quo? For example: it is useless going on holiday in a sports club full of activities instead of choosing a really restful venue as the problem of fatigue will just be worse upon the mentee's return to work.

---

**Mentor's take-away**: It is not necessary to ask the eleven questions to check the quality of an objective or an action. However, it is of paramount importance to have it scrutinised through the SMARTEC acronym: Specific, Measurable, Achievable, (sometimes Agreed), Realistic (or Relevant) and Time-bound, (or Timely). And we add Ecological (or Environment-friendly) and under Control – without this last point, the action is not under the mentee's decision power, neither are there accessible resources.

# 9 Monitoring progress and evaluation

Some mentors meet their mentee every month; some more often. Since each mentoring session ends with an action plan, it is important that the mentor asks for an update. 'What happened since we last met?' should be a neutral question, allowing the mentee to answer with sincerity. If the mentee did perform the action plan, it is important to celebrate. If it is not the case, then the mentor should react with kindness, sometimes with firmness, but always in a way that does not block the mentee's motivation to move on.

## Celebrating, celebrating and celebrating again!

Every little step, every progress is an opportunity to celebrate. Congratulate, celebrate any progress achieved and suggest to the mentee that they take ownership of the joy and pride, giving them permission to celebrate the small and large achievements.

Yet, it might sound quite difficult to do so for some mentors. Either they tend to imprint a fast rhythm to the follow-up process as they have their own drivers and speed-of-action criteria, or they are very demanding and satisfying them seems out of reach. In the corporate world, many mentors encourage their mentees to be ambitious, bold, daring, and this is quite positive indeed. Hence, too many mentors forget that their mentees are facing another reality: they are starting in the business, or they do not yet have the competence at a mastery level, or they do not dare or cannot rely on a wide network, and so on. Mentees have their own environment, their own constraints, their own workload. Perhaps the objectives were not as SMARTEC as they should have been, perhaps they were overoptimistic, overambitious and they need to be corrected. As a result, both mentor and mentee must determine if the action plan was adequate and made on a timely basis.

If trust is present at all moments, mentees will dare expressing their distress in front of a situation or obstacle. If not, mentees would tend either to be in a Submissive Child Ego State (see Chapter 3 on Building the Relationship) and accept the mentor's suggestions and challenges. We witnessed several cases where mentees were really fearing the next encounter with their mentor. Their self-confidence had been challenged and they were ashamed to show that they did not comply with their own action plan. This is a pity as the alliance is broken and trust is fading away. Or they might adopt a Rebellious Child Ego State and use any possible excuse or argument not to perform their action plan, that could lead to even disqualifying the mentor and the mentoring process.

At the opposite end of the scale, when the relationship is sound and mutual understanding is present through a non-judgmental attitude, they might be in an Adult Ego State and start negotiating terms with their mentor. Here, they would simply express the difficulties met during the implementation phase of their personal actions, and the mentor would understand and empathise with them. Temenos leads to authenticity and trust, and this is the basis for success for the duo.

> I (Sylviane) always find an opportunity to celebrate with all my mentees. As soon as they narrate a success, even tiny, I usually take my drink and toast my mentee's cup or glass with a large smile. The mentee feels automatically empowered and proud of the progress accomplished. It is even funny to see how they await that moment of celebration.

## Overcoming obstacles

Many mentees face unforeseen obstacles during the implementation phase of their action plan. Not that they lack motivation or competencies but they are faced with burdens which overcome their ability to move on, or they lack strategies to overcome them.

Effective mentors are there to support and to analyse together some other circumvention strategies, other options, and seek remedial actions: did the mentee analyse the whole system? Did they reckon on all possible resources, external and internal? Did they try different pathways before they abandoned their efforts? It is important to measure the effort invested and to trust the mentee's ability to find a solution or, at least, to find the necessary resources leading to an acceptable solution.

Even with repetitive encouragement, some mentees do not manage to implement their announced actions. The challenge, for the mentor, is not to enter a Critical Parent Ego State and adopt a posture that would lead to a Parent–Child relationship, yet sometimes Normative or Nurturing Parenting seems necessary. The mentor will then repeat their trust to their mentee, recall the process of mentoring and both side's obligations, and mainly continue offering support.

Not completing an action could also be generated by a pattern, which is a repetitive behaviour that emerges from a limiting belief based on a past negative experience. You may track it through the meta-model: never, always and but are common words to track a limiting belief, for instance (see Chapter 4).

Fear of failure or fear of success are common limiting beliefs that may hinder a mentee's actions. I (Sylviane) often check if any loyalty to a mentee's family member prevails. Quite often, women leaders will be loyal to generations of women before them, who were submissive and remained in their husband's shadow. It happens rather often that a mentee remains loyal to a family member who had financial challenges e.g., a bankruptcy, in the past, and failed to properly budget and manage available funds, or are afraid to lend money, for instance.

What about the mentees who procrastinate? The question that emerges here is: Would the mentee fail in waking up at 4 a.m. if they had to fly to meet their girlfriend in a holiday resort? So, in the framework of procrastination, the real mentoring questions would be: Is this action meaningful to you? What was the rationale behind the decision to plan this action?

Our belief is that procrastination often comes with a lack of meaning or real motivation to perform, or a loss of self-confidence in one's ability to perform. The mentor's task is thus to lighten the burden and to seek what makes the mentee paralysed; always with lots of kindness and understanding, of course.

At the end of the day, this all leads to the right balance between the carrot and the stick, as the human being needs recognition to move forward but also, from time to time, a bit of compelling obligating them to do so.

**Mentor's take-away**: Follow up by asking questions about the actions to which the mentee has committed. Adapt the work to the mentee's own rhythm, considering their availability and speed of learning, while maintaining sufficient pressure on the necessity for change.

## Understanding the change process and dealing with resistance

Resistance is one of the necessary stages of a change process, allowing it to pass from situation A to situation B, although not always for the better.

The difficulty often lies in the lack of prospects. If a person moves to a better position and a better work environment, they accept the change immediately. If this is not the case, they need to grieve for a situation they believed would have been better, and in the process, they pass through various stages of grieving. It might sound strange that we speak about grief, but we are surrounded by grief, from impactful losses – loss of a person for instance – to smaller ones: loss of an animal, an expensive object, and also loss of an expectation, a desire, a dream, an image of ourselves and sometimes even an illusion. Grieving/change is part of our day-to-day life.

These stages of grief and therefore change have been described by Dr Elisabeth Kübler-Ross,[37] a psychiatrist of dual Swiss and American nationality, and former professor of behavioural medicine at the University of Virginia at Charlottesville and Chicago (United States).

It was she who paved the way for assistance to the dying; realising that support for the family was just as important as that for the dying. She originated some of the earliest written work on grief and contributed to the birth of the hospice movement for palliative care.

Elisabeth Kübler-Ross discovered that grief goes through five stages – denial, anger, bargaining, depression, acceptance. Further on, consultants and psychologists refined the model, and added other stages in a graph that displays energy/self-confidence through time.

Let us imagine several common business situations: the mentee discovers that their beloved leader is leaving for another country and will find themselves as an orphan, or the desired promotion has been granted to a peer who seems less competent or was perceived less deserving of merit. Or that their department will be merged with another one, or that the policy of country/function delegation has been replaced by a centralised one and their region or country will lose their prerogatives. Or that the mentee now realises that they are not able to fulfil the requirements of a project or position. Or that the mentee's life partner is fed up with the lack of activities done together due to their excessive workload and is on the verge of separation. And many situations that occur in the corporate and family contexts. The process will lead the mentee through different stages.

**Denial**: The first reaction to the announcement of a change is denial. Facing the news, confronted by the shock, its negation: 'No, it's not possible!' 'That cannot be!' Since there is occultation of the reality, the mentee's energy is still high, and life continues as if nothing had occurred. It is up to the mentor to, as gently as possible, unveil the reality and organise the support needed to the mentee to overcome the change or loss. Importantly, the mentor will only be able to act if the change/loss does not impact the mentee too much. In heavier cases, the person should be directed to a person's support professional such as a psychotherapist, or a psychiatrist if needed.

**Anger**: The first active reaction to a shock is anger, and the mentee may shout out loud sentences such as: 'It's unfair, why them?' 'Why me?' 'Why our department?' This explains the demonstrations held by workers and labour unions at the doors of a closing factory, or the constant bad mood of a person confronted by an unfair decision or a perception of injustice. Energy is high as anger generates adrenaline. A good mentor will first ask questions about the situation and do their utmost to understand the actual change/loss. They should encourage the mentee to express the anger, without violence. Just having the

37  Elisabeth Kübler-Ross (1969) *On Death and Dying*, New York: Simon & Schuster/ Touchstone; and with David Kessler (2005) *On Grief and Grieving: Finding the Meaning of Grief Through the Five Stages of Loss*, New York: Scribner/Simon & Schuster.

**Figure 9.1** The Grieving Curve and the Resistance to Change

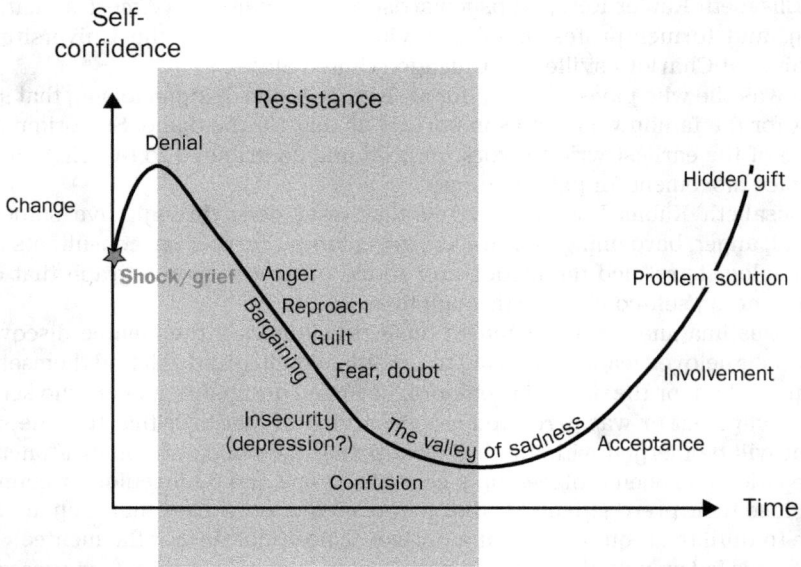

Self-confidence

Resistance

Denial

Change

Shock/grief    Anger

Bargaining

Reproach

Guilt

Fear, doubt

Hidden gift

Problem solution

Involvement

Insecurity
(depression?)

The valley of sadness

Acceptance

Confusion

Time

opportunity to dig into the emotion helps alleviate it or, even better, use this high energy to perform bold constructive actions.

**Reproach**: Further in the grieving/change process appears reproaches to the boss, to the government, to any other person who might bear responsibility for the change. 'You have no right to leave me.' 'The management did not manage properly.' 'The doctor should have warned me.' Again, when the mentee is in this stage of the change process, it means that they are progressing.

**Guilt**: 'I should have done something else.' 'I have not developed as I should.' 'I am not sufficiently competent.' Guilt creates frustration and paralysis. Past events are history. A good way out of this stage is to transform regrets into learning and commitments for the future.

**Bargaining**: 'Give me a few days.' 'I promise to finish my MBA or to accept more travel if you grant me this project/position.' This long stage is the grey area in the graph together with resistance. It encompasses several steps of the grieving/change process and is normal. We all tend to bargain with higher authority: hierarchy, government, God …

**Fear**: 'What will become of me without you, without this job, without my business?' Fear is a need for reassurance for the future. The mentor is invited to encourage the mentee to move into action based on a clear action plan and a risk assessment in an Adult-to-Adult Ego State.

**Doubts**, **insecurity** about the future, **sadness**, **confusion** are other normal steps in the change process. Here again, the mentor will help the mentee ask the right questions and accept the emotions as they come. To recognise the right emotion is already moving one step ahead.

The stages 'anger' to 'confusion' are part of the process of resistance. And it is after crossing the 'valley of sadness' that **acceptance** may come, the integration of the departure or loss, and, later in time, the discovery of a '**hidden gift**', the understanding of the lessons that can be drawn from grief.

Knowing that resistance is normal, there is no need to fight it, which will only further reinforce it. On the contrary, if we start from the axiom 'resistance and fear = unexpressed need', we can explore ways that will quickly prove fruitful to the mentee and from which action plans can develop.

Merely to explain the process of change and resistance can significantly help the mentee. It can be a relief to know that it is not they who are the problem, but a consequence of the change process. They can, above all, 'name' the experience they are facing and live their life while setting themselves at a distance from events.

I (Sylviane) systematically chase possible grief when the mentee gets emotional: anger, fear, doubt, sadness. My usual question is 'Did you lose something recently? Is it a person's presence or support, a promise of a better future, an image of yourself, or anything else?' Naming the grief is a huge step ahead and helps the mentee accept the situation is changing. Recently, the pandemic was the theatre of numerous compelling changes of habits inside corporations: loss of contact with colleagues, fear for the future, uncertainty about the business, and many others. If you analyse your reactions and the reactions of your colleagues over the last years, you may easily recognise the different steps of the change/grief process.

One type of mentee's illusion leading to a necessary grief/change of belief is to be found in the quest for many mentees to be perfect. It is especially true for female leaders who raise a family. Everything needs to be perfect, both at work and at home, and this is usually based in the belief that to be loved/recognised by their peers, they need to perform all projects with a total quality – which is impossible.

Another commonly found illusion is the fact that the company might be considered as a family by the mentee. This is a fallacy. Even though the atmosphere can be friendly, full of kindness and based on team spirit, the institution is not to be considered as a family or a group of friends. This reality is often considered as some sort of ice bucket by many mentees …

**Mentor's take-away**: We invite you to learn tracking the 'Yes, but'. Those two words are the manifestation of the mentee's inside resistance. When a 'Yes, but' is said by the mentee, immediately tackle it by asking: 'What is there inside that "Yes but"?' or 'I see that there is resistance. What does it mean?'

# 10 Selecting the mentoring process stakeholders

## Internal or external mentor?

We have already identified how mentoring can be valuable to an organisation and its participants, and reviewed major mentoring competencies. However, there are two different types of mentors – internal and external. What is the difference?

### Internal mentor[38]

This is someone from within the company or organisation. Usually, they are managers, senior experts, more experienced or senior members of the team or someone who is very good at certain things, but may be young (e.g., young experts in IT, multimedia, etc.). Internal mentors are encouraged and motivated to offer guidance and support to mentees to aid efficient learning, better performance, and develop confidence, competence and credibility.

An internal mentor is very useful and effective when someone:

- first joins a company
- is preparing for promotion
- has an internal transfer
- requires cross-function learning
- needs support to navigate the organisational cultures in which they work
- requires reorientation following a company merger or acquisition.

In many cases, internal mentors are voluntary and will not be additionally remunerated for this work, although, of course, their services will be appreciated by both the mentee and the company.

Internal mentoring develops employees in both the mentees' and mentors' roles.

---

38 Perschel Anne (2014) *Do You Need an In-House or an External Mentor?* https://www.forbes.com/sites/85broads/2014/07/21/do-you-need-an-in-house-or-an-external-mentor/?sh=2e58c74268d7

### External mentor[39]

This is an individual from outside the company or organisation. Usually, they are external experts in certain functions, who are more senior and experienced, and have received formal mentoring training.

An external mentor is particularly useful and effective when:

- there is no one at the top of the organisation with the required experience/skills to mentor the internal mentees[40]
- there is a conflict of interest. Mentors from the same organisation can never offer the truly offline space that mentees need as they are too close to the performance and promotion decisions of these individuals
- there is a willingness to find an out-of-the-box solution
- a fresh perspective is required
- there is a serious internal bottleneck/limit imposed by existing rules or regulations
- there is a desire to find new approaches to previously considered processes
- there are corporate politics requirements. Sometimes, it is hard for a senior manager to influence the mentee directly by themselves, and they need an external mentor
- an integration/activation of external resources requires a new face to energize the team.

# Who can be a mentor?[41]

A mentor is a person who has knowledge and experience to share with the mentee. Therefore, a mentor must be very knowledgeable and experienced in certain functions/industries, and be willing to share this expertise with others.[42]

There are several common characteristics in being a mentor: skill and experience in the field and industry, basic mentoring skills, emotional intelligence, desire or motivation to share wisdom and help others, enjoying cross learning

---

39    Julia Gumeniuk (2021) *Internal vs External Mentoring – what is better for your team?* https://www.femmepalette.com/blog-posts/internal-vs-external-mentoring-what-is-better-for-your-team

40    *Internal vs External Mentoring?* http://www.boardmentoring.com/InternalvsExternal.php

41    Matthew Reeves (2019) *Who Can be a Mentor?* https://www.togetherplatform.com/blog/who-can-be-a-mentor

42    Julia Martins (2021) *How to Find a Mentor in 8 Steps.* https://asana.com/resources/tips-find-mentor

between mentor and mentee, being a team player, a positive attitude, and of course, a real commitment.[43]

Very often, these people can be found around you: senior executives, older professional people, line managers, professional consultants, advisers, etc.

There is little restriction on who can be a mentor, as people of all skills and seniority levels generally have something to offer to more junior levels in their quest for personal development, career advancement, self-confidence, rapid learning and industry knowledge. This is typically called **senior-to-junior mentoring**.[44]

There is also **reverse mentoring**, where experienced young people mentor older people, for instance: a graduate IT professional mentoring a senior executive on the application of new IT technology.

# The role of the mentor[45]

The role of a mentor is simple: to provide guidance and support to a mentee to help them develop competence in professional and personal skills. During a mentor/mentee relationship, a mentor will wear different hats and take on roles that help the mentee achieve their goals.[46]

The role of a mentor is to act as the following:

- **Navigator:** Help mentees understand themselves, and ensure the mentee is doing the right things, and then doing the things right.
- **Adviser and coach:** Provide advice, guidance and feedback; share their experience; give insights into their specific industry and share expertise as appropriate; act as a sounding board for ideas and action plans.
- **Champion and cheerleader:** Offer encouragement and support to try new things; help mentees move out of their comfort zones; help mentees understand why when things do not go as planned; show support when mentees face setbacks; celebrate the big and small successes, and consistently provide words of encouragement.[47]
- **Role model:** Demonstrate their commitment to a desired goal and be willing to invest the necessary time and effort to achieve success. Mentors should not give up easily and should persevere when confronted by obstacles. Their

---

43  Alyse Kalish, *7 Qualities that Make a Good Mentor (and how to find someone who has them all)*. https://www.themuse.com/advice/how-to-find-qualities-good-mentor

44  Penny Loretto (2022) *Qualities of a Good Mentor*. https://www.thebalancecareers.com/qualities-of-a-good-mentor-1986663

45  *Mentor Roles & Responsibilities*. https://library.ucsd.edu/about/lauc-sd/5_committees/mentoring/3_mentors/1_roles.html

46  Nonprofit Leadership Center (2022) *How to be an Effective Mentor in the Workplace*. https://nlctb.org/tips/how-to-be-an-effective-mentor-in-the-workplace/

47  Julie Johnson (2017) *The Mentor and the Protégé: What, Who, and How?* https://www.astc.org/astc-dimensions/the-mentor-and-the-protege-what-who-and-how/

passion to succeed then inspires others to follow through and reach the goals they set for themselves.

- **Good listener and challenger:** Mentors must first and foremost listen and ask questions, but can also explain, advise and criticise – in a constructive way – so that mentees are challenged and are given the best possible opportunity to reflect and gain new knowledge about themselves and others.

- **Provider of resources and recommendations:** Identify resources that will help mentees with personal development and growth, such as recommending books, workshops or other learning tools; encourage mentees to expand their network and create new professional connections.

- **Facilitator of enlightenment:** Mentors use their more extensive experience to encourage mentees to see tasks and situations from new angles, to help mentees take a 'bird's-eye view' and support mentees when developing and executing action plans to achieve their goals.

- **Devil's advocate and truth-sayer:** provide tough feedback; challenge the mentee to make major decisions; push mentees to take risks when appropriate; play the opposite side and provide new angles to aid decision making; help mentees consider and weigh potential consequences of decisions and actions to avoid the pitfalls and predictable surprises that may occur.[48]

Alongside the above, the mentor also plays many other roles: storyteller, discussion partner, knowledge sharer, networker, door opener, sponsor, friend.

## The role of the mentee[49]

The mentee's role is simple: to learn and absorb as much information as they can from the mentor. A good mentee should aim to be:[50]

- **An active learner and practitioner:** The mentee is a sponge who needs to absorb the mentor's knowledge and have the ambition and desire to know what to do with this knowledge, and to practise and demonstrate what has been learned.

- **An investigator:** The mentee must maintain a flow of communication. That means asking probing and open-ended questions, following up frequently, and consistently communicating updates to their mentor.

- **Open and authentic:** The mentee should want to develop and dare to open up sufficiently to talk about things that really matter. They should be open

---

48  https://www.td.org/insights/what-exactly-is-the-mentors-role-what-is-the-mentees
49  *Mentor Roles & Responsibilities.* https://library.ucsd.edu/about/lauc-sd/5_committees/mentoring/3_mentors/1_roles.html
50  Julie Johnson (2017) *The Mentor and the Protégé: What, Who, and How?* https://www.astc.org/astc-dimensions/the-mentor-and-the-protege-what-who-and-how/

and authentic to challenges, ask unconventional questions, and propose new angles while listening to criticism, stories and good advice.

- **A self-starter:** The mentee should take the initiative to ask for help or advice and to tackle more challenging assignments. The mentee should also take the initiative to schedule meetings, provide agendas, and create action plans for their short- and long-term goals.
- **A team player:** The mentee needs the ability and willingness to work as a team player, as mentoring is a mutual learning experience for both mentor and mentee.
- **A risk-taker**: The mentee needs to understand the limitations of the mentor, i.e., they cannot be the fount of all knowledge, they will have their limitations in certain knowledge areas, working experience, etc. Also, the mentee needs to appreciate that any knowledge or experience the mentor shares can only be examples for the purpose of learning or illustration, and the conditions of the mentee's situation may be different. It is the mentee's responsibility to be a risk-taker if there is something not workable.
- **Perseverant and strong-willed:** Mentoring is a long journey. It may take a few months for the mentee to get the mentoring result they are looking for. It is not a one-day deal; therefore, the mentee should be patient, perseverant and strong-willed, even in the face of challenges.

# Mentor and mentee's responsibilities[51]

It is important for mentor and mentee to be gracious and thoughtful towards each other.

The mentor has a responsibility to maintain the right mentoring relationship by adhering to the following guidelines.[52]

- Work with the mentee on goal setting for the mentoring relationship.
- Be an active listener to the mentee, give candid feedback, sharing personal anecdotes.
- Communicate the hidden rules of the professional world; identify professional development activities.
- Take the initiative in the relationship but allow the mentee to take responsibility for their own growth, development and career planning.
- Follow through on commitments made to the mentee; meet with the mentee as agreed on a regular basis.

---

51  *Mentor Roles & Responsibilities.* https://library.ucsd.edu/about/lauc-sd/5_committees/mentoring/3_mentors/1_roles.html
52  *What are the Responsibilities Involved with Being a Mentor or a Mentee?* https://www.southampton.ac.uk/professional-development/mentoring/mentoring-responsibilities.page

- Periodically review the goals and objectives of the relationship with the mentee.
- Recognise and work through conflicts in a caring fashion, invite discussion on differences with the mentee, and arrange for a third party to assist, if necessary.
- Make only positive or neutral comments about the mentee to others. If disagreement over behaviours or values arise, share differences with the mentee and try to resolve them directly. If necessary, take steps to end the relationship and try to find another mentor for the mentee.
- Maintain a professional relationship that doesn't intrude on the mentee's personal life. Do not expect to be close friends.
- Walk the talk and do not over-promise.
- Maintain confidentiality.
- End the relationship at the agreed upon time.

Meanwhile, mentees have their own responsibilities, which include the following:

- Identify initial learning goals and measures of success for the mentoring relationship.
- Be proactive. Take an active role in their own learning and help drive the process.
- Display authentic excitement and eagerness to learn from the mentor and seek feedback.
- Appreciate the mentor's time and support. Be respectful and punctual.
- Follow through on commitments and take informed risks when trying new options and behaviours in support of their career and development goals.

# 11 Installing mentoring programmes inside organisations

## Creating mentoring programmes that work

There are many types of programmes that introduce mentoring into the workplace. Typically, these programmes require approval from the organisation's executives and are driven by the HR department.

Starting with the types of mentoring and how they work for each party, companies that adopt mentoring programmes need to determine first what is best for their end goal and the people they are invested in. Resources and time play a big part here, with different methods being suited to different situations.

Examples of mentoring programmes (which may not be mutually exclusive) include those listed here.

### Formal mentoring

Mentor and mentee are formally structurally paired, which allows for goals to be attained, and success measured with a clear, concise path. It is typically used within companies to safeguard the business's future by sharing and passing down knowledge and skills for people development. This aims to ensure the continuation of the values that define the company while invigorating the business with fresh ideas and perspectives.

### Informal mentoring

This occurs when two individuals meet professionally and establish a connection. It is usually the mentee's responsibility to ask for mentorship. This type of relationship tends to evolve naturally, as a friendship would, and advice and guidance are sought casually, especially to begin with. Informal mentors tend to be friends, family members and colleagues, but these relationships can evolve between company leaders and even 'rival' executives to facilitate broader guidance in business decisions.

## Group mentoring[53]

In group mentoring one main mentor and a group of peers help a group of mentees together. This type of mentoring allows mentees to learn from their mentor and their mentor's peers, with the mentor directing progress, pace and activities. Group mentoring is beneficial if there is a shortage of mentors, or if something needs to be delivered quickly and efficiently to impact more mentees in a shorter timeframe. It also offers the benefit of teamwork, support and inclusion, which can be especially practical for inductions and onboarding.

## Training-based mentoring

This type of mentoring occurs when mentees reach out for help with a specific skill or task. These engagements tend by nature to be shorter term.

## Traditional one-to-one mentoring

This is where one mentor and one mentee enter a mentoring relationship with the aim of guidance and support that is typically in the area of the mentor's expertise. The mentee and mentor are matched, either through a programme or on their own. The mentor can directly share knowledge and offer developmental advice that helps the mentee achieve their goals for progression.

## Distance mentoring[54]

Also called virtual mentoring, this has become more and more popular and viable in current times. It runs along the same principles as one-to-one mentoring, only without location restrictions (as the two parties are in different locations and meet virtually). Mentoring can still work just as effectively, even when offered virtually, working well in the context of the COVID-19 pandemic and the need for remote working.

## Team mentoring

This is similar to group mentoring, only involving a group of mentors who can cater for mentees with different needs and attributes. Team mentoring encourages diversity. This is common in employee resource groups or sports. It allows different viewpoints to be heard and provides a range of perspectives to take guidance from.

---

53   Julie Johnson (2017) *The Mentor and the Protégé: What, Who, and How?* Op. cit.
54   *Virtual Mentoring for the Modern Workforce.* https://www.mentorcliq.com/virtual-mentoring

## Reverse mentoring

A more junior person with specific skills or experience offers to mentor a more senior person. Both parties can learn from each other and have input. It is especially useful where companies need innovation or fresh ideas to maintain their success.

The different types of mentoring should pave a clear path for those involved in that they understand exactly why they are participating and what they are hoping to gain from the programme. Different purposes determine the specific type of mentoring required. As a company, it is important to communicate clear and realistic expectations to mentors and mentee cohorts, so that they understand the type of mentoring that has been selected for their specific purposes.

There are many examples of reasons for mentorship and these can include the following, listed here.

## Leadership development

Employees can significantly develop their leadership competence from having a mentor. Research has shown that people with mentors are five times more likely to receive a promotion than those without, and the success of such programmes means that the demand for mentors in the workplace is higher than ever before.

## Succession planning

Mentoring can speed up getting specific individuals up to competence for potential succession. Mentoring of existing talent can help individuals learn and adapt to future roles when they arise.

## Onboarding and orientation

Mentoring can help welcome new employees into the organisation, easing their transition from training and coaching into their actual job role. It is an excellent opportunity to invite experienced employees into the world of mentoring. Providing a structured onboarding programme can give employees a secure welcome into the business with a clear vision of their future there. This is a great first step for employers to present themselves as a company that takes its people and their futures seriously.

## Transition mentoring

This is designed to help employees adapt to new processes and procedures in a selected timeframe, either in group or team mentoring. Transition mentoring is implemented widely to assist employees with sudden change, to provide support and a forum to talk about concerns, as well as regular check-ins to ensure the continuation of workflow. It also helps employees get comfortable with their new setting. Transition mentoring is also a great way to encourage collaboration between team members. A good example of this is when the COVID-19 epidemic forced many businesses to close their doors in early 2020 and order employees to work from home. These unforeseen changes were a shock to many and required a period of transition for everyone.

## Upskilling

Unlike succession planning, upskilling involves retaining existing employees in roles that already exist. Using mentoring in upskilling helps to level the playing field and ensure that current employees have an equal chance to progress in their role. Group mentoring works well in upskilling, especially when it involves coaching in the same areas, as it is more efficient to deliver training to multiple people. Reverse mentoring can be highly successful in the sharing of knowledge between senior and junior employees.

## Supporting diversity and inclusion

Mentoring for diversity and inclusivity provides support for all recognised talent from any gender or cultural background, which promotes fairness in opportunities within the organisation. It can be used to promote mentees, can sometimes focus on promoting women, and help the organisation gain a new perspective and understanding of the hurdles under-represented people face daily.

### Difficulties of introducing mentoring to Chinese clients

In a long history of being a traditional mentoring country, one might think it is easy to talk about mentoring, and mentoring will be very popular. However, this is not always true. People are used to traditional mentoring, such as experience sharing, teaching by imitation, role-modelling, etc, which have quite a few limitations. That's why we need new scientific ways of mentoring. In November 2019, I (Fisher) introduced the EMCC into China, together with its qualification system and corporate mentoring technologies. At MentoringCo, it took almost three years to recruit 50 students to the EMCC accredited EQA programme called 'Associate Certified Mentor', and to obtain our first two corporate clients. We had talked to hundreds of people and explained to them the value of modern mentoring, the differences between mentoring and coaching, held hundreds of webinars to educate the market. Sometimes, I got exhausted and even I was thinking of giving up with so many failure trials. For corporate mentoring, we travelled to many cities inside China, visited many clients, did a lot of demos. Fortunately, we were accepted by the market to have our first corporate mentoring clients (which was not easy at all). Things are getting better now, and we are accepted by the market because of our perseverance and high quality of service. I should say, all my business partners in MentoringCo and my colleague Sunshine were my strong backbones when I was in high stress. I cannot achieve anything without their support. I also want to express my sincere gratitude to them in writing here.

# Key roles in mentoring programmes

Usually, there are twelve roles in a corporate mentoring programme: of which six are internal, five are external and one, the steering committee, covers both.

**Figure 11.1** Key roles in mentoring programmes

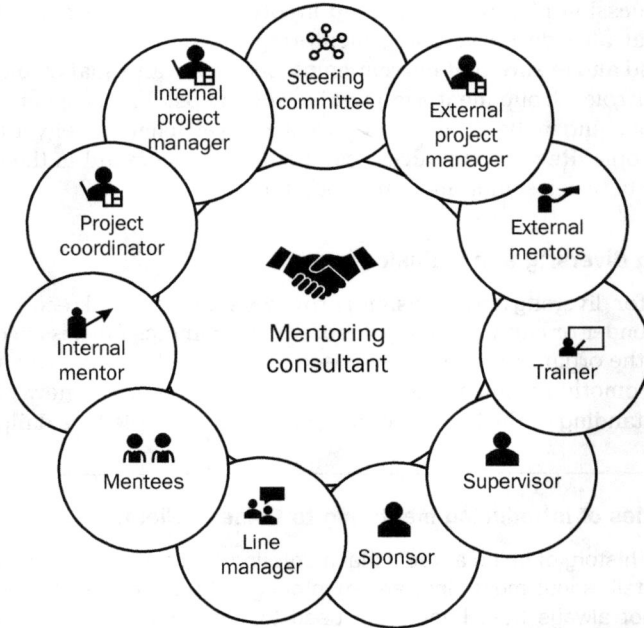

**(a) 12 roles in a corporate mentoring programme**

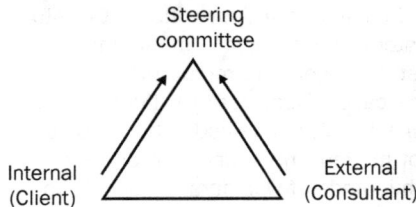

**(b) Two parties form the steering committee**

**Steering committee:** This consists of key internal and external leaders who approve the goals and objectives of the programme, agree key decisions, undertake a project review for the mentoring programme and provide all necessary support. It is the highest decision-making tier of the mentoring project (see Chapter 19 on the key role of the Programme Manager).

## Internal roles

**Internal project/programme manager:** In-house project manager responsible for managing and monitoring the mentoring programme with the external project manager.

**Project coordinator:** The person inside the company who coordinates the various channels of communication between internals and externals.

**Internal mentor:** Experienced professional inside the company ready to share their knowledge and skills.

**Mentee:** Professional who is supported by mentors to develop their skills and abilities.

**Line manager:** Offers support to mentees and is committed to the mentoring programme in line with company strategy and goals. The line manager observes the mentees' performance improvements and behaviour changes.

**Sponsor:** Sponsors can include the CEO, HR teams, senior managers, learning and development teams and others in the organisation who take the initiative to set up a mentoring programme, advocate for the programme, and provide all resources needed, whether inside or outside the organisation, to give more credibility to the process.

## External roles

**External project manager:** The person from a consulting firm who is in charge of designing, implementing and monitoring the mentoring programme.

**Mentoring trainer:** Someone who delivers mentoring-related skills training to stakeholders in the mentoring programme.

**External mentor:** Someone from outside the organisation who is invited to provide mentoring support to the client's programme.

**Supervisor:** Mentoring expert who supports mentors (and sometimes mentees) to help them reflect on their practice and solve any problems that might arise.

**Mentoring consultant:** Professional from a consulting firm who supports the client's mentoring programme.

# Transferring implicit/tacit knowledge

Knowledge transfer is a key element in many corporate mentoring programmes. There are three types of knowledge that exist in an organisation: explicit, implicit and tacit,[55] which are largely distinguished by the codification of the information. These can be illustrated using an iceberg metaphor (see Figure 11.2).

---

55   Michael Polanyi (2021) *Personal Knowledge Towards a Post-Critical Philosophy.* Shanghai People's Publishing House.

**Figure 11.2** Iceberg metaphor for three types of knowledge

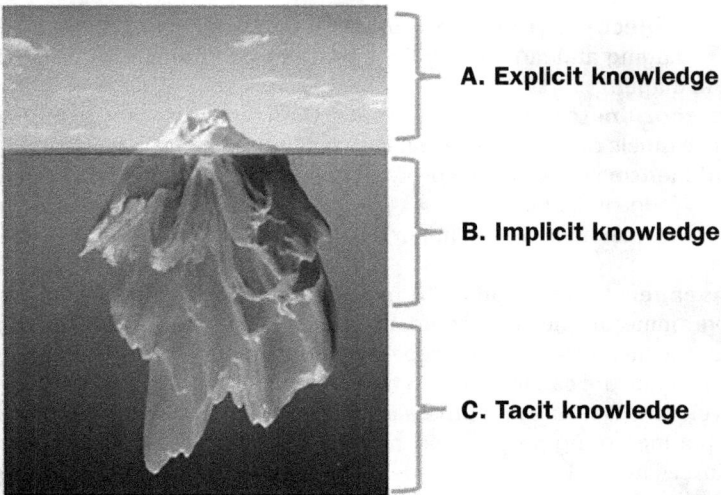

A. Explicit knowledge

B. Implicit knowledge

C. Tacit knowledge

## Explicit knowledge

This is the tip of the iceberg. It can be written down and codified in forms that can be seen, read and transferred, such as manuals, databases, white papers, reports, case studies, training documents, standard operation procedures (SOPs), guides, etc.

Sometimes the terms 'implicit knowledge' and 'tacit knowledge' are used interchangeably, but this is not entirely accurate.

## Implicit knowledge

This is made up of a team's less obvious experience and skills. In the simplest of terms, implicit knowledge is explicit knowledge that hasn't yet been documented. For example, implicit knowledge can be converted into explicit knowledge by simply recording the knowledge verbatim. Implicit knowledge is concerned with the 'how'. It tends to exist within processes and can be referred to as 'know-how'. For instance, it is the way one staff member might write better emails than others, even though they all received the same training.

## Tacit knowledge

Karl Polanyi[56] stated that 'we can know more than we can tell' (Polanyi, 1966). Tacit knowledge is a type of knowledge that is nearly impossible to document

---

56   https://en.wikipedia.org/wiki/Karl_Polanyi and Karl Polanyi (1966) *The Tacit Dimension.* London: Routledge & Kogan Paul.

or codify. It is typically acquired through experience, and it is all about instinct, gut reactions and intuitive understanding.[57] As a consequence, it is difficult to transfer this information to other individuals without professional support. Examples of tacit knowledge can include language, facial recognition or leadership skills, or even how to ride a bike; that is, things that can only be learned through personal experimentation (learn by doing). Another example would be learning a sport. An experienced player can tell you how to do something, the do's and don'ts, and even signpost books to support learning. But real learning happens only when the person is on the ground participating in the sport itself. The excellent leader is one who is able to use tacit knowledge strategically when they gain an overview through the complexity that often characterises today's business; the intuitive leader is one who simply knows what is about to happen.

### Importance of tacit knowledge extraction

Here are some benefits of tacit knowledge extraction:[58]

- **It allows people to learn from others' experiences.** The beauty of tacit knowledge sharing is that it addresses knowledge gaps and lets the mentee learn from others' experiences. When they open themselves up to others' points of view, they gain the knowledge to improve the business and its practices.
- **It helps people communicate more effectively.** The thing about tacit knowledge is that it is difficult to explain how to learn it; the mentee simply absorbs it by gaining experience within the organisation. However, relying on an osmosis-like knowledge transfer does not guarantee it will happen. Team members may not know what they do not know and continue using their usual approach instead of absorbing the better way to do things.
- **It teaches people to value different perspectives.** Human capital is a company's most important asset and leveraging each employee's experience and perspective is one of the best things a company can do. Any company can teach technical skills, but each person's tacit knowledge and experience are more valuable.
- **It differentiates the company from competitors.** Incorporating tacit knowledge gives the company a competitive advantage. Not only does it contribute to better decision making, but it can also serve its internal and external stakeholders better. Moreover, developing the best practices and demonstrating the optimal approach to tasks allows the organisation to operate at a higher level, contributing to increased productivity.

---

57  Michael Polanyi (2021) *Personal Knowledge Towards a Post-Critical Philosophy.* Shanghai People's Publishing House.
58  David Oragui (2021) *Tacit Knowledge: Definition, Examples, and Importance.* https://helpjuice.com/blog/tacit-knowledge

- **Today, tacit knowledge is a business's most valuable untapped resource.** When employees leave, they take their tacit knowledge with them, costing companies up to 213 per cent of an experienced employee's salary to find a replacement.[59]
- **It is vital to value the employees' tacit knowledge because it is irreplaceable.** Competitors can steal a company's tools and strategies, but they cannot replicate the employees' contributions and experiences.

# Ways to transfer tacit knowledge

Despite its importance, many companies do not have any systematic approach to collecting and incorporating tacit knowledge. At best, the loss of tacit knowledge is mitigated by informal procedures.

Tacit knowledge cannot be passed through written or oral instructions. Instead, it is transmitted by doing. Here are a few strategies to be considered to facilitate the transfer:

### Internal reports

For most companies, the standard best practice for recording tacit knowledge is via internal reports and any other tribal exchanges such as conversations, forum postings, chats, emails, wikis, software repository issues. However, if not enforced, this procedure is ineffective and difficult to replicate.

### Corporate mentoring programmes

Most companies prefer to organise a talent development programme via mentoring, where a new apprentice follows a veteran engineer, technician or more senior person for a few months on the job. Tacit knowledge is usually passed on during such on-site training.

### Collaboration and social networks

Online collaboration provides a community for the transfer of tacit knowledge through a process of 'socially constructed learning', which offers the opportunity to learn through shared conversations, discourses among participants and exposure to new ideas. Also, online social networks seem to be a more efficient way to transfer tacit knowledge than individual face-to-face interactions. Each person becomes a node in a network of spreading knowledge, increasing their capacity to transmit to others.

---

59  Amanda Dundas. *Replacing an Employee Cost 213% More Than Previous Employee's Salary.* https://orgvitality.com/business-costs-to-replacing-employees/

## Storytelling

This has proved itself a worthy tool in transmitting tacit knowledge. It transforms information into data and knowledge as the contents, along with gestures, expressions and tonal cues during informal meets, help the learner to understand things in a good way.

## Guided experience

The transferring of tacit knowledge through guided experience is possible by observing, practising, partnering, taking responsibility for the action and problem solving with the mentor.

## Showing the work

This is a popular strategy and includes making the work that was required to transfer the tacit knowledge visible. The strategy involves digging deeper into the mentor's expertise and demonstrating the full procedure on a live feed. Working things out verbally, narrating the steps as the mentor proceeds, and writing down what they are doing, all underpin tacit knowledge transmission.

## Tracking lessons learned

Lessons learned are a type of relevant and realistic case study. Recording and sharing these helps others benefit from the experience and is an effective way to spread tacit knowledge gained over the years.

## Reinvention

It is not always possible to transfer tacit knowledge, but what a person can do is reinvent it. This can be a slow method and involve trial and error but remember slow and steady wins the race. Reinvention makes what once was impossible, possible.

## Working in teams

Transfer tacit knowledge by working together. When people work together, especially junior and senior people, the tacit knowledge embedded within the work is transferred. This results in a retention rate of the tacit knowledge, demonstrated when the senior person leaves the organisation, but the work can still be performed satisfactorily by those who remain.

## Promote historical understanding

Tacit knowledge is often based on the history of the organisation. For example, if a company organised an event many times in the past, but the people who organised the event have moved on, the experiences have most likely left a paper trail, correspondence, procedures and participants who can provide direction as to the historical methods.

### Utilise new technologies

Social media, mobile application, big data and AI technology bring new capabilities in tacit knowledge extraction and transmission.

# Conditions for effective mentoring programmes

There are ten golden rules to follow to ensure an effective corporate mentoring programme.[60,61,62]

### Rule #1: Know the main purpose of the mentoring programme

Every mentoring programme should have a clearly defined purpose, both for the organisation and for the participants involved. Without a clear direction, it is impossible to see if the wind is favourable. A good way to begin is by evaluating skills gaps in the business. Does the business need to achieve higher sales, improve its customer service delivery, or perhaps transfer key knowledge across departments and teams? By having a clear definition of success, you will be in a better position to identify who should participate in the programme, who already possesses key skills or knowledge that would benefit others, and what individual needs and ambitions would align with the goals of mentoring.

### Rule #2: Create the methodology and the 'Master Plan'

Once the purpose is identified, the next step is to create an employee mentoring programme template. This is a tool that sets out the logistics of a mentoring programme in the workplace. It can take the form of a simple table with details about the programme, such as:

- How long will the programme run for?
- Who will be responsible for monitoring the mentor mentee relationship?
- How often will mentees and mentors meet?

60   Julia Wilkinson (2019) *Five Golden Rules for effective mentoring.* https://www.trainingzone. co.uk/develop/talent/five-golden-rules-for-effective-mentoring

61   *Best Practices for Running a Mentorship Program.* https://www.togetherplatform.com/ resources/best-practices-for-running-a-mentorship-program

62   CV Check (2019) *How to Set up an Internal Mentoring Program for Your Business.* https://checkpoint.cvcheck.com/how-to-set-up-an-internal-mentoring-program-that-will-benefit-your-business/

- How often will feedback be collected from participants?
- What are the preferred channels of communication between mentors and mentees?
- What should the mentoring relationship focus on (i.e., specific projects, day-to-day performance, or a defined plan for progressing into a more senior role)?
- How will the mentoring relationship be structured?

When it comes to structuring mentoring relationships, mentors can be paired with an individual or a group of mentees. Team or group mentoring often works better in start-up cultures, where most mentees are at a similar life and career stage. On the other hand, one-to-one mentoring is the most common approach as a corporate mentoring programme example. The most widely known type of mentoring is classic mentoring, where the mentor is more senior than the person they are mentoring. But this is not the only option. Reverse mentoring is when the mentor is junior to the mentee. This is more common when a new manager or leader doesn't have as much experience in a specific industry, company or technical skill as a more junior (but often less qualified) long-standing employee.

### Rule #3: Choose the right mentors

Problems will arise if the wrong people are chosen or matched or if a mentor lacks sufficient time to devote to their mentees. An effective mentor is someone who can challenge and support a mentee and not judge them. If they are from a different department or function, they can be more objective.

Ideally, they will be adept at the '7 Cs' of mentoring: they should be able to Coach the mentee; be a Confidant; provide Career advice; act as a Conduit to others to increase the mentee's visibility; serve as a Counsellor; be a Critical friend and provide the mentee with Choice.[63]

### Rule #4: Spread the good news

Unlike traditional training, mentoring programmes in the workplace are not easy to enforce through mandatory participation. People need to be able to choose to be involved if the programme is going to be a success. But many people are hesitant about engaging in a mentorship relationship. Mentees do not feel that mentoring is something that they need, or they fear that meetings with their mentor might be awkward. Mentors worry that the experience might not be worth their time. So, it is critical that all employees are aware of the benefits of being both a mentor and a mentee, and that they understand how it will work. The more they understand about the expectations of the mentoring programme, the less likely they are to hear criticism in their first meeting.

---

63   Julia Wilkinson (2019) *Five golden rules for effective mentoring.* Op. cit.

## Rule #5: Set mentors up for success

It is up to the organisation to set their mentors up for success because successful mentors mean successful mentees, and more positive outcomes for the business. Employers should provide core training for both mentors and mentees. This helps to set the right expectations for both parties and address any concerns on either side. Potential mentors may need coaching to help them develop or sharpen the skills and attributes they need to succeed.

## Rule #6: Make careful matches

Criteria such as personality, motivation, similar interests and hobbies, complementary experience and skills, chemistry, values and recommendations from line managers, etc. can help to pair people. Certain mentees may want specific support, or they may have an interest in a particular department. Mentees can choose their own mentors (and vice versa) or be placed by the organisation. Either way, making as much information as possible available about the other participant is key to achieving the right match. So, it can be helpful to ask mentors and mentees to complete an information sheet covering well-defined criteria. Random matching can be 'hit and miss', and the organisation will be stuck doing damage control. The best approach is to match people as well as you can – then let them have an informal meeting, such as over lunch, to see if they are comfortable with each other and let them agree how they will work together. However, it is important to offer each party a 'way out'. Therefore, if the relationship is not working, for whatever reason, either side can end it without recrimination. Forcing people to remain in mentoring relationships where there is no chemistry will be utterly unproductive.

## Rule #7: Make it appealing

Despite the time and effort involved, effective mentoring can be highly rewarding for mentors as well as beneficial for mentees. For some, it can provide a welcome new challenge. The sense of satisfaction from helping others to develop – and sharing in their successes – can be a powerful motivator, particularly if mentors are positioned as esteemed individuals who are passing on knowledge within the organisation. Also, asking pertinent questions of others encourages them to ask similar questions of themselves. The mentor must be willing to commit the time needed to build and maintain a productive relationship. Many mentors say their own practice improves through mentoring and that they benefit from the fresh perspectives of their mentees and the enthusiasm they encounter.

## Rule #8: Make it voluntary

In some organisations, all managers at a certain level are expected to become mentors. But if the role is forced upon people, they might do it reluctantly.

This can be disastrous, as mentees can think their mentor does not care about them. The best approach is to ask managers to volunteer to become a mentor. Those who come forward will often have many of the qualities required for success.

### Rule #9: Check your progress

Even if the programme management team follows all of the tips listed so far, mentoring programmes in the workplace are rarely perfect the first time around. This is why it is important to gather feedback from participants on their experience, the perceived benefits, and any recommendations they might have for future improvements. By using the knowledge acquired from every programme, the management will be able to continuously improve the effectiveness of their mentoring schemes.

### Rule #10: Develop and retain the best talent

Finding the best talent is great but keeping it can be a lot harder to do. Employees today are hungry for new challenges, stimulating work, and ongoing self-growth and development. Follow the simple tips above to leverage successful mentoring programmes in the workplace as a tool for employee retention.[64]

## Calculating the costs and the ROI

Calculating the cost and the return on investment (ROI) of a mentoring programme is possible. In many cases, you may need to combine the mentoring results of both KPIs (key performance indicators) and KBIs (key behaviour indicators) to determine the ROI of the programme. Therefore, the ROI calculation shall be heavily dependent on the specific objective of the mentoring programme.

$$ROI = \frac{\text{Incremental net profits generated from the mentoring programme}}{\text{Cost incurred for the mentoring programme}} * 100\%$$

Incremental net profits generated from the mentoring programme = incremental revenue earned, cost associated with that revenue + other costs saved

Cost incurred for the mentoring programme = incremental costs paid out for the mentoring programme

64   Nikos Andriotis (2018) *How to Successfully Implement Your Mentorship Program in the Workplace.* https://www.efrontlearning.com/blog/2018/08/how-implement-mentoring-program-in-the-workplace.html

Usually, internal costs will not be reflected in this calculation, i.e., mentor and mentee's time, line manager's time, rental for office meeting room, etc. as these costs are usually fixed not variable, which means even if there is no mentoring programme, these costs are still there.

Since the impact of the mentoring programme will usually last a long time within the company, the ROI calculation should include all economic returns of this programme in the foreseeable future; therefore, net present value (NPV) should be used for the calculation. The discounted factor can be the market interest rate of your country. For example, if the mentoring programme has improved a worker's productivity by 50 per cent, and you estimate this worker will serve the company for another 5 years, then you may need to discount the incremental value brought to the business in the coming 5 years to calculate the right ROI.

The basic formula for calculating the return on any investment is (Proceeds – Cost) / Cost. For example, €100 in proceeds from a €75 investment drives ROI of (100 – 75) / 75, which equals 33 per cent.

Sometimes, the cost of the programme is relatively easy to figure out. If you use an external provider, the cost will be whatever you pay that provider.

The harder part is determining the proceeds. The benefits of workplace mentoring are very real, but tough to quantify. The following are a couple of approaches.

**Taking KPI as an example,** retention

A common rule of thumb is that the cost of replacing an employee is 150 per cent of that person's salary. Enterprise mentoring programmes usually have a positive effect on employee retention, so it is possible to estimate how many employees will be retained, and count that as the proceeds. If the company is losing 100 employees a year before the mentoring programme, for example, and now is only losing 75, then the proceeds would be 25 people's salary, multiplied by 150 per cent.

**Taking KBI as an example,** such as career development, succession planning, diversity and inclusion or leadership development

However, when the **objective for** introducing a mentoring programme is to improve **KBIs** (key behaviour indicators), such as the ones related to career development, succession planning, diversity and inclusion or leadership development, you need to compare surveys from the beginning of the programme, at the end of each mentoring relationship and have a final survey at the end of the monitoring period, in order to effectively demonstrate results and measure the improvements over that period, then calculate the ROI.

For example, there are simple survey questions that can be used to track and compare results of a mentoring programme designed to support career development.

To determine the mentoring programme ROI, a couple of questions must be designed at different stages to see the progress, for instance: (1) before starting a mentoring relationship; (2) upon completing a mentoring relationship and (3) one year after completing a mentoring relationship.

Once the feedback from these questions is obtained, the next step is to calculate the percentage of 'Yes' responses to each question to determine the impact of the mentoring initiative. For example, if 20 per cent of respondents said 'Yes' to the 'before starting a mentoring relationship' question, and 80 per cent of respondents said 'Yes' to the 'one year after completing a mentoring relationship' question, then the programme helped 60 per cent of participants in their career development.

Those 60 per cent of participants who feel that their career has progressed in the right direction are also likely more satisfied in their career. It's a logical conclusion, then, that this was as a result of the mentoring programme, meaning those participants are also more likely to stay with the organisation long term and tell others about the benefits of working for the organisation.

With these results, it is possible to calculate a more concrete ROI because happy employees are less likely to look for work at other companies, meaning higher retention and lower recruitment costs. In any case, it is important to make sure the data is from the clients or verified by the clients.

# 12 Training and communication: keys to successful mentoring programmes

## Training for whom, and with what objectives?

To ensure the success of a mentoring programme, it is vital that people have the relevant training prior to participation.

In general, three main groups require training: mentors, mentees and project managers.

### Mentors[65,66]

The basic learning objectives for mentors are as follows:

- understand the purpose of the programme – this is the key topic of mentor training
- develop specific competencies for mentoring
- understand mentoring procedures
- be aware of the code of ethics as a mentor
- define mentor roles and responsibilities
- clarify mentor's limits and boundaries
- build and maintain motivation in the relationship
- knowledge extraction: transfer knowledge, know-how and social skills
- share experience
- use self-assessment tools to review mentee's progress
- undertake training on special topics related to the mentoring programme where necessary
- develop tips, tricks and ideas for the specific mentoring programme.

65    Smith, G.P. (2007) *Mentor Training*. https://ctl.morainevalley.edu/wp-content/uploads/2011/05/MentorTrainingOverview.pdf
66    *Topics to Include in Your Mentor Training.* https://www.get.mentoringcomplete.com/blog/topics-to-include-in-your-mentor-training

## Mentees[67,68]

It is important to train the mentee on how to get the most from the mentoring programme in a healthy way. Basic learning objectives for mentees are as follows:

- understand the benefits of mentoring
- understand the purpose of the programme – this is the key topic of mentor training
- develop reasonable expectations for the mentoring relationship
- understand mentee roles and responsibilities
- understand mentoring procedures
- adopt a proactive attitude
- understand the limits of confidentiality and the boundaries of the mentoring relationship
- know how to obtain assistance if they have questions or concerns
- develop listening skills
- commit to self-development
- define goal setting and an action plan
- give and accept feedback
- develop autonomy
- build effective personal and professional relationships.

## Project manager

The project manager provides training on how to manage the mentoring programme.

The role of the mentoring programme coordinator is to manage the entire mentoring scheme, including the development of support mechanisms, to act as the main point of contact for all stakeholders within and associated with the scheme, to be the link between the programme and top management and to troubleshoot problems.

Basic learning objectives for project managers are as follows:

- understand the purpose of the programme – this is the key topic of mentor training
- understand the project manager's roles and responsibilities
- possess competent coordination skills
- understand the criteria for selecting mentors and mentees

---

67    Judy Strother Taylor (2003) *Training New Mentees: A Manual for Preparing Youth in Mentoring Programs Guide and Handout.* https://nationalmentoringresourcecenter.org/resource/training-new-mentees-a-manual-for-preparing-youth-in-mentoring-programs/
68    Division of Human Resource Management (HRM) *Mentee Training.* https://new.nsf.gov/science-matters/nsf-101-postdoctoral-mentoring-plan

- possess good time management skills
- possess conflict resolution skills
- demonstrate sensitivity to organisation politics
- administer overall mentoring
- select and match mentor and mentee, and perform a rematch if required
- know how to arrange effective meetings
- know how to use a variety of evaluation forms for the mentoring programme
- know how to manage up and manage down inside the company.

## Communicating what, to whom and how?

Positive and effective communication is critical in a mentoring programme. Communication routes should be designed at the beginning of the mentoring programme to facilitate open communication to the steering committee, mentors, mentees, line managers and other stakeholders. Communication should include:

- **Programme expectations:** Different stakeholders need to know the purpose of the programme, the rules and policies, frequency of attendance, commitment, etc.
- **Programme contacts and their roles:** Stakeholders need clear roles, responsibilities and details of who to contact for different needs.
- **Programme goals:** Stakeholders need to know the programme's goals or expected outcomes.
- **Programme exceptions and solutions:** No matter how good the planning, exceptions do occur. Any exceptions, together with agreed solutions, should be communicated to stakeholders as required.

Once a solid communication plan is laid, the next step is to think about *how* to communicate with stakeholders. There are many methods to consider, for example: official letter or newsletter, emails, group meetings, social media, blogs, one-on-one conversations, programme website. You should also think about the frequency of communication, e.g., daily, weekly, biweekly, monthly, or as needed?

In addition, it is important to determine what information to include in the communication plans, for example:

- programme updates
- upcoming events
- programme announcements
- requests for information
- requests for feedback on the programme

- accomplishments or successes
- encouragement
- resources, information or education that might be useful for the programme
- check in on the mentor/mentee relationship or match
- concerns about behaviour or attendance
- appreciation
- opportunities for the mentor and mentee's further engagement
- pictures or videos from events.

**Mentor's take-away**: Think about the different types of information you need to communicate and how it makes the most sense to communicate it. Be ready to create a communication plan in your mentoring programme; it will pay off.

# Part 2

## Towards another dimension to mentoring with a coaching attitude – the higher purpose

# 13 Mentor's journey to the origins

*Dionysia Lagiou, Mentor, EMCC Practitioner, Coach ACC*

## Introduction

Both psychology and common experience consider mentoring a complex process, pivotal for human development.[69] Mentor and mentee *come together for the love of what they do*,[70] based on compatibility and social convention, in a relationship that encompasses guidance, knowledge sharing, socialisation into a profession, sponsoring, counsel and moral support.

It is nurtured by unconditional benevolence (*eumeneia*), empathy, congruence, competences that are essential for humanistic learning,[71] all of them being grounded in the mentor's own experience.

Mentors use their experience and influence to assist their mentees with the development of their talent and the attainment of their goals, so that they *'realise the Dream'*.[72] For Carl Rogers, whose theory of positive psychology has greatly influenced modern mentoring and coaching:

> The touchstone of validity is my own experience. No other person's ideas, and none of my own ideas, are as authoritative as my experience. It is to experience that I must return again and again, to discover a closer approximation to truth as it is in the process of becoming me.[73]

69    Eby, L.T, T. D. Allen, S. C. Evans, T. Ng, and D. L. Dubois. (2008) Does mentoring matter? A multidisciplinary meta-analysis comparing mentored and non-mentored individuals. *Journal of Vocational Behavior* 72(2), 254–67.

70    Ward E.G., Thomas E.E., and Disch, W.B. (2012). Protégé Growth Themes Emergent in a Holistic, Undergraduate Peer-Mentoring Experience. *Mentoring & Tutoring: Partnership in Learning*, Vol. 20, No. 3, 409–25.

71    Rogers C., (1969) *Freedom to Learn: A View of What Education Might Become*. (1st edn) Columbus, Ohio: Charles Merrill.

72    Levinson D.J., Darrow, C.N. & Klein B.E., Levinson, M.H. and McKee B. (1978) *The Seasons of a Man's Life*. New York: Knopf.

73    Rogers, C.R. (1961) *On Becoming a Person*, Chapter II, *How Can I be of Help?* p.33. London: Constable.

The notion of experience inherent in mentoring being primarily thought as individual may also be perceived as an intergenerational and context-bound transmission of collective experiential intelligence. This could partly explain the interest in the historical sense of a practice *'as old as the hills'* as mentoring is.[74] It matters to the mentoring profession to elicit its origins and establish its parenthood to the social cultures that shaped the *processes and transactions involved with the construction of* [its] *meaning.*[75]

What is a good approach in examining mentoring's history? In his essay, 'The Use and Abuse of History in Life' (1873),[76] Friedrich Nietzsche discusses the subjective lenses through which we see, explore and lend meaning to events and characters of the past. Nietzsche favours the way the ancient Greeks balance their consciousness of yesterday with their contemporary social, cultural and political sensibilities. His idea is that *'the unhistorical and the historical are equally necessary to the health of an individual, a community, and a system of culture'*. The emphasis he puts on history as a dynamic culture rather than the subject of detached scholarship is thought to pertain to this chapter.

## A poetic origin in Greek mythology – Homer's *Odyssey*

Homer's *Odyssey*, the epic poem from Ancient Greece, is thought to be the original source of the concept of mentoring. Odysseus is the king of Ithaca, a small insular city-state in the Ionian Sea in Ancient Greece. He joins the Greek Cities' alliance against Troy, leaving at home his wife Penelope and infant son Telemachus. He entrusts guardianship of his son and his royal household to an elder statesman of Ithaca and friend, Mentor, and to an honoured guest, Mentes, no doubt anticipating a swift return home. The war however lasts for 10 long years and then for 10 more years Odysseus is persecuted across the Mediterranean by Poseidon, the god of the seas, who seeks revenge for the killing of his giant one-eyed son Polyphemus by Odysseus. The whole journey is a quest of identity together with that of the recognition, the startling discovery produced by a change from ignorance to knowledge ('anagnorisis' in Aristotle's *Poetics*).[77] During Odysseus' absence, young local nobles, the suitors, had long occupied his palace, demanding that Penelope choose one of them in re-marriage, in the hope of usurping control of Ithaca and denying Telemachus his birthright.

In the *Odyssey*, we read that Mentor does not fulfill the royal assignment, but heroic Odysseus is far too important for the country of the Dodecatheon for his kingdom to be left in peril. Zeus charges his daughter, the goddess of wisdom, Athena to intervene and guide Telemachus into manhood and courage

74  Clutterbuck, D. (1992) *Everyone Needs a Mentor*, London: Institute of Personnel Management.
75  Bruner, J. (1990) *Acts of Meaning*. Cambridge, MA: Harvard University Press.
76  Nietzsche, F. (2019) *The Use and Abuse of History in Life* (1873). New York: Dover Publications.
77  Cassin, B. (2013) *La Nostalgie – Quand donc est-on chez soi ?* Paris: Éditions Autrement.

to defend his father's authority and his own rights to the royal throne. Athena, the divinity who protects Odysseus all these 20 years against her eternal rival Poseidon, intercedes to ensure the safe return of Odysseus.

Athena appears to Telemachus, by then aged 21, first in the guise of Mentes, to test his potential for development by encouraging him to rid the court of the suitors. The young man proves equal to the task. Later, appearing as Mentor, she sets the young man some challenges to develop his latent talents and forge his royal identity. The main challenge for Telemachus is to lead a voyage to search for news of his father, about whom only Athena knows that he is alive and well. She intervenes on the young man's behalf on several occasions. Once, she puts him into a deep sleep and takes his form in order to persuade some seamen to join the voyage in Odysseus' discovery. When Mentor-Athena feels that she has done enough, she leaves Telemachus in the hands of Nestōr, the wise king of Pylos, and his son, to help Telemachus develop further his leadership potential. At the end of the poem, Telemachus has developed all the abilities necessary to succeed to the throne as king. He becomes a vital aide to exterminate the suitors on their return. They restore the regal order and Athena's aim to earn him repute among men is achieved.

Modern mentoring literature offers different interpretations of the myth, both positive and critical. For many scholars there is much to be learned about mentoring from this myth, as an intentional, nurturing, insightful, supportive, and protective process.[78,79] Others[80] highlight the cross-gender element of the poem as a positive aspect. Others draw on the idea that an individual may have several challenging and supportive mentors,[81] a sort of developmental network of relationships, which are reminiscent of the multiple relationships enjoyed by Telemachus.

A criticism of these interpretations is that they create a philosophical narrative of mentoring that suits the context of today, which resembles very little, if at all, the male-dominated and violent societies of the time of Homer and Ancient Greece.[82] Others argue that an excessive emphasis on these characteristics of the myth could disorient people into styles of mentoring behaviour based on gender stereotypes. For them, such an interpretation misses the opportunity to see in the myth of Mentor Athena the essence of effective mentoring, which is the facility to move along dimensions, in any direction, in response to the needs of the learner at a given propitious time *(kairos)*. 'The beauty of this model is its combination of simplicity and inclusiveness.'[83]

78    Anderson, E.M. and Shannon, A.L. (1988) Toward a Conceptualization of Mentoring. *Journal of Teacher Education*, 39: 38–42.

79    Dova S, (2020): *"Kind like a Father": On Mentors and Kings in the Odyssey.* CHS (The Center for Hellenic Studies) – Online Publications, Harvard.

80    Lean, E. (1983) Cross-gender mentoring: downright upright and good for productivity, *Training and Development Journal*, 37(5).

81    Garvey, B. (2017) 'Philosophical Origins of Mentoring: The Critical Narrative Analysis', in D. Clutterbuck, D., McClelland A., Kochan F., Lunsford L. and Smith B. (eds), *The SAGE Handbook of Mentoring*. London: SAGE.

82    Colley, H. (2003) *Mentoring for Social Inclusion*. London & New York: Routledge Falmer.

83    Clutterbuck, D. (1992) *Everyone Needs a Mentor*, London: Institute of Personnel Management.

# Acting reflection and living consciousness – Socrates

The existence of Socrates is indisputable. Each historical era, however, reinvents him with its own criteria, being unable to escape from anachronism. Consequently, it is our own origin that we think and narrate through him. We know the key facts of his biography, but it is his ideal figure drawn by Plato in *Dialogues*, in *Banquet* and above all in *Apology*, that has played a founding role in the birth of philosophy. Plato's aim is not to be a chronicler, but to safeguard his mentor's legacy by transposing the character with fidelity. For this reason, his testimony can be considered as the one that best integrates what we know about the philosopher who speaks, discusses but does not teach, nor does he write anything, and who refuses to be considered as a master (Hadot, 1998).[84]

Socrates was born in Athens around 470 BCE to a midwife, Phaenarete, and a sculptor, Sophroniscus, from whom he learns the technique of chiselling. He likes to borrow metaphors from the skills of the trades – weavers, carpenters, shoemakers – which reminds us that *'sophia'* in Ancient Greek means not only wisdom, but also excellence in manual skills. In one of the *Dialogues*, Socrates recounts that he has the same trade as his mother. She is a midwife who assists women to give birth; he is a midwife who assists the birth of the spirit. He himself engenders nothing, since he knows nothing, and he only helps others to engender themselves. With his maieutic method, he completely reverses the relationship between master and disciple and only examines ideas, beliefs and perceptions, to find out through his questions whether they are coherent (which they usually are not).

During the whole discussion, the interlocutor has learned nothing, and he does not even know anything at all anymore. He has however experienced what the mental activity is, or better still, he has been Socrates himself, i.e., questioning and re-questioning, stepping back from oneself, and finally growing aware and conscious. The crucial point in this process is the path taken by Socrates and his interlocutor together, where the disciple is the opportunity for the master to understand himself, and the master is the opportunity for the disciple to understand himself. We touch on one of the possible meanings of Socrates' enigmatic profession of faith: *I know one thing and that is that I know nothing. The interlocutor disciple is thus challenged in the very foundation of his action, he becomes aware of the living problem that he himself is for himself. This is the deep meaning of the Socratic maieutic.*

By his ethical stance of *'ignorance'*, Socrates shakes the unexamined certainties and dismantles the fragile knowledge in a way that is extremely crucial for a democracy. As formulated by Plato in one of the early Dialogues: *'None of us has certainties, so we will all decide together what is just or unjust, legal or illegal in the city.'* With his *logos* and *praxis* and departing from the notion of *'aporia'*, i.e., the absence of a passage, the questioning that has no way out,

---

84   Hadot, P. (1998) *Eloge de Socrate*, Paris: Allia.

he demonstrates that to bring an answer about what is true, we will have to search during our whole life with the weapons of desire, ethics and reason. This aporia pushes us to live and throws us into action to discover that everything is decided by making our own way. As a unique and universal thinker, Socrates makes us think about life and the world from a universal and humanistic perspective. He disabuses us of our illusions, he highlights our confusions and eventually he is reinvented through our efforts to seek the truth.

It is precisely on this point that the legacy of the exemplary mentoring relationship between Socrates and Plato suffers a major breach after the former's death. In his new philosophy Plato teaches the existence of eternal truths in the World of Ideas (*the Cavern*), where the philosopher-king shapes his people according to his models, on a premise that is diametrically different from the Socratic *ignorance*: '*You have contemplated the One-Best-Beauty in the World of Ideas, you will therefore govern according to this absolute knowledge and thus the order of the world will be restored and maintained...*'.

Socrates is not *sophos*, but *philosophos*, not a wise man, but one who desires wisdom, and his individual consciousness awakens in this feeling of imperfection and incompleteness. The quest for truth and self-knowledge is a genuine mystical obsession for him, and the right way to live fully is by questioning ourselves to know us better, to reveal our dark and light sides, and to understand our true and deep essence. He attaches great value to the coherence between thoughts, words and actions, through which an individual can influence the course of things. From his ethical courage, the *parrêsia*, that targets the *psyche* of the individual and at the same time addresses the *city-polis*, derives the concept of human dignity, one of the most important contributions of his philosophy to civilisation.

## The *'tirocinium'* in the Roman Republic – mentoring in the foreground of public life

The civic education in the Roman Republic is quite a close approximation of mentoring, and a highly hierarchical and directive practice of prime importance for the coherent function of the political institutions. The Roman nobility is intensely competitive as regards the accession to political office of the Roman youth, who are *'imbued with an ethos of achievement'* and at an early age, they would have singled out their allies and competitors. The Roman orator and politician Marcus Tullius Cicero (106–43 BCE) has left a wealth of written evidence about the 'mentoring' he received from his family and other prominent statesmen.

A crucial and foundational learning relationship starts in the life of a young artician descent at the age of 16, through the institution of *'tirocinium'*. The adolescent receives the toga of manhood (*toga virilis*) and is accompanied by his father to the Forum, the Roman *'Agora'*. There, he is entrusted to a notable politician or orator who will initiate him into adulthood and the world of politics and oratory, typically through three types of functions: role modelling and teaching; sponsorship, social promoting and career development; counselling, trust and friendship. Comparative studies show the similarities, as well as the differences, between mentoring functions in Ancient Rome and today.

The Mentor in *tirocinium* behaves as a *patron*, as a successful good figure who dispenses knowledge and wisdom, acting as role model, which is an aspect also observed in contemporary mentoring.[85] Mentoring serves the Republican elite to have their sons prepared to replace them in political office. During the year of apprenticeship in *tirocinium*, the protégé commonly escorts the mentor to the Forum, to the courts, to political discussions (Tacitus, *Dialogus* 34:2), and other social instances where he is given every opportunity to build his own network of personal connections and to develop his career. The mentor promotes the novice protégé amongst colleagues, and sponsors his career prospects in the military, politics and law.[86] The benefit for himself is the respect from senior statesmen and his recognition as a praiseworthy noble Roman who nurtures fresh talent for the Republic.

*Friendship* is an essential element in Roman education. It cements with *trust, respect and affection* the relationship of the protégés with their benevolent mentors, who are more inspiring to imitate than if they were tyrannic (Quintillian, *De Officis 2:2:8)*. From Cicero's correspondence when he became a mentor, it is clear that he maintained solid friendships with many of his mentees, who revered him *'with the sacred reverence due to a father' (Epistulae Ad Familiares)*.[87]

# A historical vacuum of mentoring: the knight and squire and the master craftsman model

In the late Middle Ages, training to be a knight was very common. The squire had knighthood bestowed upon him through a religious ceremony that marked the association of his new status with Christianity. However, this kind of vocational training should not be romanticised into a modern mentoring model without due reference to the context from which it is derived. The Middle Ages was a brutal time of feudalism, injustice, disease and poverty.

Another model that aims at developing continuum in mentoring practice associates modern mentoring with the medieval and post-medieval model of master craftsmanship. This included the concept of being 'tied' to a craftsperson in order to reach a certain high level of proficiency in a trade. It is known however that apprentices were often ill-treated; some ran away, some fell ill and others died due to the hardship of their condition. In England, in the 17th

85  Levinson et al. (1978) *The Seasons of a Man's Life*. New York, Knopf.
86  Anderson and Shannon (1988) Toward a Conceptualization of Mentoring. *Journal of Teacher Education*, 39: 38–42.
87  Rawson, E. (1994) *Cicero, a Portrait*. Bristol Classical Press.

century, the system was extended to force the children of the poor into apprenticeships, which consisted of exploiting children as cheap labour in conformity with the law, despite the Guild system that helped to regulate this practice and ensure a certain fair play.

## The Enlightenment and the happiness of virtue – Fénelon, Caraccioli, Honoria

The first historical narrative of a virtuous philosophy of mentoring and a principled activity that may facilitate learning and development within a caring, supportive and challenging relationship was created in the eighteenth century by François de Salignac de la Mothe-Fénelon, Archbishop of Cambrai (1651–1715), *dit* **Fénelon**.[88] He is the tutor of the young Duke of Burgundy, grandson of Roi Soleil, Louis XIV, and future heir to the throne. Fénelon authors the most widely read book after the Bible in 18th-century France, *The Adventures of Telemachus*, first published in 1699. Fénelon rewrites the Homeric myth with a new perspective that is foreign to the mythical context of the Odyssey.

Athena disguised as Mentor accompanies Telemachus on his journey to find his father Odysseus. And more than in battles and shipwrecks, this journey is an inner and moral itinerary, under Athena's spiritual and practical guidance through supportive and challenging opinions. The vigorously moral intentions of the epic are transformed in moralising lessons of a pedagogue and a demonstration to the glory of virtue. The superhuman Greek heroes, who were confronted with destiny and ubiquitous gods, are replaced at the heart of the action with Fénelon's young mentee, the Duke of Burgundy, who gradually learns the qualities he will need to reign and the vices he will have to flee.

The *Adventures of Telemachus* is an unclassifiable work grounded in a mythological fiction that is to be read as a pedagogical manifesto. It belongs to different literary forms and is stretched between the quest for the missing father, a stable identity, foundational values and a marine adventure in foreign countries for economic profit.[89] It would be difficult to overstate Fénelon's influence as a pioneering theorist of education and rhetoric, a very influential, yet little known today, philosopher of the Enlightenment and an apostle of 'tolerance'. With immense courage, he criticises absolutism and commits to reform his country's institutions, while at the same time he instructs and mentors the heir of the most absolutist monarchy in the world.

The book met with enormous success and its influence spreads all over Europe for more than two centuries. Montesquieu is attracted by its republican philosophy, and the educational philosopher J.J. Rousseau makes it a core element of *Émile, ou de l'Education* (1762), his seminal work that restores the problem of education to its central place in philosophy, and where Telemachus

88    Garvey and Stokes (2022).
89    Cuche, F-X. (2009) *Télémaque entre père et mer*. Paris: Honoré Champion Editions.

is a guide in *Emile's* developmental journey. Diderot et D'Alembert, Louis XVI as well as his young persecutor Robespierre, they all admire Fénelon. The book is interpreted as an anti-absolutist pamphlet, and its influence extended from London to St. Petersburg, and from Brandenburg to the Italian courts, serving to educate princes and nobility. Fénelon's fame continued beyond the French Revolution, with Chateaubriand, Balzac, Stendhal and Baudelaire.

Fénelon inspired two other writers in the eighteenth century.[90]

**Caraccioli** writes *The True Mentor, or, an Essay on the Education of Young People in Fashion* (1761), a treatise on education and how to mentor. Caraccioli suggests that Fénelon's Mentor is a personification of wisdom and self-knowledge, draws on experience and acts from principle, without self-interest. His model leads to *'awareness'*, which is the overall purpose of mentoring, whilst *'true genius is stifled by a cumbrous load of dry rules, and an austere, pedantic and formal manner of education'*. Caraccioli introduces two novel ideas in his treatise that are not found in Fénelon's work: first, that a mentor needs an experienced and successful mentor as a guide, prefiguring the need for 'supervision'; and second, that mentoring is linked to all phases of life, an idea with which modern discourses on mentoring concur. Unlike Fénelon, who emphasises mentoring as an educational process, Caraccioli attributes more power in the relationship to the mentor.

**Honoria** writes *The Female Mentor or Select Conversations*, published in three volumes between 1793 and 1796. She is the daughter of the female mentor, Amanda, and she describes how her mother started with the 'virtuous education' of her own children, and how their small group later included other people's children, to finally become a learning society of adults. *The Adventures of Telemachus* are frequently referenced throughout the three volumes. In the introduction, Honoria states that *'The Female Mentor is founded on truth and nature and intended to promote the cause of religion and virtue'*. Elsewhere, the text reads that Amanda: *'...endeavoured to instil instruction into our tender minds by relating either moral or religious tales, and by entering a course of reading that was calculated to engage our attention'*.[91] Amanda has most of the mentor's qualities that are described by Homer and Fénelon, with a strong religious connection, and a main mentoring approach through role modelling.

# Conclusion

One among other possible conclusions of examining the historical origins of mentoring is that the philosophical, psychological and social perspectives it embodies today still bear at variable levels the influence of the founding Homeric myth of Mentor Athena, of Socrates, Plato and Cicero, and finally and very importantly of Fénelon and his eighteenth-century followers and successors.

---

90   Garvey and Stokes (2022).
91   Garvey and Stokes (2022).

The narratives in this chapter are thought to convey the inner workings of mentoring relationships at different moments in history. The *Odyssey* echoes the archetypal allegory of Mentor; the Greek philosophy, and the Roman political and oratory education, are embedded in contemporary mentoring, whereas Fénelon initiated a new educational philosophy and offered the Moderns the word 'mentor'. From its moral and civic forms in Antiquity, to the pedagogical rhetoric of virtue and tolerance in the French Enlightenment, this multiform legacy remains relevant for today's mentors, mentees and sponsors. It provides an account of one of mentoring's key roles as a process of knowledge creation. As a source of inspiration, of reflexive thinking and discussion, it pertains to the organisational, business, personal, educational, engagement and social inclusion mentoring, and in the other extant versions and fields.

## 14 How do Laozi and Confucius contribute to mentoring with a coaching attitude?

*Fisher Yu, CEO MentoringCo China,*
*President EMCC China*

Mentoring has existed in China for many centuries. Two of the main people who most influenced mentoring were Confucius (551–479 BCE) and Laozi (571–471 BCE). Confucius was the first person in China to open a school where students were taught in line with their characteristics and abilities.[92] This could be viewed as the origin of systematic mentoring. Laozi's method: 'Rule by doing nothing'[93] focused on developing students' strengths rather than amplifying their shortcomings and attempting to change them.

These ideas have had a huge influence on Chinese people throughout history. Of course, many people have modified these ideas over time, but by looking back at the ideas and practices of the past, we can conclude that mentoring was always regarded as important to personal growth, people development and social progress.

However, there were a lot of limitations on the development of mentoring in China. In this chapter we will also explore how today there is a call for a new style of mentoring: mentoring with a coaching attitude.

## How Laozi and Confucius contributed to mentoring

### Laozi and his theories

Laozi (571–471 BCE) was a prominent Chinese thinker, philosopher and historian. He has been listed as *a world cultural figure and one of the world's top one hundred historical figures* (according to Michael H. Hart, in his best-selling work, *The 100: A Ranking of the Most Influential Persons in History*, first published in 1978 and revised since). Hart chose people on a ranking of who had done the most to

---

92    Qijia Guo (2015) *A History of Education in China*. People's Education Press.
93    Puming Huang (2021) *Dao De Jing*. Anhui Literature and Art Publishing House.

influence the world. In 1987, *The New York Times* listed Laozi as one of the top ten ancient and modern writers in the world.

In that era, 2,500 years ago, human civilisation was entering a golden age: Socrates and Plato in ancient Greece, Sakyamuni Buddha in ancient India, and Laozi and Confucius in ancient China were among the giants of thought at that time.

Laozi served as the historian of the Zhou dynasty's (1046–256 BCE) Shou Zang Chamber (the equivalent of a national librarian or archivist) and was renowned for his erudition. Confucius asked him three times (at the ages of 17, 26 and 51) about his Taoism.[94] He wrote the *Tao Te Ching*, a book divided into two chapters, comprising 81 paragraphs of a total 5,000 words.

The *Tao Te Ching* was originally written to teach people how to practise Taoism, with *Te* being the foundation of *Tao* and *Tao* being the sublimation of *Te*. Without the foundation of *Te*, there would be no basis for *Practice of Tao*, which was later widely used for cultivating one's character, ruling one's country, using one's military and maintaining one's health.

The ideological structure of the book is as follows: Tao is the 'body' of Te; Te is the 'use' of Tao; Yin and Yang are dialectical, from heaven to mankind. (Note: in Chinese philosophy and religion, there are two principles, one negative, dark and feminine [Yin], and one positive, bright and masculine [Yang], whose interaction influences the destinies of creatures and things.)[95]

Following the way of heaven, the law of nature and advocating inaction are the essence of the *Tao Te Ching*.

## What is Tao?

Tao is the source of everything. The philosophy promotes self-cultivation through action without intention, humility, naturalness, simplicity, spontaneity, compassion and frugality. These principles informed Laozi's attitude towards mentoring.

**Tao is the Way of Heaven**. *The Tao produced One; One produced Two; Two produced Three; Three produced All Things.* It is the beginning of heaven and earth, the mother of all things and the root of all things. The *Tao* is the essential law of things, the law of nature, the origin of the universe.

**Tao is the harmony of Yin and Yang.** *All things bear Yin and embrace Yang, integrating Yin and Yang for harmony. The interaction of Yin and Yang is called Tao (the way is made up of Yin and Yang).*

**Tao is the supreme goodness.** *It is like water, which benefits all things but does not compete with them, overcoming hardness with softness and tenderness.*

**Tao is nameless**. *The Tao that can be trodden is not the enduring and unchanging Tao.* The *Tao* is ineffable and cannot be directly perceived by the human senses. Whether it is language or words or anything else, they are all

94   Xiaofen Chen (2016) *The Analects*. Zhonghua Book Company.
95   Weiseng Zhao (2020) *The Spiritual World of Laozi*. China Social Sciences Press.

signs produced by the *Tao*, not the *Tao* itself, and certainly cannot be used to interpret Tao's entirety.

### What is Te?

**Te is the attribute of the *Tao* that all things in heaven and earth need to abide by.** The attribute of the *Tao*, which is inherent in all things, and which is shown in all things, is called *Te*. *Te* is the *Tao* presented in things, and *Te* is the intermediary between the *Tao* and all things.

**If one is in conformity with the laws of the *Tao*, it is called *Te*.** Otherwise, one is in violation of the laws of the *Tao* and will be certainly punished by the *Tao*.

**Te refers to humanity.** It is the transformation from the natural order to the social order. *Te* refers to the norms of human behaviour, which, when put into practice at the level of human life, are called *Te*, i.e., what is commonly referred to as human virtues.

**Te values life.** It despises fame and fortune, keeps quiet, abstains from greed, rests the mind and ceases to act, and it is naturally inactive.

**The upper *Te* is virtuous without *Te*;** *the lower Te is virtuous without loss of Te. The upper Te does not act without thought, the lower Te acts with thought.* Those who possess upper *Te* do not manifest themselves as outwardly virtuous and are therefore actually virtuous; those who possess lower *Te* deliberately manifest themselves as virtuous and are therefore actually devoid of *Te*. Those with upper *Te* act in accordance with nature without intention, while those with lower *Te* act in accordance with nature with intention.

**Both *Te* and law are restraining forces that regulate social and human behaviours;** the realm of inaction is a upper *Te*, while law is a lower *Te*.

### The relationship between Tao and Te

**Master–slave relationship.** *Te* is vast, it is completely subordinated to the *Tao*. The *Tao* is the source of *Te*, and *Te* is the bearer of the *Tao*; *Te* cannot leave the *Tao*; the *Tao* governs *Te*, and *Te* follows the *Tao*; *Te* cannot deviate from the *Tao*.

**Cooperation.** Laozi said that there are four great ones in the universe: the *Tao* is great, the heaven is great, the earth is great, and the people are great; among them, humans follow the law of the earth, the earth follows the law of the heaven, the heaven follows the law of the *Tao*, and the *Tao* follows the law of nature. The superior goodness is like water, where softness prevails over rigidity.

### Laozi's contribution to mentoring

**Altruism:** This is the principle of benefiting others in the mentoring process. *The highest excellence is like that of water.* A person with high moral character is like water. Water is good at nourishing all things without contending its own contribution.

**Humility and modesty:** *To do, but not to be relied upon; to be successful but not to take credit for it.* Mentor helps mentee for success but retains autonomy and does not claim credit.

**Empty glass attitude:** In Taoism, an empty glass attitude is a never-satisfied mentality that challenges oneself, that is, reorganising one's own knowledge and abilities at any time, clearing out the outdated ones, leaving room for the new ones, and ensuring everything is always up to date.

In the process of mentoring, the mentor should maintain an empty glass attitude and let go of their ego. They should do so without deliberate exaggeration, without being realistic, without stubbornness, without self-righteousness, without self-aggrandisement and without self-exaltation.

**The Yin and Yang dialectic:** Yin and Yang represent opposites, dark and light, happiness and misery. Taoism explores how opposites can be complementary, even interdependent, and may give rise to each other. The Yin and Yang dialectic is that in the mentoring process, if there is a Yin there must be a Yang behind. There must be a solution to the problem and the mentor and mentee need to remain fully confident that solutions can be found. It is also possible to reframe the mentee's problem and provoke the mentee to think in a new way.

**The four levels of mentor in mentoring:** The best mentor simply knows they are there. At the highest level of mentor/mentee autonomy, the mentor and mentee are interdependent and independent of each other. In the second level, people around the mentor praise them. In the third, people fear the mentor, and in the fourth level, the mentor is despised.

**The three categories of mentee in mentoring:** The best mentee hears the Tao and strives to put it into practice. The middle level of mentee hears the Tao, and feels that it sometimes makes sense and sometimes doesn't. The lowest level mentee hears the Tao and laughs at it.

**Respect your mentor:** *If you do not respect your mentor and cherish their advice and the resources they offer, even though you are smart, you are greatly bewildered.*

**Understand self when in mentoring:** *To be able to know and understand others is called wisdom; to be able to know and understand oneself is wise. To be able to conquer others is powerful. To be able to overcome one's weaknesses is to be considered strong. To know and yet think we do not know is brilliant. Not to know and yet think we do know is terrible.* Understand self before mentoring starts.

**Actions speak louder than words:** Value the power of a mentor role model. The mentoring without words, the benefit of doing without interference, few things in the world can compare to it.

**Be authentic when in mentoring:** True and trustworthy words may not be beautiful, and beautiful words may not be true. A good person may not speak cleverly, a clever person may not speak kindly. A person who is truly knowledgeable does not show off, a person who shows off that they know a lot may not be truly knowledgeable.

## Confucius and his theories

Confucius (551–479 BCE) was a great thinker, statesman and educator, and the founder of the Confucian school in ancient China. Confucianism has had a profound influence on China and the world since then.

Confucius' father died when he was 3 years old and he was brought up with his widowed mother. Confucius once said, 'I lived in poverty when I was young, so I could do lots of menial work'.[96] He had to engage in various kinds of labour and had extensive contact with the lower classes.

At the age of 30, Confucius began to take on pupils and started the first private school in China's history, and with the spirit of 'studying without satiety, mentoring others without weariness', he trained 70 sages and 3,000 disciples. At the age of 68, Confucius returned to his home town and began to concentrate on education and compiling and spreading knowledge of ancient culture.

In his later years, he compiled the Six Classic Books (Shi, Shu, Ritual, Music, Yi and Spring and Autumn) of ancient China. After his death, his disciples and others recorded the words and thoughts of Confucius and his followers and compiled them into the *Analects*, a canon consisting of 20 chapters, 492 paragraphs and about 10,000 words.

The core of the *Analects of Confucius* is *Ren*. It is both the highest political principle and the highest moral principle in Confucius' ideal. The fundamental meaning of *Ren* is that the benevolent person loves others. In the Analects, *Ren* is mentioned 109 times and *Ritual* 75 times, which indicates their importance. According to Confucius, the essence of *Ren* must be observed by society as a whole through the practice of *Ritual*. There are three types of rituals: firstly, which refer to the hierarchy and ethical order of society as a whole; secondly, etiquette, which refer to specific etiquette ceremony; and thirdly, politeness, which refers to the moral cultivation displayed by individuals in treating others with respect, harmony and humility.

*Ren* extends to politics, which means benevolent governance. Confucius believed that to govern a country well, the ruler must attach importance to human character and morality, be trustworthy and love the people.

## Confucius' educational thoughts

Confucius loved education and devoted his life to it. He was never tired of learning and never tired of teaching. He taught not only by word but also by example, inspiring his students with his exemplary behaviour. He loved his students and they respected him, the cordial relationship between teacher and students setting a model example.

---

96   Huaijin Nan (2018) *Analects of Confucius*. Oriental Publishing House.

Confucius' educational ideas can be summarised as follows (Nan, 2018):

**The purpose of education: to help the world.** Confucius advocated the use of what one has learnt to change the world and create wellbeing for society. Only he who possesses complete sincerity can fully develop his own nature and the nature of others to help heaven and earth nourish all things, he can be juxtaposed with heaven and earth.

**The target group of education: teaching without discrimination.** Confucius advocated the idea of education without discrimination between the noble and the poor, and that equal opportunity for education should be given to all.

**Way of education: tailor-made and heuristic guidance.** Confucius was the first person in Chinese history to adopt the method of teaching students according to their natural talents. Through conversations and individual observations, he understood and familiarised himself with his students' characteristics and adopted different educational methods according to their different strengths and life circumstances, in line with their cognitive levels. Therefore, Confucius is regarded as the originator of mentoring skills. Specifically in terms of the following:

- Recognise the cognitive differences of the students: The *Analects of Confucius* stated that those whose talents were above mediocrity could study the highly sophisticated knowledge, while those who were below mediocrity should not study that.

- Understand the living environments of the students: By nature, humans are nearly alike. In practice, they become widely separated by their acquired habits. The variation in habits is caused by the different living environments.

- Value the personality of each learner.

- Recognise the talent differences of each student: Confucius had 3,000 disciples, 72 of whom were proficient in the Six Arts, and 10 of whom were the most accomplished.

- To determine the learner's willingness to learn: Confucius categorised his students as 'born to know', 'learned to know', 'dull and confused to learn to know' and 'not to learn to know', designating them 'highest class', 'middle class', 'below middle class' and 'lowest class' respectively.[97]

- Notice the various stages of the learner's life: Confucius noticed that the same person at different ages had different physical and psychological characteristics. Confucius said, *'A gentleman has three precepts: when he is young, his blood is not yet developed and stable, so he should abstain from being obsessed with women; when he is in his prime, his blood is flourishing, so he should abstain from being aggressive; when he is in his old age, his blood is weakened, so he should abstain from being insatiable.'*[98]

---

97    Hongming Koo (2013) *Koo Hongming on the Analects*. Beijing Institute of Technology Press.

98    Xiaofen Chen (2016) *The Analects*. Zhonghua Book Company.

Confucius summed up his life as follows: '*At 15, I had my mind bent on learning. At 30, I stood firm. At 40, I had no doubts. At 50, I knew the decrees of Heaven. At 60, my ear was an obedient organ for the reception of truth. At 70, I could follow what my heart desired, without transgressing what was right.*'[99] This expresses his lifelong journey of diligent study and self-improvement.

Confucius (551–479 BCE) was the first person in the world to invent heuristic teaching (heuristic teaching was first proposed in Greece by Socrates 469–399 BCE), arguing that teachers should inspire and enlighten students at just the right time when they are thinking seriously and have reached a certain level.

Confucius said, '*I do not open up the truth to one who is not eager to get knowledge, nor help out anyone who is not anxious to explain himself. When I have presented one corner of a subject to anyone, and he cannot from it learn the other three, I do not repeat my lesson.*'[100]

His disciple Yan Yuan exclaimed that Confucius was so good at guiding them in a systematic way, enriching their knowledge with all kinds of literature and disciplining their behaviour with rituals, that it was impossible for them to stop learning even if they desired to.

### Confucius' contribution to mentoring

It was Confucius' educational thoughts that contributed to mentoring as he pioneered the theory and practice of mentoring in China using individualised and heuristic education.

- He accepted students as mentees, no matter how rich or poor. He created a contractual relationship between mentor and mentee, in the form of a tuition payment, but could waive the tuition for those who were poor but motivated.
- Confucius used different educational approaches to teach and guide his students according to their cognition, life circumstances, talents, personalities, willingness to learn and stage of life, etc. This was the prototype of early mentoring, and Confucius thus became the originator of mentoring skills.

# The further history of traditional mentoring in China

Traditional mentoring culture has a long history in China. It was taught by a highly skilled mentor or teacher through word and example, and the mentee or student inherited skills through practical imitation.

---

99   Puming Huang (2021) *The Analects*. Anhui Literature and Art Publishing House.
100  Xiao Lili (2012) *Highlights on Education in Ancient Chinese Classics*. Southeast University Press.

There were two types of mentoring relationship in ancient China: one was in the official schools and the other was in folk skills.[101]

The mentoring relationship in the official school, which had huge impact on the mentor and mentee's social networks and their fates in officialdom, was the best known and most influential. The examiners of the imperial examinations usually became the benefactors of the new entrants. The students would also have other benefactors who taught them to read and write from childhood, and these two types of benefactors would identify them in officialdom and in society, and they would be influenced by them wherever they were.

Mentoring became the model for the transmission of social skills in Chinese history. Widely used in folk education, agriculture, handicrafts, arts, Chinese traditional medicine and other fields, such skills were an important supplement to the official school.[102]

Traditional mentorship was usually a method of transmission from father to son and from mentor to mentee: '*once a teacher, always a father*'. In this mentorship mode of transmission, the 'mentor' had the dual role of both 'teacher' and 'father'. The transmission was not only about passing on culture and skills, but also about passing on the virtues of the person. The mentee's character was closely related to the mentor's. The mentor must not only turn the mentee into a person who had grasped the professional skills, but also make their behaviour conform to the moral code of society. What the mentor brought to the mentee was not only the skill to survive, but more importantly, the soul of the industry. The mentor and the mentee formed a kind of community of destiny, in which all were bound in the same boat.

The folk art of mentorship, with the gift of teaching skills to make a living, could be divided into family inheritance and mentee inheritance.

In family inheritance, skills were generally passed on through the 'father to son' model. In the case of government craftsmen, the skills were passed on from generation to generation by the same family. Folk artisans, in order to consolidate their competitive edge in the industry, passed on their ancestral methods and knowledge to their families, but invariably this was only to the men not the women.

In the case of the mentee inheritance, the proposed kinship was generally established through the worship of the mentor. In some professions, the mentee left his parents and could not see them again after he joined the mentor to learn. The mentor took care of the mentee's daily life and studies and taught him professional skills.

From a historical point of view,[103] it was impossible to determine when the Chinese traditional mentorship originated, but a quick analysis of traditional mentorship reveals the following distinct phases.

---

101 Shunying Cheng (2011) *History of the Ancient Chinese Education System*. Beijing Normal University Publishing House.
102 Baoli Lu (2011) *History of Vocational Education in Ancient China*. Economic Science Press.
103 Mingan Xiong and Yan Xiong (2013) *A Brief History of Teaching Activities in Ancient China*. Chong Qing Publishing House.

## From primitive societies to the Xia Dynasty and Shang Dynasty (before the 11th century BCE)

In times when basic survival was a daily struggle, people instinctively passed on the skills they possessed to enhance the resilience of the whole community. This transfer of skills was instinctive, spontaneous, original and the most primitive way of passing on skills.

## From the Western Zhou to the Qin and Han dynasties (11th century BCE to CE 3rd century)

With the progress of social development, the increase in productivity and the refinement of the social division of labour, the mentorship began to follow certain rituals. These were reflected in the relationships and obligations of the mentee and the mentor: the mentee first had to take care of the mentor's daily life, such as setting the chopsticks and serving the rice when the mentor ate, washing the mentor's clothes, and so on, as a courtesy.

Respect for mentors was written into state law from the Western Zhou Dynasty (11th century BCE) onwards and was regulated by the state through the establishment of professional departments. Confucius pioneered the development of private learning,[104] which set the precedent for the development of mentorship in all walks of life and provided a new model for poorer people to learn skills. However, the mentorship of this period was mainly based on the 'transmission of knowledge from father to son and from mentor to mentee' model, and, once a person was engaged in a certain industry, he and his descendants were not allowed to change their profession for generations.

In those days, the copying of books was entirely by hand, which was time-consuming, tedious, and prone to errors and omissions, making transmission, teaching, interpretation and correction by the mentor particularly important. In this period, the transmission of skills from mentor to mentee was still dominated by individuals, which led to the formation of various styles of thought.

## From the Sui and Tang dynasties to the late Qing dynasty (CE 581–1911)

The main hereditary system of the nobility and bureaucrats was broken. Ordinary people had the opportunity to enter officialdom through learning. This was made possible by the establishment and perfection of the imperial examination system,[105] the development of engraving and printing technology and later movable-type printing and the promotion of the popularisation of duplicated books and other printed materials, the acquisition of knowledge and skills expanded into a variety of modes of self-learning and teaching.

---

104  Peiqing Sun (2019) *History of Chinese Education*. Eastern Normal University Press.
105  Haifeng Liu & Bin Li (2021) *History of the Chinese Imperial Examinations*. Oriental Publishing Center.

The system of mentorship flourished in various professions and became an important supplement to the official school, cultivating many practical talents for the development of society.

## From the beginning of the 20th century to the present

With the introductions of western management theories and methods into China, such as Western psychology (1920s–1930s), organisational behaviour (late 1970s), modern management (1980s), coaching techniques (late 20th century), mentoring techniques and organisational tacit knowledge extraction techniques (early 21st century), the development of mentorship entered a new stage. The transfer of skills between mentor and mentee was no longer limited to the model of the mentor doing it first and the mentee observing and then imitating. With the breaking of the traditional personal attachment relationship between mentor and mentee, the theoretical tools of mentoring became richer, the efficiency of the transfer between mentor and mentee increased significantly, and the selection, matching, content and transfer between mentor and mentee became more scientific and efficient. Today, traditional mentoring and mentorship is moving towards a modern mentoring system.

## Limitations of traditional mentorship

There is no doubt that traditional mentorship has brought great social value to human society. However, over the past 2,000 years, there were no major breakthroughs in mentoring because of the following historical limitations:

### Requirement to make a living

The scope of inheritance was mainly based on individual or family skills to make a living. The traditional mentorship in Chinese history had the characteristics of father to son or teacher to mentee inheritance. It started with seven types of people, namely, the priest, the historian, the archer, the imperial official, the doctor, the diviner and the various craftsmen. These seven types of people were not allowed to engage in other industries, and even if they had achieved success in a certain area, they could not be promoted, even if they left their home town. This later extended to martial arts, textiles, various types of handicrafts and various types of artisans. Beginner or intermediate levels of skills were handed down via traditional mentorship, while advanced skills had to rely on their own deep apprehension.

### Risks of losing core skills

Traditional mentorship might cause the loss of core skills. Because there was no protection of intellectual property rights, there was a general curse of *teaching the mentee, starving the mentor*. The mentor often kept some core knowledge to themselves, not passing it on. Some skills were kept so secret, mentors hadn't taught their mentees before their death, resulting in the loss of core skills for the craft.

### Family heritage predominance

Family heritage was a predominant force in traditional mentorship. Skills transmission was limited to family members only, with very few opportunities for outsiders. The mentorship was on a limited scale even inside the family. Sometimes, for the sake of the family's long-term competitive skills advantage, mentorship was only for men but not women. If daughters were involved, they were not allowed to get married.

### Strong attachment relationship

Traditional mentorship relied on strong dependence between mentor and mentee. The mentor had a monopoly on technical knowledge and had complete control over the mentee. If the mentee disobeyed, they would be driven out and would no longer be able to learn skills from the mentor.

### Limited to observation and imitation

The method of passing on skills was mainly based on the mentor working normally while the mentee observed and imitated, with the mentor occasionally explaining and answering questions. In many cases, the mentee was required to serve the mentor as a free long-term worker requiring complete loyalty. The mentor would test the mentee's loyalty before deciding whether or not to teach them core skills, depending on the circumstances.

### Lack of systematic theoretical support

Historically, people's education levels were generally low, the literacy level of mentors was mostly low, and skills were generally passed on orally from generation to generation as low-level direct experience, which was difficult to pass on in writing and easily lost. The mentor's direct experience remained at the level of general summary understanding. The lack of systematic theoretical support limited the sublimation of direct experience into indirect experience, i.e., theory.

### Not all mentees were equal

There were three types of mentees: those who fed the mentor, those who made a name for themselves and their mentor, and those who passed on the mentor's art. The mentor treated them in different ways, with some not ever being able to learn any skills.

*Emphasis on ethics and skills, but not on science and technology[106]*

In ancient China, there was a lack of extensive technical education, such as in mathematics and physics, which were not fundamental educational subjects. The education of society was dominated by the promotion of traditional ethics and morals, and skills knowledge was passed down from generation to generation.

# Today: a new era of mentoring in China

Today, when mentors are mentioned in China, people usually think of university professors, life tutors, entrepreneurial tutors, people who pass on their skills to others inside the company, and so on. Although many multinational companies and well-known enterprises have already implemented corporate mentoring programmes in China, mentoring is not yet regarded as a profession, and all types of mentors in China are volunteers. There are, as yet, very few professional mentors.

In China, mentors work on an individual basis, not in a team. They do not serve their clients in a systematic way; thus, the effects of mentoring are difficult to track and trace. Moreover, many companies adopt informal mentoring programmes, which although have some value, are not very effective or efficient.

Until now, no university in China has offered a specific course or degree in mentorship, and the research, teaching and application of mentorship is still in its infancy. However, the demand for mentoring technology and services has become critical.

According to the latest statistics the death figures in China for the past 10 years were close to 10 million every year with a mortality rate of 7.18 per cent – 10.14 million people died in China in 2021.[107] It is estimated that at least 20–30 per cent of these people had one or more specific professional skills. The knowledge, skills, experience and wisdom they had accumulated during their lifetime were taken to the grave before they had been effectively passed on, representing a huge waste for themselves, their families, their organisations and society. If they had been able to direct some of their energies during their lifetimes to guiding future generations via mentoring, it would have greatly contributed to the progress of society and reduced the cost of trial and error for succeeding generations.

Despite some recognition of the mentor, which is often based on fragmented personal experience and social insights, people still do not understand clearly the specific role of a mentor, how to carry out professional mentoring and how to better promote self-development through mentoring.

---

106  Guangqi Zhang (2013) *Education in Ancient China.* Huangshan Publishing House.
107  www.stats.gov.cn

In summary, there are many blanks in the field of mentoring to be filled, such as formal professional mentoring training, professional mentoring theoretical research and academic constructions, formal corporate mentoring practices, and national and international professional exchanges in the field of mentoring.

## Central government support and promotion

The Chinese government has elevated mentoring to the level of national human resource development strategy, one of the first governments in the world to take such a step. They set the policy to promote the rapid development of highly skilled personnel via the school-enterprise partnership mentoring programme and have provided government subsidies to stimulate the growing demand for talent in strategic emerging industries.

Since 2014, central government has promulgated several policies to promote the development of mentoring in society. Most of these policies have focused on the junior-level enterprise mentorship, addressing the interface between students from universities, colleges and technical schools and enterprises, and on the transmission of skills at the practical level.

## Local government support and promotion

At the same time, local governments have also introduced relevant initiatives, such as this example from the Zhejiang province:

In February 2016, the Zhejiang provincial government announced the policy of 'Notice on the pilot work of mentoring'. In August 2019, it introduced the 'Comprehensive Implementation of the New Enterprise Mentorship Initiative in Zhejiang Province', which provides financial subsidy for mentoring programmes. In June 2021, it approved the establishment of the Zhejiang Mentorship Research Centre, which was the first officially approved professional institution for mentorship research in China, and currently the Corporate Mentoring Management Measures of Zhejiang Province 'is under preparation'. Since August 2021, the Shanghai Municipal Education Bureau requires at least one mentor for every 15 students in schools at the compulsory stage of education.

## More to come ...

Mentoring has existed in China for over 2,500 years to facilitate skills transfer and people development. The long history of mentoring was consolidated by the traditional Chinese education systems and advancements in printing technology. Recently, mentoring has seen a revival, and this is a great opportunity to seize.

# 15 | How can mentoring journey with us in our quest for deeper self-knowledge and understanding?

*Dr Lise Lewis, mentor, coach, supervisor*

## Taking the spiritual path to encourage heightened self-awareness in our clients

> Come from the heart, the true heart, not the head. When in doubt, choose the heart. This does not mean to deny your own experiences and that which you have empirically learned through the years. It means to trust yourself to integrate intuition and experience. There is a balance, a harmony to be nurtured, between the head and the heart. When the intuition rings clear and true, loving impulses are favored.
>
> Brian Weiss, *Messages from the Masters: Tapping Into the Power of Love*

You may already have your own definition of mentoring and you will find others in this book (see Chapter 1 and other chapters in Part Two). Mentoring for this chapter harmonises with a coaching attitude by encouraging a client to find a way they feel confident will help them become the person they want to be without being entirely dependent on advice and suggestions from the mentor. The mentor asks the incisive questions used in coaching (see Chapter 5) to facilitate the conversation combined with an invitation to the client to reflect on responses. This approach helps the client decide on a self-generated way forward they own and that stimulates them to take action and make it happen. Combining the practice of coaching with mentoring encourages a mutuality between client and practitioner that invites unifying each part of ourselves into a higher self. A practice that connects us with our spiritual being to reveal a deeper understanding of who we truly are and want to be. In realising our spiritual self, we engage with a higher energy which for this context is a secular entity impelling us to be in service of others.

**When we're conscious of being conscious – we are self – this is who we are – this is being spiritual. We feel CLOSER and become more compassionate towards others by staying** Calm, **sharing** Love, **being** Open-hearted, Strengthening, Encouraging **and** Replenishing **others and self.**

What you can expect in this chapter is a plunge into how this higher energy springboards us into a fully functioning human *being*. How we can feel elevated beyond the limitations of human *doing* into the harmony of fertile connectivity with others. A knowing of bonding in a relational way of interdependency flourishes.

'Social being' stimulates us to access those unexploited resources within us that *deepen* a sense of self and *awakens* who we are through connecting mind, body and the higher purpose of unconditional love.

A glimpse into philosophy reveals the fundamentals of action, freedom and decision that existentialism offers us to combine with our discovered sense of self. We uncover a perhaps underused responsibility for actively engaging with systemic intelligence that goes beyond ourselves. A knowing that scales humanity to an interrelatedness between individuals for the collective good of all.

How far can mentoring take us in working towards this spiritual dimension of self? The evolution of *who* we are beyond how we perceive *what* we are? What might be gained through seeking this mode of spiritual sensitivity to access our higher purpose? What influence does existential spirituality have as a way of giving meaning and purpose to one's life and what role does spiritual mentoring play in raising levels of consciousness?

Let's explore these questions by applying the framework of 'The 6C's of Spiritual Mentoring' (Lewis, 2020) in the conversation between mentor and client illustrating mentoring with a coaching attitude; see Figure 15.1.

# Ajay's journey to deeper understanding of himself

The practitioner who mentors with a coaching attitude combines the skills of a learning partner with an ability to encourage self-discovery that liberates the client to exchange obsolete practices for new beginnings. The journey of the fictional client 'Ajay' illustrates the nuances, mysteries and treasures that spiritual mentoring with a coaching attitude unravels – places within us that want to be heard, are yet to be explored and positively exploited.

Ajay was accelerated as a fast-track talent who rapidly rose in the corporate world to secure a C-suite position; has confidence in abundance – never phased by presenting to the crowd – has tangible presence – some may use the metaphor 'a force to be reckoned with'. An enviable persona for those who long to be seen as influential and to possess this level of charisma that attracts attention.

### Courage: to discover social-emotional capability

Ajay believes he is and appears to be a high-performing individual until we immerse ourselves into mentoring conversations compared with and informed

**Figure 15.1** 'The 6C's of Spiritual Mentoring' (Lewis, 2020)

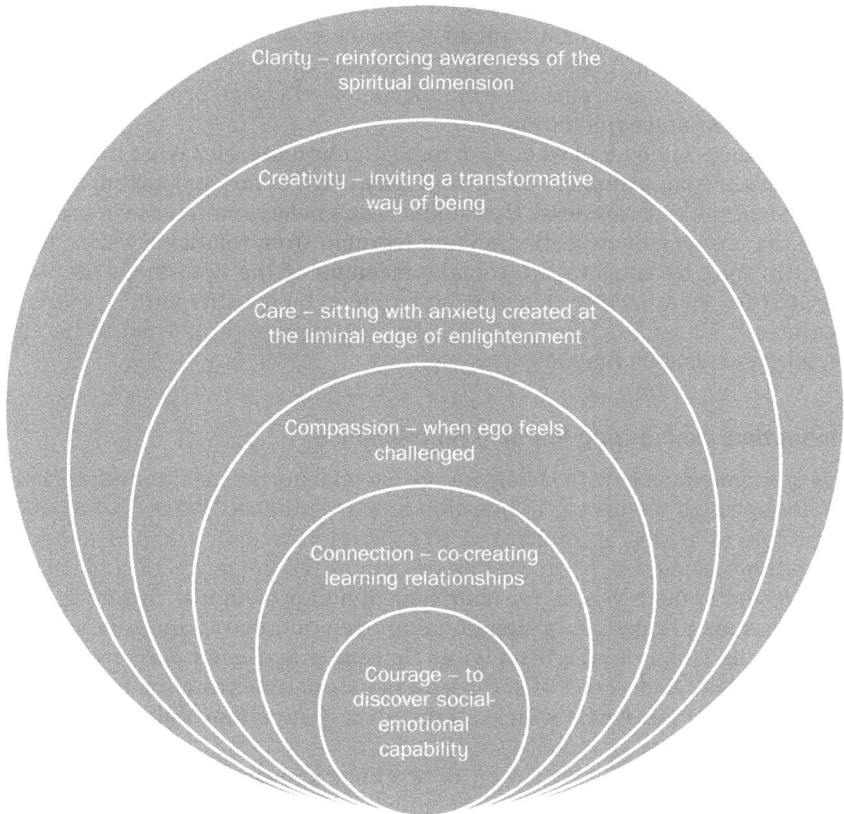

by theories of human functioning. What we believe about how effective we are as humans and how this compares with emulating a spiritual stance starts with drawing on the work of Albert Camus' Myth of Sisyphus (1942).

Camus suggests we have a desire for meaning, not just a mindless brain – a need to make sense of things. We live our lives with habitual repetition until weariness sets in tinged with amazement as we become conscious of what our lives have become. For Ajay weariness comes from agitation within – not a place that is usually visited. Bewilderment arrives when the cause of weariness can't be named beyond discomfort and – could it be anxiety – with the unwelcome exertion of failing to find a solution. Bewilderment joins other uninvited sensations as Ajay tastes the unaccustomed flavour of amazement overpowering the familiar taste buds of rationality.

Right now, Ajay isn't fully conscious of drivers that propel dislikes, desires, fears motivated by competitiveness, greed, gratitude, agreement, compromise, understanding. Ajay has the cognitive ability to use language that expresses these emotions and fears interrupted by a lack of self-knowledge impairing the ability to recognise consequences and the impact on others. Language goes unobserved as a medium of connection confined to delivery of performance expectations. Others remain vigilant to nuances of disposition and style of approach exhibiting flaws that bely the façade of compelling presence. The stifled reveal waiting to surface from this polished visage promises intentions of ruthlessness and exploitation.

Have others uncovered what Ajay really thinks and feels? What level of consciousness is Ajay genuinely operating at and how is this supporting a deeper level of emotional awareness? How might Ajay's behaviour have become habitual in the absence of reflecting on and learning from relational interactions? How can Ajay be encouraged to make meaning of the 'weariness' and to be prepared for what manifests and is undermined by questioning the source of 'weariness'? Unsettling questions that haven't apparently needed to be challenged previously by Ajay at least.

## Connection: co-creating learning relationships

Let's take a moment to reflect here before introducing the meaning of and intention for spiritual mentoring to question how we practise. What do we believe is our role in raising spirituality or to seek and summon a higher energy in mentoring sessions? Is it acceptable or only at the invitation of a client who is interested in the potential for nourishment and growth that raising spiritual awareness may bring? Does intentionality open doors to changes of modality when clients adopt exhibit behaviours that the practitioner perceives worthy of exploration? What level of self-reveal is appropriate from the practitioner? How influential can we be with esoteric practices that may only be welcomed by the few?

Spiritual mentoring isn't a way of working known to Ajay and the practice has not ventured before into this direction of working with this client. The mentor speculates on the questions asked above and reflects on the aim to encourage Ajay to move beyond the familiar comfort zone and to try new things; then reciprocity invites the same from the mentor.

'I feel a sense of overwhelm and what appears to be confusion when you talked of weariness when last we spoke. How does what I'm saying resonate with you?' says the mentor at the next meeting with Ajay.

Ajay sits a while – the tension already noticeable continues to strengthen in the jawline.

'I really don't know' says Ajay hesitantly shuffling feet – 'I'm not used to this degree of focus on me. This is different, I don't like the implication of what reference to "overwhelm, confusion and weariness" is suggesting.'

## Compassion: when ego feels challenged

Leaning on the trust developed in the relationship (see Chapter 3), and conscious of creating space for sensitivity that encourages a dialogical opening for expressing feelings, the mentor asks: 'What do you think about inviting "weariness" to sit with us and to share what emerges for each of us?'

Courage rescued Ajay to prompt a nod of acceptance. A reprieve of tranquil silence softly enters.

A compassionate exhale precedes: 'Let me share that my emotions are aroused as I sit here with you contemplating "weariness" – I have a stirring in my stomach that's calling for attention (Gendlin, 2003); a lethargy pushing aside vitality.' (Strong presence: see Chapter 4.)

'Yes – yes' exclaims Ajay, 'that sounds like the disconnect I have – my concern is that I'm losing touch with my usual rational self.'

## Care: sitting with anxiety created at the liminal edge of enlightenment

Building on this open exchange of perceptions the practitioner embraces an offering of shared engagement and takes tentative steps leading to inviting work at the edge of Ajay's cognisance.

'How do you feel about us trying a new approach to see what we discover about what might be happening to cause this situation right now? It may be that you'll find at first that this sense of bewilderment increases and invites unwelcome discomfort as we journey on this voyage of discovery together – can we see where this takes us?' The practitioner risked a 'closed' question with a tone of invitation beckoning commitment.

Hearing the 'feel' word already causes dismay and the strangeness of vulnerability floods Ajay's mind prompted by an unfamiliar fluttering of anxiety usually absented through adept emotional disconnect. Ajay recognises that any chance of regaining the reassuring sense of equilibrium beckons an untrialled antidote.

'OK' is the reluctant response.

The practitioner absorbs Ajay's palpable preference for return to the comfort of stability and cautiously avoids plunging too early into encouraging a wider conversation into untested areas. Instead, the practitioner recognises the potential benefit of opening the door to exploration of psyche through the route of reassuring rationale. Ajay releases the constraints of tension and settles down when invited to share thoughts about an article titled 'The Four Ways of Leading – Conscious Leadership' (Chapman et al., 2014).

The practitioner had summarised the content and produced a graphic interpreting what the authors of the article describe as behaviours 'above the line' and 'below the line'. Ajay was invited to say what he was noticing.

'Well, my first thought is what does "line" symbolise?' The practitioner didn't respond intending to create an 'invitation to reflect and speak' space. Replying to the silence Ajay says: 'I suppose I'm seeing that the behaviours above the line appear to be more positive than those below.'

'Yes, I agree with you, and I understand this was the authors' intention. So, when you look at the behaviours "above and below the line" what are your thoughts?' asked the practitioner.

'I think the implication of the question is that I'm being challenged.' The practitioner recognises this interruption to conversation flow as suggesting Ajay's fear of being exposed and is reminded of the words of Jampolsky (2011), 'Most of the world's belief system of how we communicate with each other and ourselves is based on fear.' The practitioner thinks of the words of Eisenstein (2013) on creating deeper connections in just 60 seconds to realise 'you're the same being I am' and meets Ajay's eyes with compassion before gently offering a reminder of their contracting conversation (see Chapter 2). How they will work together when unravelling 'bewilderment' has the potential for causing discomfort. Whether the prospect of trusting in a safe space encourages a willingness to extend into personal qualities perhaps not visited before.

'Yes, we did talk about that although right now I'm getting that sense of overwhelm again – where is this leading? I know at some level that I have to recognise and accept discomfort and work with it if I'm to achieve a way through this.'

The practitioner holds an unhurried pace of conversation and asks, 'What needs to happen to give you the reassurance to venture into new territory that may be alarming and unsettling without any guarantee of an easy solution?' (see Chapter 7).

'I guess I just have to step up and find the courage that I believe I have and that is somewhat shaken right now,' Ajay falteringly replies.

To ease the tension and attempt to build assurance for continuing to talk, the practitioner explained how our bodies naturally react when feeling under attack to keep ourselves safe and how this impairs our ability to think clearly and be rational when fear takes over. Ajay appreciated this and unprompted made the comparison with reactions experienced in the workplace when a challenge seemed evident. The practitioner thanked Ajay for sharing this observation and suggested seeing what can be learned as the session progresses about potential reactions to 'feeling threatened'.

'How do you feel about us moving on with our conversation?' prompted agreement from Ajay: 'Let's do it; I feel ready to learn.' This is a step in a positive direction as Ajay appears comfortable both hearing and responding with the word 'feel'.

'We agreed to try different ways of working today if you're willing; let's take a moment to just sit quietly together until the time feels right to continue. Can I suggest we both relax our bodies by taking and focusing on a few slow deep breaths that lets our thoughts and feelings arise on their own' (Kabat-Zinn, 2022).

The practitioner remained alert to Ajay's demeanour and to absorb energy and knowledge from the wider system; an energy that felt renewing, restorative and re-invigorating. When Ajay appeared more relaxed the practitioner enquired: 'What's going on for you right now, Ajay?' The response was encouraging, with the recognition that this was hard work in having memories emerge. Basically, feeling a lack of self-connect struggling with a willingness to continue by being both curious about and seeking answers to what was surfacing and how to leave behind this inner turmoil.

Past experience reassured the practitioner that even though in different circumstances, there was a robustness and resilience in Ajay that would be underlying this present feeling of being unsettled. What was encouraging was the reassuring engagement in willingness to continue.

The practitioner again asked how Ajay was feeling right now – maintaining connection with emotion – Ajay confirmed feeling shaky and intrigued – a sensation of 'something' wanting to be heard; something stirring – 'I want to say "awakening" although I've no idea what that can be'.

## Creativity: inviting a transformative way of being

'Can we continue with the model?' elicited an affirmative nod from Ajay.

'I guess that being "open" leaves space for creativity and new ways of learning; the opposite to what is evident in below the line as being "closed down" – fixed in our ways and likely to reject new ideas from others' ventured Ajay. The 'committed to learning' statement seems obvious – if we don't learn what's going on in our market sector then we don't have a business.

'That's true' reacted the practitioner, reinforcing the business analogy. 'What's surfacing for me beyond this model is the prospect of new beginnings. A leader who supports others to excel – a leader who is transformational and puts people at the heart of the business knowing that success is only gained through productive relationships.' (See Chapter 8.)

Another pause in conversation as Ajay breaks eye contact and gazes into the distance; beyond where both are seated; beyond the nearby view of urban life and into the far distance of blue sky and passing clouds.

A practitioner's question curiously intrudes trusting that Ajay has become more receptive to an incisive enquiry: 'When you reflect on what we've shared how would you describe your way of being as a leader?'

Ajay looked away again appearing deep in thought. This time the practitioner remained silent and still with full attention remembering the work of Nancy Kline (2015) that 'the quality of everything we do depends on the quality of the thinking we do first ... the quality of our thinking depends on the way we treat each other while we are thinking'.

After a while of further gazing into the distance Ajay's awareness came back into the room, 'Well I know I like to be right and I can see from people's expressions that they feel aggravated at times – although they don't say – and if someone does challenge me – well, I know I can be defensive and close people down – pretty sharply and efficiently! I just want to get the job done.'

The practitioner silently holds the space and maintains tender eye contact, breathing slowly, a vision of calmness and serenity.

'When I compare myself, I can see I'm leaning towards "a way of doing" and isn't that what people want from leaders? Someone who stands apart – is compelling – has all the answers – sets the pace and the vision.'

A longer pause.

'What I'm also starting to see is a new world of work prompted by turbulent times that continue from the pandemic, the environmental crisis and the tragedy of war. Perhaps the style of leadership I've cultivated and that's gained me the role I have is creating "separateness" from others.'

'Our conversation is really starting to make me think where the "bewilderment" is coming from – am I really that much out of step with others?' muses Ajay.

The practitioner attentively holds the safety of the shared relational space, while Ajay's bowed head meets protective fingers shielding tearful eyes.

'Just give me a moment,' Ajay says embarrassedly.

'Take your time,' responds the practitioner, compassionately and lovingly.

Time passes, the quality of knowledgeable time replenishes, and time unifies.

The quality of the relationship in the room denied apology crowding Ajay's lips for excusing the display of unwelcome emotion.

Meeting Ajay's gaze the practitioner asked: 'How are you?'

'Well, I'm feeling accepted, relieved, challenged and astonished that I feel all of these!' exclaimed Ajay.

'I'm also realising that I have some tough times ahead – I know I have to change and not get in my own way! To quote Carol Dweck (2017) I have to move from this "fixed mindset" of thinking I know it all – been there – done that and move to a growth mindset and see what's around the corner of new learning.'

'Congratulate yourself Ajay that you've come this far; this realisation will ease the next stage of the journey you seem keen to begin.'

## Clarity: reinforcing awareness of the spiritual dimension

'When can we start?' prompted a recovering Ajay, with a practised zeal to take action and do it fast.

The practitioner urged patience, time to allow emotion to settle into acceptance and for Ajay to welcome and become acquainted with parts of fragile self previously denied and now seeking recognition.

The practitioner also appreciated the wisdom of sessions closing with attention to client safety and found Ajay's enthusiasm to 'get started' fulfilled this purpose by exploring leadership for the future. This intervention was doubly beneficial in preparation for the next meeting and most importantly in reducing a heightened emotional state before ending the session.

This change of direction took the practitioner and Ajay into speculating the type of leadership profile emerging and evolving from the 'way of doing' to a 'way of being relational'; being in rapport gives us vitality by prompting the sharing of physical energy – we develop a lively curiosity and want to be purposeful about our contribution (Lewis, 2020).

We could say that 'how we do things around here' is demanding a sea change in business culture to become 'what will we be around here?'; the demographic influence of younger generations is creating expectations of more care in the workplace especially in recognising wellbeing as critical in these unsettled times .... and that's not all ... there are the rapid advances of technology, the preference of working patterns becoming flexible and much more.

The way of 'being with' acknowledges interrelatedness and that we're all connected. Working from home has motivated people to look at their lives more holistically and to be more family-oriented and able to choose when they work to fit in with family life. There is more recognition for the environment for future generations.

Ajay nodded recognition of this with, 'Yes my family has become very climate conscious and question the car I drive, the travel I do for business – the food we waste'.

'Yes, I relate to that too' said the practitioner, 'I'm noticing a change in what people expect from their leaders – a greater need for compassion, being kind and dare demonstrating "love" at work.' A love that shows we care and feel care about ourselves and others; 'when you choose fitting in over belonging to yourself it's painful' (Brown, 2022).

So, when you hear your family and notice what is happening in the world of work, what is this saying to us about how to connect and start to appreciate each other? How can we enable our people and ourselves to combine our work with who we are – how do we integrate both and show up as humans that want the best for each other and become more productive and make the world a better place? How do we encourage abundance and be conscious leaders who inspire, encourage wellbeing and a sustainable workforce?'

With these questions the practitioner and Ajay agreed that the next meeting will continue their exploration into the integration of self and how this will be of service to others.

The practitioner suggests Ajay may like to reflect on the conversation today and to journal thoughts arising, and to combine this with sourcing the work of Singer (2007) who talks of past pain lodging itself in our body and that can be resurrected at any time we feel under threat. This accounts for us being defensive through exhibiting a learned response that helps us avoid anticipated pain. Singer encourages us to feel the pain when it comes – to open our heart, acknowledge it and let it go. As we continue to release pain in this way, we gradually become free of it and become our spiritual selves by replacing pain with love. We learn to recognise how the pain in our heart that builds a protective shield and distorts our behaviour can be released once heard and let go. Letting go of hurt opens us to love and forgiveness.

The intention is to reinforce the learning from today and for Ajay to review this different form of expression and to question commitment to a new way of being.

'It will feel so good to be at one with myself – to feel whole, and by the way that feeling of weariness I felt at the start of the session has disappeared!' was Ajay's end-of-session comment.

# Summary

We can believe that Ajay as an executive senior level client will have attended leadership programmes, completed 360° and other psychometrics reporting on relational impact. If we accept that psychometrics is inherently biased in that responders are unlikely to be truthful about those responsible for career progression and pay awards; then direct reports have inbuilt weaknesses for raising self-awareness in managers. We also know that the transfer of learning from programme to workplace 'is essentially the crux of all learning' (Leberman, et al., 2016).

Accepting the limitations of some leadership development interventions, what can we observe in summary of what was happening for Ajay? We are formed psychologically through socialisation during our formative years and habits and patterns of behaviour become consolidated by reinforcement throughout our lives. This starts from birth; some will say before as we form in the womb, and others will say this happens even before this time through past life experiences.

In our present life, we will build on genes inherited from past generations of ancestors. To observe behaviours that impact on our relationships we first have to become aware of what impression we make on others. We know that impressions we leave range from seconds to a lifetime with transitory relationships to lifetime connections. When we decide – if indeed we do – change will benefit necessary and essential relationships in our lives. One way to support the transitions we want to make is through spiritual mentoring with a coaching approach. A combination of sharing observations with tender questioning lacking advice or judgement leading to enlightenment: reminiscent of the resulting sense of wonder and awe emergent from the deep structures of consciousness (Heidegger, 1935/2014). Through the compassion and empathy of those practising this discipline we are adeptly challenged, sensitively heard and guided along the path we wish to take. We learn how to expand our mind, make stronger emotional connections and to love unconditionally. As practitioners of spiritual mentoring our role is to 'hold that the method for recognizing the essential nature of one-self requires a reversal of attention away from the objects of experience' (Shear and Jevning, 1999, pp. 190–1) and to seek enlightenment within.

Covey's (2020) spiritual dimension fits the essence of this chapter as not taking a religious perspective rather as 'examining your life and be mindful of your actions'. His view is connecting with nature to consistently review principles and core values. Staying mentally healthy by enriching life and mind activities, connect with what you read to learn something new socially and in relationships and grow an emotionally healthy abundance mindset.

Reflecting on an extract from the work of Sinclair (2007) reminds us that spirituality has contradictory experiences. Spirituality tests our ability to sustain internal reflection blended with external connection. We are challenged to have the capacity for serious commitment and discipline alongside humour, lightness and release and to combine passion with reason.

This chapter started with a quote from Weiss and let's end with one:

> Love is not an intellectual process but rather a dynamic energy flowing into and through us at all times, whether we are aware of it or not. We must learn to receive love as well as to give. Only in community, only in relationships, only in service can we truly understand the all-encompassing energy of love.
> Brian L. Weiss, *Messages from the Masters: Tapping into the Power of Love*

# 16 Mentoring is a way of life

*Sylviane Cannio – Mentor, Coach, Supervisor, Co-founder MentoringCo*

In this chapter I would like to share my decades of experience in mentoring with a coaching attitude as well as of coaching.[108] These are reflections generated by meeting wonderful people – my life's heroes – all on a journey of professional and personal development. From these encounters have come a series of learnings that I hope will be useful to you. They encompass several themes: managing the mentor's energy, the mentor's responsibility to be a role model, the mentor's continuous personal development, the invitation to be always congruent, the taming of the mentor's ego, and the fact that mentoring has a meaning.

## Managing your energy: the oxygen mask for yourself first

In a plane, who wears the oxygen mask first if the cabin is depressurised? Always the parent, not the child. By thinking of their own life first, the parent becomes a resource for the child. The same goes for the mentor. For us to remain the pillars that mentees need, their resource persons, we must first think of ourselves in terms of emotional management and energy in general.

### Knowing how to say 'no' to non-well-matching mentees

It is common for a mentee to select their mentor: the opposite should also apply. The chemistry works both ways. It usually happens at the first meeting … when

---

108  Cannio. S & Launer V. (2009) *Coaching Excellence*, London: Lid Publishing. This book encompasses a series of coaching cases with their tools and makes the reader step behind the scenes of a coaching session. It represents a good sampling of what coaching really is. It exists in French (2008/2020): *Cas de Coaching Commentés* (3rd edition), Paris: Eyrolles and in Spanish (2008): *Practicas de Coaching*, Madrid: Lid.

we listen to our intuition. It happened that I hesitated to accept a mentee. This executive in his forties had a lot of energy, spoke loudly and was imposing. He was very strong physically and that impressed me. I thought about it for a long time and had a call with my supervisor. This exchange allowed me to identify the origin of my fear, going back to my early childhood when I witnessed the anger, sometimes wide open, of my parents, who were on the verge of getting divorced. I finally accepted the mission: the universe always sends us mentees who makes us grow and the challenge was worth taking on. Moreover, I sensed great suffering in him and, referring to the OK-Corral[109] (see Chapter 1), I recognised an inferiority complex (non-OK – OK or -/+ position) hidden under an appearance of a superiority complex (OK – non-OK or +/- position). This mentoring lasted three years, at the end of which the mentee gave me the greatest gift of all by letting me know that he had learned to love himself unconditionally (see Chapter 3).

## So, the question is: when to refuse mentoring?

I think the answer lies on two levels: the respect of our values and our bodily feelings. If a mission does not correspond to our values – for instance, the mentee is in direct opposition to our way of living and thinking – it is better to refuse it because we would spend too much time fighting against ourselves. As for our body's feelings: our body knows; it is incredibly clear-sighted thanks to its animal roots (let's never forget that we are gregarious mammals and that our animal instinct knows the sources of danger, indicates them to us, but we don't always listen to them). If we feel too uncomfortable with a potential mentee, let's remember that the mentoring relationship always remains voluntary, not forced, and that it should be a pleasure and a joy (Czikszentmihaly, 2008).[110]

That said, any assignment can help us define our own boundaries. I usually say, 'We should pay our mentees' because each one of them brings us new learnings. This is often seen in supervision, where some mentors complain about their loss of energy due to a mentee, especially when they unconsciously (or not) assume the role of the victim. The outcome is positive when the mentor manages to empower the mentee. But if the mentee continues to complain and asks the mentor to become their rescuer (see Chapter 8), the mentor better not enter such a drama triangle. A first lesson is for the mentor to have clear criteria for what is acceptable or not in terms of energy investment. A second lesson for the mentor is to analyse the way in which they allow themselves to be driven by their own drivers, notably the 'Please Other' driver (prioritising other's needs before ours), and the tendency to put the mentee's needs in place of their own, and which, in the longer term, can be detrimental to their energy management.

---

109  Harris Thomas A. (2004) *I'm OK – You're OK*, New York: HarperCollins.
110  I refer to The Flow, as defined by Mihaly Czikszentmihaly, when things are easy, natural and flowing.

## Managing the pace of work and fatigue

It took time but I had to admit that I was no longer able to deal with certain issues. I started to be bored by the repetition of very similar requests. I was reminded of this somewhat abruptly by a mentee who told me bluntly: 'I can see that I'm boring you.' I was mortified; so embarrassed. Once again, it was a matter of emotion management in front of her line manager. Once again, in my coaching attitude, I asked the questions that seemed relevant then shared the experience of other mentees, tried to explore the avenues already known and, above all, encouraged her to find new ones. I realised that I was getting tired of the path I had taken. It was too conventional, too iterative. I needed a change.

As a result, I started by only accepting requests that took me down unexplored paths: start-ups, challenging career or life transitions, more strategic and international challenges, post-Covid challenges, etc. It came naturally since, as an external mentor, I am more positioned at mentoring C-suite or top executives: corporations prefer to rely on external mentors for senior positions to keep a distance from the business in case of confidential matters or to avoid conflict of interest, for instance. My decision was made, I was going to yield my seat to younger colleagues, accept the more strategic assignments and turn to training, supervision and mentoring of fellow mentors and coaches.

It takes integrity, courage and letting go to ask these questions: What are the assignments that really motivate us? What are our favourite topics? What are we passionate about? If the energy is lacking, what is the best path we can take, in accordance with our values and that respects our freedom?

## Clearing negative emotions

Over time, negative emotions and stress can also accumulate. Personal, professional or broader crises, such as the pandemic or the war, cause mentees to share their fears, anxieties, anger and sadness on top of positive challenges. It is therefore important to find ways to decompensate these negative emotions. Just as a dishwasher needs to be cleaned to keep the dishes sparkling; we also need to 'clean' ourselves regularly.

What is the best way? Is it sport, reading, walking, cooking, contact with nature? We need to be aware of the impact that the emotions of our mentees can have on our lives, sometimes in insidious ways.

It is interesting, for our own personal development, to also adopt a 'meta-position' and analyse what can trigger a negative emotional impact, i.e., to track the 'trigger effect'. Some mentoring relationships are infinite sources of development, and the analysis of our emotions allows us to clean up negative anchors from the past that have no value or relevance today.

For me, I scrutinise my 'sugar index': turning to sugary snacks indicates that I am emotionally unbalanced,[111] despite walking my dog, gardening, meditating, watching a good comedy film, having a nice conversation with friends, doing a crossword puzzle or performing any of my routines. This is a good time

---

111   Geneen Roth explains the link between emotions and food in *When Food is Love* (1992).

to talk to my supervisor and, if necessary, to my psychotherapist when the emotion is too strong – some grief in mentees' life transitions is heavy to bear and it is best to get rid of it as soon as possible.

# We are role models: oh yes, really?

## Quite a responsibility

Whether we like it or not, our mentees will automatically be transferring on us, especially if we have grey hair. Some might be considering us as a parent, hopefully full of kindness; they might blindly follow our advice or place us on a pedestal or even see us as some kind of a guru. Are we aware of this responsibility and what we are projecting?

A former mentee recently told me that I had been the source of her decision to have a third child. What a responsibility! With a coaching attitude, I remember inviting her to explore her fears and to objectivise their underlying reasons. When she realised that her fears were irrational, and that the risks were limited for both her professional and personal life, she decided to speak about it with her husband. The process was on.

Through the years, I witnessed so many executives leave their job (resignations), or get divorced, or get back together (fortunately): each time I've taken over, I've wondered if my questions and feedback have been appropriate and as non-directive as possible. Hence the importance of adopting the coaching attitude that we talk about throughout this book: leaving as much decision-making as possible to the mentee so that it becomes '*their*' decision and not the one dictated by their mentor.

## What kind of leadership do we display?

And then, what leadership values do we convey? Would we like to be mentored by ourselves? Are we congruent with what we preach, do we really do what we say and do our words accurately reflect our thinking? I am sometimes surprised and even shocked by the lack of congruence of some fellow mentors and coaches – some claim to be champions of ethics, kindness, good values, integrity and honesty. In reality, however, their actions are not always in line with what they claim to convey. It is their actions that count, not their words or good intentions.

As for the way we live – are we in line, in our own homes, with what we encourage our mentees to be? (I remember a personal development professional who was a real domestic dictator with his wife and children.)

## Our internal state influences the way we mentor

Our mentoring style reflects who we are at our core. The problem is that very few mentees dare to give feedback to their mentor, especially if the mentor is much higher up in the hierarchy. Whether we like it or not, nature generally takes over. Like the very egotistical boss who listens to themselves talk, as if their mentee were a platform for their own purposes. Or the executive who lacks self-confidence and needs a large dose of recognition and is therefore bulimic about the successful achievements of their mentees, rather like a parent who lives their unfulfilled dreams through those (somewhat oriented according to their own dreams and aspirations) of their children.

That said, we are still human. So it may be that a mentoring session is scheduled, and we are not in shape or are under stress, with no way to reschedule. The quality of the session will also depend on our quality of presence and listening (see Chapter 4). To increase the level, there is a simple exercise leading to a **change of mindset** that consists in a three-step protocol, made in a few seconds, and that is extremely effective.

The first element (the order is not important) is **posture**. It's all about standing up straight and looking up (you can't be in a bad mood when you look up), relaxing and smiling. Get moving: a body that moves is a healthier body, the impact on the mind is immediate. Do you have your 'playlist' of 'feel good' songs on your smartphone? It can help you get in shape. Or just walking around looking at nature – trees, animals, landscapes – can help you feel better.

Second element: **language**. It reflects our capacity for positive psychology. A problem becomes a solution. A discussion becomes a dialogue. A failure becomes an opportunity for development. If we mentally place ourselves in a positive environment, it automatically increases our energy. Even if we fake it at first, it doesn't matter – fake it, fake it until you make it.

Third element: **attention (focus)** on a goal. My mentee is coming in a few minutes – what is my intention today? And what will I focus on? What is the learning element that I am going to give myself – in addition to the mentee – in today's session?

The three elements put together allow us to change our state of mind in less than a minute. I invite you to try out this little protocol and enjoy the power we have in changing our mood in record time.

# Mentoring is about developing the other person and especially yourself

### Horizontal development aimed at transferring knowledge

There are two types of development. The first is horizontal and concerns the skills acquired – activity and mental competence, learning new techniques and technologies; in short, everything that is linked to knowledge/cognition. As a mentor, this is our primary transmission objective, and this axis can be a great way to acquire skills for both the mentee and the mentor through reverse mentoring.

### Vertical development, or the invitation to leave our comfort zone

The second axis of development is vertical. It is about personal development, becoming aware of and discovering the options available to us when we step out of our comfort zone. Just as our mentee is going to learn, we too are going to have the humility to accept apprenticeship, whatever our position, age or degree of development. Isn't that precisely the first ingredient of development? Isn't it precisely asking the right questions: what in my current transformation is generated by what I am learning from my mentees? What are they passing on to me? What is my real stretch? How are they getting me out of my comfort zone? As mentioned above, the universe takes great pleasure in sending mentees (messengers) and issues (messages) in our path that make us grow. When we recall our latest assignments, we can ask ourselves: What did they teach me? Did I feel comfortable 100 per cent of the time? And if not, what did this discomfort teach me about myself?

# Congruence is a priority

I remember my early academic years in the early 1990s – I was a visiting professor at two universities, working 80 hours a week, as I combined my teaching load with my consulting practice. At less than 35, I was already teaching in an MBA programme where some of the students were 20 years older than me. Underneath the rigorous exterior, underneath my course requirements that made me look like a very strict and uncompromising professor, there was a fear of failure and imposture. Would they discover my anxiety about being a good faculty member? If lecturing in BA degrees seemed natural to me – knowing that at the time I was the only woman teaching 'hard' economic subjects such as Strategic Management and International Business – then lecturing in an MBA had set the bar even higher and activated my inner judge, uncompromisingly pointing out my imperfections and not my achievements.

We are all confronted with this obligation to perform, to satisfy our hierarchy, our clients, our own image and reputation. Then comes the experience, the maturity, the temperament and above all the confrontation with the values that we considered to be our own. I refer to the Logical Levels model (see Chapter 5). At a certain moment of our life, generally around the midpoint of life, between 35 and 45 years old, we start asking ourselves if these beliefs and values are really ours. It was at the age of 40, precisely, that I discovered coaching and followed training in Transactional Analysis, Neuro-Linguistic Programming (NLP), and the systemic approach, which really shook me up and made me question my congruence.

I was advocating the value of 'respect' but was I really respecting myself? And by demanding so much practical work from my students, was I respecting them too? Then, in the early 2000s, when I refined my corporate mentoring style to include this non-judgemental, caring and often compassionate coaching approach, I gradually came to terms with this new congruence. My corporate mentoring approach became gentler, more respectful of the learning pace of my mentees – often young women faced with the hectic pace of being a corporate executive and a mother and wife at home. As for me, what kind of example of 'life balance' was I setting when I was sending emails late at night? I was inviting my mentees to enjoy a 'carpe diem' life but was forgetting to live. I encouraged them to be strategic but often lost myself in micro-management when it came to creating new projects and/or businesses. And then there was a time in my life when I found myself repeatedly confronted by people – colleagues, partners – who prided themselves on being ethical, caring and humble and who ultimately loved the cult of personality and the spotlight. What was the message of the universe?

# From ego manifestation to self-love and the Higher Self

One answer was given to me by my own mentors. Why had I chosen them? What did I actually admire in them? There were about ten of them in the last few years who crossed my path. And, funnily enough, my mentees have been examples and sometimes counter-examples that have also allowed me to continue to grow. And it's far from being over.

### The courage to be yourself

The main lesson lies in the manifestation of the ego. It's all a question of size and measure. Some people find it difficult to position themselves, and this is a theme that we encounter very often in mentoring. Whether it is to assert oneself in a project team, a meeting, an executive committee, for example, or on social networks, or as a speaker or ambassador for one's organisation to a professional federation, the media, or whatever. Often, it is a matter of activating one's 'internal judge', the self-saboteur so well described by Tim Gallwey,[112] a sports coach who became an executive coach in the 1990s.

As soon as the mentee realises that their internal judge is useful (striving for perfection, surpassing themselves) but sometimes harmful (too critical, too demanding), it is time to start taming it. Mine is resting in Tahiti; I offered him (or her?) a nice holiday because they were close to burn-out and it is always with a lot of humour that I invite the inner judges of my mentees and students to join mine in Tahiti or to choose a dream place for them to relax. Yesterday, my mentee sent hers to the Seychelles. At the same time, I invite their internal mentors and coaches – and mine too – to step up and encourage them to become bolder, to take their rightful place, to develop the quiet strength and serenity that characterises great leaders, courageous and happy to simply be themselves.

---

112   W. Timothy Gallwey (2001) *The Inner Game of Work*, New York: Random House.

## Accepting oneself as 'beautifully imperfect'

Another key to serenity lies in accepting ourselves the way we are, and all the elements that lie outside our reach. I refer here to Eckhart Tolle[113] who nicely summed up the 'new earth' in accepting and not spending energy on all things that are beyond our control. This starts with accepting the SMARTEC goals of our mentees (see Chapter 8), both for the session goals and for their action plan. We might as well encourage them to take bold action step by step, at a rhythm that is environmentally friendly for their health and that of their team members and/or family.

And then comes the driver 'Be Perfect,' as mentioned above (Taibi Kahler[114]) – a belief generated in childhood, affirming that one can only be loved when one's actions are 100 per cent – not 99 per cent – perfect. There is no such thing as a perfect mentoring session, or a perfect mentor or mentee. This is an abstract concept. Reality makes us human, and therefore 'beautifully imperfect'. How many young managers are trapped in the 'Be Perfect' that leads to permanent self-criticism, to the non-recognition of even small successes. As mentioned in Chapter 9, let's celebrate, celebrate, and celebrate again the smallest advances or progress of each of our mentees as well as our own. It boosts self-esteem and confidence in our ability to succeed. And it allows us to accept the right to make mistakes, leading to some of our most impactful pieces of learning.

At the end of the day, isn't accepting ourselves as we are, in our magnificent imperfection, the best path to self-love?[115] Did we notice that 90 per cent of mentoring cases are about a lack of self-esteem or confidence in oneself or in one's ability to accomplish an action?

## ... and our Higher Self

Question: what would happen if we were simply accepting our Higher Self and that our life was meant to be the way it is? I strongly believe that we have a mission on earth, that all the events of our life make us grow with a purpose, that our path is written by the Greater, the Higher Self (call it the Universe, God, Yahve, Allah or Brahma or all equivalent names) *'but'* – I insist on the *'but'* – we always keep our freedom of choice upon the paths we decide to walk on (Chopra, 1989).[116] As such, there is no coincidence that we meet that mentor, that messenger in our life, as their encountering has a purpose, an impact on the course of our life. A simple synchronicity.

---

113 Eckhart Tolle (2005) *A New Earth*, London: Penguin Books.
114 https://en.wikipedia.org/wiki/Taibi_Kahler and Taibi Kahler (2006) *The Process Therapy Model*, Taibi Kahler Associates. Inc.
115 Sylviane Cannio (2022), *Le jour où je me suis enfin aimée*, Amazon. Unconditional self-love is the theme of my latest book published in August 2022 on Amazon, in French, *As I began to love myself* – structured on a poem by Kim McMillan, it is a mix of my own life experiences, the resilience stories of my mentees and clients as well as some thoughts of wisdom.
116 Chopra Deepak (1989) *Quantum Healing*, New York: Bantam Books.

As mentors, it means that our interventions are meant to be. Isn't that relieving and inspiring?

# My life has a meaning, mentoring has a meaning

### Transmitting with humanistic love – *agape*

An NLP exercise I did during my training led me to answer this question: 'What has been the common thread underlying all my actions since childhood?' and as I stepped backwards on a timeline, the answer appeared to me in the form of a verb: *'to transmit'*. I realised that this was my common denominator. From my role as a leader in the Girl Guides (Baden-Powell Scouts), to my role as a team leader, and later as a mother, to my chosen professions – consultant, teacher, author, trainer, coach and, of course, mentor. Everything made sense and became logical.

But it didn't stop there: what was behind this desire to transmit, what was the real purpose? The answer came through one word: *agape*, the Greek word for 'humanistic love' – as opposed to Eros, carnal love. Yes, if it is also a mission for you, this transmission cannot take place without a deep and holistic love of the other, without this generosity of soul and without the unfailing belief in these 'heroes of life', these mentees, and in their infinite capacity to create. Isn't this precisely the common thread that runs through the support and helping professions, from the nurse to the lawyer to the therapist? Even in these troubled and darker times, this can and should guide us in our understanding of the human being, in all its beauty. Isn't this the true definition of happiness? (Lyubomirsky, 2014[117])

### The professions meet at the crossroads

And it is precisely here that the professions meet. What a wonderful intuition the founders of the EMCC had when they bridged mentoring and coaching in 1992! They named their new association the European Mentoring and Coaching Council. Coaching would eventually adopt elements of transmission and mentoring encompass elements of coaching posture. While the International Coaching Federation (ICF) had always been dogmatic about coaching being made in 'low position' (knowing nothing, being curious, without any suggestion or advice), the federation now accepts that the coach can share information to help the client move forward more quickly. On their side, mentors are invited to adopt a coaching attitude, namely, to ask powerful questions to help their mentee 'give birth' (maieutic) to their own solution or, at least, the ways to find it.

Today, mentoring with a coaching attitude makes even more sense: as the generation of baby boomers born in the 1950s and 1960s retire, they often leave

117  Lyubomirsky Sonja (2014) *The Myths of Happiness*, New York: Penguin Putnam Inc.

their organisations with whole swathes of experience and, above all, tacit knowledge accumulated over the years. The Chinese, Indian and French governments have understood this and have included mentoring in their government programmes. In China, MentoringCo is attracting a whole range of managers in their sixties who want to become mentors to share their knowledge with younger generations – and thus also maintain their moral and physical health.

Our profession has a lot of meaning; it is a vector of transmission, of empowerment of the following generations, and provides us with an unspeakable joy and infinite gratitude (Poletti and Dobbs, 2009).[118] Growing, maturing with age like good wine, mentors will then always continue to feel useful, whether in the service of the organisation or, at large, of humankind.

*When you were born, you cried*

*And the world rejoiced*

*Live your life so that when you die*

*The world cries and you rejoice.*

Indigenous American proverb

---

118   Poletti, R. and Dobbs, B. (2009) *La Gratitude*, Geneva: Editions Jouvence.

# Part **3**

# Effective mentoring programmes in practice

# 17 Corporate mentoring: changing the paradigm

*Arshad Ali, CEO MentoringCo*

The purpose of this chapter is to challenge the reader to think about how mentoring can be used as a powerful enabler of organisation competitiveness and people strategy. The emphasis is more on the 'hard' side of mentoring (strategy, process, alignment, planning, measurement, financial outcomes) rather than the 'soft' side of mentoring (mentoring with a coaching attitude as an approach and soft skills).

The chapter is divided into four sections:

1  An exploration of organisational challenges
2  The role of mentoring in driving organisational competitiveness and organisational strategy
3  Changing the corporate mentoring paradigm
4  Practical tips on how to make mentoring stick in your organisation.

## Organisational challenges

What are the key challenges your organisation is facing? The answer will vary from industry to industry, but overall, the following challenges are industry agnostic:

*   uncertainty about the future
*   sustaining growth
*   data and artificial intelligence
*   keeping up with technology
*   regulatory changes
*   supply chain issues
*   financial management
*   strengthening the culture to support strategy and execution
*   recruiting, developing and retaining the best talent

- diversity and inclusion
- how to bridge generational gaps in the workplace
- wellbeing of staff.

This is not an exhaustive list but highlights the types of challenges most companies are facing in some way because of the VUCA (volatility, uncertainty, complexity and ambiguity) business environment. Importantly, these challenges will manifest in their own unique way dependent on where you sit in the organisation.

Ultimately, all successful organisations need to find a value-creating strategy that results in being able to serve customers in a more productive and efficient manner than the competition. In very simple terms, companies need to find ways of improving their competitiveness to survive and thrive.

Factors influencing competitiveness of an organisation are numerous and diverse. For example, they include strategy, organisational design, marketing, innovation, data, technology, culture and, of course, people – ultimately, the organisation must have people who possess the necessary skills, abilities, attitudes and commitment to drive the competitiveness of the company. We have all heard the slogan *'Our people are our biggest asset'*. Indeed, this is the one element of the organisation that cannot be duplicated easily or quickly.

Nine in ten workers will need some form of reskilling by 2030.

Research commissioned by the CBI (UK) through McKinsey in October 2020, established that nine in ten workers will need some form of reskilling by 2030. Automation and technology are key drivers for new jobs across most industries. The research found that employees will need to reskill in several key areas: digital skills, interpersonal and advance communication skills; leadership and management, and critical thinking and information processing.

This research was further supported by work carried out by Dondi et al. (2021), who investigated the skills required for the future world of work. They found four basic categories of foundational skills: Cognitive, Interpersonal, Self-Leadership and Digital.

These two research studies reinforce the need for a culture of organisational learning in order to survive and thrive. Successful organisations operating in complex and competitive environments recognise that access to a highly skilled and developed workforce is critical to achieve the desired organisation outcomes.

It is within this context that the role of corporate mentoring will become more and more important in the years to come. The integration of impactful mentoring strategies, processes and programmes into an organisation's corporate culture will contribute to its competitive advantage in many more ways than a focus just on career development or augmenting diversity initiatives (see Chapter 11).

The aim is to utilise mentoring for various strategic organisational initiatives. Although many organisations have implemented formal mentoring programmes, most have not been aligned strategically to long-term business and organisational objectives. This lack of strategic alignment can result in suboptimal and inefficient mentoring programmes. To give a greater chance of longevity and success, any corporate mentoring strategy should be aligned to the organisation's long-term goals and objectives.

---

**Points to ponder**

- What are your organisational challenges?
- Who can you speak with to gain greater insights to these challenges?
- Which parts of the organisation are affected the most by these challenges?
- What impacts are the challenges having or could have on the organisation?
- Who in the organisation has most to gain or lose from these challenges?

---

# The role of mentoring in driving organisational competitiveness and organisational strategy

Now that you have a better understanding of your organisational challenges, what is the best response? What strategies are in place to ensure the success of the company? What comes to mind as soon as the word 'strategy' is mentioned? Everyone loves using the word 'strategy' but it means different things to different people. So, before we go any further, here is a very simple definition to work with: Strategy is how the organisation should make decisions and allocate resources to accomplish key outcomes. Sounds imperfect, a little too vague? What is it we are really seeking? Is it a strategy (guiding principles) or competitive strategy or competitiveness? Have you experienced people confusing strategy with mission, vision and tactics? Ask about how the company can be more competitive and suddenly, the mental wheels will start turning.

To break things down, there are three elements that need to be considered:

1 Strategy formulation
2 Strategy execution
3 Strategy evaluation.

Structurally, there are three levels of strategy:

- Corporate strategy – the company's purpose and overall direction of travel and which businesses it will operate in.
- Business strategy – the route map on how the company aligns its resources and competes in a certain line of business to beat the competition.
- Functional strategy – this supports the business strategy and provides the direction for short-term activities, e.g., Marketing, Finance, HR, Technology.

Mentoring has many benefits for an organisation (McGee Wanguri, 1996) – some of which you will have read about in other chapters of this book (Chapters 1 and 11). What is clear is that to gain from the payoffs of mentoring, the corporate mentoring strategy and programme must be aligned to the overarching strategic direction and initiatives articulated in the corporate strategy. In essence, a corporate mentoring strategy provides a compelling business case that will help with the buy-in and ownership of the mentoring programme by the senior leadership.

## How to develop a corporate mentoring strategy

Often, organisations do not have a corporate mentoring strategy because very few people in the organisations have in-depth understanding of the dynamics, e.g., corporate strategy, strategic initiatives, structure, people skills, employee engagement levels, industry skills (current and requirements for the future) and culture. Instead, mentoring programmes are often set up to support specific people-initiatives in isolation rather than as a coherent and well-rounded corporate mentoring strategy.

The key to a good corporate mentoring strategy is alignment to the strategic position and strategic initiatives articulated in the corporate-level strategy. Here are some simple steps to help you formulate a good corporate mentoring strategy:

1  Develop a mentoring mission that is aligned to the corporate mission statement. It is important to be able to clearly articulate the strategic fit between the mentoring programme and the overall strategic positioning. By doing so, the business case for securing appropriate resources is strengthened. If the organisation already has a mentoring programme, then it is important to develop a corporate mentoring strategy based on what exists to overlay and strengthen current programmes.

2  Conduct market research on the different types of mentoring initiatives and approaches – inter and intra industry. The best practices identified should then be checked for applicability to the organisation's structures, culture and resources – *one size does not fit all.*

3  Develop an easy-to-follow mentoring process that can be used across the organisation. You should refer to sections of this book that have already covered this topic. The best mentoring processes are those that are standardised but allow the flexibility to meet the needs of different functions in the organisation, e.g., career development, orientation mentoring, etc.

4  Develop the desired outcomes of the formal mentoring programme.

In conclusion, when the corporate mentoring strategy and programme is aligned with the strategic positioning and initiatives of the organisation, there is a stronger chance of enhancing competitiveness in today's highly competitive and challenging business environment.

---

**Points to ponder**

- Who is responsible for strategy and strategic management in the organisation?
- What are the organisation's corporate, business and functional strategies?
- Does the organisation have any mentoring initiatives in place already?
- What is the strategic fit of these mentoring initiatives to the organisation's corporate strategy?
- Do you know of any successful corporate mentoring programmes in other organisations that have enhanced competitiveness? What best practices can you adapt to your organisation?
- Which stakeholders are important in developing a corporate mentoring strategy and programme?

# Changing the corporate mentoring paradigm

Most leaders would concede that mentoring is a good thing ('common sense') and can bring benefits to an organisation, e.g., improved staff recruitment, improved retention rates, improved employee engagement, improved productivity, shortened induction periods and better individual learning and career development. The list can go on. Despite all these benefits, mentoring is still not having the positive impact on competitiveness that the literature suggests it should. Why is this the case? The number of companies that have adopted mentoring programmes has increased tremendously in the past decade. These include Citibank, Coca-Cola Foods, Pfizer, GlaxoSmithKline, Procter & Gamble, British Telecom and PricewaterhouseCoopers, to name but a few, but if asked about impact on competitiveness, the response is often nebulous and, for good reasons, deliberately guarded.

To help change the corporate mentoring paradigm, we need to first explore what is happening today. Broadly speaking, there are two fundamental approaches to mentoring in companies: informal mentoring and formal mentoring.

### Informal mentoring

Mentors are selected by the mentee based on their expertise, knowledge, power and credibility. The mentor/mentee relationship often has a special chemistry and may last for many years. There is no contractual obligation within the dyad and everything is done on a voluntary basis. The relationship can extend beyond the workplace.

Since the organisation is not in control of this type of mentor/mentee relationship, there is no way of upskilling either mentor or mentee. In addition, there is no organisational recognition for the mentor. Critically, there is no way of measuring the impact and outcomes of the relationship, and in particular, the gains for the organisation.

## Formal mentoring

This is usually developed under the supervision of the organisation with clear goals, matching criteria, training, contractual agreements and key performance indicators that support the organisational strategy and goals, and are aligned to corporate culture. Mentors receive recognition for their time and expertise.

The disadvantages of formal mentoring include the risk of matching the wrong people, for example because of a lack of interpersonal chemistry. In this case, the mentee may be reluctant to open up to the mentor, which could result in frustration for the mentor too. In addition, there are risks of role overlap for the mentor and the mentee's line manager. For all these reasons, formal mentoring relationships are generally shorter compared to informal dyads.

# Change in mindset

To change the paradigm, there must be a change in mindset. Why do leaders want to be mentors? The motivation can be anywhere on the continuum of altruism to selfishness. Helping people has its own intrinsic reward and satisfaction. At the other end of the continuum are mentors who build a network of personal and professional loyalties through their mentees. They have the satisfaction of being recognised as 'king-makers' and gain referent power not only to attract talent and build loyalties, but also to gain the respect of their peers. However, when the mentor uses political influence to drive their mentee's career prospects, other employees can feel disadvantaged and despise the favouritism.

The author's argument is that informal mentoring is more focused on the benefit of the individual rather than the organisation. While this is good for the individual, less well-networked employees and minorities can be side-lined. This can result in non-egalitarian treatment of employees that can have a very negative and detrimental impact on morale.

This issue is being compounded by the growing workplace diversity caused by inter-generational values and multinational operations or language or culture. Our argument is for organisationally sponsored, leader-supported mentoring that is formalised and aligned to corporate strategy and outcomes. In essence, corporate mentoring programmes should complement and supplement other people-strategies and not be used in isolation from the broader workplace setting. This is not to say that informal mentoring should be abolished. Whatever process is put in place, informal mentoring will continue to happen by the very nature of the process – although organisations that have a culture respecting egalitarian values should be mindful of the risks associated with informal mentoring. On the contrary, it can be argued that informal mentoring for the benefit of the individual should be respected to allow employees to grow out of the company and industry if required.

Here now are some real-life stories to highlight the impact of informal mentoring.

## Vignette 1: The good

It was 2006, and I was working as an organisational effectiveness manager in the UK for a global pharmaceutical company. In my remit, I was responsible for communicating employee engagement reports to senior sales leaders and helping them develop plans to address areas of concern from the feedback they had received from their people.

One of my clients was PY, a Regional Operations Manager (ROM) on sabbatical from our global headquarters in New York. We seemed to get on well with each other and he showed a genuine interest in my future plans. He was pleasantly surprised that I aspired to work in the international setting, and in particular, emerging markets. Over the next 12 months we had quarterly catch-up meetings to discuss his engagement scores and to plan, but with time, we spent more time talking about my career development. He was easy to speak with and had amazing awareness of organisational structures and alliances.

I must confess, I never imagined at the time that I was in a mentor/mentee relationship. What I did know was that PY had been through the journey that I wanted to follow, and I trusted his judgement without any reservations.

Approximately 2 years after meeting him, he called to advise me of an opportunity that I might wish to consider in New York as a Customer Relations Director (Canada, Latin America, Africa and Middle East). We spoke for approximately 30 minutes, during which time he shared insights on the people that would likely interview me: the Recruiting Manager, Regional Marketing Head, HR Director and President of Emerging Markets. He knew each of them well enough to provide tips on what they were like and what made them tick.

For the next 2 weeks, I went through a barrage of interviews. I was pleased to be shortlisted for a final interview at our global headquarters in New York. The company flew me over to New York from London. I had listened to my mentor and prepared thoroughly with good insights on the field force size and market potential across the territories. I remember reporting to the seventh floor of the famous landmark building to learn that the President of the Emerging Markets had had to fly to Canada at short notice for a crisis meeting with Health Canada, so the face-to-face interview was no longer going to happen. Instead, I had a telephone interview. I remember my mentor's tip: 'His attention span is very short. Answer his question and be succinct. Don't waffle!' So that is exactly the approach I took. I recall answering one question at the start of the interview and spending the next 20 minutes just listening to the President's vision for the role and his business challenges. It was probably the most important interview of my life, and to be honest, after answering only one question, it was the most pleasurable! I got the job, and 13 years later, I am writing this chapter encouraging everyone to have a mentor. To note, both my mentor and I have now retired, but we still stay in touch, 15 years after that first meeting.

## Vignette 2: The bad

It was 2014 and I had recently taken on a global role with a small team based at our global HQ in New York. One of my direct reports had a similar profile to me – sales, sales management and then operations. He was a very personable team member and a joy to work with.

During a development planning meeting I noticed that he had signed up several mentors. Two of them were peers of my boss in different areas of operations, which made me a little uncomfortable. I had to wrestle with some ethical issues. Should I inform my manager? If my direct report decided to move to another function in operations, was it fair or right that one of his mentors could be a future hiring manager? Should there be an HR policy to govern such informal mentoring relationships that could bring bias to the selection process?

Through some probing, the motive of these mentoring relationships became clearer. The purpose was:

1 Visibility amongst the senior leadership team in operations
2 Gaining early news on job postings and development opportunities
3 Having early knowledge of planned functional changes.

## Vignette 3: The ugly

I had only recently been appointed to my new global role and the first challenge was to recruit for a vacancy based in our global HQ. As a policy, we always had panel interviews to minimise bias.

I had reviewed approximately ten CVs and decided to shortlist three applicants. One of the candidates was currently working on the commercial side. On paper, his CV looked good. During the interview, I sensed that he was not fully committed to the role I was offering but rather was keen to move into HQ as part of his career development. In theory, this approach is fine, providing applicants are willing to give sufficient time to prove themselves and bring value to the role, but based on what I observed during the interview, I was not convinced he was right for the job and the team. That said, he was professional, well prepared and a conscientious applicant, but in the end, I decided not to shortlist him for a final interview with my manager.

Approximately 3 days after the decision, I received a call from my line manager. He asked what I thought about the candidate and how he'd interviewed. I gave my honest opinion. He was a nice guy but not right for the role. His understanding of and commitment to the role was weak. After listening carefully, my manager then informed me that he had received a telephone call from his manager asking for the decision to be reversed. Apparently, my manager's manager had themselves received a call from a senior executive based in New York, advocating for the candidate and asking for him to be given the chance to prove himself. New in post, I was put in a very delicate situation. In the end I agreed with my manager that he should interview the colleague and make the final decision. A week later, I was asked to offer him the job.

The story does not finish there. Three months into the role, the new colleague laid his cards on the table during a development planning meeting. He wanted to move into a marketing role and asked for my help in getting a secondment. At the same time, I received a complaint from a senior client. He was not happy with the operational service he was getting from my new direct report. So now, I had to manage the expectations of an important client and consider how to coach my direct report – at the same time as helping his career development. At this point, I received another call from his mentor! Distancing myself from the threat of his mentor, I could not ignore that he had been working in the company for approximately 15 years. I felt an obligation to help him. Firstly, I had to re-deploy him so that the client would not escalate his complaint to my manager, and secondly, I needed to help him move into a marketing secondment before more damage could be done. Fortunately, my manager recognised it had been a mistake to hire him for this particular role and gave me full authority to release him for a marketing secondment without proving himself in the role he had applied for. I know that if we met in New York today, we would both embrace and remember the good times!

### Thinking differently

So how should companies think differently about mentoring? Here are some suggestions and practices that have emerged over the years across different companies:

1 **Leader-supported mentoring**

   For the past 30 years, most large corporates have invested time and energy building coaching capabilities – 'leader coach', 'player coach' – and even though mentoring has been in existence for many centuries, few companies have formalised or recognised the skills associated with mentoring. It is not uncommon for companies to use these two disciplines almost interchangeably. In terms of job descriptions, coaching often features, but mentoring is less visible. To acknowledge the value and power of mentoring, we propose that all people leaders have a clear remit to utilise mentoring in some form or other. This remit should be explicitly stated in the job profile. To support the traditional view of mentoring, i.e., 'a wise trusted counsellor or teacher' (Merriam Webster's dictionary), organisations may wish to reserve this remit for employees who have established seniority within their role, e.g., Senior District Sales Manager, Senior HR Manager, Senior Medical Representative.

2 **Philanthropic mentoring**

   As part of the company's corporate social responsibility (CSR) strategy, there should be a consideration for what employees can do for the communities they live in rather than mentoring purely for the benefit of the organisation.

3 **Project-based mentoring**

Strategic projects in the organisation should always be supported by mentors of seniority and credibility. In turn, several mentees (collective mentoring) can benefit from working as part of a project team – to gain organisational visibility, develop skills and deliver tangible benefits for the company.

4 **Matrix mentoring**

This approach has gained favour in recent times and is particularly relevant in matrix organisations or where employees are being developed for senior managerial roles that require an appreciation of multiple functions across the business, e.g., sales, marketing, finance, supply chain, etc.

5 **Internal versus external mentors**

Enlisting the support of external mentors is a powerful way of developing people in the context of strategic partnerships. For example, pharmaceutical companies should consider sending their employees for sabbaticals to the National Health Service (UK) and having mentors overseeing their development through partnership projects.

And, of course, all of the above require a formalised approach to mentoring if you are to realise a triple win (for the mentee, mentor and organisation).

---

**Points to ponder**

- Which form of mentoring is prevalent in your organisation?
- What is the dominant mentoring mindset in your organisation and why?
- How does the mentoring approach align with your organisation's culture?
- Should everyone have a mentor?
- What is the business case for formalised mentoring?

---

# Practical tips on how to make mentoring stick in your organisation

Throughout this book, and especially in Chapter 11, you will pick up on plenty of best practices to establish a mentoring programme in your organisation. In this next section, we will provide tips on how to help your mentoring programme stick. While we may revisit some of the content found in other sections of the book, the purpose here is to give practical, experiential and proven tips to help your mentoring programme survive and not be remembered as just another organisational fad that failed.

Returning to the start of this chapter, the first step is to build a robust business case for your corporate mentoring programme. This should be developed with the help of a steering group (C-Suite Leader, Business Sponsor, Line

Managers, Individual Contributors, HR, Learning & Development, Business Technology, Finance, Communications, Project Management Office).

It is prudent to select a C-Suite Leader who has either benefited from mentoring themselves or has acted as a mentor, and therefore knows about the benefits of mentoring. In addition, it is important to carefully choose a suitable project manager or mentoring programme coordinator for your initiative. This colleague should be highly networked, credible and an enthusiastic person in the organisation.

It is critical for the C-Suite Leader to be prepared to demonstrate strong, active and visible leadership for the programme. Signing off the budget is not enough. The senior leader (as well as all members of the steering group) must be committed to own the business case for the mentoring programme and be willing to engage in developing and implementing their own personalised mentoring programme action plan. Specifically, they need to be prepared to share what they will communicate (and when), how they will role model and how they will reinforce the importance of the mentoring programme.

The mentoring programme steering group should ensure that the mentoring strategy is aligned to the corporate strategy and long-term goals. If done well, senior leaders will pay attention and make the resources available for the programme (people, technology and finance). As part of the process, it is advised to have a clear mission for the mentoring programme so that everyone in the organisation can understand what the purpose is. Here are some real-world examples:

- Boost technical expertise (IBM).
- Integrate new staff into the organisation (Enterprise Rent-A-Car).
- Develop under-represented groups (Audit Commission).
- Prepare middle management for leadership roles (United Utilities).

If the organisation has no previous experience of formal mentoring, we recommend starting with a small pilot group to iron out any teething issues before scaling up. A pilot of 6 to 12 months should be sufficient to refine the programme to ensure good cultural fit and establish efficient processes.

With the steering group in place and the business case for the mentoring programme developed, an early step is to consider how to match mentors with mentees. There is much debate on the merits of formalising this process (algorithms, personality type matching, competencies) or allowing self-selection. Whichever approach you take is up to your own particular organisational needs, but it is important that the mentor and mentee have an initial meeting to get to know each other and assess if their expectations of the engagement are likely to be met. Crucially, it should be fine for either party to walk away without the fear of any repercussions.

Once the matching process has been agreed, it is critical for mentors and mentees to receive training and be given a broad framework for the engagement. This is an area we have found to be lacking with many corporate mentoring programmes, as well as general change management support to include regular communications, feedback sessions and refinements. Raja'a Yousef Allaho shares some good insights and practices from the Kuwait Oil Company case study in Chapter 21.

Finally, and importantly, the corporate mentoring programme must have clearly defined metrics to track the progress and impact for the organisation. In this regard, we have found that a balance of qualitative and quantitative metrics is required. You will find more in-depth discussion and guidance on metrics later in this book.

# Conclusions

The benefits of corporate mentoring are well documented, and more and more companies are leveraging the power of mentoring to drive organisational competitiveness. A study conducted by Deloitte in 2016 suggested that millennials are twice as likely to stay with the company over 5 years if they have a mentor. In the same survey, millennials said that they would like more mentoring time than they currently receive.

Aligning the mentoring programme to the corporate strategy and long-term goals of the organisation helps build a stronger business case and provides greater buy-in from senior leaders in the organisation.

The debate on informal and formal mentoring will continue. We believe there is a role for both, but formal mentoring (mentoring with a coaching attitude), that is well organised, supportive of the company's long-term goals and has measurable outcomes for the organisation is the agreed general direction of travel and consensus amongst mentoring practitioners.

We have found that informal mentoring is used more for sponsorship of the mentee and their career rather than development of skills and competence. In the context of skills required for the future of work, formal mentoring programmes are more appropriate in that they can help focus on what will drive the organisation's competitiveness. In addition, mentoring programmes should be designed to be flexible, allowing functional tailoring without losing sight of, and alignment to, the corporate strategy.

And finally, investing time and resources in a corporate mentoring programme is probably the most cost-efficient way of converting tacit knowledge to explicit knowledge while growing people and the organisation. Though we have focused on mentoring for corporates in this chapter, it is our opinion that entrepreneurs and small to medium enterprises (SMEs) will increase the utilisation of mentoring programmes (and importantly, mentoring with a coaching attitude) in the coming decades as a key enabler of knowledge transfer and skills building to drive their competitiveness.

# 18 Supervision of mentors and coaches

*Felicia Lauw, Supervisor ESIA, CSA*

## Introduction

How does one know that mentoring is going well? Is the mentor with a coaching attitude partnering their mentees and supporting the development of learning agility? How might the organisation and the bigger context be influencing the quality and result of mentoring? This chapter is written with an intention to encourage supervision or reflective dialogue on common challenges that mentors embodying the coaching attitude face when working in a corporate setting. Mentors with a coaching attitude work in a power-balanced relationship that supports both parties to co-learn, build generative learning muscles to stay agile and progress sustainably in complex and trying times.

**Supervision** has been referred to as the safe space where mentors further develop their skills and competence, strengthen their ethical mindedness, and recharge their energy. A supervision-enabled programme enables an organisation to generatively learn ways to maximise return on investments for their mentoring programmes. Adult learning interventions like mentoring, coaching and supervision are ever evolving to serve human development needs in a complex, fast changing and quick results era. Many corporate clients I work with have strategic intents like 'Run and Transform', 'Agility and Resilience', 'Diversity, Equality and Inclusion' and 'Climate Biodiversity'. Mentors working with (see the section on changing the corporate mentoring paradigm in Chapter 17) corporates, including start-ups, need to be agile, robust, ethical, competent, fit for purpose and more. The ask and challenge here is for all of us to hold tangential ideas and find a way to navigate with opposing forces and stay centred. Supervision provides that space for mentors to clarify the layers of weaved complexities, make sense, learn and return to their role as a mentor with increased confidence and energy.

In this chapter, the terms 'mentor' and 'mentoring' will be used, recognising common competencies between mentoring and coaching albeit nuanced differences held by some professional bodies. Mentors navigate the complex web of the mentee's and organisation's success and wellbeing and at the same time, practising with adherence to professional standards. Through supervision, many have found and introspected unconscious decisions and patterns of relations and left the session with more clarity and ease. This is an invitation to mentors and others involved in corporate learning programmes to reflect on their practices alongside a set of common challenges faced. These challenges are brought to supervision in the last decade, although each situation has its unique set of contexts and with common threads. It is acknowledged that these challenges are presented through summarised snippets of interaction, much like negative space in a painting; it is an invitation for the reader to read the cases, complete the story with their own experiences and engage in reflection of their own practice.

We have chosen to reference the European and Mentoring Coaching Council (EMCC) competency framework[119] and some common psychodynamic-related frameworks to present the reflections of these mentoring interactions. At the same time, we acknowledge there are other reputable professional bodies' competency frameworks and bodies of work that are useful and valid. We invite mentors to engage with supervision to support one's fit for purpose as a professional practitioner, with resonating frameworks of your choice.

# Why supervision?

Supervision is an integral part of a sustainable and effective mentoring programme. We position mentoring in the corporate context as a co-learning relationship. In the same way, so is supervision. Supervision has a role in supporting mentors to make sense of, reflect on their own experiences and distil personal learnings and insights, that fuel their practice, development and wellbeing. The EMCC Global accreditation process for professional mentors emphasises supervision or reflective practice as an important part of professional continuous development. To work effectively and sustainably in an increasingly complex world, supervision enables an individualised safe learning space for mentors to bring what needs to be attended to for them to continuously grow and develop for the purpose of their work.

The EMCC Global definition of supervision[120] is:

> a safe space for reflective dialogue with a practicing supervisor, supporting the supervisee's practice, development and well-being. The purpose of supervision is:

---

119 EMCC Competence Framework for Mentors and Coaches, please refer to https://www.emccglobal.org/wp-content/uploads/2018/10/EMCC-competences-framework-v2-EN.pdf

120 Updated Version 2022 – https://www.emccglobal.org/quality/supervision/definition/ For further information and resources on coaching and mentoring supervision, please refer to the document 'EMCC Global Supervision Information Document': https://emccdrive.emccglobal.org/api/file/download/R9U2woJlFi11vsy1Erp82fAwICtS8Nsea6V8TZLh

1 To ensure the supervisee maintains appropriate professional standards
2 To facilitate the development of the supervisee's professional practice
3 To provide support for the supervisee's well-being.

# Common challenges

In the next few sections, common challenges that have surfaced during supervision will be explored through short case scenarios (all names and scenarios have been masked to ensure confidentiality). These challenges are collated and synthesised from over 30 years of mentoring experience and 13 years of engagement in supervision,[121] from both positions of a supervisor and from one being supervised.

### Challenge #1: Ambiguous context and mentoring goals

The simplest view of a mentoring relationship is one where two people with distinct roles are involved, namely the mentor and mentee. However, the reality of mentoring is far more intricate than this. The learning pair sits in an organisation with interwoven systems of interest, often with different hopes and expectations of the outcome. With layers of expectations, understanding the context in which mentoring will occur and what success looks like are important considerations at the beginning and throughout the duration of the mentoring relationship.

*Case scenario 1 – Assumption of stakeholders' management and clarity of goals*

Yong (mentee) has just been promoted to manage a team of sales engineers. While excited, he was unsure about leading a team of bright and competitive salespeople. Furthermore, most of his current team were his peers. David (mentor), a senior leader from another business unit and Yong agreed to start the mentoring partnership. During the chemistry session, Yong stated his mentoring goal was to become a good manager for the engineering sales team. He additionally hoped that mentoring would help him achieve his performance indicators. During the first mentoring session, David explored with Yong his biggest challenge. Yong stated that it is to motivate his team and ensure they are growing. David shared his experience on how he motivated and coached his team and invited Yong to try it out with his team. In the next mentoring session, Yong said he attempted David's suggestions and while some relationships

---

121 Note: Insights and reflections are unique to each individual and the reader is encouraged to use the following scenarios to invite reflections of their own situation. The supervision reflections presented were reflections from the introspection and not meant to be taken as a prescribed approach or course of action. As you read further, follow your own resonance and wisdom.

improved, he had a hard time managing two high-performing individuals. He was getting anxious about the disengagement of his high performers.

As the sessions continued, David progressively felt uncertain about the value of his mentoring. Every interaction felt like a great conversation and yet David was unsure if Yong was benefiting from these conversations. About 3 months into the mentoring journey, Lisa, the HR Manager, invited Yong and David to a review session with the line manager to 'check-in'. David felt even more uncertain and doubted his value as a mentor. He brought this to supervision.

## Reflections from supervision

David reflected that he felt stuck with the request for a check-in with Yong's line manager and HR. He realised he had subconsciously left out the organisation context and assumed that Yong would communicate with the other stakeholders involved. David had a chance to re-evaluate his own assumption that mentoring was a one-to-one relationship with Yong, and he was lending his expertise. David reflected on what he could have done differently to ensure mentoring is of value to Yong and his team. We reflected on the mentoring goal and became curious how that was measuring up, what was being reviewed and followed through. We reflected on who was responsible for fulfilling those goals.

## Reflecting forward

1 What did you notice in this scenario?
2 Which voice(s) was heard and unheard in this mentoring scenario?
3 Thinking back about KPIs and KBIs mentioned in Part One, what might be useful in this scenario?
4 What else do you think is useful to elicit spoken and unspoken expectations of this mentoring relationship?

---

*For mentoring impact:*

1 Establish clearer contracting for the overall mentoring programme and each session (see Chapter 2 and Bluckett's Good Coaching Process[122]).
2 Develop SMARTEC (Specific, Measurable, Achievable, Realistic, Time-bound, Ecological and under Control) goals (see Chapters 2 and 8).
3 Support the mentee to attend to stakeholders' engagement, invite the mentee to step into their power and responsibility (see Chapters 8 and 9).

---

122 Bluckett Peter (2006) *Psychological Dimensions of Executive Coaching*, Maidenhead: Open University Press, page 11.

## Challenge #2: Power imbalance in mentoring relationships

A more experienced person tends to command expert power and, in the Asian culture, an older person or 'grey hair' is often revered because of our familial upbringing. This habitual power play exists in most mentoring relationships, and it takes conscious attention to prevent the unconscious disempowering of the mentee and the mentoring relationship (see Chapters 1 and 3).

*Case scenario 2.1 – An older, more experienced and well-regarded mentor*

John, a retired CEO of a major organisation was appointed by a start-up to mentor Alex, the younger CEO. The start-up is thriving, and Alex is wanting support from a mentor to prepare his company for IPO (Initial Public Offering). John has a good track record in this area and Alex eagerly solicited and listened to John's advice. One mentoring goal was to support Alex in his engagement with potential investors. Alex has an introverted and deep-thinking style and John is gregarious and has excellent networking skills and connections. John suggested different professional networks that Alex could join to build his connections and branding. Alex was uncomfortable but did not want to appear incompetent in front of John and he thought that, in order to be successful, he had to emulate John. Alex appeared upbeat, but he was not getting any traction with the investors' networks. John decided to bring this to supervision.

*Case scenario 2.2 – Reverse mentoring by a younger female colleague*

As part of an organisation effort to build deeper connections between Millennials and Baby Boomers, Sarah, a young, bright and tech-savvy marketeer in her twenties was paired with Craig, an older manager in his sixties from a different department, for reverse mentoring. Sarah was to help Craig learn more about digital platforms and social media applications for business to encourage innovation in Craig's business unit. Although the chemistry session was friendly and cordial, Sarah was still apprehensive about mentoring Craig. During the first meeting, there were moments of awkwardness. Craig was unsure how mentoring would play out and he felt slightly nervous. However, Craig, being the older and more experienced person, took charge of the mentoring conversation. Sarah told HR that the session went fine, and it was like a Q&A session.

*Reflections from supervision*

John reflected that Alex reminded him of a young student and he wanted to help Alex succeed. The image that surfaced was one where he was the principal and Alex was the smiling and contented student soaking up all of John's wisdom and experience. John felt appreciated and valued. With deeper reflection, John became aware that as a result of being put on a pedestal as an elder, John was unaware of Alex's natural networking preferences and abilities.

He realised that he needed to re-address the power imbalance and engage in a mentoring conversation that truly meets where Alex is now.

In the latter scenario, the importance of psychological safety is brought to the fore. At any given time, either one or both parties in the relationship might be influenced by the unspoken expectations and assumption of self and others, resulting in reduced self-trust and trust of others. There is an opportunity to support both parties to be more resourceful and work from an Adult ego-state as described in Transactional Analysis.[123] While a Q&A does provide knowledge, the conversation is one-directional, and answers were based on Sarah's current level of expertise. A co-created mentoring conversation, in addition to supporting Craig's learning and assimilation, might bring new insights and learnings to Sarah.

*Reflecting forward*

1  What did you notice?
2  What level of psychological safety was present?
3  What might be helpful to balance the power between mentor and mentee?
4  What preparatory steps or training might be helpful before mentoring starts?

---

**For mentoring impact:**

Build psychological safety for power balanced mentoring relationships (i.e., both operating more from an Adult ego-state – see Chapter 3 on ability to create trust and the temenos).[124]

5  Provide adequate preparatory training before mentoring begins to bring awareness to power traps.

6  Strengthen courage and awareness to notice when something is awry about the power positions in the mentoring relationship. Re-contract/Spot contract to re-establish how to 'be' and work with each other.

---

## Challenge #3: Mentor's personal drive takes centre stage

Many are drawn to mentoring because they aspire to be supportive of another person, to help someone else realise their potential. This is a noble and natural extension of the legacy of their expertise and experience. However, when a personal need 'to be of service and value' is over indexed, it often results in the mentor showing up as leading, directive and extremely helpful; these behaviours, when over-used, interrupt a co-learning environment where new insights, learning and innovations can be generated. In a conversation where

---

123  Eric Berne (1964) *Games People Play – The Basic Handbook of Transactional Analysis*, New York: Ballantine Books, page 29.
124  Harris, Thomas A., M.D. (2004) *I'm OK – You're OK*, New York: HarperCollins Publishers.

one person is distinctly leading or directing, the path taken will likely be one where it has been well travelled and limited by the experience and wisdom of the leader[125] (no matter how rich that experience was). Downloading as Otto Scharmer described in Theory U,[126] is based on the habitual pattern of action and thought, based on past experiences. Our VUCA (volatility, uncertainty, complexity and ambiguity) world challenges mentoring and, for that matter, adult learning to raise our learning capability to respond with agility and wisdom. Organisations today are not looking to mentoring just to deliver what was delivered before. The expectation of mentoring is to support development for performance, innovation and wellbeing. The opportunity for all of us as practitioners is to grow towards co-creating and co-evolving stages – see Connection: co-creating learning relationships (in Chapter 15).

### Case scenario 3 – Being of help became significant

Mary, a retired board member had been appointed to mentor newly appointed and experienced CFO Tom, on his board leadership and executive presence. Mary had a lustrous career in multi national corporations managing global teams and trained many CFOs under her charge. She was mindful about creating a clear agreement for their mentoring relationship and agreed on the goals that Tom wanted to achieve with the support of mentoring. As the conversation progressed, Mary tried to focus the conversation on Tom's alternatives, with mostly closed-ended questions. Tom seemed less and less capable of generating ideas and began to feel stuck. To ensure the session was of value to Tom, Mary said, 'Why don't I give you a few ideas and you go and try them out?' Tom seemed visibly relieved and thanked Mary for her options. The word 'options' stayed with her, and she brought it to supervision.

### Reflections from supervision

Mary acknowledged her ability to contract, and it was a smooth process as she trusted Tom was a seasoned professional. Tom stated that he wanted a clear plan of action at the end of that conversation. Mary, throughout her career was touted as a prized problem solver and Tom's 'clear plan' unconsciously shifted Mary into her helpful and problem-solving mode. On deeper reflection, she became aware that her belief, 'as a mentor, one should avoid giving pointed advice and options' created an internal conversation[127] and distracted her during the session. It reduced her capacity to be fully present and attentive. The internal mental negotiation of what she 'must or should do' impacted the

125  Senge, Scharmer, Jaworski, Flowers (2004) *Presence – Human Purpose and the Field of the Future,* New York: Crown Publishing, Random House, page 84.
126  Scharmer, Otto C, (2009) *Theory U – Learning from the Future as it Emerges,* Oakland, CA: Berrett-Koehler Publishers, Inc., page 19.
127  Bachkirova, Jackson & Clutterbuck (2011): *Coaching & Mentoring Supervision,* Pg 56, Using the Seven Conversations in Supervision.

quality of her ability to hold a co-learning (co-creating and co-evolving) space for mentoring.

*Reflecting forward*

1  What did you notice?
2  What is the impact of guiding and directing? When is it useful, when is it less useful?
3  What does it mean for mentors to be supportive?
4  What other significant motivations of the mentor can get in the way of the mentee's learning?

---

***For mentoring impact:***

1  Understand, resolve and calibrate personal drives to enable a partnership which supports the mentee's learning.
2  Be aware of personal preference in attending to the mentee's topic. Habitual reliance and reference to prior experience may interrupt the learning space. Shift from problem solving to leading from the future (Scharmer's Theory U, 2009).[128]
3  Have courage to pause when one detects internal mental chatter, develop a practice to return to presence with the mentee (see Chapters 3 and 4).

---

## Challenge #4: Transference and countertransference during mentoring

In many cultures, older individuals with recognised ranks, expertise, titles and successes have a high chance of inviting transference. Whilst mentoring is not a therapeutic relationship, unconscious expectations, assumptions and projections are common occurrences in human relationship dynamics. The impact of transference and countertransference[129] to a mentoring relationship is one of power imbalance and misguided behaviours and expectations during a mentoring conversation.

Transference occurs when a person redirects some of their feelings or desires for another person to an entirely different person. For example, if the mentor reminded the mentee of an ex-boss who they had a pleasant/unpleasant relationship with, that experience would be transferred to the mentor. During mentoring, the mentee may behave or feel based on their assumption and experience of their ex-boss. If this goes unnoticed, countertransference can happen where the mentor can feel and behave like the ex-boss. Transference and countertransference can happen to either party. When this happens, one or both

---

128  Scharmer, Otto C, (2009) *Theory U – Learning from the Future as it Emerges,* Oakland, CA: Berrett-Koehler Publishers, Inc.
129  Murdoch, E. and Arnold, J. (2013) *Full Spectrum Supervision – Who you are, is how you supervise,* St. Albans, Herts: Panoma Press Ltd.

parties begin to have expectations and assumptions of the other based on a previous experience of someone else. It is noteworthy that there is positive and negative transference. In supervision, these phenomena are interesting when they disrupt the quality and sustainability of learning in mentoring.

*Case scenario 4*

Jasmine was a university professor and volunteered to mentor teachers and education administrators serving schools from small villages in her country. Her mentees were highly appreciative of her wisdom and addressed her as 'elder sister'. She noticed they would arrive with questions, wanting her input. Jasmine knew that mentoring is a learning relationship and it involved more than teaching. The mentees were very satisfied when she provided them with advice, and they rated her highly as a mentor. In between mentoring sessions, they would consult her about their personal issues and would take her advice. Jasmine was in the role of the elder sister and the mentees were the younger siblings; they looked to Jasmine for advice including areas which Jasmine had no expertise in. Over time, Jasmine felt very responsible for them and expected herself to do more and more for them.

*Reflections from supervision*

Jasmine came to supervision to think about the pattern of interaction during mentoring. She realised that her mentees treated her like an elder sister and expected her guidance regardless of her expertise. She recalled that when she first started, she clarified the role of a mentor. However, when she tried to elicit answers from them, they quickly asked for her opinions instead. Their admiration and appreciation were affirmative to her and thus reinforced her actions to provide answers. While teaching and sharing was one form of knowledge transfer, Jasmine paused to consider other learning methods and what unconscious beliefs were reinforced. Mentoring is a form of facilitated adult learning and as John Heron[130] suggested for adult learning:

> To educate persons means to facilitate their self-direction:
>
> - In learning what the content of a discipline is
> - In learning how to learn that content
> - In learning whether they have learnt it

Telling reinforced the traditional education system where the teacher held the right answer. In mentoring, the most appropriate answer sits with the mentee and the best decision and action is always taken in context. This is an invitation for the mentee to learn in a different way and be effective in their own

---

130  John Heron (1999) *Facilitation and the Revolution in Learning*, an extract of Chapter 1 from https://wiki.p2pfoundation.net/John_Heron_on_Facilitation_and_the_Revolution_in_Learning

environment. Where traditional training and learning has its limits, mentoring offers an opportunity for individuals to learn with agility and critical thinking skills to meet their current and future challenges.

*Reflecting forward*

1 What did you notice?
2 What is your experience of either being the object of transference or experiencing transference with your mentee?
3 What do you notice about your mentoring behaviours? In a typical mentoring session, what ratio of time are you listening, questioning and sharing?

---

***For mentoring Impact:***

1 Notice the impact of cultural nuances on learning relationships; it can support or compromise mentoring effectiveness.
2 Awaken to over-the-top feelings in the mentoring relationship, e.g., being extremely nice and accommodative, defensive or hostile.
3 Ask 'who do I remind you of?' or 'who do you remind me of?'

---

## Challenge #5: Connected and running in parallel to the bigger system

Like fishes in water, one may not notice systemic influences because we are conditioned. We dulled our senses to patterns of behaviour in the organisation and in the wider community. We fall asleep. In the seven-eyed model of supervision developed by Peter Hawkins and Robin Shohet,[131] eye 5 and eye 7 highlight the interrelatedness to the wider system. Eye 5 looks at parallel processes that might take place during the mentoring session. Eye 7 takes an interest to forces in the wider system that may be enacting or interacting with the mentoring dialogue. Of equal interest and importance to the writer is how the effect of the mentoring conversation might ripple out and interact with the wider system. A mentee feeling anxious and stressed often represents what is also happening in the wider organisation. When a mentee leaves a session and returns to the workplace with an increased sense of calm, it feeds calmness into the wider system.

This next common challenge reminds us that we are always working in the context of a wider system, we are interconnected and co-exist with other human beings, life forms and other matters.

---

131 Bachkirova, Jackson & Clutterbuck (2011) *Coaching & Mentoring Supervision*, pages 33,35, The Seven-Eyed Model of Coaching Supervision.

*Case scenario 5*

Vivian was an internal mentor to a newly promoted partner, Karen, in a consulting firm. The organisation was going through structural changes and was merging with another company. There were many unknowns. Vivian has found in recent mentoring sessions that there was a flatness in their conversations and both of them were progressively disengaged. Vivian brought this sense of disengagement to supervision. She wanted to know what she could do differently and felt responsible for raising the energy level of Karen and, to be honest, her own energy.

*Reflections from supervision*

Vivian acknowledged her sense of disengagement started when the company announced the structural changes, and her own line of business was under review. Vivian noted that while Karen was excited about her promotion, she mentioned that she was still feeling uncertain. Both Vivian and Karen were going through a similar collective experience. Vivian noticed a parallel process during the session. The organisation was putting on a brave front to deal with the current uncertainty, and the same set of behaviours were showing up in the mentoring conversation. The expectation to ignore that sense of disengagement and soldier on was prevalent in the organisation. That realisation relieved Vivian and supported her to be honest with how she was feeling. Vivian saw this as an opportunity to acknowledge their current situation, engage in an honest conversation about one's feelings and experience, create space for both of them to discover what is most helpful in the current situation. As Nancy Kline[132] suggested, 'When it comes to helping people think for themselves, sometimes doing means not doing.'

*Reflecting forward*

1 What did you notice?
2 What might stop you from being an equal partner when you are both going through the same situation?

---

**For mentoring impact:**

1 Notice parallel feelings and behaviours during mentoring conversations.
2 Enquire into the parallel feelings and behaviours, and what might be happening in the wider systems (e.g., organisation, family, community, industry or country).
3 Encourage empathy to self and others, re-decide what might be most useful in the context of wellbeing of everyone involved (including the wider system).

---

132  Nancy Kline (2015) *More Time to Think*, page 52, What is Your Hurry?

## Challenge #6: Awareness to ethical dilemmas

Ethical maturity and sensitivity develop through a continuous process of self-reflection with empathy and compassion.[133] It is a muscle strengthened with awareness, practice, feedback and reflection over time. Adherence and commitment to a professional code of ethics requires a mentor to be awake and curious. Ethical dilemmas are edges of consideration based on professional standards, practices, personal values and qualities overlayed with context and local culture. Often when people bring an ethical dilemma to supervision, they reported that they first felt a discomfort in their body, from tension or heaviness in the shoulders or a twitch or contraction in the upper torso, usually associated with feelings ranging from judgement, disappointment to shame. In supervision we see this as an opportunity to clarify one's ethical stance and values. Through reflection of one's ethical boundaries and personal values, mentors gained clarity, expanding their capacity and confidence to work in grey areas, stay present with a centred posture of 'strong back, soft front', a phrase I first heard from Joan Halifax[134] at a mindfulness retreat; to work with principles and compassion.

### Case scenario 6

Mark, a senior leader from a different business unit has been mentoring Kate for a few years. A role opened in Mark's business area, and he thought Kate would be a perfect fit for that job. During one mentoring conversation, Mark casually mentioned the role to Kate because he remembered she was very keen to work for him. Once Mark mentioned the opportunity, he noticed a twitch in his gut. He was unsure if it was appropriate for him to bring it up as a hiring manager during mentoring and if his mentoring relationship with Kate would be an unfair privilege or a disadvantage to Kate.

### Reflections from supervision

Mark was in a bind when he arrived in supervision. He could not pinpoint what it was he was uneasy about. However, the lingering twitch when he thought about that mentoring session was enough to bring it up. He acknowledged that he really wanted Kate to have that role and, with further reflection, he noted that apart from Kate being a safe pair of hands, he was convinced of her commitment and learning capabilities. We paused on his gushing approval of Kate and reflected on what the impact was of his positive perception of Kate? What possibly was he not seeing? There was a long pause.

133 Carroll and Shaw (2013) *Ethical Maturity in the Helping Professions*, London: Jessica Kingsley, page 44, 'Ethical maturity and unethical behaviours'.
134 Halifax (2018) *Standing at the Edge – Finding Freedom where Fear and Courage Meet*, New York: Flatiron Books, Macmillan Publishers, page 59.

Mark acknowledged that their dual relationships could impact Kate's application in the shorter term and her credibility in the longer term. He wanted her to get the role but on her own merits and it was important that she and others knew that she got the role because she was fully capable. Mark was visibly calmer and stronger with this realisation. Being a seasoned leader, he knew exactly what he needed to do next.

*Reflecting forward*

1 What did you notice?
2 What are some body sensations you noticed when you faced an ethical dilemma?
3 What might be some ethical dilemmas in mentoring (e.g., diversity, equality and inclusion, climate and biodiversity)?

---

*For mentoring impact:*

1 Notice any discomfort in the body, it is likely a first indication that we are closing in on our ethical boundary.
2 Approach with curiosity and compassion.
3 Celebrate this opportunity to strengthen one's ethical sensitivity muscle and capacity to serve.

---

# Conclusion

> The greatest danger in times of turbulence is not the turbulence – it is to act with yesterday's logic.
>
> Peter Drucker (1980)

Mentors and supervisors, alike, need to grow with individualised learning and remain impactful to the evolution of businesses. At the point of writing, supervision is generally more accepted and practised in Europe. In Asia Pacific, supervision is relatively new, and more is needed to explain the purpose and impact of supervision as an important support for mentors. The EMCC accreditation process included minimal hours of supervision to encourage mentors to adopt reflective practice in their professional development. Whilst it is early days for us in Asia Pacific, through interviews and feedback from supervisees, supervision was found to be extremely useful to them as a practitioner and as a person. In MentoringCo, we included supervision as a continuous professional development activity for mentors who trained with us and incorporated it as part of our programme management and delivery process. Having a reflective practice supports mentors to consciously awaken to our unconscious and to our weak spots, grow in competence and capacity and be fit for purpose.[135] This ultimately contributes to our professional assurance to our clients and the beneficiary communities.

We invite you to look for supervision support in your local chapter of your professional body.[136]

### The Oldest Thirst There Is

Give us gladness that connects with the Friend, a taste of the quick,

you that makes a cypress strong and jasmine jasmine.

Give us the inner listening that is a way in itself and the oldest thirst there is.

Don't measure it out with a cup.

I am a fish. You are the moon.

You cannot touch me, but your light can fill the ocean where I live.

Rumi, *The Essential Rumi*[137]

135 Turner, S. and Palmer, E. (2019) *The Heart of Coaching Supervision – Working with Reflection and Self-Care*, London: Routledge.

136 There is a global network of supervisors listed on the AoCS website: https://www. associationofcoachingsupervisors.com/supervisors/search and the EMCC accredited supervisors website: https://www.emccglobal.org/directory/.

137 Barks, C. (1995), *The Essential Rumi*, New York: HarperCollins, page 311.

# 19 The key role of the programme manager: case analyses from France

*Dominique Cancellieri-Decroze and Danielle Deffontaines,[138] Cap Mentorat, France*

## Introduction

Mentoring has been developing very rapidly in France for the past 10 years, after more than 40 years of existence in Anglo-Saxon countries. As seen throughout this book, mentoring is a helpful tool to value and develop skills and talents of all generations and it is increasingly appreciated by companies and organisations that see it as a way to reconcile individual development, collective intelligence and global performance (see Chapter 17). However, mentoring is far from having reached its full potential, as it is still too often implemented without any real organisation or follow-up, at the risk of making the process fail. A survey conducted by EMCC France (2015)[139] among 10 international companies belonging to various sectors – automobile, energy, agri-foods, cement, banking services, audit and consulting – showed that most of them had hired external mentoring experts but had no in-house professionals to support the programme. As a result, the evaluation of these mentoring programmes showed poor results.

The particularity of this type of support (within organisations) is that it includes both a **relational aspect** (between mentors and mentees) and an **organisational aspect** (the mentoring programme).

All the international studies show it and our experience with organisations confirms it: mentoring only works if it is led by an experienced professional, the 'mentoring programme manager' (internal and/or external) capable of monitoring all the stages of the process (from the needs analysis to the evaluation) and at the same time of managing the relations between mentors and mentees.

---

138  Authors of *Le Mentorat, Mode d'emploi*, (2020) Le Mans, France: Editions Gereso.
139  Imloul I., 'Étude qualitative sur le mentorat en entreprise', université de Haute-Alsace, 2015.

His or her role is crucial to guarantee the effectiveness and sustainability of the whole programme. It is therefore important that he or she understands and embraces the philosophy of mentoring as well as the principles of coaching (see the benefits of developing a coaching attitude in Chapter 1). This is particularly necessary since the mentoring programme manager must be able to provide mentors with the appropriate training so that they can share their experience while helping mentees develop their potential.

Our purpose here is to show, from our point of view as mentoring experts as well as certified coaches, how the mentoring programme manager is key to the success of mentoring programmes and why they should be familiar with coaching practices. So, we'll detail their various roles and tasks and illustrate the importance of their contribution through a few case studies. We chose three companies (Seqens, A. Group) where we provided different types of expertise, including a needs analysis before launching a mentoring programme, some training for internal mentoring programme managers as well as training for mentors and mentees.

## A key player essential to the success of the process

Organising a mentoring programme requires real know-how. Mentoring is fashionable and seems simple to set up. Just type in the word 'mentoring' on the internet and you'll come across a multitude of articles on mentors (how to become a mentor or how to find a mentor) without knowing what distinguishes mentors from coaches or mentoring from coaching. On the other hand, the literature is quite limited on the role of the mentoring programme manager.

Therefore, it is useful to remember the following:

- Mentoring in organisations is above all a collective process that involves the matching of several mentor–mentee pairs (then referred to as 'cohorts' or 'promotions'), essential to generate a strong sense of community as it brings together people from different departments, regions or even countries who otherwise would have rare occasions to meet.
- The mentor in this type of programme belongs to the organisation but he or she is not a specialist in coaching or mentoring (even if he or she will receive training to prepare for his or her role).
- The programme manager is a professional who must possess (or acquire) specific mentoring skills and knowledge. Few articles in the literature give it its full place.

Indeed, the person in charge of the operational implementation of a mentoring programme designs, plans, monitors, supports and evaluates the programme (see Figure 19.1). They must be trained in the principles of coaching and

**Figure 19.1** The different roles of a mentoring programme manager

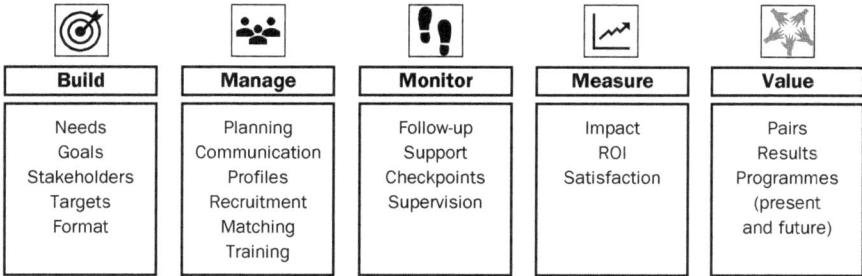

| Build | Manage | Monitor | Measure | Value |
|---|---|---|---|---|
| Needs | Planning | Follow-up | Impact | Pairs |
| Goals | Communication | Support | ROI | Results |
| Stakeholders | Profiles | Checkpoints | Satisfaction | Programmes |
| Targets | Recruitment | Supervision | | (present |
| Format | Matching | | | and future) |
| | Training | | | |

mentoring and have a real mastery of project management. The greater the number of pairs, the more complex the tasks.

# Essential skills specific to mentoring

Managing a mentoring programme requires a significant investment of time, money, energy and qualified personnel on the part of the institution or organisation that implements it. The mentoring programme manager is a key figure who guarantees the quality of the process, ensures that schedules and costs are respected, supports the pairs throughout their journey, and verifies that the approach is always in line with the objectives set by the management committee. The success and effectiveness of mentoring depend largely on the skills of these professionals to accompany the process. It is important that these skills are recognised and valued.

# A multiple role in the long run, from diagnosis to implementation

### The organiser

The role of the project manager is essential, first, to help decision-makers ensure that mentoring is the right solution to their problem: does the approach complement actions already underway to foster employees' personal and professional development? What are the objectives? What results can be expected?

Once the decision is made, the internal or external programme manager will help the executive committee, or the management committee, decide how the mentoring programme should be structured. Among their tasks they will need to: identify priorities, set goals, prepare milestones, plan the key points of progress, and estimate the necessary resources (in time, skills, costs and so on).

It will then be necessary to define how the pairs should work: rhythm of meetings, modalities of recruitment and matching, information and training of all stakeholders, ethics, etc.

## The facilitator

But beyond this first function, the person in charge of the mentoring programme will be a facilitator: the one who makes exchanges flow smoothly, allows different points of view to be expressed, listens, rephrases, advocates and asks questions. That means understanding what mentoring with a coaching attitude means (see Chapter 1). In some cases, they will have to manage conflicts within a pair or with other stakeholders. Therefore, this function is often entrusted to an internal company coach, an HR manager who needs to wear the different 'hats' of a coach, project manager and mentoring expert.

## Business Case 1

*Mentoring at Reed Midem, managed by an internal coach belonging to the HR team who needed occasional support from external professionals.*

The first business case is a good illustration of the different 'hats' worn by the company's mentoring programme manager. When he contacted us, as a member of the HR team and as an in-house coach, he was already fully aware of what mentoring was and he knew the close relations between mentoring and coaching. What he needed was the external vision and experience of mentoring experts to convince his management committee that mentoring would meet their needs. His company already fully appreciated his coaching attitude and practice which allowed him to know about what kind of training mentors needed: the techniques of mentoring with a coaching attitude.

Reed Midem (which became RX France in 2021), is a member of Reed Exhibitions, a world leader in the organisation of professional and public events, with more than 500 events in 30 countries, covering 43 sectors of activity, and which employs more than 33,000 people worldwide. Since 1963, Reed MIDEM has been organising professional and international events for key players in industries such as TV, music, real estate and tech.

The company had been deploying a 'Talent Programme' for several years (since 2019) aiming to support employees in their development. Feedback with the beneficiaries highlighted that mentoring, experienced by some of them on individual initiatives, could be an asset to enrich the programme.

**Jean-Yves Coent, HR Project Manager and Internal Coach, was appointed to pilot the mentoring programme with the management committee from 2019 to 2021:**

*To begin with, the senior executives decided to move forward through an acculturation phase on what mentoring was and was not, the benefit or not of a programme, the link with the needs and expectations of both the company and the participants.*

*On this basis, a 'Mentoring discovery day' was organised for the top management and led by Cap Mentorat. This day enabled us to validate the launch of a first programme that I structured and deployed. The intervention of Cap Mentorat for the acculturation phase was strategic for the success of the programme and its implementation.*

*For our first edition, we chose to accompany 10 pairs during a one-year pilot programme. The mentors, all members of the top management and volunteers in this programme, accompanied the mentees (also on a voluntary basis) from the Talent Programme or employees with responsibilities in the company's transformation programmes. The objective was to ensure the success of key projects for the development and transformation of the company.*

*I had two sponsors, members of the steering committee, as interlocutors. This role is essential for the implementation and maintenance of the programme. I was fortunate that these sponsors were both the HR Manager and a Profit centre Manager, thus combining complementary visions.*

## Managing the process

*I managed this project by structuring and deploying it. To begin with, I managed individual commitments and organised a one-day kick-off meeting to launch the programme. This day, co-facilitated with a pair of coaches, allowed us to share about the meaning of the programme, to continue the acculturation to mentoring, and above all, to create a link between mentors and mentees. Throughout the day, meetings were organised to lead to the pairing stage. This choice was structured around the desires of the mentees; the only limit was their hierarchical and operational links with mentors. Each participant received a booklet with the rationale of the programme, an interview guide for the first steps, and a calendar for the meetings, as the programme was structured around a monthly meeting of 1.5 hours for each pair.*

*I remained the interlocutor of all the participants to bring them structural support because their exchanges remain obviously confidential.*

*A half-day meeting was organised in the middle of the programme, after 6 months, to give a collective sense to these interpersonal actions and fuel the dynamics. This time was devoted to bringing together the mentors on the one hand and the mentees on the other hand in sub-groups. They reflected on the benefits of the relationships, the points of improvement, the expectations and the hidden gifts of the programme.*

*We concluded this programme with a half-day of collective regrouping by specifying that if the programme of this first session was closed, the relationship created between pairs belonged to them and that they remained responsible for making it live or not.*

## Some benefits of the programme

*It has brought together the company's senior managers and the employees involved. The links created helped reinforce the meaning of actions, the sharing of visions, and the role of each person in the company and as an individual. This programme has also enhanced the visibility of our company within the Group, as well as its specificity and attractiveness.*

## Difficulties observed

*The lack of criteria on individual expectations during the recruiting phase between mentors and mentees may have reduced satisfaction. This point was considered for the second edition by sharing the expectations of each individual in advance.*

## Skills required

*Project management skills seem to me to be essential to carry out the structure of the programme successfully. Launching a mentoring programme is a project with all its stages of framing, planning, deliverables, measuring activities and results, as well as communicating about the project. At the same time, knowledge of the mentoring practice, postures and techniques of interpersonal communication, coaching techniques and group facilitation are essential resources that also reduce the need for external services and strengthen the company's involvement in the programme.*

## Time devoted to the programme

*This function has been one of my parallel projects over the past two years. I can estimate about 10/12 days per year to carry out and monitor the programme.*

## Evaluation of the process

*The result of the first year was measured three times based on the participants' satisfaction: after the launch meeting, after the mid-term grouping and then after the closing. The very positive results, with a recommendation rate of 86 per cent, allowed us to launch a second edition the following year with 14 pairs.*

*With the experience of the Talent Programme, we were aware that measuring effectiveness required a longer timeframe than the programme itself. The Transformation projects associated with the objective were at the halfway point. However, it was observed that the mentors, after five months in the programme, considered the meetings as 'refreshing moments'.*

*If I can give one piece of advice, it is that mentor training is essential: everyone can have an opinion on what mentoring is, but it is essential that this point be clearly defined and shared by everyone. Reinforcing the position of mentors is a major asset.*

*Likewise, setting up a structured programme is essential. In the past, we had individual initiatives: but our feedback showed that the initiatives ran out of steam and the lack of corporate objectives reduced the impact for the group.*

*And finally, the involvement of management is key and indispensable to the effectiveness of the programme.*

### Lessons learned

The mentoring at Reed Midem was led by an HR Project Director who was also an internal coach. He had both project management skills and coaching skills. This dual skill set allowed him to be more autonomous in the organisation and management of the process. Mentoring was only a partial activity in his schedule as the number of pairs was limited but he relied on external expertise for certain tasks:

- the facilitation of a workshop allowing the members of the Executive Committee to discover mentoring and to validate the relevance of the programme to their needs
- the programme-launching phase with a preparation of mentors and mentees for their role
- the mid-term meetings of the pairs and at the end of the programme.

## Communicate to convince management and sponsors

During one of our interventions at an energy company, one of the company's top managers told us that he was very supportive of mentoring and had high expectations for the upcoming programme, which was designed to boost the careers of local managers and bring them closer to the field. He actively supported the mentoring programme at first, but then unexpected organisational changes diverted his interest from the process. Fortunately, we had convinced some influential people in the organisation to become sponsors of the mentoring programme and to accompany us throughout the process.

Thanks to this initiative, the programme was able to continue with the full support of the sponsors and the hierarchy, which allowed all participants to feel valued and supported until the end of the programme.

## Coordinate internal and external stakeholders

Usually, in organisations where mentoring is already well established, external professionals work together with internal staff who have been trained and have learned new skills. Here we summarise the many steps involved, since mentoring is a long-term process.

To ensure the success of the process, several steps are necessary, as outlined here:

- assess the organisation's needs
- identify the programme's objectives and, at the same time, the result indicators
- verify that they are consistent with the company's orientations
- convince and get the management's support
- find the right contacts
- define the format of the programme
- plan the steps
- choose mentors and mentees
- match the pairs
- train them
- ensure that everyone understands the process
- provide supervision to the mentors and group practice exchanges to the mentees
- monitor and evaluate the process
- promote the programme.

Like any large-scale project, the management of a mentoring programme requires availability, expertise, perseverance and conviction.

## Business Case 2

*Mentoring within the A. Group is carried by an internal pilot with the support of external professionals. Launched in October 2021, it is still in progress.*

In this second case, the company knew nothing about mentoring and did not know how to structure and organise a mentoring programme. The mentoring programme manager who had been appointed from the HR team knew neither coaching nor mentoring. Our support lasted more than a year: from the initial training of the mentoring programme manager to the follow-up of the process, including the training of the mentors and mentees and the performance evaluation.

The A. Group is present in 45 countries on 4 continents and employs 25,000 people worldwide. Its core business is international communication dedicated to retail.

**The mentoring programme manager is the HR Manager for one of the group's business units. She has a co-pilot for certain tasks.**

*Our mentoring programme was initiated in response to a major issue of young recruits leaving after a few years in the Group. Then, it was found that employees felt there were few exchanges between our different structures especially at the international level and our international structures felt that they were not integrated enough into the processes organised by the head office .*

*In October 2021, we launched our first experimental programme with 21 pairs, including 9 abroad, and for a period of 9 months. The programme sponsor is the Head of the Group's HR Department. The Group's CEO is himself a mentor. The programme has two objectives:*

1 *Break down silos*
2 *Clarify the vision and perspectives of the company.*

*The mentees, young talents that the Group would like to 'retain', were chosen by co-optation after an interview with the programme leader. The mentors are senior executives, business unit directors, and all are volunteers.*

*The most difficult part was the recruitment phase, because at the beginning the criteria were not really precise enough. To ensure that the co-optation of mentees was carried out correctly, the line managers had to advocate the mentoring programme. This took time. Matching was also complicated because of time differences, languages, and profiles of mentors and mentees.*

*Cap Mentorat provided training for mentors and mentees: one-day training for mentors and half a day for mentees, face to face for the French-speaking persons and remotely for the internationals.*

*There was no kick-off meeting because it was difficult for the internationals. We sent each mentor and mentee a short video of their pair (pair reveal). The mentee was responsible for making the first contact. We set up Slack communication between the mentors and the mentees.*

## Follow-ups

*Two months after the first meeting, in December, we organised a first feedback session through a questionnaire (via Google Forms) to check that everyone had really started the relationship, that the objectives had been set and that the rhythm of the meetings and the framework had been chosen. Most pairs meet every month or 3 weeks. The duration of the meetings is 1 hour to 1h 30.*

## A key point

*We work a lot with the sponsor, the Group's HR Department, and the Communications Department, which produced some presentation videos and a **programme logo** that everyone can use in their signature.*

## Among the benefits of the programme

*At the time of writing, the programme is still underway, but in France, the mid-term results are very positive. It is a real success in terms of knowledge of the Group's businesses and creation of links between entities.*

### Difficulties observed

*The difficulties mainly concern the internationals, as the pairs do not always find subjects to work together: the issues are very different from one BU to another and from one country to another. For a V2, we have planned to better identify the different issues per country before the matches.*

### Skills required

*With my co-pilot, we were trained beforehand by Cap Mentorat. This was essential for understanding our role and structuring the actions. I was able to use many tools that made my job easier in organising the programme: mentoring guide, questionnaires, etc.*

*To be a good pilot, listening is essential as well as patience while keeping focused on the objectives. It is necessary to structure the programme well so as not to forget key actions such as communication.*

### Time dedicated to mentoring

*This function is one of the projects I manage since I am HR Manager in one of the BUs. We are two co-pilots to support each other and divide the workload. It is not my main activity and for the moment it is a pilot programme with a limited number of pairs.*

### Evaluation of the process

*We have identified some quantitative and qualitative KPIs:*

- *level of peer satisfaction*
- *ability to move forward in one's career plan and identify areas for improvement*
- *quality of the exchanges*
- *number of meetings and duration.*

*An evaluation questionnaire for mentors and one for mentees is currently being developed.*

## Lessons learned

This company's mentoring programme is managed internally by an HR manager and assisted by an in-house co-pilot. They relied on an external professional to train and support her in certain tasks, notably the training of mentors and mentees and the mid-term evaluations. The programme is international in scope, with mentors and mentees of different nationalities and cultures, which made the recruitment and matching phases more complex.

## Tasks that can be delegated or performed in-house

The use of an external professional who specialises in mentoring will depend on the size of the structure, the number of pairs and the culture of the organisation. Most of the time, the tasks are shared with in-house professionals. If the organisation does not have sufficient resources in-house, it will rely on an external mentoring expert who will take on all or part of the tasks. However, the consultant will need to have a contact person within the organisation, such as a member of the HR department, who can work alongside them to manage the programme and ensure its coordination. For example, many companies outsource tasks, such as programme design and structuring, training, supervision (see Chapter 18) and evaluation. The in-house team then takes care of the communication, recruitment, matching and follow-up phases and coordinates the entire programme.

## Business Case 3

*Mentoring at Seqens is carried out by an internal programme manager with the operational support of an external professional throughout the process.*

In this company both the mentoring programme manager and the CEO asked for some training to understand about the mentoring process. Our support which lasted one year helped them launch and follow up the process, train their mentors and mentees, and introduce them to mentoring with a coaching attitude.

Seqens, a real estate subsidiary of the Action Logement Group (20,000 employees, more than 1 million housing units), was created through the merger of six social housing companies. With a portfolio of nearly 100,000 housing units, it is one of the major players in social housing in the Île-de-France region. With its 1,500 employees, Seqens relies on their expertise to meet the diverse needs of residents.

In January 2020, a few months after the creation of the company, the Executive Committee wanted to set up a mentoring programme to:

- encourage the bringing together of its employees
- create a common culture shared by all
- facilitate the integration and development of its employees
- improve internal cohesion to unite teams around new projects.

**Florence Samyn, Director of Human Resources Development and Administration, has been appointed as the person in charge of internal mentoring.**

*After a presentation of mentoring to the members of the Executive Committee by a professional from Cap Mentorat, followed by a meeting with the top management, it was decided to set up a pilot mentoring programme for a period of 12 months with about 12 pairs. Most of the mentors were members of the Executive Committee and top managers, and the mentees were in management positions. The validated objectives were to:*

- *develop a culture of professional support programmes*
- *facilitate the exchange of knowledge*
- *strengthen team cohesion*
- *improve individual and collective performance.*

## Managing the programme

*My role was to support and coordinate the various stages of the programme, from defining objectives with the Executive Committee to organising the programme's highlights (launching, mentor/mentee training, co-development meetings, closing the programme), including identifying pairs and defining internal communications.*

*My contacts were the CEO, who was also Chairman of the Steering committee, the top management team, the mentors, the mentees and sometimes their N+1 (manager), as well as the Communications department.*

*We relied on a member of Cap Mentorat to help us monitor the mentoring programme, and more specifically, to launch the programme, conduct the training for mentors and mentees separately, facilitate the mid-term co-development sessions and evaluate participants' satisfaction.*

*I was trained by Cap Mentorat to understand mentoring, its differences and complementarity with other forms of professional support approaches (such as coaching or tutoring) and to learn about the different stages of the programme.*

*In my opinion, to be a good programme manager you need to have good listening skills, curiosity and availability. It is necessary to devote time to make the programme live, and to develop periodic informal exchanges with all stakeholders.*

## Among the benefits of the programme

*As soon as the programme was launched, we observed a strong involvement of mentors and mentees, with the development of strong links between pairs and between mentors and mentees themselves. What was particularly appreciated was:*

- *the implementation of an innovative process for the company*
- *the discovery of a different and rewarding posture for mentors and mentees.*

## Difficulties observed

*The monitoring of the programme was made difficult in the context of the pandemic. Lack of time was a difficulty noted by participants too, especially when most meetings and exchanges were done remotely.*

## Time devoted to mentoring

*Managing the mentoring programme was not my main activity and it is difficult to estimate the amount of time devoted to this mission: a few days of preparation, communication and organisation over the duration of the programme.*

## Evaluation of the programme

*Despite the difficulties related to the health crisis, the programme's satisfaction ratings were really positive (over 80 per cent satisfaction) for both mentors and mentees.*

*The mentees indicated that they were able to take a step back with the help of their mentors, gained confidence and improved their managerial posture after this first experience. The mentors also indicated that they had developed their active listening posture and appreciated being able to see their mentee evolve. After this pilot experience, we launched a second cohort with more mentors and mentees, and all the previous mentors (except one) offered to accompany new mentees again.*

## Lessons learned

This company's mentoring programme was managed internally by an HR manager, assisted by an external professional, in the context of a difficult health crisis. This approach was strongly supported by the Executive Committee and general management, and promoted internally, notably through regular communication.

The tasks delegated to the external professional were:

- the facilitation of a mentoring discovery workshop (2 hours)
- training the internal pilot and the CEO (half day)
- training of mentors and mentees during a launch day (1 day)
- separate meetings for mentors and mentees (half day)
- evaluation of the process and collective presentation of the results during the closing day (2 hours).

More and more organisations wish to make mentoring accessible to all employees. As they must deal with a greater number of pairs, some have decided to hire a full-time mentoring project manager (and sometimes a whole team, in the case of high turnover, to avoid losing information) to handle all mentoring activities. Recently, in France, many institutions have been designated to implement a government-funded programme dedicated to helping young people with their orientation and employment issues (the '*1jeune-1mentor*' initiative). We were recently asked by one of them to train their new hired Mentoring Project Manager, Gérard Druelle from GIP Réussir, whose task is to implement a whole programme for 120 mentees per year.

### Bringing together and facilitating exchanges within the steering committee

The success of the mentoring programme depends on the quality of the exchanges between all the stakeholders involved in the programme. One of the mentoring manager's first tasks is to set up a steering committee and to bring together all the department managers with whom they will be working: communications, human resources, management, etc.

An example of these tasks is provided by Tammy Allen:[140]

> As an example, one of the companies we interviewed has an executive steering committee, consisting of the programme sponsor and several other senior executives, that meets quarterly to discuss how the mentoring programme is working, see how the relationships between the pairs are evolving, identify any difficulties, and provide solutions to identified problems. The committee also receives periodic feedback on the challenges and experiences of the mentors and provides assistance as needed.

# Qualified professionals

In summary, the knowledge and skill set required of the mentoring expert or internal project manager revolves around the following skills and abilities.

- Knowledge of mentoring: definitions, specificities, principles, philosophy, techniques.
- Project management: managing a complex project with numerous stakeholders.
- Ability to communicate, convince and mobilise, to get everyone on board and to obtain support over time.
- Facilitation/mediation to ensure the 'smooth running' of the pairs and good relations with all stakeholders.
- Knowledge of tools and methods of coaching and pedagogy to ensure the training of mentors and mentees.

As an example, Cap Mentorat produced a summary of the skills required for this new function, as seen in Figure 19.2:

---

140 Allen T.D., Finkelstein, L. and Poteet, M. (2009) *Designing Workplace Mentoring Programs*, Chichester, UK: Talent Management Essentials, Wiley-Blackwell.

**Figure 19.2** The skills framework of the mentoring programme manager[141]

| COMPETENCIES | KNOWLEDGE | SKILLS | ATTITUDES |
|---|---|---|---|
| Designing a mentoring programme. | Explaining the fundamentals of mentoring, its specificities and differences from other forms of professional support. | Analysing the issues and needs of public or private organisations. | Adapting behaviours and attitudes to all stakeholders to optimise the quality of your exchanges. |
| Implementing a programme over time and following all steps. | | Conceiving a comprehensive programme meeting the needs of the organisation. | Questioning, rephrasing, making sure you understand the need. |
| Bringing support throughout a programme. | Building a mentoring programme and knowing all the steps involved. | Writing a proposal. | Uniting around common objectives. |
| Adapting to each organisation. | Knowing about mentoring tools and coaching techniques. | Presenting effectively both in writing and orally. | Regulating, facilitating and resolving difficulties. |
| | Knowing how to facilitate meetings and working groups. | Mastering communication skill. | |
| | Knowing how mentors and mentees need to be trained. | Assisting in defining an objective and defining result indicators. | |
| | Designing and maintaining follow-up dashboards and providing regular feedback on the progress of the programme. | Building and giving effective training programmes for mentors and mentee. | |
| | | Suggesting pairs recruitment methods. | |
| | Developing a budget, optimising it and monitoring it (cost control, envelope monitoring, etc.). | Setting the framework and enforcing it. | |
| | | Managing communication for all programme stakeholders. | |
| | Knowing about evaluation method. | Prioritising and establishing actions according to the programme's challenges. | |

141  Danielle Deffontaines and Dominique Cancellieri-Decroze (2020) *Le Mentorat Mode d'emploi*, Le Mans, France: Editions Gereso.

# Developing a training offer

Today, this knowledge, know-how and interpersonal skills in mentoring can be acquired through training. Below is a description of the training offered by Cap Mentorat. The aim of this training is to provide the necessary knowledge to those who wish to develop a new skill, in order to manage a mentoring programme in any type of structure.

---

**Sample content for mentoring programme managers' training**

**Training objectives**
- Understand what mentoring is, its objectives and its applications.
- Define a project to implement mentoring within an organisation.
- Structure a mentoring programme.
- Facilitate and evaluate the programme.

**Content abstracts**
- The definition of mentoring, the differences, and specificities between mentoring and other types of support.
- The various mentoring actors.
- The components of a mentoring programme and the conditions for its success.
- Diagnosis methods, recommendations, support for decision-making.
- Designing a framework for a mentoring programme.
- Recruiting mentors and mentees, forming pairs.
- Training mentors and mentees.
- Communicating about mentoring.
- Problem solving.
- Monitoring and evaluating the progress of the programme.
- Mentor–mentee contract, ethical charter, operating rules.
- Supporting mentors and mentees over time.
- Evaluation tools.

---

# A role to be valued

In today's increasingly competitive business environment, external or internal mentoring programme managers must constantly prove their usefulness and demonstrate the ROI (return on investment) of the processes they organise and supervise (see Chapter 11). Their intervention makes it possible to organise effective and sustainable programmes. In organisations where the resources devoted to the development of individuals are limited, mentoring programme specialists can become indispensable assets for implementing innovative and qualitative approaches that have powerful impacts on individual and collective development. It is therefore important that these professionals feel supported and valued. If all participants perceive this support, the individual and collective benefits of mentoring will be more tangible and its results more effective.

Many companies or organisations still wish to embark on the mentoring adventure without qualified professionals, which in the end is a waste of time, energy and money. However, sometimes all it takes is one qualified person to make it work. With the growing demand for mentoring in all areas, we can hope that the situation will change in the near future.

# 20 Mentoring at Bristol Myers Squibb in Brazil

*Cicero Carvalho, coach, mentor,*
*Senior Partner MentoringCo*

## Case background

As we saw in Chapter 1, a mentor acts with a coaching attitude when they believe their client knows more than they think. Often this attitude is not properly channelled within organisations. Below, we shall discover an excellent example of implementing an organisational mentoring programme with a coaching attitude.

The practice of mentoring in Brazil, as well as in several other Latin American countries, has become an increasingly frequent phenomenon. The case presented refers to a large biopharmaceutical company in which I had the joy of being able to contribute for two years.

Bristol Myers Squibb (BMS) is a centenary American biopharmaceutical company that has been operating for almost 80 years in Brazil and has a great reputation within the global and local market.

BMS recognises the value of their high-performing employees as a key competitive advantage and they would like to accelerate the development of talents that represent diversity, such as women in leadership roles in the commercial area.

To support this critical need to develop diverse leadership in rapidly changing conditions, internal talent assessment was used as the first round of criteria for participant selection. For BMS, mentoring became a key component to the overall leadership development approach. In particular, mentoring is being used as a catalyst in accelerating skills and competencies across the organisation.

## The process

Broadly speaking, the programme had some important milestones that made it a great success:

1 **Goal and sponsor** – from the beginning it was defined that the general development of minds and the acceleration of talents that represented

diversity would be the main pillars. The President and the Leadership Team then became the sponsors, setting the tone from the top of the programme's importance.

2 **Selection** and capability building – the mentors and mentees chosen for the programme participated in training on roles and responsibilities and best practices for a successful mentoring relationship. Part of this workshop included a group activity to introduce mentors to the potential mentees, similar to a 'speed dating' dynamic, where each mentor was given a minute to share their experiences and areas of expertise. At the end of this session, each mentee could select up to three preferred potential mentors.

3 **Matching mentoring pairs** – based on the mentees' development objectives and their selected three preferred mentors, Human Resources made the match between mentors and mentees. With this, each mentor received a list of their mentees, for a final validation.

4 **Preparation** – after this stage of finetuning, both groups received a kick-off communication, detailing the programme's timelines and supporting resources, such as opening questions for the first meeting. A maximum date of 12 months or 9 meetings was set for the process to develop.

5 **Action and evaluation** – the one-on-one mentoring sessions began soon after the performance evaluation discussions, where each mentee had defined their development plan with their managers. A survey was held in the middle and closing of the programme, to assess the evolution and gather feedback to improve future cohorts.

# The challenges

Talking to the Human Resources Director, she commented that some points were challenging for the good running and, mainly, the sustaining of this type of programme in the medium and long term. These included the following points.

- Number of mentees compared with mentors – finding an appropriate balance between the number of people who want to be mentees versus the number of mentors who can commit to this extra activity in their routine, was the first point raised.

- Agenda to preparation – this was another challenging point, with much work involved in getting together an agenda for such a diverse audience, with activities that occupy much of the day, adding a time for selection, matching, etc.

- Keeping pace – as seen in Chapter 4, a strong presence is one of the keys to the good continuity of the mentoring process. In the case of BMS, especially after the first few years, maintaining the cadence, the time available and the level of engagement can be challenging, and relies a lot on mentees' accountability to schedule their encounters.

# The outcomes

BMS knew that measuring the mentoring outcomes could provide insight as to the effectiveness of this strategy against their goals and would dictate the frequency and scope of future programme rollouts. In Chapter 11, we discussed the ROI calculation. Although I cannot share the exact numbers because of internal compliance, in general, the main outcomes shared by the HR Director were these:

- Keeping track of the promotions, it was noticed there was an increase in representation and a reduction in the gap in diversity representation, such as gender in the leadership team, especially in the commercial area.
- Improved relationships in management and increased self-confidence in mentees were noted, as well as a series of new insights generated in senior executives which came from younger mentees.
- After a year of the programme, many pairs of mentors and mentees continued to meet in a more informal way; this generated benefits for everyone, including for the company.

# The lessons learned

Despite recognising a great success in the implementation of this programme, the HR Director agreed that some points could be improved in their approach:

- Instead of asking the leadership team to nominate the mentees in their respective areas, the application should be spontaneous on the part of the mentee – aligned to their development plan.
- Blocking out time in people's calendars, at the very beginning of the sessions, is helpful to ensure a good cadence of meetings during the year.
- Implement some kind of technological support or application to be able to optimise the matching process, scheduling of sessions and a place to store insights and annotations.

Generally speaking, everyone at BMS is proud to be part of the company, especially those professionals who have been able to participate in the mentoring programme. When there is a defined goal, a strong sponsor and a well-structured process, the benefits for individuals and the organisation are immense. The BMS example is a good illustration of this principle.

# 21 A mentoring case in the Middle East-based corporation

*Raja'a Yousef Allaho, professional coach, mentor and supervisor*

## Introduction

Kuwait is a country with a 4.5 million population and organisations in Kuwait allocate huge budgets for training and development. Informal mentoring and coaching are tools in the employee development kit. Organisations in the oil sector, banks, private sector and telecommunications invest in coaching and mentoring. According to my own research and experience in working with these organisations, my findings are that there is no structured formal process in transferring knowledge and expertise from professionals to new and junior employees that achieve a return on the company investments in their staff. People in Kuwait retire at an early age of between 45 and 60, leaving their organisation with a wealth of knowledge and experience, not allocating the time and the process to transfer and develop others within their work context.

Based on my passion for developing others, and feeling a responsibility towards organisations in my country, I took on the role of implementing a professional coaching and mentoring programme in a leading organisation in Kuwait, to create a successful example for other companies to follow.

Mentoring is a learning relationship between two persons – mentor and mentee – which results in gaining learning and knowledge for the partners in this relationship by utilising coaching skills and competencies such as building rapport, active listening, asking questions, requesting and providing feedback for continuous development for the two partners – mentor and mentee – and providing a safe space for learning and reflections. These skills and competencies are part of the professional mentoring programme where we train participants in understanding and mastering the mentoring skills – applying mentoring with a coaching attitude to support organisations in creating a learning culture.

In the case study I am presenting in this chapter, Kuwait Oil Company was the first organisation that implemented the professional accredited mentoring programme in 2017. Today Kuwait Oil Company has a pool of certified and credentialled mentors.

I want to start my case study in the Middle East by presenting this story of Surah Al-Kahf from the Holy Quran, which we are requested to read every Friday to remind us about how we deal with the four main challenges in life: 1) dealing with personal faith/beliefs; 2) managing a healthy relationship with money/fortune; 3) coping with learning and knowledge; and finally, 4) qualities of leadership. AbdukalHaq Altuweel wrote the story in his article 'Principles of learning in the story of Moses and Al-Khidr, peace be upon them'.

## Principles of learning in the story of Moses and Al-Khidr[142]

Contemplation on the story of Moses and al-Khidr is mentioned in Surat Al-Kahf. A review of the course of its events and the solid indications and signs that it contained mainly related to the subject of learning. It can lead to the deduction of the essential principles and foundations upon which we can build our edifice as the foundation of our education. We aim to achieve quality and prepare learners whose main characteristics are diligence and perseverance in every educational act. Moses's story is a good reminder of what can be considered as a statement of the most important of these principles (numbers between brackets are referring to the verses of the holy Koran with Moses' words).

In the story related in the holy Koran, while walking, Moses told his servant that he would not cease traveling until he reaches the junction of the two seas or continue for a long time. At the junction, they forgot their fish, and while passing beyond it and feeling the fatigue, Moses asked the boy to bring his morning meal. He also asked him if he had noticed that they had forgotten the fish. Moses said: "None made me forget it except Satan - that I should mention it" (63). Deciding to go back following their footprints, they found Al-Khidhr, another servant who could transfer some knowledge and Moses asked him if he could follow him on the condition that he would teach him what he had been taught of sound judgment.

When Al-Khidhr asked Moses if he would be patient with him, Moses answered: "You will find me, if Allah wills, patient, and I will not disobey you in [any] order". (69) The servant accepted that Moses follows him. When embarking on the ship, Al-Khidhr tore it open, and Moses told him that he had done a "grave thing" (71). The servant reminded him that he had promised to have patience. Moses asked then Al-Khidhr not to blame him for what

142 AbdukalHaq Altuweel: www.alukah.net/social/0/126135

he had forgotten. On their way, they met a boy that Al-Khidr killed. Here again, Moses reacted strongly, stating that he had certainly killed a pure soul and that it was unfortunate. Again, Al-Khidhr reminded him that he had pledged to have patience, but Moses told him not to keep him as a companion if he wouldn't have questioned him about the boy. Getting on their walk, they reached a town and asked people for food, but they refused to offer them hospitality. A bit later, they found a wall that was about to collapse and Al-Khidhr restored it. When Moses told him that he was surprised that Al-Khidhr didn't take any salary for the work done, he answered that Moses was still missing patience. Then he started providing explanations: the ship belonged to poor people that he had to protect against a king who was seizing every good ship by force; the boy was the son of believers and could have overburdened them by transgression and disbelief. He said: "So, we intended that their Lord should substitute for them one better than him in purity and nearer to mercy" (81). Finally, the wall belonged to two orphan boys in the city and was containing a treasure for them, but the Lord preferred that they reach maturity before benefitting from it. Al-Khidhr concluded: "I did it not of my own accord. That is the interpretation of that about which you could not have patience". (82)

What are the learnings on mentoring we can draw from this story?

## Sacrifice for the sake of learning

That is because Moses left his family, companions, and his country and went out seeking knowledge to a destination that only the Knower of the Unseen, Glorified and Exalted be He, knows. In his Sahih, on the authority of Ubayy bin Ka'b, God said: The Messenger of God addressed us and said: 'Moses stood as a preacher among the Children of Israel, and he was asked: Which people know best? God to him: I have a servant in the complex of Bahrain who is more knowledgeable than you; Moses said: O Lord, how can I meet with him? He said: You take a whale with you and put it in a lump, so sacrifice and hardship are necessary wherever the whale is lost.'

*Reflection*

The importance of science and learning should be explained and the learners should be encouraged to spend time and effort on learning for personal and professional development .

## The need for a helper

When Moses decided to go out to seek knowledge, he chose a boy to accompany him. He is Joshua bin Nun, whose job was to carry provisions, prepare food, and do other things that if the student of knowledge did himself, he might miss valuable learning time.

*Reflection*

The need to learn by joining and being a team member, to be supported in your learning journey and emphasis on the team spirit – Learning Teams.

## An unbridled desire to learn

That is because Moses, despite his high status, his knowledge and his support for revelation from God Almighty, complied with the direction of his Lord and went out looking for the man (Al-Khidr) whom he would teach, and he was eager and eager to find him, which was achieved at the rock. Where the whale was lost, as soon as it was found, it made its request, saying: Moses said to him, 'May I follow you on [the condition] that you teach me from what you have been taught of sound judgement?' AlKahf (66). Emphasising his desire and eagerness [Moses] said, 'You will find me, if Allah wills, patient, and I will not disobey you in [any] order.' AlKahf (69).

*Reflection*

One of the most critical responsibilities of a mentor is to motivate their mentee to learn – the desire to continue learning and make a difference between people is the degree of learning, considering it the responsibility and a mission.

## Humility

When Moses met Al-Khidr, he did not crudely say to him: I am Moses, a prophet among the Children of Israel, and God sent me to you to teach me, so teach me! He did not say that, but instead, he asked for it with kindness and gentleness in complete humility: Moses said to him, 'May I follow you on [the condition] that you teach me from what you have been taught. Of sound judgement?' AlKahf (66).

*Reflection*

Essential ethics for the learner–mentee must include humility and respect.

## Contracting

This is because successful learning opens with an agreement between the teacher and their learners about the conditions and mechanisms of learning. So that each party knows what they have and what they owe, without exaggeration or negligence, he said, 'Then if you follow me, do not ask me about anything until I make to you about it mention.' AlKahf (70) Moses accepted that and said, 'You will find me, if Allah wills, patient, and I will not disobey you in [any] order.' It was agreed, and the educational journey began.

*Reflection*

Having a mentoring agreement as part of a professional relationship will support and organise the learning relationship between the mentor and mentee. It is a reference point that clarifies partners' roles, responsibilities, goals and processes, and minimises conflict opportunities.

## The combination of what is theoretical and what is practical

This is because Al-Khidr did not sit down, and Musa taught him what God wanted him to teach him but took him to the field; to show him after the trials (breaking the ship, killing the boy, building the wall), believing that what Moses will hear and what he will inevitably see will be firmly entrenched in his mind, unlike if he was only communicating knowledge.

*Reflection*

The importance of applying and utilising a variety of tools in mentoring, based on the learner style and personality triads.

## Be patient and wait

It is important not to rush to deny or interrupt the teacher until they finish their speech: because any address may have an apparent and an inward meaning. They got what they wanted.

*Reflection*

It is vital to develop professional mentors who understand and practise mentoring ethics and competencies and are role models for the mentees.

## Respect the learner and allow them to learn

This is because when Moses denied boarding the ship out of forgetfulness, Al-Khidr did not directly exclude him from learning but gave him another opportunity for Moses to repeat his denying what is worse than the breach, which is the killing of the boy without an apparent excuse, forgetting him again to get the last chance after his apology and his request for forgiveness from him: [Moses] said, 'If I should ask you about anything after this, then do not keep me as a companion. You have obtained from me an excuse.' AlKahf (76).

*Reflection*

Mentoring ethics – being patient and understanding about learning styles and personality styles.

## Respecting and appreciating the teacher

This is because Al-Khidr was treated sublimely by Moses, from the beginning of the educational journey to its end. Where we found Moses at the beginning asking to follow his teacher as mentioned above, with kindness and leniency, without imposing or exploiting the position of his prophethood, then once he forgot and denounced what he did not deny, he proceeded to apologise with complete humility without scorn or boredom, and in that of appreciation and respect for Al-Khidr.

*Reflection*

Mentoring ethics – understand and practise mentoring ethics in respecting your mentees.

## Satisfying the learner's desire and putting an end to their confusion

This is because Al-Khidr did not leave Moses until he explained to him every-thing that was hidden from him, thus bringing an end to all the questions that circulated in his student's mind and exhausting his mind. It can provide us with this, a model for the successful teacher, and the dedication that should be on him in the performance of his duty, to explain and clarify tirelessly despite boredom, even in the most challenging circumstances.

*Reflection*

Being a mentor is a mission motivated by passion and responsibility. Building a relationship based on a win–win relationship is essential for each mentoring relationship.

## An Arabic definition of mentoring

The EMCC has a clear definition of mentoring (see Part 1) but the Arabic culture provides us with another one (literal translation): '*Assist individu-als to increase and integrate their growth in the areas they wish to enrol in*' (Ibn Manthoor, 1232–1311). This definition aligns learning and development for individuals with their interest, passion and willingness. The mentor's role is to support mentees in defining their needs, interests and desires to ensure a continuous learning journey.

# Popular misconceptions about mentoring

In his publication *The Mentor Handbook* (2013) David E. Gray[143] presents popular misconceptions about mentoring. It is also valid for the Middle East; it was essential to design our solutions and practices to address these misconceptions in Mashar Professional Mentoring Programmes, our Middle East culture.

### Misconception 1: A mentor has the potential to exert power on the mentee

'One of the most common and troubling myths about mentoring is that a mentor can exert tremendous power over the mentee as a powerful and influential entity', David E. Gray said. Mentoring usually occurs between experienced senior professionals in superior positions and joiner fresh graduate professionals. It was a clear, challenging perception that we faced during mentoring training to work on understanding that being the expert is not necessarily to have the power over the mentee and to have all the answers. Understanding the professional mentoring relationship balances the partners' power and builds a healthy and professional mentoring relationship in a partnership which comprises mutual trust and respect.

### Misconception 2: The mentor is older than the mentee

'A common misunderstanding prevailing across the mentoring world is that a mentor is always an older, white-haired professional mentoring a relatively younger person', David E. Gray said. We overcome this misconception by including reverse mentoring in the programme curriculum to bridge the gap between the generations and encourage mentees to be effective partners in the mentoring relationship by playing the role of mentors in supporting senior employees and executives in the area of technology.

### Misconception 3: Mentoring is a time-consuming process

'Practice mentoring needs time, and we have limited time to complete our daily tasks' – this is what mentoring students usually say when discussing professional mentoring practice.

---

143 David E. Gray (2013) *The Mentor Handbook*, European Centre for Development of Vocational Training.

Another misconception is that mentoring is a time-consuming process. The duration of the mentoring process is variable, unique to the objectives the trainee wishes to achieve. Typically, individual mentoring sessions last between 1 and 2 hours. It was essential to work on this misconception by focusing on the following:

- Learn and understand the benefit of mentoring for mentors, mentees and the organisation.
- Mentees' and mentors' professional development should be linked with the performance evaluation by including mentoring practice/hours.

## Misconception 4: Mentoring is a one-way process

David E. Gray said, 'Potential mentors believe that mentoring as an intervention contributes only to the mentee's knowledge enhancement, leaving minimal benefit for the mentor. However, mentoring is a two-way street to success that offers a knowledge and experience exchange for the trainer/mentee, their mentor, and the organisation they are integral to.'

Understanding mentoring as a two-way learning process is essential for the mentors during their mentoring learning. Being open to learning from their mentees is a significant shift in their perception and supports them in building a relationship based on partnership.

## Misconception 5: Mentoring deals only with personal problems or has no limitations

In this misconception, David E. Gray said: 'The view which holds that mentoring has no limitations is a misconception, as is the idea that mentoring deals only with personal problems.' Generally, mentoring deals with specific professionally related issues faced by the mentee/trainee and provides a generic supportive mechanism for mentee/trainees to familiarise the novice mentee with the working environment of the organisation or department. It was essential to consider focusing on developing mentors' skills and competencies to work with and support their mentees in a holistic approach to professional and personal aspects.

## Misconception 6: Mentoring is a face-to-face process

David E. Gray said, 'Traditionally, mentoring is believed to be a face-to-face intervention. A mentoring relationship can be pursued via various modes of communication such as telephone, emails, and video conferencing.'

Due to the COVID-19 pandemic, during 2020 to 2021, coaching, training and mentoring moved from face-to-face to virtual interactions. These circumstances forced leadership and employees to accept the change, use technology in their daily interactions, meetings, mentoring, coaching and training, and to achieve great success in considering virtual forums and mentoring.

# The process developed for Kuwait Oil Company

Kuwait Oil Company (KOC) was established in 1934 by the Anglo-Persian Oil Company, known today as BP (British Petroleum), and Gulf Oil Corporation, now known as Chevron. Since its inception, KOC's activities have included exploration operations, onshore and offshore surveys, drilling of test wells, developing producing wells, and crude and natural gas exploration. In 1975, the Kuwait Government took 100 per cent control over Kuwait Oil Company and, by 1980, the Kuwait Petroleum Corporation was established to bring all state-owned oil companies under one entity.

Today, KOC continues to live up to its stated mission of exploring, developing and producing Kuwait's hydrocarbon resources for its customers worldwide in an environmentally sound and economically viable way. There are more than 8,000 employees working in the Kuwait Oil Company.

## Awareness sessions

Creating and marketing mentoring programmes in different organisations requires creating interest and linking the value of mentoring to achieve the company's vision, mission and strategies. I started meeting training and development managers in different organisations that apply to coaching and mentoring as part of their organisation development tools. I also present coaching and mentoring workshops to teach coaching and mentoring concepts: methodology and skills as an awareness workshop. We raised and discussed coaching and mentoring as development tools during the workshops. We gathered their feedback, suggestions and challenges in applying formal coaching and mentoring practices to develop their staff and peers.

### Workshop findings

After completing the first two awareness workshops, we can summarise our findings as follows:

- There was misunderstanding between coaching and mentoring.
- Coaching practices are informal mentoring where the senior-level staff coach (mentor) junior levels by giving advice and answering their questions.
- The mentoring sessions are completed as part of the performance evaluation process and do not measure the mentee's learning and knowledge transfer.
- There is no balance of power in the coaching (mentoring) relationship built according to seniority in positions and experience.
- There is no structured process for implementing the coaching (mentoring) practices.
- There is a need to learn mentoring skills and competencies (contracting, building relationships).

## Developing an accredited mentoring programme

Following the awareness workshops, we started developing a professional mentoring programme focusing on aligning mentoring engagements to achieve companies' goals and objectives. Also, we researched and gathered information from potential mentoring clients regarding the following:

* client's mentoring and coaching culture
* outcomes, feedback from the previous coaching and mentoring programmes/ workshops
* client's needs/challenges regarding developing newcomers, peers and talent pool.

The main success factor (criteria) of marketing and implementing a professional development programme in the Middle East is to achieve certification and accreditation from a professionally recognised global association for the programme. Organisations in the Middle East prefer to invest in these programmes to ensure the quality of the knowledge and learning for their employees.

Mashar coaching and training worked together with the EMCC to complete all the requirements to award the accreditation for the programme EMCC. Accredited programmes help us gain the trust and confidence of our clients, who constantly request high-quality programmes.

The Mashar training programme structure can be seen in Figure 21.1.

**Figure 21.1** Mashar Certified Professional Mentoring Programme

**Certified Professional Mentoring Programme** – Mashar Coaching and Training – Kuwait

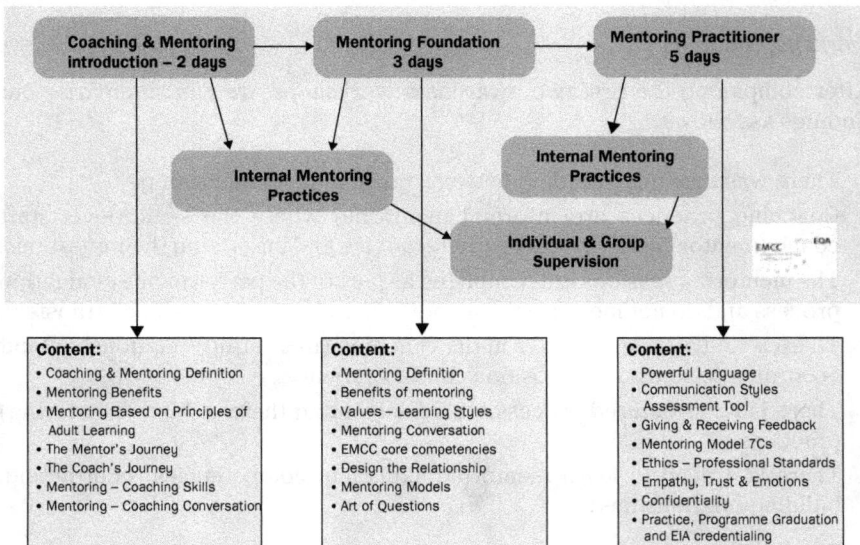

**Figure 21.2** Mentoring model related to EMCC Competencies

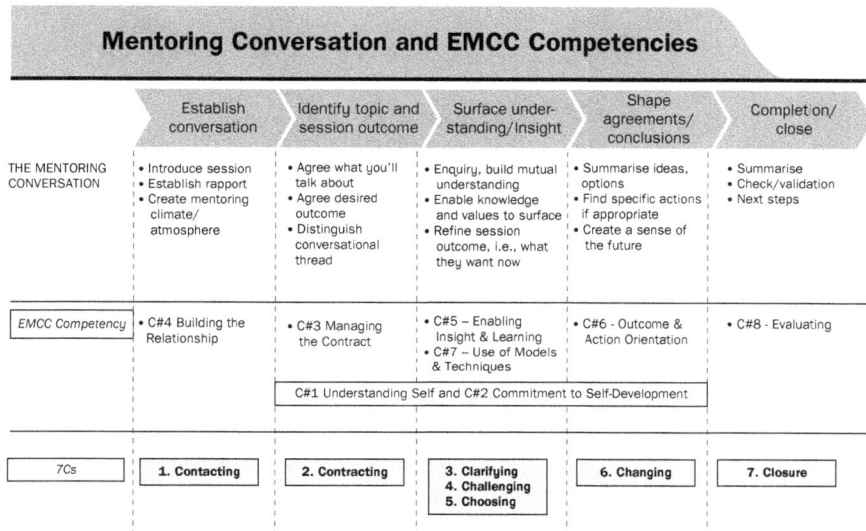

The KOC mentoring model (see Figure 21.2) was developed and adapted from the Oasis School of Humans and the 'Skilled Helper' model[144] (Egan, 2009). This model's 7Cs cover the seven mentoring steps: Contacting, Contracting, Clarifying, Challenging, Choosing, Changing and Closure. It focuses on the three main stages of the mentoring conversation process: exploration, creating new understanding and action planning.

KOC adapted the 7Cs model as the formal model for their mentoring practices. They developed all necessary automated processes for mentoring to be applied to all company staff and monitored electronically by mentors and leadership.

## Programme implementation

Our strategy as programme leaders is to support organisations in successfully implementing professional mentoring programmes as a step towards creating a learning culture. Our case study on Kuwait Oil Company included a group discussion and exercises during the first three programmes. For Foundation and Practitioner Programmes, we applied the following methodology:

- Request participants on each table to define challenges that work as barriers to mentoring methodologies and practices and list them on a flipchart.
- Each group will visit other groups' lists and add their suggested solutions to the challenges.

---

144  Oasis School of Human Relations 2003 & the 'Skilled Helper' model. Egan, G. (2009) *The Skilled Helper*, Belont, CA: Wadsworth Publishing.

- Each group will spend 15 minutes on other groups' lists to develop suggestions and solutions.
- At the end of the exercise, the main groups will return to their list, revising and finalising all the solutions and suggestions.
- Our responsibility as programme leaders is to communicate these challenges to the leadership and sponsors in the organisation to apply these recommendations as part of programme success.

## Kuwait Oil Company (KOC) challenges with mentoring

Creating a mentoring culture within the client's organisation is essential to ensure the success of mentoring initiatives and achieve programme objectives. In this framework, we faced a series of challenges where we engaged the programme's students and their leaders to develop suggested solutions for the challenges.

*Challenge #1: Marketing mentoring practices and communication (including tools)*

Sub-challenge: **Lack of awareness and understanding**
Sub-challenge: **Building mutual trust**
The solution proposed to address this first challenge included the following steps:

- Conduct awareness sessions at the group level at KOC (what is mentoring, its benefits, how will it help the group?).
- Training on mentoring for seniors and others who want to be or have the potential to be mentors – the goal is to increase the number of mentors and skill set of mentors (for both mentors and mentees).
- Organise a large-scale conference on mentoring.
- Go to other Kuwait oil companies and see how they are approaching the challenge of raising awareness of mentoring – get best practices to implement in KOC.
- Awareness of formal process for mentor and mentee.
- Public relations and information in KOC media about mentoring (Training and Development feeds information).
- Conferences and workshops (interactive, internal).
- Best Practice Forum (annually focus on achievements).
- Conduct annual forums (current best practices, success stories, etc.).
- Introduce mentoring like Health, Safety and Environment – HSE moment for every meeting.
- Relate mentoring to KOC strategies/values.
- Utilise KOC intranet (website) in introducing mentoring.
- Present mentoring in Tuesday Talks through video clip, 1–2 minutes.

- ToolBox talks.
- Create a mentoring logo.
- Design and create brochures/pamphlets about mentoring.

## Challenge #2: Prioritise mentoring

Suggested solutions to overcome this challenge were:

- To add mentoring as part of the annual Key Performance Indicators (KPIs) in measuring managers' and team leaders' performance.
- To be part of QPR (Quarterly Performance Review) for managers.
- To be part of promotion requirements for senior employees and mentors in completing a certain number of mentor hours for under training – UT/Under development – UD.
- To include completed mentor hours as part of SOP (Summary of Performance – financial end of the year).
- To include mentoring as part of a Personal Development Plan – PDP.

## Challenge #3: Effective use of workforce resources

To overcome this challenge, we suggested the following solutions:

- Build criteria to see who is eligible to be part of the professional mentoring pool.
- Establish a process and procedure (how mentor chooses mentee, include an entire mechanism for all KOC, roles, responsibilities, etc.); have a flow chart of the process and this responsibility for training and career development.
- Develop an action plan scheduled for procedure and mentors (related to KPIs).
- All to be supervised and initiated by the leadership (aligned with roles and responsibilities of the procedure).
- Follow-up left to planning and support groups responsible for following up on KPIs.
- Bring in a specialised company to conduct training for mentors and mentees.
- Exchange mentors between Kuwait oil companies in technical areas.

## Challenge #4: Recognition

Solution: It is important to develop adequate incentives to enhance the overall motivation. We, therefore, proposed a list of incentives, including the following:

- Adding in financial incentives.
- Recognition of performance-based achievement.

- Appreciation in team meetings (weekly or fortnightly) with team leader approval.
- Recognise in KOC media and communication (publishing photos, achievements, etc.), announcing certified mentors to motivate others to be professional mentors.
- Mentoring accreditation supported by KOC.
- A pool of expertise for all Kuwait oil companies.
- Presenting a success story through the conference, internal media or another form of communication.

### Challenge #5: Sustainability

The 7Cs process for mentors was used for sustainability and to increase this, we suggested a series of solutions:

- Standardising analysing and measuring indicators (so all mentors are working on the same page and using the same tools).
- Continuous analysing and encouraging feedback.
- Customise the KOC process from the 7Cs (including contracting, feedback, clarifying, etc.).
- Creating a database based on a 'structure of the job training' (SJOT) for mentees and mentors through training and career development.
- Adding mentoring strategy to the 2040 KOC strategy.
- Ensure top management commitment over time (possibly through KPIs and other tools).
- Develop a recognition programme for mentors and mentees.

# Conclusion and lessons learned

From this business experience of the mentoring work at Kuwait Oil Company, we can draw some conclusions.

First and foremost, it is crucial to obtain top leadership approval and support in investing and implementing the mentoring methodology. The investment in the mentoring initiative must relate to the return on investment to measure the value and benefits of mentoring on organisation objectives and goals.

Applying mentoring as part of the employee's development methodologies will improve learning and development skills for employees at all levels of the organisation.

Also, mentoring practices are a good way to develop the partnership between mentoring parties and create learning opportunities for mentors and mentees. They are a good way to support building a professional relationship based on trust and respect.

Moreover, when implementing a new methodology such as mentoring it is essential to create awareness among company employees. This can happen by conducting workshops and one-day events to ensure an acceptable level of understanding about mentoring and customising the implanting plan, based on the readiness and capabilities of the staff.

And, finally, it is of vital importance to provide supervision sessions for the programme attendees to support them in their learning journey.

# 22 Mentoring with a coaching attitude in Médecins Sans Frontières

*Wiet Vandormael, Mentoring and Coaching Programme Manager MSF, Mentor and Coach, and Aurélien Marechal, Logistics Workforce Coordinator, Mentor and Coach*

Over the past few years, various mentoring initiatives have flourished across the different Médecins Sans Frontières (MSF) Operational Centres, aiming to support managers in the field in a timely way so they can better contribute to the success of MSF operations. Since 2012, the mentoring offer has been consistently tried and tested by Operational Centre Brussels (OCB) and today, it is widely recognised as a valued tool in supporting and developing MSF staff in key positions while on the job. Currently, all five[145] MSF operational centres are running their own mentoring programme. Knowledge and findings are shared among the different programmes, which helps to improve our practice and our offer. Most MSF mentoring programmes today rest on the same principles and mechanisms. The MSF Mentoring Programme is open to all MSF staff.

## History of mentoring in MSF

Mentoring has probably existed from the very beginnings of MSF: experienced staff members supporting new staff to understand their role and the ins and outs of the organisation. However, the first structured offer for mentoring began in Geneva and Barcelona around 2007. Mentors were sent to the

---

145 Geneva, Brussels, Amsterdam, Paris and Barcelona. Upcoming Operational Centres will be included soon (Western African Central African Section (WACA); Southeast Asian Australia Pacific Section; South African Section; and others will follow).

field to accompany first-time coordinators in their new roles and responsibilities. In 2012 the mentoring programme of MSF in Brussels was introduced and is now the 'model' that is commonly offered across the organisation. Today mentoring and coaching are embedded in the organisational culture. It is increasingly used as an additional resource for learning, good management and leadership.

# Mentoring in MSF

With several definitions available for mentoring, MSF sees mentoring as a process of learning from a senior colleague. The mentor supports the development of the mentee using a self-discovery approach and provides advice when appropriate, shares knowledge and experiences. The mentoring relationship accompanies the mentees while they address issues in their work environment. While the mentor does not fix issues in the project/mission, the mentor does help the mentee to identify their own solutions, remaining outside the mentee's management line.

Within the learning and development approach of MSF, it is aligned to the 10-20-70 model, where 10 per cent of learning takes place in formal learning environments, 20 per cent in peer-to-peer discussions and exchanges (social learning) and 70 per cent on the job. MSF believes that mentoring and coaching has an impact on both the 20 per cent and the 70 per cent. Creating the space for people to learn and develop on the job is the main focus of the 'Coach mindset in management' programme that was launched in early 2022 and will be discussed below.

Mentoring with a coaching attitude is part of the MSF strategy to change organisational culture. All the mentors and coaches involved in the MSF programme are MSF employees. A core of specific abilities, like active listening, powerful questioning, unlearning triangle or feedback, is taught to the participants of the mentoring and coaching programmes.

Mentoring and coaching for the Brussels Section aims to have an impact on both an individual's professional development and the organisational culture.

Continued learning and development enhances the capabilities and capacities of all staff and the entire organisation: how meetings are run, the type of conversations had, and the level of responsibilities people are taking, including for their own development.

A coaching and mentoring culture exists in MSF when all staff and other stakeholders experience a coaching and mentoring approach as a key aspect of how engagement takes place. This will be true at all levels and in all functions, and the result will be increased individual, team and organisational learning, enhanced performance, high levels of engagement and a sense of shared value for all stakeholders.

# Key concepts of mentoring in MSF

Coaching and mentoring are complementary to other personal and professional development initiatives. Both mentoring and coaching are based on the principles of voluntarism, confidentiality and non-interference (see Chapters 1 and 11). In addition, there is a strict policy to avoid any conflict of interest between mentors/coaches and their mentee/coachee.

### Voluntarism

The element of choice is all-important for mentoring and coaching to be successful and for talent development to really happen. The openness to questioning oneself and being challenged that is necessary for genuine learning can only happen with commitment from mentees.

### Confidentiality

Trust is essential between mentor and mentee, at a time when the mentee is taking on a challenge, such as starting in a new position. The mentee must feel confident that their welfare and development is primary to the mentor/mentee relationship.

### Non-interference with Operations

Mentors guide mentees in their analysis of the situations they face in their work, and they are clear that the responsibility for decisions rest with mentees and their line managers.

# Mentoring process

At the start of the process, the mentee undertakes a self-appraisal where they reflect on the transversal competencies needed for the role they will take on. During this exercise they indicate a few top priorities they wish to work on with the mentor. This, in combination with their development goals, forms the basis of the mentoring relationship. Throughout the mentoring relationship the mentee can choose to engage with their respective HR referents and/or line management and align with their goals and objectives.

Once the objectives are clear for the mentee, the mentoring programme manager takes the time for a one-on-one conversation to explain the programme, the broad goals of mentoring, and explores specific preferences with regards to the potential mentor.

Based on this induction, the programme manager proposes two mentors for the mentee to contact to initiate a discovery conversation to get to know each other. Consequently, the mentee decides which mentor to start the relationship with and informs both mentors and programme manager about the decision.

Both the line manager and HR referent are then informed by the programme manager about the relationship and the main principles.

During the relationship both mentor and mentee can make use of a set of tools to structure their relationship. Initially, there is the mutual agreement outlining the atmosphere they wish to create, setting the objectives and necessary logistics (frequency, communication means, etc). At the midpoint of the relationship there is a moment to give each other feedback, through a prescribed list of questions. In closing the relationship, a structured debrief is available to support the transition.

Throughout the relationship they are reminded of the above structure and the objectives of the mentoring.

# Quality assurances

### Collaboration and guidance

From the onset of the programme in 2012, MSF has been guided by the EMCC when it comes to building the mentoring education and impact evaluations. In 2021, the introduction to the mentoring workshop was EQA[146] Practitioner level accredited, as well as the coaching education and the coaching skills workshop for managers. This collaboration also led to MSF being rewarded the gold level ISMCP[147] accreditation, first in 2017 and again in 2020.

In addition, MSF and the EMCC have worked on enabling MSF mentors and coaches to apply for EIA accreditation as part of their continued collaboration and intention to further professionalise the in-house mentoring and coaching programme.

### Impact evaluation

In September 2017, MSF Mentoring and Coaching Hub (MCHub), Oslo, Norway, commissioned a two-year impact study[148] of how mentoring supports the personal and professional development of MSF Field Managers and contributes more broadly to the strategic priorities of the MCHub. The intention is that this study will inform the ongoing monitoring of the MCHub's mentoring programme and provide a framework and model from which other Operational Centres can implement and adapt to evaluate mentoring impact/s. It is hoped that this study and subsequent engagement across the movement will secure the MCHub as a centre of excellence and best practice in mentoring. The study was conducted by JHM Professional Development Consultancy, chaired by Dr Julie Haddock-Millar.

The research team adopted a mixed method longitudinal approach, encompassing the views of mentees, mentors and key stakeholders. The research

146 EMCC Global Quality Award for Coach/Mentor Training
147 International Standards for Mentoring and Coaching Programmes
148 https://mentoring-coaching.msf.org/wp-content/uploads/2019/08/MSF-MCHub-Mentoring-Impact-Evaluation-FINAL-Short-Report.pdf

engaged participants involved in the mentoring programme since the beginning of 2014, with significant participation results. Mixed methods included an online survey for mentees and mentors (27 per cent and 48 per cent participation), semi-structured interviews with matched mentees and mentors, in addition to non-matched participants and key stakeholders (18 per cent and 52 per cent participation). Participants also provided visual representations as metaphors to demonstrate the impact of mentoring.

Overall, the results show that the mentoring programme is having a positive impact on mentees in supporting their personal and professional development. The most valuable outcomes relate to increased self-esteem, confidence, leadership and management capability. This also has a positive impact on mentees' intention to stay with MSF at the end of their mission. Knowledge transfer between mentees and mentors is evident as mentors also benefit by seeing how the mentee finds certain solutions for a dilemma or challenge. Emerging opportunities for improvement include the development of a community of practice for programme participants, specific training and tools to address mentees' needs in the field, and fully harnessing results of current and future programme evaluations.

The recommendations of the study led MSF to work on the following topics:

- Strategic positioning of mentoring within MSF: in 2020, the Strategic Orientations of MSF describe the need for coaching and mentoring to be at the cornerstone of their management culture. Furthermore, during the last two years, the programme offer has increased so more staff can now seek the support of a mentor, focusing on increasing the variety of languages, and cultural and gender diversity in both mentors and mentees.
- Wellbeing and self-care for field workers: mentors have received a module on self-care and psycho-social support since the beginning of 2020. Other continued professional development (CPD) options are available to the mentors and some of them focus on the wellbeing of staff members in the field.
- Professionalisation: EIA accreditation is now being offered to mentors with a set of requirements. Continued evaluation of the programme is structured through a pre and post relationship survey. Results of the survey are shared, and the programme adapted accordingly. Lastly, several CPD activities are being set up (group supervision, mentoring café, community of practice and webinars).

## ISMCP golden award

The MSF mentoring and coaching programme has received twice (2017 and 2020) the International Standards for Mentoring & Coaching Programmes (ISMCP) golden award. This accreditation adds both substance and credibility to programmes, and bolsters internal business cases for employee development. The framework ensures programmes are designed to align with participant and business objectives, under the professional umbrella of the EMCC Global standards and Global Code of Ethics. It helps us create a qualitative structure that adheres to international standards.

MSF is proud to be awarded this accreditation and uses the feedback to continue improving and monitoring the quality of its mentoring programme.

## Evolution to the coach mindset in management

In addition to the work done by the MSF Learning and Development unit on leadership and management, mentoring and coaching is complementary to the shift set in motion after the People Development and HR Strategic Orientations highlighted the need for the MSF manager to possess mentoring and coaching skills when leading and growing MSF individuals, teams and relationships. In 2021 a project was launched to further define how MSF OCB defines the concept of the MSF leader.

The 'coach mindset in management' concept refers to a manager or supervisor serving as a coach, facilitator or mentor of learning in the workplace setting (70 per cent learning), in which they enact specific behaviours that enable their employee to learn and develop. Managerial coaching can be highly structured but is often considered to be an informal learning strategy by managers to help employees learn, grow and improve their performance. Despite the importance of coaching as a managerial activity, the 'managerial coach' is often a rare species and 'managers infrequently engage in coaching'. Managers vary in their willingness, competencies and skills to be a manager coach. Yet for those managers who do perceive themselves as managerial coaches, or want to be, a 'coaching mindset' or a set of beliefs about being a managerial coach are considered to be necessary prerequisites, along with specific skills and capabilities that enable the manager to coach effectively.

Ellinger and Bostrom (1999)[149] and Beatie (2002)[150] taxonomies identified managerial coaching behaviours that included both empowering and facilitating behaviours. We have been inspired by this, resulting in the following:

- Which behaviours allow you to support staff in developing their reflection and problem-solving capacity?
  - Reflective or prospective thinking
  - Working it out together: talking it through
  - Using analogies, scenarios and examples
  - Stepping in to shift perspectives
  - Broadening team members, perspectives – getting them to see things differently

149 Ellinger, A.D. and Bostrom, R.P. (1999) Managerial coaching behaviours in learning organizations. *Journal of Management Development*, 18(9): 752–771.

150 Beatie, R. S. (2002) *Line managers as facilitators of learning: Empirical evidence from voluntary sector.* Proceedings of 2002 human resource development research and practice across Europe conference. Napier University, Edinburgh, January.

- Which behaviours can secure and support team members?
  - Being a resource – removing obstacles – sharing knowledge
  - Caring: support, encouragement, approachable, reassurance, commitment/involvement, empathy
  - Setting and communicating expectations – fitting into the bigger picture
- Which behaviours can give more autonomy to staff?
  - Transferring ownership to team members – delegation/trust
  - Holding back – listen more, talk less
- Which behaviours can foster a learning environment?
  - Providing feedback to team members
  - Soliciting feedback from team members
  - Creating and promoting a learning environment
  - Engaging others to facilitate learning
  - Challenge team members to stretch themselves

Other studies point out that these managers believed that coaching employees and facilitating their development is their role and what they are expected to do.

MSF has identified coaching and mentoring skills that can enable managers to create such a coaching mindset. Of course, these skills need to be translated into practice and be accompanied by behaviours that enable managers to perform in a 'coach mindset in management' capacity.

# In practice, the Field Recentralisation project (FRC)

Field Recentralisation is the change process towards an organisation (OCB) that puts decision-making as close as possible to the medical-humanitarian act and its beneficiaries.

In the past decade, MSF has grown both in size and complexity. Our operational responses have become more technical and diverse. The places where we work are more and more volatile, uncertain and complex.

The aim is to place the centre of decision-making – as much as possible – with those closest to our beneficiaries and communities, putting our project teams firmly in the centre of the organisation.

Initially, the team was given the mandate to work on possible new models to support MSF operations in Southern Africa, while following the implementation of a new set-up for the Italy mission. Currently, the Central Africa region is undergoing a similar process.

In essence, the FRC's key characteristics are:

- **Tailor made**: The structure is adapted according to the needs/reality of the projects in a particular region. There is not one model for all.
- **Subsidiarity**: Decisions are taken as close to the patient/humanitarian act as possible and grounded in context reality.

- **Consultation principle**: Teams are autonomous, yet not independent, with a duty to collect the necessary expertise/knowledge to be able to take an informed decision.
- **Accountability**: Clarification of who will take which decisions/has final responsibility, and at what time.
- **Distributed teams**: Aiming to maximise added value of MSF capacities existing in the region, working together in a network.
- **Reactivity**: Improving overall reactivity and agility as an emergency organisation.

The coaching and mentoring mindset works with a combination of individual and team coaching efforts, making the 'coach mindset in management' a priority for these contexts. Together with the main stakeholders, specific plans and activities will be organised to facilitate the change and support the people in their management responsibilities.

# Challenges and opportunities

### Clinical mentoring

Through close collaboration and transparency with the MSF South Africa Medical Unit (SAMU) and the MSF Academy for Health Care, MSF wishes to come to a common understanding of what mentoring and clinical mentoring have in common and how to promote mentoring practice from a developmental and clinical approach.

### Harvesting knowledge from coaching and mentoring practices

As an organisation with an internal mentoring and coaching programme, there is much to learn from these practices and how that can serve the organisation. The launch of a community of practice, mentoring cafés, supervision sessions, etc. are a start. Furthermore, facilitating strategic discussions, change management initiatives and management/leadership ambitions are all areas we feel we can have an added value.

### Efficiency of resources on mentoring and coaching

The dreams within the mentoring and coaching community across the movement are the following:

- Create greater access to mentoring and coaching, for national staff and expanding job profiles.
- Arrive at harmonising processes across the movement when managing the pool of mentors (similar to coaches' pool). At some point, sharing mentors across the

movement should be a given. Alignment on the criteria for the recruitment of mentors, quality standards and practices are the first steps towards this.

- Anchor mentoring and coaching (M&C) in learning and development (L&D) across the sections. A first concept note was written and the L&D in the different sections have taken steps to integrate M&C in their strategy and key services.

Furthermore, MSF would like to advocate bringing the mentoring and coaching offer closer to its operations. Some regional offices, HQs and partner sections have proposed ideas around boosting the capacity in their region (Middle East, Latin America, West/Central Africa). Together with the other sections, there is the ambition to look at this holistically and propose initiatives.

## Diversity of the pool of mentors and mentees

Looking at the reality in the field, MSF realises that a more balanced representation of mentors is needed to cover the needs. Diversity here means professional profile, gender, cultural background, age and experiences. However, the complexity of reaching the corners of the organisation to recruit mentors and mentees to the programme remains the greatest challenge to this goal.

# Case studies

In order to illustrate the implementation of the programme, two case studies were carried out. For each of the case studies presented, the mentees' first names and geographical locations have been changed to preserve anonymity.

The process of matching a mentor to a mentee was identical for each of the case studies. The first meeting included the initial introduction leading to the matching and the first mentoring session.

At the initial session a structured introduction in the form of a contract was used to define the environment of the relationship (what kind of set-up the mentee wants to have), building trust with a sense of security, confidentiality and respect for integrity. Elements relevant to the case study will be developed in the section on linking.

All the mentoring sessions were conducted remotely using the different technological means available to the mentees. They were free to choose the system that best suited them, with the proviso that they could use video, where the quality of the connection allowed.

## Case study 1

### Presentation of the mentee

Mickael, Water and Sanitation Officer, is Ugandan and had been working in South Sudan for 2 months when his mentoring programme started. He is responsible for a national team of five people and also interacts with a team of five international mobile staff. Mickael has a 9-month contract.

Mickael has a long experience with MSF as locally recruited staff in Uganda and is a first-time international mobile staff member. He is 35 years old and is no longer sure he wants to continue working with MSF as the relationship with these colleagues seems complex with so little recognition.

### First discussion, definition of objectives and expectations

Due to the distance between Mickael and his mentor, the whole mentoring programme was done at a distance. The first discussion took place on the basis of the self-appraisal filled in by the candidate a few days before this first contact. The mentee's objectives seemed clear enough at first glance and were explained as follows:

- To have good communication with the people I supervise and work with.
- To have a good grasp of the project's strategic documents and to be able to understand the water and sanitation activities to be implemented.

During the initial discussion the candidate's understanding of the mentoring exercise became increasingly confused until the need for coaching replaced the need for mentoring. The mentee's request was mainly triggered by negative feedback from his hierarchy and colleagues on the way Mickael communicated ('I would like to understand why everyone criticises the way I communicate and interact with my colleagues and why it is described as such in my evaluation'). So, his goal, in the first instance, seemed to be to understand, not necessarily to change.

Mickael's second objective, 'to have a good grasp of the project's strategic documents and to be able to understand the water and sanitation activities to be implemented' was also motivated by negative feedback from his superiors and colleagues on his ability to develop an operational strategy. So, likewise, Mickael seemed to want to understand more than to change.

### Connection mentor/mentee

The first approach adopted by the mentor in the coaching posture was to transform the desire to understand into a desire to learn and change. To enable Mickael to become aware of his internal state (emotions) and hindrances (limiting beliefs, limiting behaviours, saboteurs) the mentor in coaching posture conducted introspection and values clarification exercises to stimulate the desire for transformation (rippling) and professional skills development in a mentoring programme. Once Mickael had become aware of his desire to develop and reveal his best self in his professional activity, he was ready to return to the mentoring programme. This time of introspection in a coaching approach took place over two sessions.

## The accompaniment

Mickael wanted to meet once a week and was keen to experiment. It was necessary to find a balance between the mentor/mentee and coach/coachee relationship and, on several occasions, it was necessary to switch from one to the other and to develop a ritual of passage so that Mickael could differentiate and adapt his expectations according to the nature of the relationship. A mid-term evaluation made it possible to assess the impact of this atypical method and to correct what needed to be corrected, while respecting Mickael's expectations and integrity.

## The impact

Mickael experienced a decisive turning point in his search for development when he discovered the person he wanted to be and not the person that his hierarchy and collaborators asked him to embody. He developed new communication strategies and was able to discover and begin to learn how to preserve the values that are so important to him. Mickael entered a process of professional development which he wished to continue but in a different mission with new objectives.

## Conclusion

Mickael felt that he had gone beyond his mentoring objectives but that the start had been painful and tedious because the self-examination required 'looking at one's negative emotions and his barriers'. He admits that he had not been prepared for this phase of questioning and had initially hoped to find a support that gave him reason to be a 'victim' in these situations of judgement about his communication skills. Mickael recognises that becoming an expatriate after having been a national staff member for many years presents several challenges. First of all, the managerial culture of internationally mobile staff was for him Euro-centric and therefore far from his culture of relating to others and his way of managing (maieutic).

The mentoring programme helped Mickael want to continue his professional development with MSF and allowed him to see different professional perspectives.

The mentor pointed out that the company culture is sometimes so powerful that in some situations it is difficult for the employee to be themselves.

## Case study 2

### Presentation of the mentee

Patrick is Tanzanian and is a first-time logistics coordinator in Guinea. He has over 10 years' experience as locally recruited staff in MSF logistics in his home country. Patrick is an international mobile staff member for the second time. He started out as a logistician. Patrick likes organisation and is very happy with his professional development. For his next mission he would like to be able to obtain a family contract allowing him to bring his wife and two children.

### Connection mentor/mentee

Patrick sees the mentoring programme as an opportunity to develop himself and the recognition that the organisation has of his potential, but also to have a neutral space for discussion where everything can be expressed without the risk of being judged. He expects his mentor to be a good listener and to ask powerful questions that allow for introspection. Patrick wished to have a session every 2 weeks to allow him to step back and experience new things, and asked for more frequent sessions if he had difficulties.

### Setting objectives and expectations

Before starting the mentoring programme, Patrick had thought long and hard about the professional skills he wanted to develop. To help him in this process Patrick used the self-assessment of the function of logistics coordinator and his job profile. Patrick's first objective was to be 'able' (in his words) to develop a strategic vision of logistics, one that was anchored in the operational needs of MSF in the country where he worked. The lack of strategic vision was the main criticism his career manager had for him, so his motivation was based first and foremost on improving evaluation.

Patrick's second objective was to develop his assertiveness in coordination meetings, to be able to structure his arguments to be as convincing as possible and to develop effective communication strategies.

### The accompaniment

For each session Patrick came with issues from his daily life. He briefly described the situation and engaged in a dialogue with his mentor. Patrick had little awareness of the skills he had developed, and the mentor's first task was to enable him to recognise them and to make them more accessible.

For example, Patrick complained about the lack of support from his supervisor. Patrick felt that when he presented a problem or sought approval for his proposed solution, he rarely got a positive opinion from his supervisor. He did not understand why his supervisor did not have a stronger opinion on his issues.

As the sessions progressed, Patrick realised that what his supervisor was reflecting to him was a mirror image of the way in which he brought up and argued his points and decision making. And that by developing more assertive communications, his supervisor would have more direct, stronger reactions. At some times of stress or doubt, Patrick asked to have more frequent sessions. During such sessions the emotional load was heavy, more complex and sent him back to his most present saboteurs. These sessions allowed him to become more aware of them and to work on strategies to gain control over them. Patrick often sought advice or shared experiences, and the framework of mentoring had to be clarified several times so that the mentor did not replace the role of the functional or hierarchical supervisor. According to the mentor, there were no situations where a precedent was set.

### The impact

By doing perspective-taking exercises, taking meta positions and allowing Patrick to put himself in the shoes of the different people he was interacting with, he was able to reflect on the internal states of his supervisors and some of his colleagues, and understand why his supervisor was reacting passively to his positioning requests. These exercises and this awareness of his ability to understand others allowed Patrick to define new communication strategies. These new strategies were a win–win for all parties. Firstly, for himself, because he learned to structure his arguments, to relate to his interlocutor, to understand that he was responsible for the quality of the interaction and the dialogue, and that he could have some control over the outcome.

Patrick developed a better awareness of his potential. This enabled him to gain self-confidence, and he was able to develop an assertiveness that allowed him to significantly improve his relationship with others. He also became aware of the complexity of managing interculturally, especially in relations with his teams, colleagues and supervisors.

### Conclusion

Patrick's level of transformation during the mentoring programme was impressive. The big challenge for him was to be able to maintain and anchor his transformation in a sustainable way. Patrick was grateful to have been accompanied by a mentor. At the end of the mentoring programme, he was a little stressed about having to continue his career path without a mentor and said that the skills he had acquired were still fragile and that it would take a lot of effort before they became automatic and present in all circumstances.

## Mentor's conclusion

The mentor who initiated the case study has been part of the development of the mentoring programme with the logistics department since its inception. He has been a mentor through the internally developed, EMCC-certified programme. The mentor was also trained as a coach through the in-house training programme developed by MSF, training accredited by ICF (Approved Coach Specific Training Hours – ACSTH).

According to the mentor, the mentor matching process is smooth and the match between mentor and mentee well prepared. In most cases the mentee had a good understanding of the scope of mentoring before the first meeting with the mentor. And the prior discussion between the mentoring HUB and the mentee always allowed the mentee to be ready to enter the mentoring programme fully and confidently.

The training scheme developed by MSF is undoubtedly of high quality. In addition to a 3-day training course, the programme has set up a system of exchange between pairs, reflection and enrichment on mentoring practices through mentoring cafés and meetings. This allows the mentor to enter a process of continuous development, to reflect on their practice and to be inspired by the experiences of others to improve their practice.

Mentors have little training in coaching, and coaching postures can, in some cases, improve the quality of the relationship and its outcomes. The main difference is that the coach does not give advice and is not necessarily an expert in the coachee's professional field. The mentee regularly faces certain barriers such as limiting beliefs or limiting behaviours. The mentoring programme provides little training for mentors to work on these aspects.

All functions, regardless of their functional level, should have access to mentoring programmes. But the pool of mentors does not seem to be large enough, which reduces access to the programme. The size and complexity of the organisation also makes this difficult.

The Mentoring and Coaching HUB has developed an online tool to establish and structure the relationship between mentor and mentee. This tool is well constructed and allows for follow-up in the mentee's journey.

For the mentor, the mentoring programme at MSF is exemplary in every way. It is a smooth, clear and well-supported process for both the mentee and the mentor. The community of practice of the mentors allows for continuous development, which is essential for the mentoring function.

The mentoring programme contributes to the success of its humanitarian operations by making individuals more efficient, more autonomous and more connected to their teams. Mentoring promotes systemic performance rather than individual performance. Success depends on the ability of teams to perform well.

# 23 Mentoring in Euroclear

*Sophie Bocquet, Lead Coach and Head of Mentoring*

Mentoring was born in Euroclear as a complementary product to coaching. The company started offering coaching by internal coaches to its employees in 2009.

Gradually, another type of demand emerged: people who wanted to benefit from the experience of others. Sometimes it was also access to the network that was requested, or the transmission of knowledge. From there, we started to offer another type of service: the allocation of a mentor.

We decided to formalise mentoring to ensure that it had the best chance of success. This did slow down the roll-out, but we have always given priority to quality over quantity.

The potential for mentoring is huge, as we could eventually draw on a significant portion of Euroclear's leaders and experienced employees. This can become a viral way of connecting, breaking down silos and accelerating the transmission of mentoring within our company.

Regarding the style of mentoring adopted within Euroclear, the coaching attitude has always been considered as crucial. Indeed, the ability to listen, and letting mentees think for themselves, experiment and find their own solutions are considered crucial for the mentors at Euroclear. As for a coaching journey, it is made clear that, for a mentoring journey, the mentee is in the driving seat and is responsible, with the precious support of the mentor.

The persons driving and giving support to the mentoring programme are all either professional coaches or individuals with a strong affinity for coaching and receiving adequate support from coaches. Moreover, the inductions and support given to the mentors and mentees were always done in coaching style, by coaching professionals. In other words, coaching has been systematically embedded into the Euroclear mentoring programmes.

## Context and strategic choices when starting up different mentoring initiatives

To respond to demands and to capitalise on the appetite for mentoring, we launched various initiatives. This saved us from having to generate further demand. We preferred to start on a small scale with quality support.

As the human element is crucial for mentoring, we also wanted to put this element at the heart of the guidance.

It was essential to interact with the mentors when we recruited them, when they started their mentoring journey with their mentee, and possibly halfway through and at the end of the journey.

We discussed why we were mentoring, what we expected from them, what involvement was needed to make it work, what their goals were in joining a mentoring initiative, the benefits for themselves, their mentee and the organisation, what they needed to become even more effective mentors and how best to improve the mentoring initiatives.

Even though we started small, the effort to support the above, especially if mentoring is new to your company, should not be underestimated. Follow-up ensures that there is sufficient focus on mentoring.

For example, planned intermediate sessions with a mentor–mentee pair could help the mentoring pairs realise that they had slackened their focus on mentoring. Most of the time they conclude that this was a pity and decide to restart the follow-up and to reinvest in mentoring with the commitment needed.

There must be a sponsor for each initiative, who wants the mentoring to happen, who gives steering and who is an advocate for the programme. They can fulfill the role in several ways: helping to define the right communication channels to recruit mentors and mentees, serving as an example by taking on a mentoring role themselves or discussing the value of the initiative with their peers.

Our sponsors have often helped us to create appetite among senior managers at Euroclear. This has enabled us to mobilise high-quality mentors, in terms of seniority, level of experience, styles and willingness to get involved. Sometimes just mentioning the sponsors' names opened doors for us to initiate discussions with people we wanted to involve in the initiative.

For some of the initiatives, we really wanted to involve people at the highest level of the company. We were pleasantly surprised to see how many senior executives responded positively to our call. Very few declined our offer and, when they did, their reasons were always valid. Those who told us that it was not possible at that time all told us that we could come back at a later date, once they had come out of the intense period of work they were in.

They all played the 'game' as we asked them to make themselves sufficiently available for their mentees, to take the time to follow an introduction and to ensure a real quality in the exchanges with their mentee. The icing on the cake was that at the end of the journey they all, without exception, told us how happy they were to be mentors.

We recommend that leaders who want to start or strengthen mentoring in their company do not put any barriers in the way of involving mentors. It just might work.

## Some examples of initiatives

*Launching an initiative was always the consequence of a specific need or demand*

In one department, there was a desire to integrate young newcomers. The initiative worked well overall, but we realised that it was a bit premature to start mentoring immediately as a junior joiner, while focusing on taking on a new position, role and starting in a new company. Young newcomers were not yet asking themselves a lot of questions about their desire for development. It would probably have been worth waiting a little while before starting the mentoring. A buddy system could be more appropriate, with one person guiding the newcomer.

For one country, the challenge was for the young population to gain much-needed experience. In this case, the aim of the mentoring initiative was essentially to pass on experience. For another entity, the need was to present credible profiles when management positions opened.

An initiative focused on the need to have a greater sense of ownership among employees.

Another interesting experiment was conducted at the borderline between peer coaching, peer mentoring and buddying: creating pairs to support the learning objectives of each member of the pair. The results confirmed both a better focus on learning and satisfaction that came from the human interaction.

During the COVID-19 lockdown, Euroclear switched to a completely remote mode of operation. For some managers, it was not always easy to adopt the new online collaborative working tools. But it was important that they did adopt these new tools to set an example for their divisions and teams.

As part of the deployment of new office automation tools, reverse mentoring was set up to help senior management to discover the new tools. The idea was to create pairs between these managers and young mentors who would give them technical guidance on the digital possibilities that could best support remote operation, such as the use of an electronic whiteboard.

During one of the mentoring pilots, we noticed that mentees sometimes also took on the role of mentor. We understood that establishing pairs with a young mentee and a senior executive could give our senior management an opportunity to receive specific insights from millennials, and so two-way mentoring was born.

We observed that the mentee also took the mentor role in the pairs where the mentor proactively supported that approach. Some mentors set learning goals for themselves, and the mentoring sessions were designed to balance the goals of the mentee and the mentor.

Other mentors shared with their mentees their doubts and difficulties in situations they encountered and asked for their opinion in a very sincere way. One mentor took a mentee to a workshop on a specific theme, bringing a fresh and youthful perspective to the topic. Another mentor asked his mentee to proofread a communication to send to the department. He completely revamped it after receiving feedback from his millennial mentee and was able to be much more relevant for his young population. The mentee can share their network to the mentor and vice-versa. They can reflect on a mentor's own leadership style.

Euroclear's 'Leaders for the Future' programme was launched shortly before the lockdown. Its intention is to develop the potential leaders of the company with the tools, skills and attitude required to become these leaders in the future. Mentoring is definitely a tool to be used and we chose to approach the senior leaders of the company to take the role of mentors.

At the beginning of the lockdown, we wondered whether mentoring could continue. Even if face-to-face sessions are more desirable, lockdown was probably the time when there was the greatest need to support employees working from home, given the lack of direct social interaction. Employees working remotely did not easily have opportunities for nurturing human exchanges in an informal way. It was therefore particularly appropriate to provide access to mentoring.

### The human component is the main lever of a mentoring relationship

To stimulate this component, we wanted to mobilise it in all the interactions we had with mentors and mentees. We co-created our mentoring initiatives with the participants. The idea was to try the adventure with some pilot initiatives, with guidance focused on the human aspect.

People supporting the initiatives were either qualified coaches or people with an interest in coaching and its attitudes. The launch of a first mentoring pilot can take place in a very simple way and serve as a learning base to expand to a larger population. With good follow-up, companies can dare to succeed without the model being too complicated.

Questions arose with no ready-made answers. We took an emergent approach to create the answers. For example, we asked the mentors to reflect on the difference between the roles of mentor, coach, manager and sponsor. They described the specific intention of each of these roles, identifying differences and commonalities. A mentor seeks to pass on experience, to guide and support, to help the mentee grow, to bring in other perspectives. The mentor's main asset is their experience, whereas the main assets of a coach are their attitude and tools.

Coaching is one of the things a mentor can bring to a coachee, but it is far from the only thing. For the future, other issues will need to be addressed and developed in additional mentor support workshops. They may concern ethics, the mentor's attitude and how to support the mentee. For example: how do you ensure that there is a two-way component to mentoring? Can one move from mentoring to sponsorship? How do you ensure that confidentiality is respected in discussions?

Theoretical models for mentoring are not abundant; it is a field that is only beginning to be structured and there is still a lot of potential for development. We were therefore asking ourselves certain questions to which we felt the answers were uncertain. In this case, we chose to trust our mentors and mentees to help us come up with answers that were sufficiently nuanced and reflected the human reality. We relied on collective intelligence during the start-up sessions with the mentors and we gradually obtained definitions that corresponded well to the reality of Euroclear.

# The mentoring process and the training of mentors and mentees

As the different initiatives unfolded, we learned and then integrated our learning into subsequent initiatives. There were a number of difficulties and benefits that we observed.

Whatever the structure of the mentoring initiatives, the first step is always to go out and recruit the mentors and mentees. It is very important to ensure that the desire and commitment is there. To ensure that mentoring is not just a 'box ticking' exercise, it is always optional. Notably, what people gain from the experience is proportional to the effort they put in / invest. With the best mentor in the world, there will be low value if the mentee doesn't put heart, desire and energy into the initiative. This applies to the time spent, the focus, the mental bandwidth and the heart.

Those mentees who open themselves up, who reveal themselves as they are, will give their mentor all the keys for an authentic discussion, to get to the heart of the topics that really matter. Similarly, a mentor who really shows who they are, in all their humanity, will inspire the mentee much more than a perfect, completely smooth superhero.

### 'Mentorability' is a key success factor

The mentee's desire to be mentored strongly influences the results of the mentoring process. The few failures or lesser successes often came when the mentees did not decide by themselves to ask for a mentor. A somewhat more passive attitude of the mentee sometimes resulted in sessions not taking place or there was less progress, due to lack of enthusiasm. Hence, we included steps that would induce a real voluntary approach from the mentee. For example, we asked them to confirm their willingness to participate in the process, and we did not call them back when they had to complete their form. The intention was to ensure they were fully active and responsible in the process.

To find mentors we always asked persons to volunteer only if they wanted to. We needed to make sure the grit in the oyster was their guiding principle.

### Induction sessions for mentors

Once the desire is there, both for mentors and mentees, they must understand the framework in which they can operate and receive the basic tools to start.

They should be given the opportunity to reflect in induction sessions conducted for small groups.

- How do they want to contribute?
- Who are they?
- What do they need?
- What is their unique personal offering as a mentor?

- What are they looking to learn?
- What kind of mentees would they like to have?

The mentors reflect collectively on the questions.

A definition of mentoring was co-created:

> A distinct relationship where one person, the mentor, supports the learning, development and progress of another person, the mentee.
>
> A mentor provides supports by offering information, advice and assistance in a way that empowers the mentee.
>
> The mentor–mentee roles can and should be exchanged between the two persons.

## Benefits of mentoring

Mentors exchanged their views on the benefits of mentoring. Here are some examples of what they identified. The mentee gets the opportunity to talk to someone who has experiences to share, to discuss the challenges they are confronted with. It provides them with comfort and reassurance. They can see a manager in a different way and better understand their role. The mentor can be confronted with a reality that sometimes they do not see anymore. They better understand the difficulties encountered by employees and can act upon them. For Euroclear, mentoring can contribute to a culture change and offer connection between different teams and departments. It helps employees to dare to be fully themselves and therefore contributes to a diverse workforce. It is an excellent way of demonstrating that management cares and driving development means increasing engagement.

### Ethics and confidentiality

We then introduce the code of ethics, using the EMCC global code of ethics as a reference.

Confidentiality creates a safe space for the discussion, so that the mentee and the mentor feel totally free to speak about what they have on their mind in their discussions. There should not be any reporting of the content of the mentoring discussions, or even of the progress of their mentee, neither to human resources nor to the line manager. If the mentor chooses to open themselves authentically, what they are revealing should not be repeated outside of the discussion. If exceptions are needed to that confidentiality rule, they should be discussed upfront, and the person should give explicit permission to share the information.

### Integrity and authenticity

We also recommend integrity and authenticity – no facades.

Mentoring should demonstrate that a point of view can be personal and that nuances exist outside of the usual standard corporate messages. If the conveyed message is not the intimate conviction of the person giving it, it is often detected and has a negative impact on trust between the two persons. The mentors should be clear that they have the best interest of the mentee in mind. We invite the mentors to be curious and non-judgemental when they are confronted with different personalities. It is an opportunity to open their minds.

### Roles and responsibilities

We discuss the roles and responsibilities for the mentor and for the mentee and we give them an idea of the qualities that would be the most useful for a mentor, originating from curiosity, courage and compassion. Emotional intelligence is a great asset for a mentor: self-awareness, social awareness, self-management and relationship management. A mentor should be easy to relate with and always make mentees feel comfortable. They should be listening carefully and asking good questions to 'get the mentee'. They should be finding connections to the mentee and build respectful rapport. They should raise awareness of the mentee and empower them to solve their problems. They should dare to drop the mask and reveal their own vulnerabilities, for example by sharing their own stories and experience.

We also spent some time reflecting on what the impact of presence could be for the mentors and how they could be fully present in the session.

At the end of the induction sessions, mentors had to complete their application form and participate in chemistry sessions upon invitation of mentees who might be interested in having them as mentors.

### Induction sessions for mentees

For some of the mentoring initiatives, we also planned induction sessions with the mentees, again in small groups. We gave them some common elements with the induction for mentors: the definition of mentoring, the roles and responsibilities of the mentor and of the mentee.

We observed that it is much less obvious for the mentees to define their objectives for the mentoring journey, especially when they are junior. We therefore let them reflect on their expectations of their mentoring path. They discussed what could be great qualities for a mentee, such as willingness to learn, accepting responsibility for their own learning, integrity and authenticity.

We let them reflect on the way to get full benefit of their sessions and on how to get prepared for them. And we gave them the ground rules: the code of ethics, the fact that they were in the driving seat and were expected to plan and prepare the sessions.

The mentor is a resource; it is then up to them to make the best use of the opportunity they are receiving. When they met a potential mentor for a chemistry session, they could easily express their expectations, which allowed these discussions to easily take on a certain depth. Our mentors confirmed that they liked to feel that their mentees came to the chemistry discussions mentally prepared.

## Capturing what mentors and mentees want

After the induction session, mentors and mentees filled in application forms that we use as an important input for the matching.

For the mentees, we ask for some organisational and practical information. Then we ask them to formulate their needs and what they expect from the mentor–mentee engagement, such as developing their communication skills, reflecting on their career and next steps, being inspired, and so on. They were asked to specify what they wanted to learn and the type of person they wanted to be a mentor. For example: someone with a very good knowledge of the organisation's business; someone who has worked outside Euroclear and can describe other practices and bring a fresh perspective, etc.

For the mentors, we also collect practical information. We ask them about their unique personal offering as a mentor, what they expect from the mentor–mentee engagement and what they want to learn. They explain what kind of individuals they want to mentor, for example: an introvert, a young person with a lot of potential. We check their areas of expertise in terms of hard and soft skills.

## Matching the mentors with the mentees

The allocation of a mentor to a mentee, called matching, is of paramount importance. Through the application form, we try to understand the needs and wishes of both people involved. We also sometimes listen to our intuition, especially if we know the mentor or mentee well. The personalities can also come into play: their emotional intelligence, their ability to navigate the business, and sometimes even their personality preferences – introversion or extroversion, a tendency to focus on facts or relationships in decision making. For example, we will not favour the same personality traits for a mentee who needs to be challenged as for someone who needs to develop confidence. Doing this maximises the chances of helping the mentee to develop their self-awareness. Some of our mentors are trained in coaching, which they may or may not practise. We keep it in mind when allocating mentees.

We ensure that the mentor is focused on the mentee's best interest and not on their own interest and/or the interest of the division. Therefore, in most cases there must be some sort of organisational distance between the mentor and the mentee to reduce the risk of conflict of interest. It also removes the difficulty of managing a dual relationship: confiding in someone who is also the person who evaluates, influences promotions and assigns priorities in the team can sometimes be more complicated than talking to someone with whom one has no supervisory relationship.

Some topics benefit from a certain neutrality from the mentor: a difficult relationship with the manager, a desire for progression that cannot necessarily be addressed within the mentee's current role, a desire for promotion where their direct supervisor may feel threatened, etc.

While these phenomena should ideally not exist, it is important to recognise that they can sometimes occur in companies. Ideally, these topics should also be discussed with the manager, but it can be very helpful to start the discussion with someone who can hear things without them already being crystallised. This helps the mentee to understand themselves, what they really want and to prepare an action plan and a communication strategy with the people involved.

We often get the matching right, but we could also be wrong. If the match is not right for one of the two parties, it can derail the mentoring journey. In that case, we add in safeguards and we plan for the possibility of dealing with a possible mistake.

During the induction session we make it clear to both mentees and mentors that if a match does not suit them, they have the possibility of a 'no fault divorce'. They do not have to give an explanation, but they must close the mentoring process properly, with a closing session between the mentor and the mentee. The mentoring team must be informed and, if the mentee wishes, a new mentor can be proposed. This 'no fault divorce' possibility is hardly ever used, but its mere existence is already a very good protection against relationships that do not work out.

Another protection mechanism relies in 'chemistry sessions'. We will describe these later.

## Another possibility for matching: speed dating

When launching some mentoring waves, we invited all mentors and mentees so they could meet each other in a speed-dating format. A mentee could meet several mentors and get an impression of what a mentoring pathway with each person might look like. After this meeting, each mentee handed in a list of three mentors they would have liked to choose, with a brief explanation of the reasons for their choice.

We did not wish to let the choice be made completely at the meeting session because we were afraid that it might be painful for a mentor not to be chosen by anyone. This is a recurring theme: how do you take care of a mentor who is disappointed at not being chosen?

## The chemistry session

Mentees were offered one to three mentors. In order to verify the proposed matching, mentees have a 'chemistry session' with each offered mentor. The mentee gets a taste of what the mentoring relationship could look like and should be equipped to choose as consciously as possible the most appropriate mentor for their needs. The mentor should be able to confirm that they feel they could help that mentee. Approximately two-thirds of the talking should be done by the mentee, supported by opening questions asked by the mentor.

The mentor can start by introducing themselves and give the needed permissions, such as, for example, the kind of questions that could be asked. The topics to be covered are respective expectations, basic ground rules, what the mentee wants and the kind of mentor the mentee is hoping for.

Globally, the possibility of choosing the mentor and the chemistry session was highly appreciated. It implicitly gives the message to the mentee that they are in the driving seat. From feedback, we learned that it can be difficult for the mentees to go back to a non-selected mentor, especially if they are a very senior person in the organisation, to tell them that they have not been selected. We will have to tackle this in our future mentoring initiatives. Also, because we are giving the choice to the mentee, we are sometimes left with a pool of very valuable leaders who did not receive any mentee. We will have to find ways to take care of these mentors in the future, for example by nurturing the community of mentors.

### Which objectives for a mentoring journey?

The essence of mentoring is to allow the mentee to grow. This opens the door to many topics and objectives. The mentee's career concerns can cover development opportunities, the need for change, the search for a new challenge. Mentoring can help to develop the mentee's confidence and self-esteem. Relationships and communication also come up regularly, which can have a fairly general impact on many of their interpersonal interactions. Leadership-related topics also appear quite often. A better understanding of the company and its business model may be sought. Priority or time management would also make sense. The mentor and the mentee can share their network.

Some of these topics can also be covered by coaching. In that case, it is a matter of understanding what is best for the person who needs guidance, keeping in mind that the mentor can take a coaching attitude in some cases. It is even highly recommended.

### The mid-term session

It is quite useful for the mentoring team to check in with the mentors and mentees during the course of the mentoring. Sometimes the simple fact of scheduling a mid-term session can revive a mentoring relationship.

During intermediate sessions, the mentor and mentee share the benefits they are bringing to each other, thank each other and celebrate successes. They can consider how to further accelerate their journey. These sessions are very valuable when we take the time to conduct them. It allows us to take the pulse of the mentoring relationships and to better capture the benefits.

Sometimes, we also took stock during group sessions with the mentors and with the mentees, focusing on the same topics and with the same intentions.

# A few learnings

### Offer mentoring at the right time

Mentoring is not necessarily the best tool when the mentee starts to work in a company and is focusing on the content of their role, getting to know new colleagues and even the physical space. At this point, it is probably more appropriate to give them a buddy who will support them in finding their way around their new role and company. One exception, which we have not yet explored sufficiently, is for highly experienced newcomers. It would probably be worthwhile to offer them a mentor to whom candid questions can be asked in a safe space, about the company, its business, its culture.

This could be done in several ways, depending on both the needs of the person joining Euroclear and the possibilities for mentoring: assigning a more senior person for classic developmental mentoring, lining up a peer for a two-way mentoring relationship, or even setting up two-way mentoring with a young employee. It also makes a lot of sense to offer mentoring when a person is taking a new role, especially if it is a first management or leadership role.

## Beware of mentee commitment

It doesn't work to assign a mentor to a mentee just because somebody thinks it is good for them, to motivate them, because they are a talent. The mentee must choose to initiate the process. In some initiatives, we let the management determine the mentees and assign them into the initiative. It was in these cases that we experienced the highest drop-out rate. Afterwards, we made sure that the mentee was volunteering. We avoided, for example, too many reminders to the mentees as they went through the steps they had to take before a mentor was allocated to them.

## It is not always easy for a mentee to define their goals

These goals will determine the contribution of mentoring to the mentee's growth. A coach is often confronted with a coachee who arrives with an unclear request and has the tools and the approach to bring out the coachee's goals, or even to go and find the hidden requests. A mentor is not necessarily experienced in this exercise. Hence, during the introductory session, we let the mentees reflect on their expectations of the journey. This impacted positively on the quality of the chemistry sessions as the mentees came up with the topics that were important to them, giving more focus and relevance to the discussions.

## Mentoring can help the mentors to become better leaders

Mentors find joy and energy in the mentoring moments. We asked ourselves who could be a mentor and what makes a good mentor. We defined the following qualities: self-awareness, listening, caring, curiosity, courage, compassion. A person who wants to become a mentor does not necessarily have all these qualities immediately. If we give mentors choice to opt in for the right reasons, they will be able to further develop the required qualities along their mentoring experience. The key condition is that they volunteer to participate.

The framework we set in the induction sessions also helps them to understand the attitude we expect from them. Developing as a mentor can influence leadership style by developing new attitudes.

## Mentoring and diversity

It is important to be aware of unconscious bias. In one of our first initiatives, we found ourselves with a majority of female mentors and a minority of female mentees. What a paradox when mentoring is an excellent tool for developing diversity and inclusion! When we shared this experience, we realised that we were not the only ones to whom this had happened. We wondered if this could be because women are more conditioned in caring for others, but we could not analyse this further. Afterwards, we paid attention to the ratio of men to women among the mentees and were able to correct this quite easily. Mentoring is a powerful lever to include and develop any individual.

# 24 Mentoring at Unilever and Bosch in Poland

*Piotr Ciacek, Mentor, EQA programme owner*

Mentoring is a process that, in a way, goes against the grain of corporate culture. How so? Mentoring does not mesh with KPIs; it is not subject to reporting and control in line with well-worn corporate rules. Mentoring means working with people who are not our subordinates, and in a way puts the master (the boss) in the position of student, which can be emotionally tiring. In fact, it's hard to say who is under the most stress in the process – mentor or mentee. The sponsor of the process also risks a lot, for the outcome is unforeseeable.

The coaching attitude is crucial. Using open questions by you as a mentor somehow can make you feel that 'you lose control' on the one hand (because you are 'out of your mind map'). On the other hand, without open questions you cannot show your curiosity, and without curiosity you cannot build a rapport with your mentee. Therefore, I usually spend a lot of time teaching my 'new mentors' that while using coaching attitudes, you are not losing control. In fact, you are supporting your mentees in building their self-awareness, thus, they can better control themselves – which is one of the most important aims of the mentoring process.

I would like to present two different models of how I worked with two different corporations that decided to implement a mentoring programme. Each company has global reach, a well-established position and excellent internal procedures. I would like to share how in each case I went about determining their needs, how the integration of the mentoring programme enriched the organisational culture as a whole and how the programme ran.

## Setting up mentoring at Unilever

This case involved going from QFR (Question for proposal) to needs identification at Unilever. In the summer, I had received a standard email, a request for an offer to start up a mentoring programme for about 20 people in a company. The deadline for submitting an offer was 7 days away. The request was enigmatic. The message was signed at the bottom by the contact person and there was a telephone number. It was the middle of the summer holidays when I called. A very young-sounding person picked up the phone. He was open and willing to talk. I thanked him for the request and began asking questions.

- Has a mentoring programme ever been run in the company before?
- What are the goals of the programme?
- Who is to be the mentor, and who will choose them and how?
- What is their level of knowledge and experience?

My interlocutor said that, unfortunately, he wasn't actually able to answer any questions. I asked him where the idea about mentoring had come from and who I should speak with. He told me it was part of the company's global programme, that it was already up and running in a prepared format outside Poland, and that an order had come from headquarters to their department – not HR, but Inclusion and Diversity – to start up such a programme. I told him it would be very difficult for me to submit any offer without even knowing the basic parameters of the programme. He promised to get in touch with his colleagues from the department and call back within a few days.

After hearing nothing for a week, I called again – I had deliberately ruled out email communication on the premise that at this stage it wouldn't help build up a relationship. The same person answered at once and apologised, asking me to be patient for a few more days because 'my colleague who's responsible for the programme is on leave'.

## What are we talking about?

After another week, the phone rang. A different person this time, David, asked for a meeting on Zoom, to be attended by the whole team and, at which he hoped, 'You'll hear answers to all your questions'. So, 3 days later, there we were on Zoom. Me on one side, and four very young people on the other. I felt a bit dejected. We introduced ourselves. I proposed we address each other informally and asked how much time we had; the answer was 30 minutes. A lady named Iga Iwanek quickly took the helm. She said that in fact all she knew was that they had to get a mentoring programme going by the autumn of this year, that such programmes were already functioning in other countries, that it had its own format, and in principle all they expected was training for mentors. I asked for more information on how things work in Holland or Germany – but they said they couldn't provide any.

I asked if I could tell them how I implement programmes in companies and what standards I work to. They agreed. Using PowerPoint, I explained the particular stages of implementing a process, from setting organisational and developmental goals for both the mentees and the mentors, to how to identify and qualify those willing to be a mentor or mentee, to the role of application questionnaires and communicating the intra-organisational rules of the mentoring programme, with particular emphasis on confidentiality. I explained why a mentor cannot be a mentee's superior, why it is important to have a properly constructed system for training mentors and mentees, and what that involves.

At that moment our time ran out – which I announced, asking, 'What next?' and Iga quickly answered that I could continue if I wished. So, I also spoke about the rules of the process, EMCC standards and the Code of Ethics. I said that if I were to take responsibility for the process and its effects, we'd have to ensure that the mentors had the possibility of intervision and supervision, as well as training during the process. I explained the importance of these to the mentors, but also to the mentees and the whole process within the organisation. Finally, I mentioned the need to evaluate the programme at the end and to hold a final meeting for all participants with a presentation of results, some kind of speech and a celebration.

I had the impression this was quite a lot for them. 'Wow,' David said at the end. 'We had no idea. We thought this was a pretty banal thing, we'd take care of it ourselves. But it looks like maybe not, exactly.'

## Just do it! ... But 'Why'?

'Could you write it all up and send it to us?' Iga asked. 'Kind of like crib sheets, and if you could immediately give us a max and min programme you could handle to meet at least the basic standards.'

I agreed but asked them to first send me what they expected from the programme – the goals to be achieved in the context of the whole company and the programme participants. 'Without that I won't lift a finger,' I said.

'Okay, but we haven't got much time, because the company expects the first training to start in September,' Iga put in. I said I understood, but couldn't send an offer on something unspecified, and certainly couldn't calibrate the programme. I promised them that if I got their goals in 3 days, I'd send a full offer with options within a week. That's how we left it.

After that meeting, I had no idea what direction the talks were going in. But I knew there were several conditions without which I wouldn't want to run the programme: total trust between the mentor and mentee; no subordination between mentor and mentee; free will on both sides to take part in the programme; compulsory training for all mentors, including practical exercises; training for the mentees; at least two group supervisions during the process; and a final evaluation based on an anonymous questionnaire for the mentors and mentees.

I received information on the programme goals within 2 days, as follows:

*Unilever mentoring programme 2021/22*

The goals of the programme are:

1   To support the development of young talent in the organisation.
2   To demonstrate and equip leaders with tools they can use to work on themselves, with their team and within the organisation as a whole.
3   Networking: to create opportunities for managers and employees to get to know people from beyond their own division/department; to expand

knowledge on how the organisation operates as a whole; to show 'young' employees that they can help managers from outside their division.

4 To enhance communication within the organisation; to create opportunities to experience and understand other perspectives and points of view.

In response, and before sending an offer, I wrote up a framework and rules for the programme. For me, these were vital. I also knew that they had to give the highest possible sense of security to programme participants (see Chapter 20).

### Programme framework and rules

The proposal had to comply with the framework and rules; this means respecting the following criteria:

1 Pairs were chosen by the external company based on mentor and mentee applications in which both sides had to define the development areas they wanted to work on. The mentors were asked to indicate what areas they felt particularly competent in, and the mentees what areas they wanted to develop in or which they believed they were lacking. In no case should the mentor and mentee be in any way dependent on each other professionally.

2 The process was totally confidential for both parties, except for the programme supervisors (trainers), to whom both mentors and mentees could turn for help at any time (the 'red line').

3 Pairs were to meet at least once a month but no more than once a week (a minimum of six meetings during the process). Of course, there could be more than six meetings, depending on the contract agreed by a particular pair.

4 The process could be discontinued by either party at any time. The procedure for stopping the process was as follows: The party wishing to discontinue communicates this to the supervisor. They meet to discuss the participant's reservations and reasons for wanting to end the process. If, after that meeting, the participant still wants to stop, they communicate this to the other party, explaining their reasons. When the process is discontinued, the mentor is not assigned another mentee and the mentee does not get another mentor.

5 The process ends with an evaluation made by both parties, in the form of an anonymous questionnaire provided by the external company running the programme. The results are published and made available to all participants and sponsors, in the form of a summary presented during the official programme closing ceremony.

On this basis, I prepared and calibrated an offer containing three versions: maximum, together with an option for certification of the mentors, where the training would be in line with the EQA Mentor Foundation course; extensive, but without certification; and minimum, with training for the mentors and mentees, two supervisions and a final evaluation.

## Go!

Ten days later, the client called and said they had approval for the maximum programme, in which we were given complete control over the process, the applications and putting pairs together. The issue of certification would be left up to the mentors themselves; for those wanting to become certified we were to run supplementary sessions just after the end of the programme. We worked out the details of the schedule, the contact persons from the client's side and the coordinator from my side. The client also wanted us to take care of writing a letter introducing the programme and encouraging people to take part. I didn't want to agree to that, for I thought it should come from the client, though I did offer to consult on the content. I felt that the number of people volunteering for the programme would be a kind of measure of the amount of trust employees had in the company and would show how much the programme was meeting actual needs.

The client expected about 10 responses from people wanting to become mentors (together we drew up threshold criteria for potential candidates) and about 20 from willing mentees. The results exceeded our expectations. There were almost 30 candidates for mentor and almost 50 for mentee. I was glad that in the application form I'd included a declaration for wanting to work with more than one mentee; that is, I was pleased, but on the other hand I had to double-check the programme assumptions in terms of the schedule and costs. Another difficulty was that the client had also sent the invitation to employees in other parts of Central and Eastern Europe, which meant the training would have to be in English, something we hadn't foreseen in the initial offer.

## Stop ... and go

I proposed renegotiating the schedule and contract in three aspects. We needed a second workshop for the mentors (there couldn't be 30 people in one workshop because we wouldn't be able to see how everyone was doing the exercises or give adequate feedback), so I suggested we divide the mentors into two workshops, of which one would be in English. I also asked for more time to prepare (for the trainers, and for the materials, handouts, etc. to be translated), and for more time to go through the process of forming and verifying pairs. The client agreed to the schedule change but, for changing the price, chairman acceptance was absolutely necessary at this stage.

After a moment's hesitation, Iga made the call, and it turned out the chairman was available to speak. He turned out to be a very friendly, open person. With the others, I described the programme and the problem that had arisen from our unexpected 'success'. The chairman asked us to send him an outline of the programme and promised to get back by that same evening.

In the evening, I got a call from Iga. 'Piotr, I have good news – two things, in fact. The chairman approved everything. He also said he wants to be a mentor in the programme, can you imagine? He said he took part in something like that in France, but when he saw our outline it's really professional and he wants to be part of it – in the training, too.'

## Work in progress

At this point, we had completed all the training and the intervisions. About 10 people took part in the intervisions – one-third of the participants – and these were not compulsory. It was not accidental, though, as to who took part in them. Their involvement, openness and readiness to work on themselves showed they had 'caught the mentoring bug'. For some of them this process wasn't completely new – it was obvious that they have experience – however, others found themselves in totally new roles which were more difficult than they had anticipated, yet which were also extremely interesting and challenging. For most of them the process was not just enriching but transformative. They saw how the process of conducting the mentoring process developed not just the mentees but themselves also. In the end, they all declared their willingness to undertake further training to earn accreditation.

The reports from the mentors showed that the pairs were well chosen and that the work had gone full steam ahead. The evaluations of the training showed that they had been run at a very high level in terms of their content, practical value and appropriateness, as well as the outstanding skills of the trainers. An outstanding 10 out of 30 mentors decided to go for EMCC Mentor Foundation certification – which is a remarkable number. (Especially if you consider that they made the decision when they were not aware that Unilever would pay for that.)

In my opinion, the success of this project was due to the trust I managed to establish with the client. That trust resulted from the fact that, from the very beginning, I concentrated on identifying the client's needs, on listening to them, and that I set my own conditions and priorities very clearly. Client education played a key role here, as did my refusing to assume that 'the customer knows best'. Respect and openness from me, and from the client's team as well, enabled us to function as one team. Also important, I believe, was being responsive, meeting deadlines and conversing directly – this enabled me to learn the client's language so I could explain the process in a way they could understand. I also set clear limits, and explained why I was doing so, with respect for the client's perspective.

Credit also goes to the organisation for its readiness to implement solutions that met local needs, for its courage to depart from or modify the global format, and for its willingness to learn. Without such an approach, it wouldn't have been possible to run such a programme.

## Outcomes

The evaluation was made at the end of the programme. Above all, 100 per cent of the mentees declared that they reached their goal, 95 per cent said that their mentor was engaged. For 77 per cent, the process was inspiring and helped in career planning. For 72 per cent, the process widened their perspective. On top, 95 per cent would recommend the programme to others. For the mentors, it was an inspiring experience and, thanks to it, they learned how great it is to use feedback in a coaching way. They also found that being a mentor is an effective method of self-development and, due to their mentoring and coaching attitude, they could improve their leadership skills. In addition, 85 per cent of them said they will recommend the programme to others. Finally, 10 mentors (out of 23) decided to take part in an additional mentoring course, allowing them to obtain their EMCC Foundation level certificate for an EQA awarded course.

# Bosch – A story of engineering

Robert Bosch is one of the most stable employers in Poland, with people who have worked there for 15 to 20 years. Turnover is low and growth steady – based both on sustainable, tested procedures and a conscious effort to innovate. I was put in contact with Bosch through the Business Leader Foundation, with which I used to cooperate as a supervisor of their mentoring programme, a programme in which Bosch employees – the head of HR and the CEO – took part as mentors. They asked me if I would like to introduce a programme at their company, with five directors as mentors and ten mentees. The programme sponsor would be the CEO and her right-hand woman, the HR Director.

## Set up

First, I met the CEO. She was experienced and had quite a clear conception and ideas about the programme. It would begin with the Hogan test for the mentors, followed by setting the goals the mentees were to work towards during the process, in agreement with their supervisors. In this way, the bosses of the mentees would be drawn into the process and would indirectly be judging the results achieved by both the mentees and the mentors.

This conception was very much in line with the culture of the corporation, but would distort the essence of the mentoring process, which is founded on three principles: it must be voluntary, there must be complete confidentiality and the mentee must be able to change the goal during the process. The process described by the CEO would not guarantee confidentiality. Worse still, it would subject both the mentors and mentees to unnecessary control. In this way, the programme would not comply with EMCC principles, or with my own.

On the other hand, Bosch offered me a very tempting nugget; I knew that if I agreed to the conditions proposed by the CEO, I would get the contract. But I didn't want to go for such a compromise. I knew I would feel bad about it, and that it wouldn't be good for the client, either – it could be the end of mentoring at Bosch for many years, or at least until the next CEO.

What was crucial was to understand the risks of the new programme for the organisation, how these were perceived by the CEO, and to find out what effect the stakeholders expected the programme to have. So, I told the CEO that I'd make a firm offer after getting to know the company's culture better. The CEO left it at that and turned me over to the head of HR.

At my meeting with her, I asked for a list of key people in the organisation who I could talk with about the corporate culture who would be involved in some way with the potential mentoring process. I was given a list of 10 people: the CEO, the HR Director, the Talent Manager, Directors of Trade, middle managers and potential mentees.

The interviews turned out to be a great idea. The organisation ran like a well-oiled machine. Everyone knew their place, procedures were clear and adapted to reality; employees knew what they had to do to advance and what not to do… People treated each other with trust and respect. Nevertheless, through its system of 'divisions', the company had created permanent 'silos' – hermeneutic 'mini-companies' within the corporation. While there was a free flow of communication within a given silo, there was practically none between silos. The firm did not make full use of its own experience since nothing was shared among different departments or divisions. This was conducive to an unspoken rivalry between divisions – each headed by an experienced leader who had been associated with Bosch for many years. Internally, then, it looked something like a football league where everyone is playing the same game in the same organisation, but each team a bit differently, and a bit against the others. Naturally, rivalry is needed, and can help an organisation grow, but at the same time, without cooperation and sensible means of transferring knowledge, it can turn dysfunctional (see Chapter 17).

I had a meeting with the CEO and HR Director at which I presented my conclusions from the interviews. They took it well; in fact, they told me that the main aim of the mentoring programme was to 'break up those silos, instigate horizontal communication, transfer knowledge and best practice among divisions, integrate employees'. In which case, I suggested, the form of the programme initially proposed would have no chance of achieving those things. Both the mentors and mentees would be striving for goals that were not their own but came from their 'silo'. They would be working in closed pairs, without exchanging experience with other pairs, and so there would be no integration among mentors. Finally, if this was to be a programme for developing talent, we had to assume that, if things went well, one indicator of this would be mentees changing their goal, and that it was vital for motivation that a mentee should work towards a goal they have set for themselves and internalised. I also mentioned the discomfort the mentors would experience as, while it was fine for them to have a mentee from another division, it was unacceptable to have the mentee's line manager set the goals or assess whether the mentor had led the mentee towards achieving them.

## The offer

My arguments hit home, and I was asked to come up with a programme that could achieve the goals defined by the CEO and HR Director.

My proposal was as follows:

### A. Selection and preparation of mentors

1  Individual analysis of the level of soft skills and motivation of the mentors (interview of up to 2 hours).
2  Hogan diagnostic tests for the mentors.

3  Hogan Personality Inventory (HPI).

4  Hogan Development Survey (HDS).

5  An inventory of motives, values and preferences (MVPI); discussion of the results achieved by the mentors with a certified Hogan consultant in the presence of the project supervisor (1.5–2-hour session).

6  Initial session combined with a discussion of the mentees' EASI test results. The EASI test identifies what psychological traits make people tick.

## B. Programme candidates pairing session

Session in mentor/mentee pairs (2-hour meeting) based on the application questionnaires.

## C. Preparation of mentors

A 6-hour workshop based on my EQA Mentor Foundation training module.

## D. Supervision of mentors

This would consist of mastermind group workshops (once per quarter) – each about 3 hours, conducted by me; and individual supervision for the mentors.

## E. Supervision of mentees

Feedback session with mentees (once per quarter) plus telephone consultations on an ad hoc basis.

## F. Closing session and programme evaluation

Programme evaluation to consist of a presentation of the results of anonymous surveys completed by the mentees and mentors at the end of the programme.

## Guiding principles

At the same time, I proposed some guiding principles for the programme as a pre-condition for my participation.

1  The mentors and programme sponsors must familiarise themselves with and sign the EMCC ethical code.

2  The process must be confidential.

3  The company must inform employees about the programme in a clear manner, with particular emphasis on the criteria in accordance with which mentors and mentees are invited to take part.

4  No mentee can be paired up with a mentor to whom the mentee reports or who has direct influence on the mentee's career path, whether they are given a pay rise/bonus, etc.

The programme also contained a timeframe and was to run for no longer than 8 months, where the pairs should meet no more than once a week and no less than once a month.

## The work

Five pairs began working together. In accordance with the schedule, the programme began with a discussion on the results of the Hogan tests, conducted by a certified user of that tool, in my presence (with the mentor's consent). The test results were not revealed to anyone else.

I must admit that this was a valuable experience – both for the mentors and for me. I observed their reactions to information that was not always easy to hear. This usually involved a description of the situations in which those weaknesses appear – which provided me with a pretext for introducing an element of mentor self-reflection in the process.

Another positive element of the Hogan tests was that they prepared the participants for corrective feedback from me. I referred to the tests during our supervisions, showing at the same time how they could give their mentees' feedback (assessing behaviour, not the person).

The third benefit for me was being able to see the personality profile of the mentors, which made it easier to communicate with them later and to establish a relationship with them before the training day. In this way, the group entered the training process very quickly and smoothly.

I was very surprised to learn during the training that the participants found themselves all together for the first time (each of them had been working at Bosch Polska for more than 15 years). Also, that this was their first-ever training that was 'soft', i.e. not strictly technical.

They treated the programme as an 'exploration into the unknown' and I encouraged them to do so. It was particularly difficult in the beginning for them to speak about themselves, their thoughts and emotions, to ask open questions, to focus on the other person while remaining in contact with themselves. Some of them found it very moving to discover their own mental maps and the significant differences that existed between members of the group. The process was able to move forward thanks to their mutual good will, openness, sense of humour, and the fact that they all discovered that no one in the room was 'better' than the others.

It was hard for them to accept that there would be no KPIs in the mentoring process, and that the mentees could look for their goal over three sessions and then change it at any time during the process. They instinctively tended to want to 'programme' the process and take responsibility for the result.

But you cannot change old habits during a single training programme. For me, what was key was that they understand why it was worth working on such a change, that they discover the sense of working in another tempo, style and paradigm.

In this context, the mastermind sessions were especially useful. The mentors began cooperating with each other. They saw that they have similar problems, doubts about their own competencies and the quality of this new type of work of theirs. I made sure that, apart from being confidential, the meetings were run in an atmosphere of relative freedom, were not too long (up to two hours) and were relevant. Of course, I had a plan I had prepared, but I preferred that they raise topics/questions/problems. We worked out a system for searching for options and alternative solutions and, in this way, I taught them techniques for working with their mentees.

Another particularly difficult element for the mentors was how to perceive progress and particular traits in their mentees, and how to give them feedback that would motivate and strengthen them. 'Here we don't pat people on the back; doing something well is just considered doing your duty, and for that you get paid, not praised.'

When everyone had proposed their own solutions/ideas, I changed the group into a 'group of experts' whose task was to evaluate each of the options put forward.

The participants quickly began to go beyond conventional thinking. By the end of the second session, it was clear they'd formed a kind of 'support group', and after the third session, for the first time in history they went out together for a beer.

Over time, they began to see that each of them had their own unique, individual style and different skills – which they began to share with each other and mutually benefit from.

All of the mentoring processes ended successfully. That did not mean in every case that the mentee achieved their goal during the process, but it did mean that each began an autonomous journey towards that goal, using their own resources and accompanied by their mentor.

## Outcomes

After 8 months of the programme, most of the initial goals were achieved, notably the integration and the transfer of knowledge and experience among departments at three levels, the directors, the managers and the members of the HR Department. They addressed the following issues:

- building talent within the company
- increased innovation
- better use of the unique talents of the mentees and the mentors
- acquisition by the mentors of new leadership skills, notably the development of autonomy and initiative among their employees
- implementation of best practice in their departments or in other departments.

During the preparation of the second edition of the programme, the existing CEO left the company. The new CEO invited me for a talk but, at that time, he was not interested in continuing the programme. One year later, he got back to me and asked: 'What do I have to do to take a course as a mentor?' 'Just sign up', I said.

Since December 2021, the current CEO of Bosch Polska has been a certified mentor at EMCC at the Foundation level and, as he put it, 'I haven't said the final word on the subject yet.'

In July 2022, another batch of four mentors decided to take an additional Mentor Foundation course. All of them succeeded and obtained their certification at the Foundation level.

We're starting up again.

# 25 Turning job seekers into job creators through entrepreneurship mentoring at Bharatiya Yuva Shakti Trust (BYST), India

**Authors:** *Dr Chandana Sanyal, Dr Julie Haddock-Millar, Dr Leandro Sepulveda, Dr Robyn Owen, Dr Stephen Syrett and Dr Neil Kaye*

**Original Content Narrator**: Lakshmi Venkataraman Venkatesan, Founding and Managing Trustee, Bharatiya Yuva Shakti Trust (BYST), India

## Introduction

This case study showcases a volunteer business mentoring programme of Bharatiya Yuva Shakti Trust (BYST) in India, based on extensive longitudinal impact evaluation research conducted between 2016 (Phase 1) and 2018 (Phase 2), involving nine mentor–mentee paired interviews and survey questionnaire responses across Phases 1 and 2. In April 2022, a follow-up review was conducted with key personnel at BYST to capture the programme evolution, new developments and BYST's current enhanced vision of leading mentoring globally.

**Voluntary business mentoring** is defined as personalised support that helps young entrepreneurs develop their abilities and insights as they start and grow their own business. The mentoring relationships demonstrate that the volunteer entrepreneurship mentors offered help and support to maximise potential and enhance careers (Kram, 1985; Parsloe, 1999; Apospori, Nikandrou and Panayotopoulou 2006) and also aided in the transition and development of the entrepreneur in their new business role (Wallace and Gravells, 2007; Clutterbuck and Ragins, 2002).

The primary roles of the entrepreneurship mentor are sounding board, guide and role model. The mentor supports the mentees' psychosocial needs, building confidence and self-esteem. Alongside this, the mentors adopt a coaching attitude, providing non-directive support, unconditional positive regard (Rogers, 1957), minimising potential power dynamics to empower the mentees, addressing both the intellectual as well as the emotional needs. In mentoring with a coaching attitude, the mentor may share experience with detachment, by inspiring, encouraging and supporting (see Chapter 1).

## About BYST

The Bharatiya Yuva Shakti Trust (BYST), a non-profit organisation, was set up in 1992. It was inspired by the then HRH The Prince of Wales to replicate the Prince's Trust youth entrepreneurship support model to help disadvantaged young people in India develop business ideas into viable enterprises with the guidance and support of a mentor. BYST is an established locally led member of Youth Business International (YBI). YBI is a global network made up of over 50 member organisations in 46 countries around the world, providing mentoring programmes for young entrepreneurs. The programmes support young, underserved people to start, grow and sustain their businesses, enabling entrepreneurs to contribute to the entrepreneurial ecosystem through job creation, community interaction and people development.

Celebrating its 30 years of service to the nation and the young people of India, BYST has helped young entrepreneurs across Indian cities, such as Delhi, Pune, Hyderabad, Chennai as well as rural areas of Haryana, Tamil Nadu, Odisha, Jharkhand and Maharashtra. BYST works with young people in the age group 18 to 35 years, who are either unemployed or underemployed. Individuals with sound imaginative business ideas, along with the will and determination to succeed, are encouraged to participate. Business proposals from potential entrepreneurs are welcome directly or through vocational schools, entrepreneurial training institutions and well-established grass root and non-governmental organisations (NGOs). BYST give assistance to help formulate these proposals which are screened by an Entrepreneur Selection Panel comprised of experts from the industry in marketing, finance and management. On approval of the proposal by the panel, BYST provides a whole range of business development services such as training, business plan development, monitoring, mentoring and networking as well as supplementing financing (ranging from 6,189 to 123,349 euros respectively, as at 8 August 2022).

In the last decade, BYST has supported a wide variety of business activities and sectors: desk-top publishing, construction, manufacturing, handicrafts, electronics, organic tea blending, catering services, garment making, furniture making, herbal cosmetics and many more. Through continuous outreach and counselling initiatives, as of 31 December 2021, BYST had reached out to nearly 925,000 youths, financed (through banks) and mentored over 25,000 entrepreneurs with a total funding of more than 55,997,935 euros (as at 8 August 2022). These efforts have generated over 337,000 employment opportunities and many BYST-supported entrepreneurs have gone on to win national and international awards, emerging as successful youth icons – 69 national awards and 27 international awards. Ten per cent of BYST entrepreneurs have become millionaires (in rupees) with an annual turnover between 13,500 and 14,500 euros.

## BYST mentoring programme

BYST has developed a mandatory mentoring programme for disadvantaged entrepreneurs which starts from the time the entrepreneur makes a loan application with support from BYST and continues for the next 2 years of business development. Each entrepreneur is offered one-to-one mentoring in the urban and rural areas including a mobile mentoring clinic for some rural areas when one-to-one mentoring is not feasible. The interviews highlight that, although mandatory for 2 years, several mentoring relationships have continued to flourish over 7 or more years as successful entrepreneurs have grown and expanded their businesses.

The traditional Indian 'Guru-Shishya' relationship is encouraged where the teacher or the 'mentor' not only teaches, but also guides and helps the mentee, in this case to develop the business disciple. The mentor provides personalised advice, maintains regular contact, monitors progress and helps to build and grow the business. The mentor, in turn, gets a wide range of first-hand business experience and the satisfaction of helping a disadvantaged young person.

The mentoring programme is designed to operate alongside a range of other business development services such as professional advice, financial guidance, training and education to support the entrepreneurs to start, grow and stabilise their business. Mentoring is a prerequisite; it starts during the loan application stage and is mandatory after loan disbursement followed by a 2-year 'handholding' period. An entrepreneur may have more than one mentor during this period.

Mentors are business volunteers and are recruited through social organisations, existing mentors' references, business exhibitions, conferences, associations and professional networking sites. The approach to mentor–mentee matching is broadly similar across the regions and pairings examined. Mentors are assigned to entrepreneurs by the Mentor Advisory Panel based on geographical area, expertise, gender and occasionally religious beliefs; this panel keeps track of mentor–mentee relationships, intervenes, troubleshoots, inducts new mentors and oversees mentor accreditations.

The role of the local mentoring manager/officer is vital in ensuring that the mentor–mentee matches are nurtured and supported in the beginning with early interventions if there are any signs that the matching may not work. Here, BYST has a clear process to support the local mentoring officers through the

Mentor Advisory Panel who offer guidance and advice on managing and monitoring the mentor–mentee matches and relationships.

BYST has an innovative 'Mentor Online Learning' (MOL) programme for mentors, comprising of key concepts, knowledge, behaviours and skills required as volunteer business mentors. Among the knowledge, behaviours and skills are the elements of non-judgemental unconditional positive regard, empowering mentees to take responsibility for their development and entrepreneurship journey, focusing on the dual aspects of entrepreneurship identity and business growth (see Chapter 1). Ultimately this leads to mentee autonomy and entrepreneurial success (see Chapter 8). The mentors are accredited with the internationally recognised City & Guilds certificate after the completion of both the MOL course and 10 hours of mentoring practice. The entrepreneurs receive specific guidance on mentoring and their role and responsibility of being a mentee.

The mentoring programme is centrally managed and aims to be consistent in approach across all operational regions. Mentoring is clearly differentiated from other BYST business development services offered to the entrepreneur such as financial and professional advice, training and education. Mentoring is seen as an essential and specialist support, requiring personalised guidance through regular contact, problem solving, monitoring progress and helping to build and grow the business. The key focus is on skills development, typically in relation to sales and marketing, building confidence, developing business networks, financial management and technical trading issues and regulations. The mentor, in turn, gets a wide range of first-hand business experience and the satisfaction of helping a disadvantaged young person. The mentor–mentee contacts are face to face and over the telephone once a month or sometimes more frequent when required.

BYST has developed a robust tracking system for recording, maintaining and reporting the personal and project profile of an entrepreneur. The mentoring programme evaluation is undertaken using a Business Performance Tracking Sheet (BPTS). The BPTS tracks mentor–mentee interactions such as date of meetings, mentor–mentee action plan, mentee's monthly sales, turn over, profit margin and instalment, number of employees and customers, as well as development/diversifications and business challenges. The main topics covered in mentoring conversations were finance, accounting, bookkeeping, business/product development, marketing, diversification, dealing with customers, licensing, contracting, environmental sustainability, corporate social responsibility, export/import, competition and business processes.

# Essence of the programme – mentoring with a coaching attitude

At BYST, mentoring is perceived to have enormous added value for the disadvantaged young entrepreneurs. In the context of small businesses, involving an experienced entrepreneur (mentor) to support a nascent or novice entrepreneur (mentee) in their personal and professional development is considered good practice (St-Jean and Audet, 2012). Mentoring is viewed as one of several support functions, assisting in knowledge acquisition, choice-guiding and decision-making, enabling behaviour and attitudinal change, business development and continuity (Sullivan, 2000; Gravells, 2006; McKevitt and Marshall, 2015). While non-directive guidance by the mentor is best practice (Clutterbuck and Megginson, 1999; Gravells, 2006), McKevitt and Marshall (2015) propose that mentorship within small and medium-sized enterprises (SMEs) may have different needs, and for mentoring to be effective more direct support needs to be included within the mentoring process. It is also recognised that a non-judgemental approach, holding the mentee with unconditional positive regard underpins mentoring practice and a coaching attitude (see Chapter 1). In all examples illustrated in this case study, the mentors adopt the coaching attitude, while also taking a mentoring approach, providing guidance and role modelling. This is necessary in the case of the novice entrepreneur, where navigating the entrepreneurial ecosystem requires a heightened level of self-insight, confidence and self-esteem. Core mentoring skills with a coaching attitude include active listening, powerful questions and reflection (see Chapters 4 and 5).

The mentor–mentee interviews highlight that in most cases the mentor took the responsibility for initiating and managing the mentoring relationship in the preliminary stages. The interviews highlight that, at the start of the relationship, the mentors offered guidance on loan sanction, product development, people and management structures. One mentor observes that his mentee was *'afraid and hesitant to ask questions in the beginning, so I told her to feel free and talk about her problems; once I gave that comfort zone, she discussed about lots of things …'* It was evident that where the mentee had limited education and exposure to the world of business and was therefore lacking in confidence, the mentor was in the driving seat in the mentoring relationship, to give structure to the process and guide the entrepreneur to set up the business, at least in the initial stages.

Alongside support with development and growth of the entrepreneur's business, the mentoring also built confidence and improved their people and business management skills. This is where mentors shifted their approach, to include coaching skills such as enabling insight and learning, with an outcome and action orientation (see Chapter 7). This quote describes what a mentee gained personally from the mentoring relationship.

> I learnt the meaning of the word entrepreneur from my mentor, I got the award, my total life changed, it changed my personality … changed the way I dress, I used to be scared to face people, now my confidence has gone up. Before in a group I would not speak in case I was wrong but now I give lectures in board meetings … My mentor helped to build my confidence, communication skills and my attitude.

This illustrates that the mentor supported the entrepreneur in enhancing his sense of personal identity and belonging (St-Jean and Audet, 2012; Terjesen and Sullivan, 2011; Baluku et al., 2018). Here, the mentoring fosters the entrepreneurs' mental and emotional mastery, including their ability to self-evaluate, developing their self-awareness, self-insight and reflectivity skills, developing both as an entrepreneur and a person (St-Jean and Audet, 2012; Johannisson, 1991). This demonstrates mentoring with a coaching attitude.

# Evolution of BYST mentoring programme

There has been significant development and some changes within BYST in the last 4 years.

## BYST Highflyer Club

A significant development within the programme was the introduction of the BYST Highflyer Club offering an opportunity to showcase successful entrepreneurs and their mentoring relationships. The mentees and mentors can also network and learn from each other's practices. Over the last four years, there is clear evidence that the Highflyer Club has become a strong platform for BYST's success stories. In some instances, the entrepreneurs in the Highflyers Club have now been identified as potential mentors and several successful entrepreneurs are now BYST mentors.

## Programme expansion

BYST has widened its mentoring scope across India through the new Government of India initiative 'Mentoring India'. Alongside the core voluntary mentoring programme, in 2017, BYST launched Mentoring India. This is BYST's new vertical programme, where it is leading on training a pool of mentors at every touch point to guide and support the entrepreneur through each stage of their entrepreneurial journey. The Mentoring India programme is actively developing a mentoring environment through training, research and consultancy, at every touch point of financial, government/private institution that an entrepreneur is likely to interact with, especially for SMEs. The overarching aim of the programme is to create a facilitative ecosystem to increase the viability and success rate of young, first-generation entrepreneurs in underserved communities in India. At present, the programme has trained and accredited 3,521 institutional mentors; this has helped motivate around 14,000 young peope to select entrepreneurship as a career option. The Director of Rural Self Employment Training Institute, India (RSETI) highlights that: '*This is excellent training on mentoring by BYST. It's very much required for the nation as we need entrepreneurs in all fields to excel in every aspect of life.*' The upgraded learning management system has systemised the matching process and tracking of the 'learner's' progress.

Alongside, expanding across regions in India, BYST as a founding member of the YBI has also set up similar programmes globally, enhancing its international links and network. BYST has supported the establishment of mentoring programmes in Mauritius, Sri Lanka, Philippines and Nepal.

By consistently bringing on board the Indian corporate sector in all aspects of its operations – financing, project evaluation and review, training and mentoring, BYST has created a model for corporate executives to accept their social responsibility and participate voluntarily in the process of nation building through volunteer mentoring. BYST's Board of Trustees comprises leaders from the top business houses in India and the corporate partners include national and multinational organisations such as the Confederation of Indian Industry (CII), HDFC Bank, Bajaj Auto, JP Morgan India, JK Paper, Info Edge, IKEA Foundation, Foreign, Commonwealth & Development Office (FCDO UK) and YBI. These partnerships contribute significantly to supporting, nurturing and empowering young dynamic, disadvantaged entrepreneurs, and integrating them to the economic mainstream in eastern and southern regions in India.

# Opportunities and challenges

BYST's long-term vision is to position BYST as global leader in mentoring young Grampreneurs[151] at the grassroots level by creating a pool of mentors to counsel and support Indian youth in building sustainable micro enterprises. BYST will continue to turn job seekers into job creators through entrepreneurship mentoring. The goal is to create and support 1 million Grampreneurs to generate 50 million jobs by 2050.

Some of the identified challenges are as follows:

* Identify and reach out to potential mentors in underserved areas.
* Sensitise policy and decision makers in government and financial institutions about the need to promote mentoring, to help build viable businesses and reduce the incidence of 'bad loans'.
* Continued engagement and motivation of mentors nominated by BYST institutional partners.

# Mentor–mentee case study examples

This section presents three case study examples of mentee/mentor pairings to illustrate the BYST programme implementation and mentoring impact. The case studies describe the following:

* mentee and mentor profile
* relationship focus
* reflections on the mentoring relationship and perceived value.

---

151 *Grampreneurs* are micro-entrepreneurs with value chains spread across small towns and villages.

For each of the case studies presented, the names of mentors and mentees are withheld in order to preserve anonymity. In each case study, mentors and mentees are referred to as Mentor 1 and Mentee 1, and so forth. The process of matching and mentoring the relationships followed the programme structure and processes described in the section on the BYST mentoring programme. The mentoring sessions were conducted using a range of methods – face to face, telephone and online as convenient for the mentors and mentees.

## Case study 1: Plastic polymer start-up

*Introducing Mentee 1 and Mentor 1*

Mentee 1 is 28 years old, from a small village in Western India. His parents were originally farmers but migrated to the city and worked as labourers for their livelihood. Mentee 1 and his brother often could have only one meal a day. Through government education he completed his graduation and for a while did odd jobs to meet his daily expenses and contribute to the family income. He then decided to attend a 2-year course in an Industrial Training Institute on Plastic Processing Operation; he learnt about polymer products and decided to start his own business to manufacture such products. In 2011, he was able to get a loan of 12,345 euros through BYST to buy machinery; at the same time, he was allocated a mentor.

Mentee 1 now manufactures a wide range of mulching films that help to retain soil moisture, provide weed control, decrease leaching of fertilisers, and reduce labour and electricity for a sustainable model of farming in India. He has also expanded into manufacturing industrial packaging material, supplying across the western region of India, Maharashtra and three other states, and is currently contemplating exports of industrial packaging material. He is passionate about his product as the mulching technique (mulch is a technical term meaning covering of soil) helps farmers to save up to 60 to 70 per cent water by retaining high moisture and improving the health and quality of the soil. This addresses a vital social need for farmers and the agricultural community in rural India. Mentee 1 received the YBI Social Entrepreneur of the Year in 2015. Between 2020 and 2021, he has managed to get an impressive turnover of more than 256 million euros employing 53 people to work in his unit.

Mentor 1 is 55 years old, a commerce graduate and has had his own business in engineering and fabrication since 1991. He is an experienced mentor and has mentored other BYST entrepreneurs. Initially, he did not receive any mentoring training but now regularly attends BYST Chapter meetings which he finds especially useful and motivational as there is good interaction with other mentors. His expertise is in the areas of finance and commerce – essential in setting up successful businesses.

*Relationship focus*

The mentoring relationship has continued for 10 years since the start of the business in 2011. As Mentee 1 had no experience in setting up a business, his mentor helped him enormously in the initial stages to understand the essential require-ments of starting his business. Mentee 1 says *'without the specific and right direction'* from his mentor this would not have been possible. His mentor's expe-rience in finance has helped him to successfully access other government loans to expand his business. The mentor's advice and guidance on ensuring that loan payments were made on time was great learning for Mentee 1. He realised the importance of this as he was able to access further loans based on his record of repayments. His mentor also helped him to self-evaluate, developing and increas-ing his self-awareness, self-insight and reflectivity skills, helping him to build his identity as an entrepreneur. The entrepreneurship mentor adopted the roles of coach and mentor, providing guidance and empowering the mentee to have the confidence to take the first steps in accessing finance to start and develop the business (see Chapter 1). He continues to meet his mentor regularly, face to face, and also has mentoring conversations on the phone as required. The mentoring conversations now mainly focus on marketing, particularly international mar-keting, and further improvement of business processes.

Mentor 1 observes that the mentoring relationship worked well because his mentee is a good listener, and he follows through on suggestions and was able to achieve the result. *'I ask my mentee to get information on raw material from a particular place, he will follow up immediately and report back to me. That is why there is good bonding.'* Mentor 1's steady guidance and support contributed significantly to Mentee 1's spectacular business success.

*Reflections*

Initially, Mentee 1 had no understanding of mentoring and did not know what to expect from his mentor. In his first meeting, his mentor asked him about his family, why he wanted to start a business and what he wanted to achieve. Mentee 1 remembers that his mentor made him feel free and comfortable and he spent 2 hours talking to him. He says that it is an excellent quality of his men-tor; he is able to reach out to his mentor whenever he needs help and guidance:

> He is more than BYST, he is my friend, I can say anything I want to say, I can call him anytime and say I have a problem and he will ask me to go and see him ... he always has a solution, he will not do it for me but ask me questions which make me think – if you want 1 million turnover, do you have the machinery, the marketing plan? Then I have to come up with the answers.

When asked what support he has received for this success, he replied that *'the most important support received is the confidence, the moral support to move forward you can say, which is very important and necessary for a new entre-preneur.'* Mentee 1 attributes the success of his business which started with a small loan from BYST to his mentor's guidance and direction.

Mentor 1 too says that: *'I mentor him like a friend and there are no losses in this relationship; if there were losses nobody would be interested in mento-ring.'* He acknowledges that he has strengthened his own confidence through the success of his mentee entrepreneur: *'If my mentoring is getting the results then definitely the same thing will happen to my business also.'* He also observes that there is a need for more committed and experienced mentors to support more entrepreneurs within BYST.

## Case study 2: Health food manufacturing start-up

*Introducing Mentee 2 and Mentor 2*

Mentee 2 is a 25-year-old male entrepreneur who comes from a southern coastal town in Tamil Nadu, India. His father was a carpenter and supported Mentee 2's education with his meagre earnings. He completed his first degree and applied for an educational loan to do an MBA. As there was a delay with this, rather than look for a job, he decided to start *'something on my own – a dream I always had'*. He started selling fast food snacks, but lack of experience and debts forced him to close the business. He decided to take up entrepreneurial courses on food products and, after much research into the health food sector, decided to start a business with a few friends – Strawberry Group, producing health food products, specifically dealing with millets, nuts and lentil-based mixes. The initial response was positive and there was demand for millets, but he needed funding to continue and expand the business. He contacted BYST after finding out about the organisation while searching for loan options on the internet. His business proposal was approved by the BYST Internal Entrepreneurs Sectional Panel, and his loan was sanctioned by the BYST Bank Entrepreneurs Selection Panel. He received training and was allocated his mentor.

Mentor 2 is a serial entrepreneur in software products and runs his own company. He has been selling his own products globally since 1995 and worked with SMEs in America, Australia and Europe. He has the experience of collaborating with several companies to scale up their web, e-commerce and mobile technologies. He is also an experienced mentor and has mentored start-ups in the technology sector as well as within BYST. His expertise is in marketing strategies, product positioning and development. His reason for joining BYST is to *'spend more time outside my own core business to help others, on non-profit activities'*.

*Relationship focus*

The mentoring relationship started in early 2014, as soon as Mentee 2's BYST loan was sanctioned. Mentee 2 had no experience of being mentored before, but he says that *'after BYST training I understood about mentoring support'*. Both the mentee and mentor confirm that the match worked well and the mentor was able to connect with the mentee to build an authentic relationship (see Chapter 3). The mentoring relationship continued over 5 years with regular mentoring conversations once a month face to face and three to four times by telephone during this period. Initially, Mentor 2 steered mentoring conversations: *'I took the initiative to create a platform to ask questions, now he floods me with questions.'* He also introduced his mentee to his friends who are in business to help with networking and exchange of business ideas.

The main topics of mentoring discussions have been marketing, product development, finance, export–import, competition, branding, current and future trends, and expansion. Key mentoring outcomes have been steady rise in sales, improved focus on marketing strategy, developing a process for tracking expiry of food which has reduced food rejection, preparing for the global market and considering new products for business expansion. Alongside business guidance and advice, the mentoring has also focused on Mentee 2's motivation and wellbeing as well as developing an entrepreneurial mindset, which reflect coaching elements within the mentoring conversations. This included enabling self-insight and learning, with an outcome and action orientation (European Mentoring and Coaching Council – Mentoring and Coaching Competence Framework, 2017; see Figure 1.1 in Chapter 1). The mentor minimised the power distance, enabling the building of rapport and a safe space, where the mentee was able to be open and honest about challenges, issues and concerns.

### Reflections

Mentee 2 says that his mentor is friendly and knowledgeable; his expertise in e-commerce, marketing and product development in particular has helped his business enormously. The mentor's personal contacts have helped to expand sales of products to other parts of India. He has increased the number of employees and the turnover between 2014 and 2019. His mentor has also supported him with media interviews and online branding. He says that he would not like to change anything about the relationship, it is the *'best mentor and mentee relationship'*.

Mentor 2 reflects that the mentoring relationship developed significantly over the 5 years and during this time Mentee 2 and his business partners have become franker and more open in their discussions, sharing both personal and business concerns with him. A personal benefit for him is the satisfaction of seeing the growth of the business and development of the products, and how his support has contributed to this success.

Unfortunately, Mentee 2's business has been severely affected by the pandemic as the production process was manual. The company is no longer in operation. Mentor 2 has supported the mentee through this challenging time, guiding him through challenging decisions when considering several options, including dissolving his current company.

### Case study 3: Kitchen and cookware manufacturing start-up

*Introducing Mentee 3 and Mentor 3*

Mentee 3 is a 32-year-old female entrepreneur based in the south-central part of India. She is the only child of her parents; her mother had a saree business and her father was a contractor but also had a business in precious stones. Unfortunately, he fell ill when Mentee 3 was at high-school leaving age and she had to take responsibility for the family. She did part-time jobs and attended evening college to complete her undergraduate degree. Following graduation, she joined a German company in the jewellery department. The same company also manufactured cookware which required far less oil and water to be able to cook healthy and nutritious food. Along with her primary work of selling jewellery, Mentee 3 started selling this cookware as well. The product was exceptionally good, but it was not affordable for everyone. The company was also not interested in reducing the cost of the cookware. Mentee 3 felt this product could become a great addition to the Indian kitchen and help Indians to eat nutritious food. She decided to collaborate with a business partner with 18 years of work experience in similar products. The demand for the product has increased with the rise in health consciousness. But as the cost of production overseas is high, she and her partner wanted to utilise their experience and started product development in India. They engaged in R&D for around 2 years, successfully developing the product and now have many satisfied customers. Mentee 3 secured a loan of 24,685 euros from BYST to buy raw material for mass production of the cookware in India. At this time, she was allocated a BYST mentor to support the development and growth of her business.

Mentor 3 is a technology entrepreneur and has been promoting and encouraging young people to take up businesses in technology. He is an electronics engineer and a management graduate and has supported many individuals with access opportunities in technology businesses. He has been associated with BYST for over 20 years and currently supports two entrepreneurs, Mentee 3 being one of them.

*Relationship focus*

The mentoring relationship started in 2018, as soon as Mentee 3's BYST loan was sanctioned. Mentee 3 explained that her mentor became her guiding light at every step of her business. She now understands how to manage her assets, has learnt how to deal with her employees and develop operation procedures, as well as how to create an effective marketing strategy. Her biggest order recently was worth 80,220 euros. Mentee 3 referred to the emotional support alongside the technical guidance from her mentor, particularly during the pandemic. She was able to talk through her ideas of 'taking her product from offline to online' as well as build her resilience and maintain her emotional wellbeing through her mentoring conversations. She says, '*I am clear about my business goals, and I have my mentor as my guru to provide guidance and direction to achieve my goals.*'

*Reflections*

Mentee 3 explained that her mentor was both directive and challenging as well as nurturing and facilitative in building networks and social connections to develop and grow her business. The mentor's guidance, direction, as well as his influence and motivation has helped her to expand her start-up significantly. Her company hired 24 employees directly and 150 indirectly.

Due to the pandemic, the turnover for last year was reduced to 43,190 euros but this year they are aiming for 123,407 euros. Her mentor is guiding her to explore opportunities for export to the UAE and Singapore where there is a high demand for the product. Her vision is to turn job seekers into job creators by encouraging women to take up entrepreneurship. She wants to take nutrition to every kitchen in the metropolitan cities and urban towns of India. This would also provide opportunities to other women to start their own enterprises by using their cooking skills, which is otherwise just a daily chore. The mentor adopted the role of guide and role model, sharing his experience and knowledge at key transition stages. Alongside this, the mentor demonstrated a coaching attitude, supporting the mentee's psychosocial needs, building her confidence and self-esteem (see Chapter 1). Furthermore, the mentor was able to support the mentee to develop key behavioural indicators, imperative for the novice entrepreneur (see Chapter 2).

## Final thoughts

The BYST mentoring programme in India clearly demonstrates the power of voluntary business mentoring in addressing the barriers experienced by young entrepreneurs, including access to institutional networks and alliances, acquisition of skills, information and professional advice. BYST continues to build a mentoring programme with a coaching attitude that harnesses the power of personal connection and professional support to benefit thousands of underserved young entrepreneurs.

# Morocco: Mentoring at Hassan II University of Casablanca and women in politics

*Samira Siham Raïssouni, LPRH President, Coach, Mentor and Trainer*

I wish to share with you the change we are undergoing in Morocco. A rich human experience that is still going on thanks to all the contributions of people who have participated in the mentoring projects.

## Background

This chapter includes two mentoring cases that took place between 2019 and 2022: the first in the field of education (two projects) and the second in the arena of politics. I will try to answer the following questions:

- Why mentoring and not another mechanism?
- How did the process operate?
- What contributions did it make and what results were obtained?
- What were the difficulties or obstacles encountered in the implementation of the two projects as well as the lessons learned?
- Is there a cultural specificity to mentoring or not?
- Can it be implemented in the same way in Morocco as elsewhere?
- Can its beneficial effects be measured?
- What are the factors that act as a lever to make the mentoring process a success?
- If it were to be redone, how could it be done differently?

Both projects were implemented in a challenging context, as if mentoring found its essence in the need to renew itself, innovate and think differently. The experience is related here in several parts:

- background of the project
- objectives

- process
- gains
- key success factors, and
- testimonials by mentees.

I am contributing to this book because I worked to promote mentoring with a coaching attitude at the Hassan II University of Casablanca with the support of the President, and in political parties with the collaboration of the Konrad Adenauer Stiftung foundation.

At the Hassan II University of Casablanca (UH2C) level, the training included the transmission of coaching tools and posture (professional attitude of listening, benevolence and openness), plus the definition of the mentoring and coaching professions, in their points of intersection and distinctions. The beneficiaries, which consisted of doctoral students, played the role of mentor with a coaching attitude with first-year students, their mentees.

The supervision sessions allowed the doctoral students to sharpen these tools, to listen to each other collectively in a group and to deepen the learning in a practical way. The pleasant observation is that they engaged in the process with professionalism and determination.

For political parties, the transmission of coaching tools and the importance of the mentoring process were highly appreciated by the mentors. Awareness sessions on the mentoring process were carried out collectively, bringing together all political parties, and sessions for the transmission of coaching tools and posture were carried out by the political party.

As the group of mentees was made up of women, the values of female leadership were reinforced. The benchmark with other German and American foreign experiences was a mirror of the positioning of women in the East and in the West with bringing together what is happening in Morocco and elsewhere. It was also about relaying spirituality in female leadership by taking the example of the Prophet's wife (Sallahu Alayhi Wa Salam). Lala Khadija (RA) was a very important lever, which honours the identity and the strength of the Muslim woman, as a pioneer, independent, strong and supportive, and whose values of respect, integrity, sharing, transmission, support and love are essential. RA stands for 'Radhi Allah Anhu' meaning 'May Allah be pleased with him/ her'. Mentoring has a noble mission that gives meaning to people's lives, enlightens and illuminates their paths.

# Education: Mentoring within Hassan II University of Casablanca (UH2C)

### Innour Mentoring: a project launched amidst a pandemic

The idea of setting up a mentoring project within Hassan II University of Casablanca (UH2C) emanated from a working session with the University President, currently Minister of Solidarity, Social Integration and the Family.

The President's wish was to support two targets: (i) doctoral students, and (ii) first- and second-year students in difficulty, who are at risk of dropping out of university. It should be noted that being a woman at the head of 18 institutions within the university reveals particular competence and real leadership; the President proved to be very sensitive to the development of interpersonal and communication skills, along with self-confidence.

The idea is that mentoring is an adequate and sustainable response to specific needs, namely the development of the skills of doctoral students, who are called upon to act as mentors for undergraduate students. This will contribute to the creation of a community of mentors within UH2C and its educational ecosystem.

*Project start-up and prerequisites*

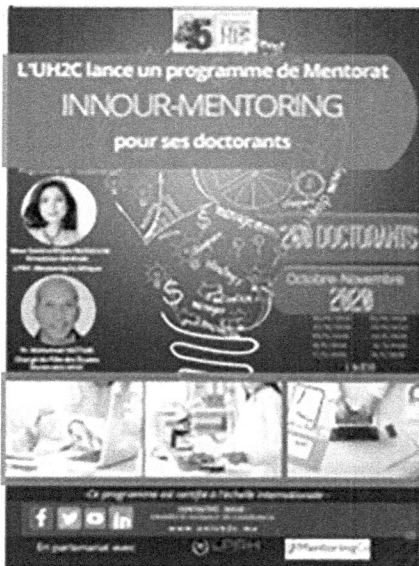

'Innour Mentoring' Project was launched in October 2020, in collaboration with the University's Doctoral Center led by Dr Mohammed Hattabi, during the COVID-19 pandemic. This compelled us to carry out our actions in digital mode.

The name 'Innour Mentoring' was coined from **IN** for **Innovation**, **NOUR** for **light** (in Arabic) and **MENTORING** for the **mentoring mechanism**. It was the very first mentoring project for doctoral students in any of the various educational tracks at UH2C, including scientific, economic, legal, literary, engineering schools, etc.

We set out by establishing selection criteria for doctoral candidates, because we had to check their commitment value to ensure that they would follow all the stages of the process and that they were capable of transmitting the tools learned and the experience lived (transmission generosity). A call for applications was sent to the various UH2C institutions, asking potential candidates to fill in a questionnaire. At the end of this phase, approximately 80 per cent of the applications were accepted.

An internal and external dissemination was carried out to give visibility to the project, namely the design of a poster to be posted in the various institutions.

*A certifying and international process*

Let us start with the venture that followed UH2C President's request. We had agreed that the project could lead to an official certification and be backed by an international experience. I, therefore, proposed to Professor Sylviane Cannio, a seasoned coach and mentor, to join me in this project. I had a relevant and warm professional exchange with her during the third coaching session organised by the Morocco Coaching Association. This Association was supported by the International Coaching Federation (ICF) Association, which I chaired from 2011 to 2013, and which aims at promoting professional coaching in Morocco. I had kept a very positive image of her professionalism, quality of self-assertion and open-mindedness. I felt that these values of openness, sharing and humility could serve as a basis for this transformation project.

In her turn, she proposed that I join the international platform MentoringCo and to involve the internationally renowned mentors: Fisher Yu and Cicero Carvalho in the project. Currently, I represent this rewarding platform in French-speaking Africa.

Thus, the seeds of Innour Mentoring Project were sown and our working group created to support doctoral students from all educational tracks to acquire the position of 'Mentor with a Coach Attitude'.

### Phase 1: mentor training

The project was divided into three phases: the first phase consisted in organising 10 webinars on mentoring, with a view to transmitting mentor tools and position, with coach attitude, to doctoral students. Several themes were discussed: the coach attitude, the mentoring agreement, positive and inspiring communication, strategies for asking powerful questions, knowing how to give and receive feedback, the SWOT efficiency of the mentor, self-assessment matrices, and finally the societal impact of mentoring.

The exchange with doctoral students was very rich throughout the webinars; a human relationship was created, albeit through screens. 'The heart has its reasons that reason does not know' applied in this context, because the doctoral students felt and saw, through the webinars, that what drives us, in addition to the transmission of tools and position, is this real sharing of our professional and personal experience.

Fisher Yu and Cicero Carvalho were part of the 'game': getting insight into what is being done in China and Canada provided doctoral students with a wide range of know-how in the practice of support, positions of experienced mentors, who respect the mentoring sense, the sharing and transmitting values, along with the position of a mentor with coach attitude (see Chapters 1 to 7).

The webinars were concluded with a backdrop of cheers and nurturing feedback.

### Phase 2: support through practice (peer groups)

In the second phase of the programme, doctoral students organised themselves into practice groups of 5 to 7 members, to get trained and appropriate the tools. In sub-groups, they alternated in role-playing mentors, mentees and observers.

Group work is rewarding. It allows you to know yourself as a person in your relationship to yourself and to other members of the group.

- Am I comfortable within a group? Will I be able to talk about the difficulties I encountered easily or not (and why)?
- Am I clear enough in my requests and in the expression of my need(s)?
- Are the goals I want to achieve SMART?
- From what position am I making my request: independent position, victim or counter-dependent position? (See Chapter 8.)
- Have I tried actions or not? If not, why this lack of action?
- Am I a good listener? Am I in empathy or in sympathy (emotional sponge)? Have I entered a dramatic triangle, in the position of a victim, a rescuer or a persecutor? Does this apply in my personal or professional life?

To capitalise on this rich human experience between people who did not know each other before, doctoral students were asked to provide a document of no more than five pages, reflecting their experience during this second common experience: what they learned, what they appreciated, what was difficult and their suggestions (mutual learning process).

We left it to the groups to arrange themselves according to their affinities, and we advised them to be heterogeneous to maximise the learning opportunities.

We conducted several webinars (before, during and after phase 2). The first enabled us to explain the processes and listen to their questions on this phase of the project. We then fixed a date to receive the articles we asked them to provide, after the tool appropriation work carried out in sub-groups.

During all the webinars, we listened to their needs and complaints. We were able to discuss specific requests. The reports related the experiences lived: how had they appropriated the mentoring tools? How had they managed to set themselves up as a working group? Did they see each other face to face or did they resort to the digital environment? How did they liaise with each other? How did they help each other in capitalising on mentoring tool learning? Was it easy to play the different roles: mentor, mentee and observer? What did they think? (See Chapters 4 and 6.)

We received all the reports on time, which shows the doctoral students' interest in and commitment to the project. The documents were rich and diversified, demonstrating the strong involvement of doctoral students in the Innour Mentoring Project.

Leadership actions emerged, in particular the desire to create an association of doctoral students, which we found magnificent.

### Phase 3: support to doctoral students' practice and supervision

The third step is that the doctoral students start mentoring first and second year students in difficulty. Being newly graduated from high school, they strongly needed support to succeed in their university life (transition from high school life to university life).

This step enabled us to validate the commitment of doctoral students to support the undergraduate students, transmit tools to them by adopting their position of mentor with coach attitude. It allowed them to capitalise on the knowledge and positions learned during the mentoring project.

A student database was provided by UH2C administrative services. This stage was also very insightful for the doctoral students. Indeed, some undergraduate students did not agree to be accompanied, which generated frustration among some doctoral students. We then suggested that they make it into a mirror of themselves and see how a doctoral student would cope with the difficulties encountered and with surprises in their life.

During this stage, we organised supervision sessions after 6 weeks, to support the doctoral students and see where they got in relation to their work with the undergraduate students. We asked whether they had specific needs to impart to us. The supervision also aimed to maintain their motivation and appreciate their work, their successes and their areas of progress (see Chapters 8 and 9).

A strategic element that we did not think of, and which was a challenge for us, was the difficulty certain male doctoral students had in calling in female undergraduate students: parents were a little surprised and sceptical about the process, because they had not been informed beforehand by the university.

This is a cultural element that we have faced. The doctoral students suggested that a specialist from the university be indicated as a contact person for parents to secure a doctoral student–undergraduate student relationship. We took this relevant request into consideration and asked the Director of the Doctoral Centre to hand out the project flyer in all the university's institutions. We emphasised that the heads of such institutions inform their respective student services of the existence of the mentoring project and of the support of undergraduate students by doctoral students.

### Project gains

To date, a whole series of gains have been made:

- Emulation around mentoring, its tools, the mentoring position with coach attitude (listening, feedback, reformulation, positive communication, etc.).
- Enhanced atmosphere between doctoral students through work in subgroups: task distribution, respect of timing, organisation of face-to-face or digital meetings.
- Commitment of doctoral students to undergraduate student mentoring.
- Improved quality of the relationship between the management of the university's Doctoral Centre of doctoral students: closer relationships and smoother connections.
- Positive projection with regard to university life: doctoral students expressed the desire to continue to meet, work together and create an association of doctoral students within UH2C.
- Development of a quality human relationship with mentors to date.

*Key success factors of Innour Mentoring Programme*

To succeed, a mentoring programme requires real commitment of stakeholders, perseverance and patience (see Chapter 12). We benefited from:

* the commitment of UH2C presidency
* the professionalism of the management of the Doctoral Center
* the motivation and commitment of the selected beneficiaries
* the spirit shared by all project stakeholders
* mentors sharing the same values and working enthusiastically in mutual respect.

The success of Innour Mentoring within UH2C, manifested by doctoral students, enabled us to implement a second, women-specific, mentoring project. It was launched on International Women's Day in March 2021.

## 'Women Mentoring Women for Success' (WMW) within UH2C

For this new 100 per cent female experience, Ms Meryl Frank joined the team of mentors. Ms Frank is a former UN Ambassador for the Status of Women (2000–2010) and Mayor of Highland Park, New Jersey, USA.

*The process of the WMW project*

The 'Women Mentoring Women for Success' project started in April 2021. It followed the same steps: organisation of webinars, group work among doctoral students, undergraduate student mentoring and supervision.

Target specificity required that we adapt the themes of webinars in relation to the specificities of female leadership in a Moroccan cultural context: assertiveness, mental workload and priority management, learning how to say 'No', to dare coming forward, learning self-protection and self-care, positive communication through Transactional Analysis and Neuro-Linguistic Programming.

This beautiful and pioneering adventure within UH2C, with a 100 per cent female audience, coincided with the timing during which the Ministry of National Education was in the midst of a pedagogical transformation, in particular by the introduction of 'soft skills' in all the disciplines of public university education.

*Testimonials*

**Testimonial 1**: One of the most beautiful utterances heard during this rich human experience was: *ALLAH YERHAM AL OUALIDINE*, literally translated as 'May God bless your parents'. This phrase is uttered in the Moroccan context when one wishes to thank someone warmly. Some mentees shared their successes with us: achieving a good ranking in an international article competition, birth of a baby, heartfelt emotions, joy, gratitude, million thanks, flow of good energy, and so on.

One sentence particularly touched me: 'My life has changed; there is now a "before" and an "after" Mentoring.' By participating in mentoring projects, we think we are giving, but in reality, we are receiving a lot: good energy, joy, etc. I learned a lot from doctoral students, from their sincere exchanges and from their experiences. I am deeply grateful!

**Testimonial 2**: Here is the faithful text of a doctoral student who succeeded in obtaining a position as a research laboratory officer. She wrote:

> The mentorship training gave me the opportunity to enrich my life skills, know-how, as well as to expand my social network. Thanks to our mentors, I had the pleasure of acquiring mentoring tools and applying them in my personal and professional life.

> The mentoring sessions helped me a lot, when I was tested positive for COVID-19. Indeed, I was able to manage my stress, focus on the future and set the goals I wanted to achieve after recovery. Finally, I may summarise this exceptional experience by this little proverb I invented myself: 'Find a mentor or become one...'

These testimonials showed us the benefits of mentoring.

*Innour Mentoring programme nominated by EMCC*

Another joy we shared with the whole team, Sylviane, Fisher, Cicero and myself, was that the UH2C Innour Mentoring programme was nominated by the European Mentoring and Coaching Council (EMCC) in 2022 as the best mentorship programme.

While the mentoring programme was being deployed within UH2C, another mentoring programme was emerging in the arena of politics.

# Political arena: mentoring of women in political parties

## Mentoring women in politics in Morocco

We would like to point out that the project 'Mentoring of Women in Politics in Morocco' is part of a large project managed by the German foundation

Konrad Adenauer Stiftung Maroc KAS as leading partner. It is sponsored by the European Union under the theme 'Let us commit to more women in politics in Morocco and Benin in general'.

In this section, we focus on the project 'Mentoring of Women in Politics in Morocco', for which I collaborated with KAS in the collective implementation of the mentoring scheme with four political parties. The project 'Mentoring Women in Politics in Morocco' was funded by the European Union.

### Objectives of the project

The project 'Mentoring Women in Politics' had several objectives:

- To participate in the construction of a female leadership system in political parties.
- To create cooperation between women in the political arena, by heightening their awareness of the importance of positioning themselves and helping each other to achieve, together, greater success in the political field.
- To assist mentors in their support to mentees, to enable them to succeed in their involvement in a political party, and benefit from their political expertise and experience in the party.
- To raise women's awareness of a common cause, i.e. the importance of women positioning in politics: regardless of the party chosen, there is only one cause: to strengthen women's positioning within parties.

### Background of the project

It should be noted that 2021 was an election year in Morocco. This project started in July 2019. It involved four political parties.

The project coincided with a positive context: the will of the highest authority in the country to raise women's position in society, in politics and in civil society, with committed actors: Constitution 2011, Moudouwana (Family Code), and representation quota in political parties.

However, the progress made in women representation fell short of the ambitions of women involved in politics to advance laws and, thereby, Moroccan society.

In June 2019, the rate of female parliamentarians was 20 per cent in Morocco, 30 per cent in Tunisia and 61 per cent in Rwanda. Once these figures were posted, women realised the importance of fighting in this political arena and the opportunity of being assisted through the mentoring project.

### Project approach

We chose to start with a SMARTE (e for ecological) objective, with a team of 12 people per political party: each three mentors were assigned three mentees. Mentors were men and women with experience in the political field; they included former ministers, members of the party executive bureau, presidents

**Figure 26.1** Representation of women in politics

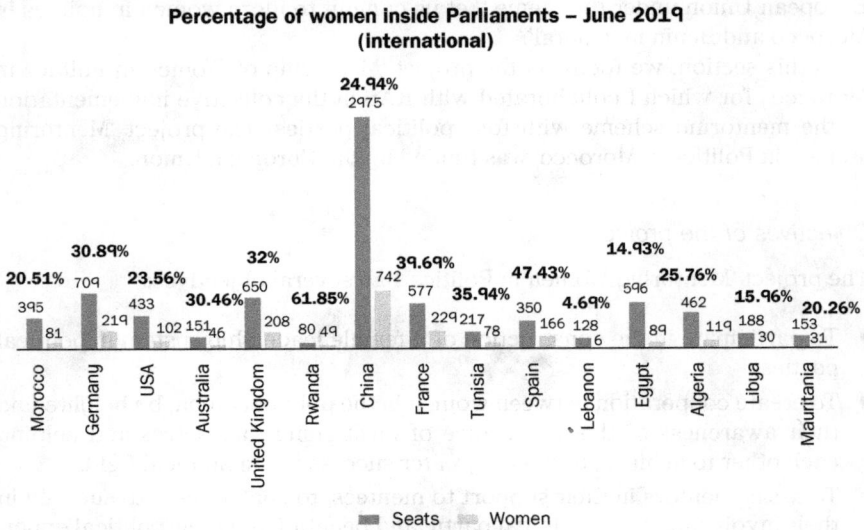

**Percentage of women inside Parliaments – June 2019 (international)**

Source: Inter-Parliamentary Union website

of party women federations, parliamentarians and top-tier persons in parties. Mentees were all women, since the project is about women.

Objective criteria for mentees' eligibility were presented to the party to ensure transparency and objectivity.

As this was a pilot project, once succeeded in the field, political parties could appropriate the scheme and deploy it at their level on a large scale.

*Project process*

The project was divided into five stages, including three main activities (see Chapter 2):

- A project launching workshop
- Activity 1: matching mentors and mentees
- Activity 2: facilitation and delivery of one lecture per political party
- Activity 3: facilitation and delivery of one global lecture per political party, in conjunction with international partners
- Closing of the project.

*Project launching workshop*

The launching workshop had multiple objectives and challenges. First, to present the challenges and objectives of the 'Mentoring Women in Politics' project;

secondly, to present the principle of mentoring (what it is and what it is not); thirdly, to clarify a mentor's role and position, the mentee's role and position, and the project supervisor; fourthly, to define the values to be shared by the group in order to unite the whole team around a common objective.

Then, team building was undertaken, during which the Director of the German foundation, Mr Steffen Krugler, reminded participants of the objectives and challenges of the project. Exercises were devised so that participants could get to know each other, appreciate working in a group and give meaning to the project in its strategic dimension: to raise the position of Moroccan women in the political arena.

### Project Activity 1: formation of mentor–mentee tandems

The highlights of Activity 1 were to support mentors and mentees in acquiring political mentoring tools, raise awareness among mentors and mentees regarding the importance of more involvement in the process of recruiting women into their political party, and develop further cohesion between mentors and mentees.

Political mentoring tools were shared: Political Map Diagnostic, tools for effective communication and strategy for building a future career in politics. The idea was to get to know each other, achieve personal development and look positively to the future.

The aim of the Political Map Diagnostic was to enable participants to position themselves within their internal and external environments, give them the opportunity to get to know themselves and connect to their strengths. This requires devising a strategy and adequate action plan, according to their political ambitions, but also to allow them to know their areas of improvement and the threats for which adjustment strategies should be put in place.

The communication tools were highly appreciated. Women expressed the idea that they work a lot, but do not often take the lead to make themselves or their work known. (False belief: let me work and my work will certainly be appreciated. Sometimes, it is a lack of audacity; in Moroccan culture, women are not supposed to come forward and position themselves too much. Other times, it is the 'Be perfect' hindrance: I must say things meaningful and perfect, or keep silent.)

The identification of the strategy and action plan to be implemented for the construction and development of a political career enabled mentors and mentees to clarify and lay the foundations of their work. (What political position am I aspiring to? How do I get there? By what means: electoral campaign, recruitment of voters, people to contact and mobilise in the party or the entourage?) Above all, it considered how to look positively to the future with a defined action plan and a positive and mobilising energy (see Chapter 8).

A discussion was held with stakeholders to clarify the key success factors of the project:

- mentor–mentee relationships should be confidential and non-hierarchical
- mentor–mentee relationships should be based on tolerance, respect and honesty

- mentor–mentee tandem meetings should be focused on developing both a short-term and, for the mentee, a long-term goal
- the mentee must be willing to open up to her mentor, and the mentor must be willing to offer guidance, based on her experience and knowledge of the party
- both mentor and mentee must be committed to the values outlined in the Mentoring Charter of Ethics, which was described on the day of their first meeting
- tandem partners commit to meet according to their mutual agendas and to contact the project coordinators, if necessary.

Mentors and mentees expressed their satisfaction, which was revealed by photos posted on social networks.

*Project activity 2: facilitation and delivery of one lecture per political party*

Activity 2 of the project had several objectives:

- To create a dynamic of learning and exchange between party mentors and mentees on a topic chosen by the party.
- To give mentees an opportunity to ask questions and express themselves freely in relation to the topic.
- To give mentors an opportunity to pass on experience to mentees and challenge them as well.
- To create more links between mentors and mentees through the topic.

To implement Activity 2, a questionnaire was sent to mentors so they could choose an appropriate topic that would enable mentees to better manage their political position during the COVID-19 crisis.

The topics chosen by political parties were:

- The role of women politicians in crisis management (during and after COVID-19 pandemic confinement).
- How to maintain and strengthen further trust with citizens during and after confinement.
- How to manage the post-confinement period. What role should the politician play with citizens?

As the context was a particular one with the COVID-19 crisis, mentors and mentees wanted to discuss the impact of the crisis on the implementation of the actions planned, and how to be innovative to make it into a lever for change and not a constraint.

Mentees learned that in order to succeed, they needed to have a working strategy. They needed to draw on mentors' experience in order to learn from them and persevere in the political field. They needed to establish strong links with mentors and undertake networking action within the political party. Exchanges were fruitful, sincere and authentic, given the constraints and difficulties women were facing. They now had a positive and determined look at how to achieve greater success in the political arena (see Chapters 3, 4, 5, 6 and 7).

The evaluation undertaken at the end of the activity allowed for participant mobilisation during this period of crisis; mentors and mentees shared their views; mentees learned from mentors' commitment, despite mentors' great professional and political responsibilities; and finally a transfer of mutual experience took place.

A strong point was the communication of this activity by communication officers in parties on social networks, both before and after the event.

### Project activity 3: facilitation and delivery of one global lecture per political party, in conjunction with international partners

Activity 3 was about benchmarking, including international experiences with highly qualified leaders in the field of politics, namely: Ms Doris Pack, a distinguished German political leader, President of EPP Women, President of Robert Schuman Institute and Member of the European Parliament, and Ms Meryl Frank, American, as previously introduced, Ambassador to the UN Commission on the Status of Women (CSW), appointed by President Obama in 2009.

Participation in this activity included several Moroccan ministers, including two women ministers. This is important to note because we believe in modelling and, therefore, mentees can make a positive projection of their political careers.

Experience sharing between national and international partners was very rich. It showed that women positioning in the political arena is not only a national but also an international cause. A feeling of international sisterhood was experienced. This produced more motivation to fight on the Moroccan political scene, as women deserve to be raised to decision-making positions in the political field.

The sharing of experiences, tips and advice was welcomed by mentees and mentors. They felt enriched by these international experiences, with women leaders of exceptional backgrounds.

The topic chosen by political parties was 'Communication and political marketing: how to build an image to mobilise voters'.

Guests gave an overview of their political careers in Germany, USA and Morocco. They gave an account of the levers that enabled them to position themselves in politics (taking into account the specificity of their campaigns in their own countries): marketing, communication, financing, mobilisation strategy, etc. They also shared the obstacles and hindrances they faced, and how they overcame such situations. In terms of political marketing, they shared the tools they have used, as well as the experiences drawn therefrom. A fruitful debate followed, focusing on whether such methods could be used in Morocco, based on the German and American experience.

This learning dynamic was comforting and reassuring. Women felt understood in their demands. They touched down, in a human way, on the fact that we are one, regardless of the country we are in. We move forward together, even if places and countries are different. This mobilised women in a positive atmosphere.

The exchange focused on the importance of mobilising for women's causes in general. Men within the party who believe in women should be identified. A pool and a network should be established to allow for taking into account the contribution of women in the political arena, as they are deserving and competent. The winner is the party, in the first place, by mobilising women's skills, and society at large, as they represent a cultural–political mirror.

The results of the mentoring project have been positive: we have received several direct testimonials from various women who expressed their gratitude. They said that they have gained confidence, learned a lot from each other's experience and from the mentors' values of perseverance, humility and determination.

### Closing of the project

**Mentoring is cited today as a success story.**

For 670 beneficiaries of the global project 'Let's Commit Ourselves' in Morocco, 220 candidates competed in the 2021 elections: 99 were elected, including 9 MPs and 1 Councillor.

Women who collaborated in the mentoring project now hold political positions in municipalities, the Parliament, professional chambers and the Chamber of Councillors.

What characterises them today is that they generate a different energy, an assumed feminine leadership with a clear vision, a sense of meaning in their work, a declared determination and a willingness to strive for a balance between professional, personal and political life.

These women believe further in women's networking within the party. They have become more assertive, to the extent that when they succeed in something, they are happy, and when they do not succeed, they learn the lesson and keep going. One feels that they are more fulfilled in their work, in a political world that is often not easy and where the stakes are high.

# My conclusion

I wanted to share with you this image, where two beautiful seeds of two beautiful trees of mentoring were sown in the Moroccan soil: one in the field of education and one in the field of politics. These seeds will blossom over time into two fruit trees, each with a head that is proud of its values of sharing, connection, empathy, determination, courage, and a trunk that is strong enough to represent confidence and strength, in a fertile and nourishing land.

# 27 Mentoring programmes in two universities in China

*Fisher Yu, CEO MentoringCo China,*
*President EMCC China*

Since 2009, I have been engaged in various mentoring programmes in China to support different groups of people. I have seen many mentees benefit from such programmes. In addition, many business schools and universities in China have adopted successful mentoring programmes to help their students.

From these examples, two cases stand out that I would like to share with you, as they may help you understand how different mentoring programmes work in Chinese universities. These are the CEIBS and CEDAR mentoring programmes.

## The CEIBS MBA mentoring programme

In the 12 years that I have been engaged in the China Europe International Business School (CEIBS) mentoring programme, I have witnessed significant developments in this one-to-one mentoring model and am very proud to have been part of its success.

### About CEIBS

CEIBS was co-founded by the Chinese government and European Union (EU) in 1994. CEIBS has campuses in Shanghai, Beijing, Shenzhen, Accra in Ghana and Zurich in Switzerland.

CEIBS is China's only business school to originate from a government-level collaboration. It is committed to educating its students to become responsible leaders in line with its motto of 'Conscientiousness, Innovation and Excellence' and promotes the concept of 'China Depth, Global Breadth'.

Leaders from the Chinese central government and the EU, respectively, have lauded CEIBS as 'a cradle of excellent executives' and 'a role model of EU–China cooperation'.

CEIBS offers these courses: MBA (Master of Business Administration), FMBA (Finance MBA), EMBA (Executive MBA), Global EMBA, Hospitality EMBA, DBA (Doctoral of Business Administration) (Switzerland) and an EDP (Executive Education programme). CEIBS was the first business school on the Chinese mainland to be accredited by both EQUIS and AACSB. EQUIS and AACSB are international quality standards for Economics and Business Schools awarded to universities with high scores on education and internationalisation (among other aspects). When a university is EQUIS and/or AACSB accredited, this indicates that this is an excellent university. CEIBS has been placed in the top tier of the *Financial Times* ranking of global MBA programme for 6 consecutive years (2016 to 2021) and has been ranked in the top five on its global EMBA list for 4 consecutive years (2018 to 2021).

Most recent figures, until 2022, show that CEIBS has more than 26,000 alumni from over 90 countries around the world and has provided a broad range of management programmes for more than 200,000 executives in China and abroad.

## Purpose of the CEIBS mentoring programme

CEIBS was the first business school in China to adopt a mentoring programme in its formal MBA education. It was designed to provide current MBA students with valuable advice beyond the classroom to help them grow and develop as business professionals. It started in 2004, eventually becoming integrated in 2016 into a required academic course – the 'MBA Leadership Journey' – to promote classroom learning with practical experience from the field. As part of the requirements for graduation from this course, every student must select a mentor from CEIBS.

Students take the experiential and classroom learning from the Leadership Journey course, developing their career competence with the help of their mentor's valuable knowledge. This includes offering guidance, sharing experiences and assisting in network expansion. Mentors provide feedback to their students, helping them reflect on their performance to specifically strengthen their skills for the future. This programme has been so successful that many MBA students, alumni and mentors have benefited from it. It is now a flagship for the MBA at CEIBS.

This programme is also intended to connect its MBA students with the broader community of CEIBS and draw upon the expertise and experience of their EMBA students and alumni. It aims to prepare and inspire MBA students to become the next generation of strong business leaders.

## How it works

**Figure 27.1** CEIBS mentoring programme flow

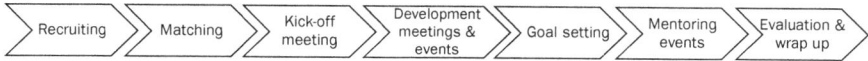

Recruiting ⟩ Matching ⟩ Kick-off meeting ⟩ Development meetings & events ⟩ Goal setting ⟩ Mentoring events ⟩ Evaluation & wrap up

### Step 1: Recruiting

This mentoring programme is 8 months long. It is managed via an online system that facilitates mentors and mentees and allows the MBA office's project manager to easily monitor the status of the programme.

Before recruiting, the MBA office will hold promotional events for prospective MBA students, EMBA and alumni, which include information about the programme values, recruiting criteria and the schedule for the programme.

Both mentors and mentees need to register their information onto the system to qualify. Mentors also need to indicate how many mentees they can take in the programme, and the type of mentee they prefer, if any. Mentors are usually EMBA students and alumni with rich working experiences.

### Step 2: Matching

After the registrations, mentees screen the mentors' profiles, then there are three rounds of mentor/mentee matching. In each round mentees can only apply for one mentor. Three students can apply for each slot, based on a 'first come, first served' policy.

If the match application fails in the first round, then the process moves to the second round, and if necessary, finally to a third. In the end, each mentee will get one mentor, while each mentor can have up to a maximum of three mentees. This limit ensures a reasonable workload for the mentor. When the match is completed, both mentor and mentee will receive a confirmation email, and the mentee is encouraged to take the initiative to contact their mentor and start the mentor/mentee journey.

### Step 3: Kick-off meetings

Usually, the MBA office will organise an opening ceremony for the programme. Mentors are invited to the school campus or remotely to meet each other, refresh the mentoring objectives and programme journey, receive basic mentoring skills training and meet with mentees. There will also be some learning and sharing from previous years' mentors and mentees.

## Step 4: Development meetings and events

The mentee needs to meet at least twice (either virtually or face to face) with their mentor. These meetings will be used for personal development, as part of the Leadership Journey course, and are a required component to pass the course. Students are strongly encouraged to have regular interactions with their mentors over and above this required academic component.

## Step 5: Setting goals

Setting goals that both mentor and mentee can work towards is essential at the beginning of this process so that the mentor can better understand the mentee in order to help them in their personal development.

## Step 6: Mentoring events

The mentoring events sessions can be face to face or virtual and can range from personal development topics to company visits, project opportunities, networking opportunities, and so on. Students are encouraged to be very proactive and make full use of the time spent with their mentor to get the appropriate feedback and advice.

## Step 7: Evaluation and wrap-up

At the end of the session, both mentor and mentee are encouraged to give formal feedback to each other. A closing ceremony is organised by the MBA office for evaluation, celebration, summary of learning and to express appreciation.

In my 12 years of intensive involvement in this programme, I have mentored about 30 MBA students in total; they were from more than 10 countries in 5 continents. We all keep in regular contact even many years after the programme had come to an end.

One thing I should mention is that when I was a mentor, all mentees were requested to provide me with their personality/characteristic reports, which helped me to better understand them. Then, we jointly defined the mentoring objectives for the mentoring journey, and I used various coaching skills like active listening, clarification, powerful questioning, challenging feedback, etc. to inspire them and dig out their potential. Of course, some solutions/answers will also be shared with mentees.

In a word, I adopt mentoring with a coaching attitude to help my mentees *Do the Right Things, then Do the Things Right.*

## Summary of learning

From talking to my colleagues and based on my own personal experiences in CEIBS's MBA mentoring programmes, we have identified the following success factors:

- EMBA students and alumni are passionately motivated to support this programme for mutual learning and contribution.
- Mentors equipped with basic coaching skills make the CEIBS mentoring programme very productive and effective. Sometimes, if a mentee's area of weakness has not yet been identified, then typical knowledge and experience sharing may not help them until the adoption of *mentoring with a coaching attitude*.
- The mentoring programme is integrated with the Leadership Journey study, which focuses on specific targets and objectives for each MBA student. This contrasts with informal mentoring, which is unstructured and just for networking and advice.
- Although it is a compulsory element, all MBA students are very proactive in taking the opportunities with their mentors. Even after coming to the end of the programme, mentors and mentees often keep in touch, extending their mentoring relationship for a long time.
- CEIBS's support is essential to the success of the programme. They have designed a comprehensive system to facilitate the overall mentoring programme.

# The CEDAR mentoring programme

I have been involved in this unique programme for the past 9 years (2013 to 2022) and would like to show you how it works.

### About CEDAR

The CEDAR mentoring programme was set up in October 2012 by a group of alumni from CEIBS. It is a non-profit organisation, and its name comes from the abbreviation of its five hopes for its mentees: Creative, Efficient, Disciplined, Ambitious and Responsible.

CEDAR operates across cities, regions, universities and functions. To date, this programme has involved approximately 100,000 students and 2,000 mentors in over 200 universities in 40 cities. It is now a nationwide mentoring programme and the biggest mentoring programme in China so far.

### Purpose of the CEDAR mentoring programme

CEDAR aims to inspire young university students from rural or deprived areas and enhance their abilities in the community and workplace. It seeks to clarify possible career pathways, build a positive attitude in its participants and it supports each young person to see more possibilities in their future.

CEDAR calls on experienced entrepreneurs and senior managers to be voluntary mentors and help the students in adapting quickly and successfully to life in a big city, as well as offering university life planning, career advice, etc. It also creates a platform for many successful professionals to give back to the community and helps to build a better society. It is an 8-month programme, starting in October every year and ending in June the following year.

## How it works

The mentorship programme has grown from humble beginnings to a more mature system for mentoring. It is a group mentoring programme, which means a group of 2–3 mentors will serve a group of mentees from different universities (limited to 10 students). Every five groups form a 'Big Group', with group leaders being elected from experienced mentors. Group leaders oversee the overall mentoring activities of the five groups.

The 8-month programme takes the following form:

- Before October: Preparation – recruiting mentors and mentees.
- End of October: Opening ceremony – launch of the programme, including matching mentors with mentees in a group.
- November–January: First chapter of the mentoring events – smart goal setting and facilitation to achieve the results. Each meeting or event focuses on one objective collectively owned by the small group team (8–10 mentees). Group sharing is also available online to all mentees. Usually, topics include tips for mentees to quickly acclimatise to life in a big city and facilitates communication with new students and new people.
- February: Mid-year review – all mentors are invited to attend a meeting face to face or remotely to review the progress and milestones of the programme, and discuss any improvements needed.
- March–May: Second chapter of the mentoring events – best practice learning from other groups, additional objective setting and facilitation. Usually, the focus is on life planning in university, career planning, competence improvements, and so on.
- June: Wrap-up – reflection and appreciation.

## Summary of learning

The CEDAR programme has championed many innovations in mentoring:

- Group mentoring rather than one-to-one mentoring. This involves a group of 2–3 mentors mentoring a group of 8–10 mentees.
- A hierarchy system to manage the mentoring programme. Each city is divided into several sections, then into sub-sections consisting of several groups. Each city, section, sub-section and group is assigned a leader to monitor it.
- Mentees are from different universities, and many did not know each other before they met in the mentoring programme. This helps to improve the network and communication skills of all participants.

- There is a disparity in mentoring resources between relatively large, rich coastal cities, inland and smaller cities. With this programme, experienced mentor resources can be shared across many different locations.
- The programme helps set up new students at the very beginning of their university journey, providing them with orientation and direction.
- Many professional volunteers have been inspired to join the programme, and it has already recruited over 2,000 voluntary mentors.

# Conclusions

Mentoring programmes have been proven effective to assist university or business school students to connect with seasoned business professionals, help identify and achieve their goals and explore professional opportunities available after graduation. Through these programmes, mentees learn professional and life skills that they can carry into their careers; mentors use their expertise to guide the next generation of business leaders and can also improve their mentoring skills.

I have summarised the following 11 tips for a successful mentoring programme, which I think will provide a useful reference.

- **Define mentoring objectives and identify suitable senior leaders.** If there is no objective, then it is hard to know what success looks like at the end of the programme. Make sure to identify a senior leader to support the programme.
- **Find a strong, passionate programme manager.** A strong programme manager doesn't guarantee success, but a weak one will guarantee underwhelming results. Passion, excellent communication and organisational skills are a must for such a manager (see Chapters 11 and 19).
- **Build flexibility into the programme.** Mentoring is about individual students' learning and growth, which means participant needs will vary in terms of desired outcomes and preferred methods of learning. When planning a mentoring programme, identify areas that require flexibility and build them into the structure.
- **Advertise your programme.** The absence of effective promotion may result in fewer potential alumni mentors and student mentees, with neither side understanding the benefits and resulting in low participation rates. It is essential to promote and offer information about such programmes to potential mentees, mentors, school leaders, and so on.
- **Encourage alumni or outside mentors.** Identify alumni's needs and issues, look for creative ways to reinforce positive drivers and lower the hurdles of negative ones throughout the mentoring process. Also, make sure to be respectful of their time, and ensure recognition, appreciation and reward strategies for all participants. Formally recognising mentor involvement can be very motivating and help attract new participants. Things to think

about are how mentoring can benefit their current job, and how their organisations will relate to a younger generation of future employees.

- **Prepare for all stakeholders' success.** You need to do whatever you can to help all participants stay on track and get the most out of the programme.
- **Appropriately match your mentor and mentee.** A critical step in the mentoring process is matching mentors to mentees. Mentoring management software can improve and speed up the matching process for any size of programme and is especially useful with a large volume of participants.
- **Track, measure, listen and modify.** Software can help you track programme progress and generate metrics. Ask participants and stakeholders how well the mentoring programmes meet their goals and the goals of the business school. Also ask them for their ideas for improving the programme.
- **Ensure positive closure for everyone.** Create milestones to encourage participation and design a formal process that brings closure to the mentoring experience. Provide an opportunity for both the mentor and mentee to reflect upon what was learned, discuss next steps for the mentee and provide feedback.
- **Broadcast successes.** There are likely to be many potential student participants out there who just need to know more about mentoring and encouragement to join a programme. At the conclusion of each mentoring programme, recognise participant contributions and spotlight successes to demonstrate the value of the scheme. This will bring energy to the programme, expand participation and increase overall support within the business school or university.
- **Mentor with a coaching attitude.** Properly integrating coaching skills into mentoring sessions will help mentees to identify their potential, overcome obstacles, set positive attitudes and a willingness to listen to the proposed solutions, even to create brand new ideas and behave in a proactive way.

I hope that you have learned a few best practices for making your mentoring programme a success. Good luck!

# References

## Part One

### Chapters 1 to 9

Bandler, R. and Grinder, J. (1975) *The Structure of Magic I: A Book About Language and Therapy*. Palo Alto, CA: Science & Behavior Books.

Bateson, G. (1972) *Steps to an Ecology of Mind: Collected Essays in Anthropology, Psychiatry, Evolution, and Epistemology*. University of Chicago Press.

Berne, E. (1964) *Games People Play – The Basic Handbook of Transactional Analysis*. New York: Ballantine Books.

Berne, E. (1975) *What Do You Say After You Say Hello*. London: Transworld Publishers.

Cannio, S. and Launer, V. (2011) *Coaching Excellence*. London: Lid Publishing London.

Clutterbuck, D. (2014) *Everyone Needs a Mentor* (5th edn), Chartered Institute of Personnel & Development.

de Saint-Exupéry, A. *Le Petit Prince*, published in French in 1943 by Reynal & Hitchcock and published in English by Wordsworth Editions Limited, Ware/England, 1995.

Dilts, R. (1995) *Strategies of Genius* – free pdf at: www.academia.edu/39219222/Robert_Dilts_Strategies_of_Genius_Volume_One_M_E_T_a_Publications_1995_.

Ernst, F.H. (1971) The OK Corral: The Grid for the Get-on-With, *Transactional Analysis Journal*, 1(4): 33–42. https://doi.org/10.1177/036215377100100409

Goldsmith, M. (2012) Try Feedforward Instead of Feedback: https://marshallgoldsmith.com/articles/try-feedforward-instead-feedback/#:~:text=Feedforward%20can%20be%20a%20useful,not%20imply%20superiority%20of%20judgment

Goleman, D. (2005) *The Varieties of Meditative Experiences*. New York: Most Tarcher/Putnam Books.

Hostie, R. (1987) *L'âge adulte, Analyse Transactionnelle*. Paris: Interéditions.

Jung, C. (1980) *Psychology and Alchemy (Collected Works of C.G. Jung Vol 12.)*. London: Routledge.

Karpman, S. (1968) Fairy Tales and Script Drama Analysis, *Transactional Analysis Bulletin*, 7(26): 39–43.

Kolb, D. (2015) *Experiential Learning: Experience as the Source of Learning and Development*. London: Pearson Education.

Kübler-Ross, E. (1969) *On Death and Dying*. New York: Simon & Schuster/Touchstone.

Kübler-Ross, E. and Kessler, D. (2005) *On Grief and Grieving: Finding the Meaning of Grief Through the Five Stages of Loss*. New York: Scribner.

Lenhardt, V. (2002) *Les Responsables porteurs de sens*. Paris: Insep Consulting.

Luft, J. (1969) *Of Human Interaction – The Johari Model*. San Francisco, CA: Mayfield Publishing Co.

Mehrabian, A. (1971) *Silent Messages* (1st edn). Belmont, CA: Wadsworth.

Paul, R. and Elder, L. (2002) *Critical thinking: Tools for Taking Charge of your Professional and Personal Life*. New Jersey: Financial Times/Prentice-Hall Press.

Poulsen, K.M. (2008) *A New Way of Seeing Mentoring – benefits for mentors: Mentor+Guide*. KMP+ Forlag. https://kmpplus.com/wp-content/uploads/2014/02/A-new-way.pdf

Rogers, C. (1951) *Client-Centered Therapy: Its Current Practice, Implications and Theory*. London: Constable.

Vaughan, F. (1988) *Awakening Intuition*. New York: Anchor Books.

Watzlawick, P. (1993) *The Language of Change: Elements of Therapeutic Communication*. New York: WW Norton & Company.

Xiaofen Chen (2016) *The Analects*. Zhonghua Book Company.

## Chapters 10 to 12

Andriotis, N. (2018) *How to Successfully Implement Your Mentorship Program in the Workplace*. Efront. https://www.efrontlearning.com/blog/2018/08/how-implement-mentoring-program-in-the-workplace.html

Dundas, A. (2012) *Replacing an Employee Cost 213% More Than Previous Employee's Salary*. OrgVitality. https://orgvitality.com/business-costs-to-replacing-employees/

Gumeniuk, J. (2021) *Internal vs External Mentoring – what is better for your team?* Femme Palette. https://www.femmepalette.com/blog-posts/internal-vs-external-mentoring-what-is-better-for-your-team

Johnson, J. (2017) *The Mentor and the Protégé: What, Who, and How?* Association of Science and Technology Centers. https://www.astc.org/astc-dimensions/the-mentor-and-the-protege-what-who-and-how/

Kalish, A. (2020) *7 Qualities that Make a Good Mentor*. The Muse. https://www.themuse.com/advice/how-to-find-qualities-good-mentor

Loretto, P. (2022) *Qualities of a Good Mentor*. The balance. https://www.thebalancecareers.com/qualities-of-a-good-mentor-1986663

Martins, J. (2021) How to Find a Mentor in 8 Steps. Asana. https://asana.com/resources/tips-find-mentor

Nonprofit Leadership Center (2022) *How to be an Effective Mentor in the Workplace*. Nonprofit Leadership Center. https://nlctb.org/tips/how-to-be-an-effective-mentor-in-the-workplace/

Oragui, D. (2021) *Tacit Knowledge: Definition, Examples, and Importance*. Helpjuice. https://helpjuice.com/blog/tacit-knowledge

Perschel, A. (2014) *Do You Need an In-House or an External Mentor?* Forbes. https://www.forbes.com/sites/85broads/2014/07/21/do-you-need-an-in-house-or-an-external-mentor/?sh=2e58c74268d7

Polanyi, M. (2021) *Personal Knowledge Towards a Post-Critical Philosophy*. Shanghai People's Publishing House.

Reeves, M. (2019) *Who Can be a Mentor?* https://www.togetherplatform.com/blog/who-can-be-a-mentor

Smith, G.P. (2007) *Mentor Training*. Moraine Valley Community College. https://ctl.morainevalley.edu/wp-content/uploads/2011/05/MentorTrainingOverview.pdf

Strother Taylor, J. (2003) *Training New Mentees*. National Mentoring ResourceCenter. https://nationalmentoringresourcecenter.org/resource/training-new-mentees-a-manual-for-preparing-youth-in-mentoring-programs/

Wilkinson, J. (2019) *Five Golden Rules for Effective Mentoring*. Training Zone. https://www.trainingzone.co.uk/develop/talent/five-golden-rules-for-effective-mentoring

### Useful websites/web pages

Virtual Mentoring for the Modern Workforce. https://www.mentorcliq.com/virtual-mentoring

CV Check (2019) *How to Set up an Internal Mentoring Program for Your Business*. https://checkpoint.cvcheck.com/how-to-set-up-an-internal-mentoring-program-that-will-benefit-your-business/

Mentor Roles & Responsibilities. University of California San Diego. https://library.ucsd.edu/about/lauc-sd/5_committees/mentoring/3_mentors/1_roles.html

What are the Responsibilities Involved with being a Mentor or a Mentee? University of Southampton. https://www.southampton.ac.uk/professional-development/mentoring/mentoring-responsibilities.page

Division of Human Resource Management (HRM). *Mentee Training*. National Science Foundation. https://www.nsf.gov/

Best Practices for Running a Mentorship Program. Together. https://www.togetherplatform.com/resources/best-practices-for-running-a-mentorship-program

Internal vs External Mentoring? Board Mentoring. http://www.boardmentoring.com/InternalvsExternal.php

Topics to Include in Your Mentor Training. Mentoring Complete. https://www.get.mentoringcomplete.com/blog/topics-to-include-in-your-mentor-training

# Part Two

## Chapter 13

Anderson, E.M. and Shannon, A.L. (1988) Toward a Conceptualization of Mentoring, *Journal of Teacher Education*, 39: 38–42.

Bruner, J. (1990) *Acts of Meaning*. Cambridge, MA: Harvard University Press.

Caraccioli, L-A. (1761/2018) *Le Véritable Mentor, ou l'Education de la Noblesse*, Liège: Editions de Bassompierre. Translated into English in 2018, *The True Mentor, or, An Essay on the Education of Young People in Fashion*. Online: Gale ECCO.

Cassin, B. (2013) *La nostalgie – Quand donc est-on chez soi?*, Paris: Editions Autrement.

Clutterbuck, D. (1992) *Everyone Needs a Mentor*. Institute of Personnel Management, London.

Colley, H. (2003) *Mentoring for Social Inclusion*, 2003, London & New York: Routledge Falmer.

Cuche, F-X. (2009) *Télémaque entre père et mer*, Paris: Champion Editions.

Dova, S. (2020) *"Kind like a Father": On Mentors and Kings in the Odyssey*. The Center for Hellenic Studies. https://chs.harvard.edu/stamatia-dova-kind-like-a-father-on-mentors-and-kings-in-the-odyssey/

Eby, L.T., Allen, T.D., Evans, S.C., Ng, T. and Dubois, D. L. (2008) Does mentoring matter? A multidisciplinary meta-analysis comparing mentored and non-mentored individuals, *Journal of Vocational Behavior* 72(2): 254–67.

Fénelon, F. (2003) *Les aventures de Télémaque*. Paris: Editions Gallimard.

Garvey, B. (2017) 'Philosophical Origins of Mentoring: The Critical Narrative Analysis', in Clutterbuck, D., McClelland, A., Kochan, F., Lunsford, L. and Smith, B. (eds) *The SAGE Handbook of Mentoring*, London: SAGE.

Garvey, B. and Stokes, P. (1994/2022) *Coaching and Mentoring, Theory and Practice*. (4th edn). London: SAGE Publications (2022: new Kindle edition).

Hadot, P. (1998) *L'éloge de Socrate*, French Edition, Petite Collection éd. Paris: Allia.

Lean, E. (1983) Cross-Gender Mentoring: Downright Upright and Good for Productivity, *Training and Development Journal*, 37(5).

Levinson, D.J., Darrow, C.N., Klein, B.E., Levinson, M.H. and McKee, B. (1978) *The Seasons of a Man's Life*. New York: Knopf.

Nietzsche, F. (2019) *The Use and Abuse of History in Life*. New York: Dover Thrift Editions: Philosophy, Kindle Edition.

Rawson, E. (1994) *Cicero, a Portrait*. Bristol Classical Press.

Rogers, C.R. (1961) *On Becoming a Person. A Therapist's View on Psychotherapy*. London: Constable.

Rogers, C. (1969) *Freedom to Learn: A View of What Education Might Become* (1st edn). Columbus, OH: Charles Merrill.

Rousseau, J. J. (1762) *Emile ou De l'Education*. Paris: Jean Néaulme (Duchesne).

Ward, E.G., Thomas, E.E. and Disch, W.B. (2012) Protégé Growth Themes Emergent in a Holistic, Undergraduate Peer-Mentoring Experience, *Mentoring & Tutoring: Partnership in Learning*, 20:3, 409–25.

## Chapter 14

Baoli Lu (2011) *History of Vocational Education in Ancient China*. Economic Science Press.

Guangqi Zhang (2013) *Education in Ancient China*. Huangshan Publishing House.

Haifeng Liu & Bin Li (2021) *History of the Chinese Imperial Examinations*. Oriental Publishing Center.

Hongming Koo (2013) *Koo Hongming on the Analects*. Beijing Institute of Technology Press.

Hart, M. (2000) *The 100: A Ranking of the Most Influential Persons in History* (2nd edn). New York: Citadel Press.

Huaijin Nan (2018) *Analects of Confucius*. Oriental Publishing House.

Lao Tsu (alternative spelling for Laozi): *The Ancient Chinese Book of the Tao*, translated by John Minford, London: Penguin Classics.

Mingan Xiong and Yan Xiong (2013) *A Brief History of Teaching Activities in Ancient China*. Chong Qing Publishing House.

Peiqing Sun (2019) *History of Chinese Education*. Eastern Normal University Press.

Puming Huang (2021) *The Analects*. Anhui Literature and Art Publishing House.

Puming Huang (2021) *Dao De Jing*. Anhui Literature and Art Publishing House.

Qijia Guo (2015) *A History of Education in China*. People's Education Press.

Shunying Cheng (2011) *History of the Ancient Chinese Education System*. Beijing Normal University Publishing House.

Weiseng Zhao (2020) *The Spiritual World of Laozi*. China Social Sciences Press.

Xiaofen Chen (2016) *The Analects*. Zhonghua Book Company.

Xiao Lili (2012) *Highlights on Education in Ancient Chinese Classics*. Southeast University Press. http://www.stats.gov.cn/ztjc/zthd/lhfw/2022/lh_sjjd/202202/t20220228_1828031.html

## Chapter 15

Brown, B. (2022) *The most eye opening 10 minutes of your life*. YouTube: https://youtu.be/6j7DbxtMbpQ

Camus, A. (1942) *Le Mythe de Sisyphe*, Paris: Editions Gallimard. Translated in 2013 *The Myth of Sisyphus*. London: Penguin Modern Classics.

Chapman, D., Dethmer, J. and Kemp, K.W. (2014) 'The Four Ways of Leading – Conscious Leadership'. *From the 15 Commitments of Conscious Leadership: A new paradigm for sustainable success* Article, August 23, 2020.

Covey, S. (2020) Excerpt from YouTube https://youtu.be/o82axA-Ntq0 *Summary of The 7 Habits of Highly Effective People* by Stephen Covey Free Audiobook.

Dweck, C. (2017) *Mindset – Updated Edition: Changing The Way You Think to Fulfil Your Potential*. London: Constable and Robinson Ltd.

Eisenstein, C. (2013) *The More Beautiful World Our Hearts Know is Possible (Sacred Activism)*. Berkeley, CA: North Atlantic Books.

Gendlin, E.T. (2003) *Focusing How to Gain Direct Access to Your Body's Knowledge*. London: Rider, Ebury Publishing.

Heidegger, M. (2014) *Hölderlin's hymns 'Germania' and 'the Rhine.'* Bloomington, IN: Indiana University Press. (Original work 1935) sourced in Hunt, H.T. (2019). Intimations of a Spiritual New Age: III. Martin Heidegger's Phenomenology of Numinous/Being Experience and the 'Other Beginning' of a Futural Planetary Spirituality, *International Journal of Transpersonal Studies* Vol. 38 (1) 3.

Jampolsky, G.G. (2011) *Love is Letting Go of Fear.* (3ʳᵈ edn). New York: Celestial Arts/Crown Publishing (Random House).

Kabat-Zinn, J. (2022) *A Guided Meditation on Observing Thoughts* – Jon Kabat-Zinn. Sourced in Mindful @ https://www.mindful.org

Kline, N. (2015) *More Time to Think. The Power of Independent Thinking.* London: Cassell (Octopus Publishing Group Ltd).

Leberman, S., McDonald, L. and Doyle S. (2016) *The Transfer of Learning. Participants' Perspectives of Adult Education and Training.* London: Routledge.

Lewis, L. (2020) *Relational Feedback: Why Feedback Fails and How to Make it Meaningful.* London and New York: Routledge.

Shear, J. and Jevning, R. (1999) Pure consciousness: Scientific exploration of meditation techniques, *Journal of Consciousness Studies*, 6 (2–3): 189–209. Sourced in APA PsycNet, 2022.

Sinclair, A. (2007) *Leadership for the Disillusioned. Moving beyond myths and heroes to leading that liberates.* Crows Nest, NSW, Australia: Allen & Unwin.

Singer, M.A. (2007) T*he Untethered Soul: The Journey Beyond Yourself.* Oakland, CA: New Harbinger Publications, Inc.

Weiss, B.L. (2008) *Messages from the Masters: Tapping into the Power of Love.* London: Hachette.

## Chapter 16

Cannio, S. (2022) *Le jour où je me suis enfin aimée.* Amazon.

Cannio, S. and Launer, V. (2009) *Coaching Excellence.* London: Lid Publishing.

Chopra, D. (1989) *Quantum Healing,* New York: Bantam Books.

Czikszentmihaly, M. (2008) *Flow: The Psychology of Optimal Experience.* New York: Harper Perennial.

Gallwey, W.T. (2001) *The Inner Game of Work.* New York: Random House.

Harris, T.A. (2004) *I'm OK – You're OK.* New York: HarperCollins Publishers.

Kahler, T. (2006) *The Process Therapy Model.* Little Rock, AR: Taibi Kahler Associates. Inc.

Lyubomirsky, S. (2014) *The Myths of Happiness.* New York: Penguin Putnam Inc.

Poletti, R. and Dobbs, B. (2009) *La Gratitude.* Geneva: Editions Jouvence.

Roth, G. (1992) *When Food is Love.* New York: Plume Books.

Tolle, E. (2005) *A New Earth.* London: Penguin Books.

# Part Three: Effective Mentoring Programmes in the Practice

## Chapter 17

Branson, R. (2022) Why Mentors are the Key to Successful Teams, Maddyness Newsletter, 11 January: www.maddyness.com/uk/2022/01/11/why-mentors-are-the-key-to-successful-teams/

CBI (2020) A Radical New Strategy for Lifetime Reskilling must be the Bedrock of UK Economic Recovery – CBI, 19 October: www.cbi.org.uk/media-centre/articles/a-radical-new-strategy-for-lifetime-reskilling-must-be-the-bedrock-of-uk-economic-recovery-cbi/

Deloitte (2016) *The Deloitte Millennial Survey 2016: Winning over the Next Generation of Leaders*: www2.deloitte.com/al/en/pages/about-deloitte/articles/2016-millennialsurvey.html

Dondi, M., Klier, J., Panier, F. and Schubert, J. (2021) Defining the skills citizens will need in the future world of work. McKinsey & Co. https://www.mckinsey.com/industries/public-and-social-sector/our-insights/defining-the-skills-citizens-will-need-in-the-future-world-of-work

McGee Wanguri, D. (1996) Diversity, Perceptions of Equity, and Communicative Openness in the Workplace. *The Journal of Business Communication* (1973), 33(4): 443–457.

## Chapter 18

Bachkirova, T., Jackson, P. and Clutterbuck, D. (2011) *Coaching & Mentoring Supervision Theory and Practice*. Maidenhead: Open University Press.

Barks, C. (1995) *The Essential Rumi*. New York: HarperCollins.

Berne, E. (1964) *Games People Play – The Basic Handbook of Transactional Analysis*, New York: Ballantine Books.

Bluckett, P. (2006) *Psychological Dimensions of Executive Coaching*, Maidenhead: Open University Press.

Carroll, M. and Shaw, E. (2013) *Ethical Maturity in the Helping Professions*, London: Jessica Kingsley Publishers.

Drucker, P. (1980) *Managing in Turbulent Times*, p.X (preface). Routledge.

EMCC Supervision Centre for Excellence (2022) *EMCC Global Supervision Information Document*, https://emccdrive.emccglobal.org/api/file/download/R9U2woJlFi11vsy1Erp82fAwICtS8Nsea6V8TZLh

Halifax, J. (2018) *Standing at the Edge – Finding Freedom where Fear and Courage Meet*. New York: Flatiron Books (Macmillan Publishers).

Harris, T. (2004) *I'm Ok – You're OK*. New York: HarperCollins Publishers.

Hawkins, P. and Shohet, R. (2000) *Supervision in the Helping Professions*. Maidenhead: Open University Press.

Heron, J. (1999) *The Complete Facilitator's Handbook*, London: Kogan Page.

Kline, N. (2015) *More Time to Think – Listening to Ignite the Human Mind*, London: Cassell.

Murdoch, E. and Arnold, J. (2013) *Full Spectrum Supervision – Who You Are, is How You Supervise*. St. Albans, Herts: Panoma Press Ltd.

Scharmer, O.C. (2009) *Theory U – Learning from the Future as it Emerges*. Oakland, CA: Berrett-Koehler.

Senge, P., Scharmer, C.O., Jaworski, J. and Flowers, B.S. (2004) *Presence – Human Purpose and the Field of the Future*. New York: Crown Publishing/Random House.

Turner, S. and Palmer, E. (2019) *The Heart of Coaching Supervision – Working with Reflection and Self-Care*. London: Routledge.

## Chapter 19

Allen, T.D., Finkelstein, L. and Poteet, M. (2009) *Designing Workplace Mentoring Programs*. Chichester, UK: Talent Management Essentials, Wiley-Blackwell.

Deffontaines, D. and Cancellieri-Decroze, D. (2020) *Le Mentorat Mode d'emploi*. Le Mans, France: Editions Gereso.

Imloul, I. (2015) *Étude qualitative sur le mentorat en entreprise*. Université de Haute-Alsace.


## Chapter 21

AbdukalHaq Altuweel: www.alukah.net/social/0/126135

Egan, G. (2009) *The Skilled Helper*, Belmont, CA: Wadsworth Publishing.

Gray, D.E. (2013) *The Mentor Handbook*. Thessaloniki, Greece: European Centre for Development of Vocational Training.

Oasis School of Human Relations 2003 & the 'Skilled Helper' model.


## Chapter 22

Beatie, R.S. (2002) *Line managers as facilitators of learning: Empirical evidence from voluntary sector*. Proceedings of 2002 human resource development research and practice across Europe conference. Napier University, Edinburgh.

Ellinger, A.D. and Bostrom, R.P. (1999) Managerial coaching behaviours in learning organizations. *Journal of Management Development*, 18(9): 752–771.


## Chapter 25

Apospori, E., Nikandrou, I. and Panayotopoulou, L. (2006) Mentoring and women's career advancement in Greece, *Human Resource Development International* 9(4): 509–527. doi:10.1080/13678860601032627

Baluku, M.M., Leonsio, M., Bantu, E. and Otto, K. (2018) The impact of autonomy on the relationship between mentoring and entrepreneurial intentions among youth in Germany, Kenya, and Uganda. *International Journal of Entrepreneurial Behavior and Research*, 25(2), 170–92.

Clutterbuck, D. and Megginson, D. (1999) *Mentoring Executives and Directors*. London: Routledge.

Clutterbuck, D. and Ragins, B.R. (2002) *Mentoring and Diversity: An International Perspective*. London: Routledge.

Gravells, J. (2006) Mentoring start-up entrepreneurs in the East Midlands – Troubleshooters and Trusted Friends. *The International Journal of Mentoring and Coaching*, 4(2), pp.3–23.

Johannisson, B. (1991) University training for entrepreneurship: Swedish approaches. *Entrepreneurship & Regional Development*, 3(1): 67–82.

Kram, K.E. (1985) Improving the mentoring process, *Training & Development Journal*, 39(4), 40–43.

McKevitt, D. and Marshall, D. (2015) The legitimacy of EM, *International Journal of Entrepreneurial Behavior & Research*, 21(2), 263–80.

Parsloe, E. (1999) *The Manager as Coach and Mentor*. London: CIPD Publishing.

Rogers, C. R. (1957) The necessary and sufficient conditions of therapeutic personality change. *Journal of Consulting Psychology*, 21(2): 95–103. https://doi.org/10.1037/h0045357

St-Jean, E. and Audet, J. (2012) The role of mentoring in the learning development of the novice entrepreneur, *International Entrepreneurship and Management Journal*, 8(1): 119–40.

Sullivan, R. (2000) Entrepreneurial learning and mentoring, *International Journal of Entrepreneurial Behavior & Research*, 6(3): 160–75.

Terjesen, S. and Sullivan, S.E. (2011) The role of developmental relationships in the transition to entrepreneurship: A qualitative study and agenda for future research. *Career Development International*, 16(5): 482–506.

Wallace, S. and Gravells, J. (2007) *Mentoring in the Lifelong Learning Sector*. Exeter, UK: Learning Matters.

## Chapter 27

CEIBS (2023) 'Mentoring Programme'. https://www.ceibs.edu/mba/mentoring-programme

Shanghai Cedar Highrise. 'Voluntary Project', University Student Support. http://www.cedarcharity.org/index.php/Home/Page/index/id/37/n/3.html

Wang Pingping (2022) 'The total population has maintained growth and the level of urbanisation has steadily increased'. China National Bureau of Statistics. http://www.stats.gov.cn/ztjc/zthd/lhfw/2022/lh_sjjd/202202/t20220228_1828031.html

# Index

Page numbers in italics are figures; with 'n' are notes.